Victors and Vanquished

Victors and Vanquished

The German Influence on Army

and Church in France after 1870

by Allan Mitchell

The University of North Carolina Press

Chapel Hill and London

Library of Congress Cataloging in Publication Data

Mitchell, Allan.
   Victors and vanquished.

      Bibliography: p.
      Includes index.
         1. France. Armée—History—19th century.   2. Catholic
Church—France—History—19th century.   3. Church and
state—France—History—19th century.   4. France—
Church history—19th century.   5. Germany—Relations—
France.   6. France—Relations—Germany.   7. France—
Politics and government—1870–1940.   8. France—History,
Military—19th century.   I. Title.
UA702.M5   1984   355'.00944   83-25917
ISBN 0-8078-1603-5

Contents

Tables and Maps

Tables

Maps

Preface

This book is both a sequel and a prologue. The second of a projected trilogy, it follows directly from a preceding study of the German influence on politics and economics in the formative phase of the French Third Republic. At the same time, it is intended to provide background for a comparative social history of republican France and imperial Germany between the wars of 1870 and 1914. Throughout, my objective is the same: to demonstrate that one of the essential elements for a clear understanding of French public life is an appreciation of the nation's special relationship with Germany. In the present account the optic has been altered and the focus broadened to bring into view the institutional development of the French republican army and the Roman Catholic church. These two organizations were of course very different in certain regards. But I shall try to show how their history was interrelated and why both were substantially affected by the connection with Germany. I do not claim to have discovered a golden key that unlocks the mysteries of French history. But I do hope to provide an added perspective that is illuminating and, I maintain, indispensable.

Some of my findings have been published as essays in the *American Historical Review, French Historical Studies*, and the *Journal of Strategic Studies*. The editors of those three journals— Otto Pflanze, John Rothney, and Amos Perlmutter respectively— have kindly granted me permission to revise the articles and to incorporate them here. For technical advice I am likewise indebted to George O. Kent and Peter Lundgreen. Nor can I neglect to commend the remarkable skill of my copy editor, Trudie Calvert, whose care in preparation of the manuscript has been so valuable.

In the preface of the earlier volume I was able to express gratitude to several colleagues who have offered their professional assistance. Yet over the years a number of other persons have also aided me more indirectly to gain a better understanding of my subject or of myself. I want to use this space to thank them: Tom Angress, Susanna Barrows, Hans-Christoph Bömers, Stanley and Peggy Chodorow, Istvan Deak, Christl Jacquot, Peter Jones, Lawrence Joseph, Paul Kennedy, Klemens von Klemperer, David Luft, Arvid Möller, Gabriele Ouellette, Michael Parrish, Earl Pomeroy, Armin Rappaport, Fritz Ringer, Robert Ritchie, Alejandra Ruiz, Edith Scott, Marie-Hélène Sénéchal, Cecil Smith, and Judith Woodard. All will recognize why their names appear here, and I trust that each will consider the mention as a measure of my affection and esteem. If the quality of life may be judged by the company one keeps, I can rest easy. The only question is: can they?

La Jolla, California
December 1983

Introduction

Because the close juxtaposition of military and religious affairs may not be self-evident, it should be useful to begin with an explanation of the reasons for this particular choice of topics. In doing so, a certain familiarity with the political and economic circumstances of the early Third Republic is assumed. My preceding volume has already provided the context within which the French army and the Catholic church attempted to reconsolidate their prerogatives after the defeat of 1870 and the collapse of the Second Empire. The creation thereupon of a new republican regime obviously presented an initial parallel between the army and the church insofar as both were widely blamed for the recent debacle. Hence, from the beginning, they shared a marginality among republican institutions, at least in the eyes of those politicians who henceforth ruled and who had reason to regard them with some suspicion. Because of the favored status formerly accorded to the army and the church by royalist or Bonapartist authorities, in other words, neither institution was altogether secure within the still fragile framework of a republic. Thus the relationship between old institutions and new regime could not be taken for granted. It had to be negotiated, painfully and sometimes precariously, in the decades that followed.

Another similarity was structural. Here generals, sergeants, and recruits; there bishops, priests, and believers. Both the army and the church were hierarchical organizations that spanned the social spectrum from the elites to the masses. Decisions about their competence or composition therefore affected, at times in the most direct manner, the daily existence of millions. This fact was especially crucial after 1870 because of the urgent thrust for reform and, specifically, for the introduction of universal military conscription and compulsory primary education. Certain elements within the military and religious hierarchies were resistant to such reformism. They deliberately and at times successfully sought to impede institutional changes that might undercut their traditional authority. As we shall observe in some detail, however, neither the army nor the church was in fact single-minded; and a simplistic division into right and left did not always render accurately the terms of debate. Yet those republicans who were bent on genuine reform surely realized that their measures would often need to be implemented over the objection of professional soldiers and Catholic prelates. This dynamic tension was quintessential to the course and character of the reform movement, which must occupy a central place in any analysis of the republic's emergence.

A third criterion for matching the military and religious questions is that the story of both in the early Third Republic found a traumatic *terminus ad quem* in the Dreyfus Affair. Naturally there is something arbitrary about the selection of a stopping point. Yet by any standard this affair constituted a disruption in the progress of public life under the republican regime. The initial impact, to be sure, was not identical in the two cases under consideration. During the 1880s the army was beginning to enjoy an entente with the republic, whereas the circumstances of the church were becoming increasingly disturbed. But as the plot thickened in the succeeding decade, both tended to join forces against the dreyfusard side, only to see themselves soon driven into the defensive, not to say disgrace, once the innocence of Alfred Dreyfus became apparent. Thereafter, like the onset, the outcome was again different: the army, buoyed by a nationalist revival, managed to regain public respectability as the threat of a European conflict grew, whereas the church was condemned to face the consequences of a total separation from the state. In short, the divergent trajectories of the 1880s were resumed when the crisis dissipated. That extension of the story, however, belongs to the period of *avant guerre* and does not figure in detail here. This study instead concludes by establishing the principal tendencies of the late nineteenth century, for which the Dreyfus Affair proved to be an extraordinary hiatus.

Finally, each in its fashion, the army and the church both became deeply involved in the nationalistic competition between France and Germany. At home and abroad, the French attempted to keep pace with their most formidable neighbor. Humiliation is always the best teacher, and the lessons of the lost war seemed clear: that it was imperative for France to adopt German models of conscription and education. If they were to compete, the French would need to imitate. Thus the rivalry with Germany became a compelling rationale for reform, particularly because the most vaunted slogans of the time—"science," "progress," and "modernity"—became associated in the minds of many Frenchmen with Teutonic superiority. Accordingly, it is necessary to document the manner in which the public life of the republic was thereby affected.

A few indications are required concerning the sources and the structure of this volume. Once more, as in the treatment of political and economic matters, I have made an effort to uncover the archival base upon which every scholarly analysis of this sort must ultimately rest. Received ideas and ambiguous generalizations would not suffice. Fortunately, there is no penury of documentation; and in fact, like most modern historians, my problem was to find sensible delimitations for the field of research in order to avoid being swamped by the sheer quantity of directives, memoranda, and dispatches. This venture took me everywhere from Vincennes to the Vatican. In the course of my survey I was especially able to benefit from the availability of nearly complete minutes (along with supporting documents) of two important bureaucratic organisms: the Conseil Supérieur de la Guerre (CSG) and the Conseil Supérieur de l'Instruction Publique (CSIP). During the years in question, these groups were sequestered forums for debate of reform issues before they entered the public arena. Their records are of crucial significance, I believe, not only because of the convenient institutional parallel between CSG and CSIP but because they enable us to penetrate to a level of discussion and decision more profound than the public record. In the interpretation of motives, to borrow a phrase from Freud, I would suggest that we are able to fathom the latent content of reform legislation and need not rely solely on the manifest appearance of parliamentary debates or newspaper editorials, indicative as these sometimes were. The confidential proceedings of committees and subcommittees may not be everyone's idea of a thrill, but they permit us to move behind closed doors, they afford access to real (not just rhetorical) issues, and they disclose the intimate thoughts of those who wrestled with the problems of reform. In my view, such sources are relatively more ingenuous, more "honest," than those spoken or written for publication, and I have consequently given them special weight.

As for the structure of this volume, I must forewarn the reader not to be deceived by its ostensible symmetry. True, each of the two parts has an equal number of chapters, and each chapter has a corresponding number of sections. But the principles of organization are not identical. That is so because the army and the church were not entirely parallel institutions, they did not always pose similar problems, and the available archival resources are not the same. There is, however, a unified chronological conception. Both parts of the book have their focal point in the first two decades of the republic, with briefer attention devoted to the origins of reform before and the consequences of reform after that period. Yet the military question is examined according to the various branches or services of the army (infantry, artillery, cavalry, and so on), which are treated seriatim. The religious question, on the other hand, is divided into its political and educational aspects, which are analyzed alternately. I trust that these somewhat different strategies of presentation, justified by the disparate nature of the issues with which French reformers had to cope, will create no insuperable obstacles to comprehension.

A preliminary word also needs to be added here concerning the "German model." That term presents a problem that should be directly addressed. My task could not be to write an extensive history of German institutions or, in particular, to set the record straight in detail about the evolution of the German military and educational systems—for which, in any case, competent studies already exist. I took my assignment, rather, to be the delineation of the French perception of German examples. During the decades after 1870 *l'outre rhin* was much studied and often visited by the French. But rare were those observers who possessed adequate training or leisure to gain a comprehensive view of the German way of life. Instead, they resembled the legendary blind men tapping about at random on the anatomy of an elephant. For my purposes, then, to describe a totally consistent and distinct profile of German institutions would in a sense be to falsify the contemporary record in France by imagining an intellectual coherence where none existed.

Nonetheless, we may legitimately assume that various aspects of German society were more or less accurately recorded and that a certain consensus emerged among French reformers about the nature of German institutions. It is that consensus, misapprehensions and all, which is understood here as the "German model." Lest that explanation appear unduly elusive, one brief illustration should clarify the point. French commentators invariably oversimplified the German system of secondary education, the complexity of which they (not alone) found bewildering. Above all, they failed to grasp the development of a basically tripartite structure in which pupils could pass through either the *Gymnasium*, the *Realgymnasium*, or the *Oberrealschule*—not to mention some variations in rural areas. Although that pattern was usually unclear to the French in the 1880s, they at least seized the simpler notion that the classical *Gymnasium* still dominated German education, whereas the "modern" (*Real*) alternative was gaining importance despite its socially inferior status. It was this duplex model upon which the educational debate in France turned, and my discussion of French reform proposals is framed accordingly. In the pages that follow, I repeat, our primary concern is to clarify the French perceptions of Germany, as well as the ideas, the arguments, and the actions that sprang from them.

Part One: The Military Question

Chapter 1

The Impetus to Reform

The German Civil War and the Niel Law

If the shot from Prussian cannon at Sadowa in 1866 was not heard around the world, it was at least audible throughout France. No one could ignore the reverberations: not the French emperor, not the military leadership, not the ministers and deputies, not the press, and certainly not the millions of ordinary Frenchmen whose personal lives were to be affected by the reforms—or lack of them—that henceforth came under consideration.[1]

After decades of institutionalized lethargy, the need to modify the structure of France's military establishment was conceded even by those who merely wished to limit change to certain "opportune innovations."[2] Not the theoretical necessity of army reforms but the practical scope of them was the issue raised by the Prussian triumph over Austria and the creation of a North German Confederation, which could no longer be counted as France's military or demographic inferior. Among the outspoken critics of the prevailing French inertia was the lead editorialist of the famous *Revue des deux mondes*, Eugène Forcade, who emphasized "the inexorable law of numbers." The population of the territories directly dominated by the Prussian crown had just been increased from 19 to 29 million. Given the current rates of birth and death, Forcade calculated, the new German state would increase in population by a half million souls annually, whereas France might expect the same increment only every five years. Yet demography alone was not the key. With a population approximately equivalent to that of France, the North German Confederation could efficiently place a million men under arms, although the French were able to call barely half that total and in actual combat strength, far fewer.

Thus France needed to adopt "virile resolutions" to raise its own army of a million; and the "most practical and most efficacious" means to do so, Forcade concluded, was "the imitation of the Prussian system."[3]

Of course, a question so central to the life of a great nation as military reform, especially during a span of several troubled decades, cannot be reduced to a simple formula. But Forcade was surely near the mark. He was, moreover, not alone in his assessment. We know that Napoleon III was predisposed to evaluate the problem in much the same terms, that he communicated such a conception to his political entourage, and that the contours of the ensuing debate were largely shaped by the same controversial proposition: to compete with Germany, France must imitate Germany.[4]

The emperor's admiration for the Prussian military system had long been a matter of public record. Well before 1866 he had written unabashedly that "the Prussian system . . . is the only one that accords with our democratic nature, our egalitarian mores, our political situation."[5] Sadowa was bound to confirm such a view. So, too, did the reports of the French military attaché in Berlin, Colonel Eugène Stoffel. He reminded Napoleon that, after a crushing defeat by the first Bonaparte, Prussia had introduced the principle of compulsory military service for all its citizens. By taking a page from revolutionary France, the Prussian reform movement of the early nineteenth century had envisaged and eventually achieved "le peuple en armes," thereby providing, Stoffel wrote, the Prussian military with "an element of superiority lacking in all the other armies of Europe." He expanded further on the advantages of the Prussian system in numbers, morale, and efficiency; and he pointed out that required military service was complemented in Prussia by universal primary education as "a very notable element of superiority." Better than France or any other major European state, Prussia had solved both military and social problems by enlisting members of all classes in one great national effort. Such was the example that the French should now emulate.[6]

There are several reasons for dwelling on these first reactions to the war of 1866. First, they demonstrate that the impetus to reform in this sector of French public life, among others, can be located before the Franco-Prussian conflict of 1870. In addition, they document that the notion of "prussification" was central to the military debate from the outset; as we shall observe, this was not simply *one* fashion of stating the issue, but it became *the* manner in which the entire military problem was habitually framed. Finally, these first statements were notable for their quality and clarity, and they were seldom surpassed in substance by later rhetorical versions. One must add, however, an important caveat: in retrospect it is apparent that those who early sought to advocate the Prussian military system were inclined to exaggerate its democratic virtues. A greater realism about the true character of German military organization came only gradually as it was submitted to a more searching technical analysis. Early French reformers, for instance, were dazzled by the prospect of introducing a version of the Prussian *Landwehr* system—without realizing that the prevailing current of military opinion in Germany was more and more to absorb militia elements into the regular army. To that extent the much invoked Prussian example, whether vaunted or denounced, was often only a mirage. Suffice it now to establish, in any event, that this was nonetheless the lodestone of the French military debate toward which the needle of every compass pointed.[7]

Official notification of the imperial regime's intention to seize some reform initiative was published in mid-September 1866. Although this first communiqué by no means suggested that France was in any immediate danger, it did assert "the necessity of perfecting without delay our military organization."[8] The minister of war, Marshal Randon, busied himself with soliciting various reform proposals; and at the emperor's personal request he appointed a blue-ribbon commission composed of twenty-two military leaders and cabinet members.[9] These actions were promptly hailed by Eugène Forcade as encouraging evidence that the demand for a new million-man French army was receiving the broad popular and political support it deserved.[10] Such optimism was unwarranted, however, and it scarcely outlasted the colorful foliage of that autumn. As for public opinion, there is no proof whatever of a groundswell in support of adopting a vastly more stringent conscription law or of abolishing a lottery procedure, dating from 1818 and modified in 1832, which allowed most Frenchmen to escape the draft. Napoleon III may have been greatly stirred by Sadowa, but his people, it would appear, remained exceedingly temperate in their enthusiasm for things military.[11] Nor were the propertied classes eager to forego the convenient procedure of "exoneration," in force since 1855, which allowed them to purchase an exemption from the draft in case one of their sons unfortunately drew a *mauvais numéro*.[12] For their part, French military men were far from unanimous in approving the transition from professional cadres to a citizen army *à la prusse*. The emperor had his supporters—prominent names such as Fleury, Berthaut, and Marshal MacMahon—but he met with stubborn resistance from Randon, Vaillant, Ducrot, and others.[13]

Even before it met, then, the reform commission was seriously divided; and the division, when seen as a matter of issues rather than personalities, was over the question of prussification. A general chronology of the deliberations is already known and is unproblematical. Thus we may pass directly to a brief analysis of the results announced in the *Moniteur* on 12 December 1866. The effects of a compromise were visible in every paragraph. The necessity of augmenting the size of the army was balanced against the budgetary need to restrain military appropriations. Introduction of the "principle of equality" was matched by deference for "established customs." The lengthening of liability for military service was compensated by the shortening of actual time required in the regular army. Three categories would be created: the active army (six years), the reserve (six years), and the *garde nationale mobile* (three years). A lottery system was maintained so that conscripts served either in the active army or in the reserves; then all would pass into the national guard. Exoneration would be kept, although somewhat restricted, and other exemptions would be generous. All in all, France would ostensibly be endowed with a fully staffed and equipped army of more than a million men. This level, to be sure, could not be attained before another six years.[14]

There was less to this projected solution than met the eye. In reality the emperor's reform proposals had been emasculated at their first test. Compulsory service remained a myth. Active duty was to be required of only a small portion of those recruited (even apart from exemptions and exonerations) because military service was not reduced to the three years mandatory in the Prussian system.[15] The French reserve structure also differed importantly insofar as it was not placed strictly on a regional basis of recruitment as in the North German Confederation. Finally, the *garde nationale mobile* was something of a fiction. Its four hundred thousand members would be mostly retired from the army or the reserves with whatever equipment and training they possessed. They would meet seldom and irregularly; as the commission announced in a tone intended to reassure the populace, their "service in ordinary times will be practically nil."[16] If ever a military document created paper divisions, this was it. France had adopted a prescription for continued inertia and, as soon became apparent, for failure.

In the first step along its tortuous legislative path, the commission's project was sent to the Conseil d'Etat for formal drafting. There it bogged down once more in the details of compromise, and Napoleon's irritation began to flare. Not only was time being frittered away, he fumed, but the entire process hardly seemed an adequate response to his expressed concern about "the imperious necessity . . . for a military revolution."[17] The emperor therefore dismissed Randon from the war ministry in January 1867 and replaced him with the more compliant Marshal Adolphe Niel. Yet it was soon evident that a new personality could not basically alter intractable issues. The somewhat revised reform bill advanced by Niel in fact retained all the main features of the previous proposal. When the emperor reconvened the Conseil d'Etat at the Tuileries palace in early February, therefore, the most that could be expected was a standoff. After four lengthy deliberations during the ensuing month, the Conseil d'Etat adopted the Niel plan, further modified, and forwarded it to the Corps législatif.[18]

The French parliament had meanwhile been convoked at a joint session in the Louvre on 14 February. Napoleon's opening address to the deputies gave no hint of the discord within his regime. He attempted instead to justify the strict neutrality that France had observed in 1866 during the struggle "on the other side of the Rhine," and he made an urgent plea that new legislation be passed to assure an increase of France's defensive capabilities. The conditions of war, he said in obvious allusion to the North German Confederation, had been changed so that "the influence of a nation depends on the number of men that it can place under arms."[19] These words retained some of the rhetorical flavor of earlier reform statements just after Sadowa. But the more stilted bureaucratic language of the Niel project, which the parliament was being asked to consider, gave a far more accurate notion of the retreat that had already occurred: "We do not hesitate to declare impractical in our country any legislative measure which tends to render personal military service compulsory." Hence the Niel reforms would essentially amount to no more than a reaffirmation of the principles of the 1832 military law. The Prussian system, after all, "would be incompatible with our organization." The net effect was at most to be an increment in the number of men available for military duty through the devices of an expanded reserve force and a newly created *garde nationale mobile*. To make this increased obligation more palatable, Niel advocated that the length of active service for draftees be reduced to five years.[20]

Thereupon the question of military reform formally entered the public domain. At this juncture we may leave a detailed narration to others and concentrate on an analysis of the fundamental options available to those who participated in the open debate. Even the most precise definitions could not possibly incorporate every minute variation, of course, but it is arguable that only four identifiable positions were available. Naturally there was some wavering among them. Yet to choose one was to preclude the rest, and there were very few French orators or editorialists of the late 1860s who did not finally advocate one of the following alternatives.

1. *A professional army*. Among the French military leadership, as well as in parliament, there were those who regarded anything beyond minor tampering with the traditional structure of the army as a mistake. France possessed, they insisted, a professional corps that had served the nation well in continental and colonial enterprises for half a century. Sadowa had not altered the fact that the French could still claim to have Europe's preeminent military force—an assertion usually accompanied by the claim that the Prussian victory over Austria was to be explained largely on political rather than military grounds.[21] Prussian military prowess should therefore not be exaggerated. In truth, all that France required was a disciplined standing army in instant readiness to fight, which was to deny the primacy of numbers. In combat, success depended not on how many men were hypothetically under arms but on how many could be effectively deployed. The larger the scale of operations, the less significant the literal ques-

tion of numerical superiority. A vastly expanded system of reserves would be unwieldy; and the proposed formation of a *garde nationale mobile* would be both economically wasteful and militarily ineffectual. In this regard, one of the most widely publicized spokesmen of the professional army, General Nicolas Changarnier, cited the heavy losses sustained by the Prussian *Landwehr* in 1866; and he admonished: "Let us not envy this institution."[22]

Underlying such arguments was the assumption that a long military service was necessary to instill in recruits the proper instincts of unquestioning obedience. A popular army could never attain a sufficient degree of professional discipline. The ambiance of a professional corps was necessary to sustain solid cadres of noncommissioned officers who would make a career of the military and who formed the backbone of basic training for conscripts. There was also self-evident need for lengthy service to develop and use the aptitudes of those soldiers who entered such specialized branches as the artillery, the cavalry, or the corps of engineers. Beyond these technical considerations was a mystique that the best soldier is a seasoned veteran. Some expansion of the French army to countenance Prussian aggrandizement was undoubtedly desirable but not at the expense of professional competence and esprit de corps. The annual contingent of draftees should be kept moderate in size, and the individual soldier's length of duty should preferably remain at least seven years.[23]

Consequently, proponents of a professional army followed Changarnier in favoring the abandonment of the Niel reform project because "it tends to denature the character of our army."[24] This viewpoint was represented in the Corps législatif by no less an orator than Adolphe Thiers, who, while deploring the political ineptitude of the imperial regime's timorous handling of German affairs, stated frankly that he was not a partisan of the Niel law because it would "disturb the population . . . and at the same time, instead of strengthening the army, will weaken it."[25] Although Thiers's skepticism failed to sway the French parliament at the outset of 1868, he was nevertheless to persist for several years thereafter.

2. *The Niel compromise.* The case for moderate reform can be stated more succinctly because the main provisions of the proposal have already been outlined and most of its axioms are apparent. The tone had been set by the welcoming speech of Na-

poleon III at the parliamentary convocation in the Louvre in November 1867, when he carefully avoided any reference to a *reorganization* of the army. Rather, he pretended that his own reformist inclinations were "independent of the circumstances" created by recent events in central Europe and that it was merely in the normal course of affairs "to perfect our military organization." Hence the "simple modifications" of the 1832 law now being suggested by Niel were pursuant to objectives he had long sought: a reduction of military service in time of peace and an augmentation of French strength during war.[26]

In formally introducing the military bill to the Corps législatif, however, the parliamentary reporter Edouard Gressier was far more candid in admitting that "the government, always solicitous of public opinion, has consented to abandon its initial project in order to revert to the law of 1832."[27] From all the heat and bother created in the imperial coterie by Sadowa, there thus remained fifteen months later only the advocacy of two noteworthy modifications: a reduction of mandatory service for draftees from seven to five years, to be followed by four years in the reserve; and an amended version of the *garde nationale mobile*.[28] Of these, the first represented an increase in the size of the standing army, not a challenge to its character; and the second proved to be a dead letter from its inception. Yet Marshal Niel could still hope that some valuable precedents might be set by such legislation and that, with steadily increasing appropriations in the future, he could eventually encourage a much larger and stronger army. Although he had originally favored a more forceful reform, Niel was sufficiently disabused to realize that current political realities made infeasible a scheme similar to the Prussian model. He was therefore willing to temporize and to obtain whatever was possible.[29]

In defending this compromise, Niel was forced to contend with objections to any vast addition to the number of Frenchmen under arms. Such attacks came both from professional military circles, for reasons previously examined, and from more liberal factions in the Corps législatif, who charged that the government intended to convert France into a military encampment. To his critics the marshal replied bluntly: "You do not want to make of France a barracks; take care that you do not convert it into a cemetery."[30] With that remark he touched a nerve of apprehension among military professionals and liberal parliamentarians alike that the army of the Second Empire might no longer be equal to the task of confronting a resurgent Germany. To assuage such fears, a vote for the Niel law was a small price to pay, and most French deputies were prepared to do so.[31]

3. *The Prussian system.* Early proponents of a French military reform patterned after Prussia felt that the various amendments adopted by the commission, the Conseil d'Etat, and the Corps législatif had progressively strangled their original purpose. In the *Revue des deux mondes* Eugène Forcade continued to argue in vain that France and Germany were destined to be competitors on the European continent, that each must learn from the other, and that France therefore faced the necessity of increasing its army to an equal size and proficiency. Because the Prussian system was both more egalitarian and more economical than the French, an adaptation of it was clearly desirable.[32] Likewise, Colonel Stoffel submitted more technical data to undercut objections that the institutional forms of a particularistic Germany were not well suited to the established traditions of a more unitary French nation. Although the issues were not yet as sharply defined as they would be following the war of 1870, regarding the related questions of recruitment and a regional system of reserves, Stoffel maintained in effect that the Prussian scheme was indeed feasible.[33]

The most ardent advocate of prussification in the parliament was the deputy Alexandre Glais-Bizoin. He even proposed to go France's eastern neighbors one better by reducing the length of active military service to only two years so the French could gain parity with the North German Confederation "thanks to the same organization and material." If the French army intended to copy Prussian weaponry, he asked, "why not borrow its military organization?" But as the parliamentary appetite for reform abated in late 1867, such a question could be largely ignored and the proposal behind it not even brought to a vote.[34]

Wider circulation and more serious attention were accorded to the views of General Trochu. A military officer who was thoroughly professional and yet programmatically flexible, Trochu had been deeply shaken by the Austrian collapse at Sadowa, which struck Europe, as he said, like a thunderbolt. It had exposed the myth that an army of recruits would invariably be overmatched by an army of professional soldiers. In 1866 Prussia had demonstrated, contrary to French expectations, that its military force was as great in the field as on paper.[35] Trochu challenged the conventional wisdom that seemed inherent to the revised versions of the Niel project: that France could maintain a military esprit de corps and yet keep a system of exoneration which inflicted military service mostly on the poor; that new units of reserves or national guard to match the German system could be obtained without a substantial increase in the annual budget; or that veteran soldiers were incomparably better than conscripts despite long years of idleness in provincial garrisons. Ideally Trochu wanted France to make a fairly literal adaptation of the Prussian model. The spectrum of possibilities stretched from a short term of service for all, as in Prussia, to a long term of service for a few, as heretofore in France. "The first is incontestably the most equitable and *in time*—that it to say, when it has entered profoundly into popular customs—it is the best." For the moment Trochu was willing to accept five-year active service instead of three, but the long-range drift of his thinking was to move away from a professional army and toward a nation in arms. As of 1868, however, his was still a minority view.[36]

    4. *A popular militia.* A small but articulate faction not only opposed the Niel reforms but wished to abolish the standing army altogether. Although they did not speak in unison, these voices retained some coherence and were to be of subsequent importance in the formative period of the Third Republic. Their cutting edge was an open attack on the "caesarism" of the imperial regime. That term was introduced into the debate by Jules Simon, who, when challenged to do so, defined it as "democracy without liberty." The evident ideological overtones of liberalism were altogether deliberate, and the stance of Simon and the like-minded on military reform was explicitly attached to a campaign to secure greater freedom of speech and assembly. Their primary charge was that the Niel bill would deprive parliament of the right to determine the size of the annual contingent of recruits; instead, the emperor would determine whether a national emergency existed. Hence the abuses of personal power, blatantly revealed by the disastrous French expedition to Mexico, would be further magnified. An enlarged army removed from parliamentary restraint might then lead France to financial ruin or to war—or perhaps to both.[37]

The financial issue rested on the objection that a large stand-ing army would represent a permanent burden too great for the French people to bear. This fault was all the more glaring because France's traditional military system made the per capita cost of sustaining the army much higher than the more efficient Prussian model. The deputy Joseph Magnin presented to the Corps législa-tif a detailed comparison of the two 1868 military budgets, which, he claimed, proved that the Germans were receiving about twice as much value for their money as the French. If such a comparison was imprecise, Magnin was unambiguous in his critique of the government's retrogressive military policy: "Certainly the future belongs to democracy and not to permanent armies."[38]

Another recurrent theme among liberal critics of the 1832 law and of the Niel revision was that they only deepened France's demographic dilemma. Because marriage was forbidden for sol-diers in active service, to increase the standing army was to create an even greater statistical deficit by foreclosing early marriage to a greater percentage of the young male working population. Niel's willingness to reduce the length of duty for draftees to five years was partly in response to this objection. But it did not appease those such as Ernest Picard and Jules Simon, who argued that any short-term gain would be more than offset by eventual losses in production and reproduction. The Corps législatif nevertheless dismissed out of hand a proposal, signed by seventeen liberal dep-uties, that would have required the government to make a public investigation throughout France of the effects of military organi-zation on "the interests of industry, agriculture, and the popula-tion." The attempt of these few deputies to relate the military question more closely to the social question thereby, for the time being, failed.[39]

The same was true of a motion, presented to the parliament by Simon and others, which began with an unequivocal assertion that "every French citizen owes military service to the state." This phrase reiterated the underlying premise of those who favored a Prussian style of universal conscription. But the intention in this case went further to demand replacement of the regular army by a national militia much like that of Switzerland. In debate Simon indicated that his militia plan was also similar to the Prussian *Landwehr* system introduced by Gerhard von Scharnhorst in the early nineteenth century; but it was the Swiss model that he chose to defend.[40] Outside the parliament the most militant proponent of this scheme was Gustave-Paul Cluseret, a career officer soon to be better known as a military leader of the Paris Commune. More radical in expression than Simon, Cluseret insisted that modern science had rendered all war illegitimate and offensive war impossible. In the Prussian system he saw both virtue and fault. It could boast of the most excellent high command in Europe and also of the best educated and best trained soldiers. Yet its one-year volunteer system favored the wealthy and imposed a disproportionately heavy load on the poor; as a democratic institution, Cluseret charged, the Prussian army was "a hypocrisy from top to bottom." The adoption of a militia system would be adequate to ensure national defense, and therefore the Swiss model was the only one appropriate to France's "principles and necessities."[41] Cluseret's vision of a nation in arms was thus quite different from that of those who favored the Prussian example because, if literally implemented, it would have altogether decentralized control of military affairs. That the radical implications of this proposal ran contrary both to deep-seated French traditions and to the political inclinations of most Frenchmen would be confirmed by later events.

As one reconsiders the totality of these four contending positions and the actual results of the legislative process, there seems to be little reason to revise the contemporary judgment of Colonel Stoffel that the Niel reform effort in fact produced "an abortive law."[42] We have already observed the obvious discrepancy between the original design and the final version. Moreover, the Niel reforms, even as modified and amended, proved to have far less support than initially supposed. Apathy and skepticism had already regained the upper hand by the time a parliamentary vote was finally accomplished. The appropriations requisite to implement the military law were consequently not forthcoming in the months thereafter; and following Niel's death in 1869 a new Ministry of War under General Leboeuf quietly allowed much of the reform legislation to sink out of view.[43]

In the succeeding decade it was frequently to be contended that France was defeated in 1870 because the nation's military establishment had been in a period of transition. But precious little was in fact being done before the war to realize the Niel reforms. Yet that is not criticism enough. The truth is that even had the reforms been fully operative by 1870, they would have been unlikely to affect the outcome in the field. The reserve system was too slow and cumbersome for rapid mobilization, and the *garde nationale mobile* did not represent an adequate strengthening of France's military capacity. Germany was to be victorious not because France was momentarily ill prepared for combat but because the imperial army was not competitive in size or in strength.[44]

The Lessons of L'année terrible

Reduced to its simplest terms, the impact of the Franco-Prussian war on French military planning was to narrow the spectrum of four options by eliminating the extremes. First, the professional army was discredited by the disastrous reverses on the German frontier that culminated in the surrender of Sedan and the capitulation by Marshal Bazaine at Metz. Then the frenetic attempts of Léon Gambetta to stave off ultimate defeat by organizing a vast *levée en masse* brought to grief the notion that national defense could be adequately sustained by a popular militia force. The relentless German juggernaut finally ground them both down and therewith reduced the basic alternatives for military organization to two. Immediately after the war of 1870, then, the military question was to acquire its starkest possible definition: should France adopt the Prussian system? Without entering into the details of combat, we need to examine how this situation came to be and also to determine why the Paris Commune provided little more than an ugly postscript to the outcome of the war.

Initial French reaction to the opening of hostilities was enthusiastic and optimistic. Indeed it was generally assumed that France would quickly take the offensive and that the conflict would be fought mostly on German soil.[45] The first adverse news of border skirmishes and of advancing Prussian forces was disconcerting; but even former critics of the Bonapartist dynasty supported the war effort with their wishful thinking and false hopes. In this "fateful and inexorable struggle," despite a few painful surprises, the French army would eventually prevail because of the inexhaustible resources of the populace. So one could read.[46]

The reality is all too familiar to warrant another recounting here. The French military was tried by Germany and found inferior in nearly every crucial respect: rapidity of mobilization procedures, logistics, cavalry tactics, effectiveness of artillery, communications, engineering, and above all leadership. Germany simply brought to bear a greater force than France could withstand. German superiority was partly a question of numbers—Helmuth von Moltke had nearly twice as many trained and equipped troops under his command as Napoleon's generals could muster—but it was mostly a matter of organization and concentration of firepower.[47] The French regular army was swept aside with astonishing rapidity, and the initial German advantage was widened with every week. Although French soldiers in the field did not lack courage, they soon learned that personal heroism counted for little in the midst of confusion resulting from inept generalship, insufficient matériel, and inadequate preparation. The dispiriting truth of this "egregious disarray" was fully revealed when Mac-Mahon's exposed and pursued troops found themselves utterly helpless to thwart the Germans at Sedan. The professional army had failed.[48]

While France's first line of defense was disintegrating, a second was being created. In August 1870 the imperial government decreed that all able-bodied male adults under forty should be incorporated into the National Guard. The militia phase of the war was thus to begin with the formation of small territorial armies. France seemingly had no other recourse. As Léon Gambetta said in support of the measure: "What we have before us is Prussia; it is the entire Prussian nation armed. . . . To confront a nation armed we must also raise an armed nation."[49] This same rationale—based, one must reiterate, on an imprecise conception of Germany's military prowess—was maintained as the basis for the military policy of the Government of National Defense after 4 September. In Paris the expanded National Guard held massive demonstrations under the salute of General Trochu; and in Tours a new War Council was established by Gambetta to ensure the "consistent direction" of military operations in the unoccupied provinces.[50] Gambetta's subsequent claims that he had somehow raised a huge popular army out of nothing were exaggerated; in reality the recruitment was already under way by the time he reached Tours and took command. The actual problem, in any event, was not to find enough men but to organize and equip them. To meet these difficulties Gambetta and his chief civilian lieutenant, Charles de Freycinet, resorted to various improvisations: creating an "auxiliary army," encouraging village militia units, revising conscription rules, calling up volunteers, suspending promotion procedures.[51] The justification for these measures was later stated by Freycinet without apology: "The enemy was at our door." Without such a display of raw energy, France would undoubtedly have capitulated to Germany much sooner. Yet when directly confronted with Moltke's disciplined troops, the hastily formed French units rarely provided any serious opposition. One glorious episode—the victory at Coulmiers in early November followed by the reinvestment of Orléans—did not a campaign make; and by the beginning of December the inflated hopes of the French were dashed. Gambetta's brave words proved to be hollow: "The Prussians can now judge the difference between a despot who fights to satisfy his whims and a people in arms determined not to perish."[52] In the end Gambetta's ragtag guerrillas fared no better than had Napoleon's professional troops. Both were obliged to bow in humiliation to German superiority.

Despite all the diplomatic maneuvering that went into it, the armistice of January 1871 was as unavoidable as any historical event can be. No less inevitable were the dissatisfactions and recriminations in France that followed the admission of defeat. It was a time for finding scapegoats. Bazaine was one;[53] and for shamefaced officers wishing to restore a modicum of order in the military, Gambetta was another. As General Véronique wrote to the acting minister of war, General Le Flô, the improvisations in Tours had been of "dubious utility" because "the moment was singularly ill chosen to make reforms." Gambetta and Freycinet had indulged in an "orgy of promotion," Véronique complained: "Nothing stopped them—not *rules* nor *traditions* (which they called routine) nor *personal prerogatives*." Then he added stiffly: "It is therefore not without reason that some very regrettable measures and a certain responsibility for our disasters have been attributed to their inexperience." Under the circumstances, however, no one could deny that the army also bore a "certain responsibility" for the French calamity. Consequently, the Bordeaux government was left with no practical choice but to discard as many shattered military remnants as possible and to admit, as Adolphe Thiers openly did, that "there are no longer grounds for maintaining the present organization of the army." Among other things, this meant both disbanding the *garde nationale mobile* and rescinding most of Gambetta's wartime directives. Thus the first military policy of the Thiers regime was simply to clear away some of the wreckage of the war.[54]

Although the eruption of the Paris Commune in March severely shook the new French government, the final result was only to consolidate Thiers's control and to confirm the *faits acquis*. This was true for two reasons: because the army was enabled to regroup and to restore some measure of self-confidence and because the objective of crushing the communards was shared by the Germans, from whom Thiers obtained military cooperation as well as a commitment of political support. At most, from the standpoint of military reform, the Commune delayed any serious reorganization and prolonged the postwar period of improvisation.[55]

A full military history of the Commune from the perspective of the communards has never been written, probably because it would be an incoherent tale of desperation. When General Cluseret arrived in Paris to lend his support to the insurrectionaries, he was appalled to find the military command in the hands of three men, only one of whom had any previous military experience (as a sergeant) and all of whom were "ignorant as fish."[56] Convinced that the task of organizing an effective defense of the capital would be hopeless, Cluseret at first refused the Ministry of War; but after artillery shells began to drop on the city in early April, he relented and took charge. The pathetic account of his frustrations with indiscipline and inefficiency are recorded in Cluseret's memoirs, written soon after the event from his exile in Switzerland. They recount in detail the dilemma of attempting to combine professional military procedures with the assumptions and attitudes of an egalitarian political democracy. After twenty-eight days Cluseret was arrested, relieved of his command, and soon replaced by the journalist Charles Delescluze, presumably as a demonstration of the primacy of civilian over military priorities. But as Cluseret's interim successor, Louis Rossel, observed of Delescluze, "When it came to technical questions, he was absolutely bewildered."[57] A unified command was never created and, instead, small autonomous free corps units began to appear in the month of May just as barricades were being erected throughout the city. The disorganization of the Parisian National Guard was thus hastened without at the same time providing much compensating weight for the defense. The Commune thereby set no military precedents for the future of the Third Republic, except perhaps in a negative sense.[58]

The dilemma of amalgamating professional and popular elements, inherent in every massive military organization, was also evident in the formation of the invading army of Versailles. The indicative difference, however, was that any ambiguity in this instance was consistently resolved by Thiers in favor of the officer corps. One of the earliest responses to the outbreak of the Commune was a resolution, passed by the National Assembly on 30 March, which directed that "every department should place at the disposal of the government one or more battalions of volunteers," preferably chosen from veterans of the army, the navy, the National Guard, or the *garde nationale mobile*. The officers of these new units, it was stipulated, would be appointed by Thiers himself. A week later the army of Versailles was formally constituted with Marshal MacMahon as commander in chief, General Vinoy as head of the reserves, and the three army corps under generals Ladmirault, Cissey, and Du Barail. That these names were all to be prominent in the military affairs of the early Third Republic was not coincidental. With the collaboration of the German general staff—which returned prisoners of war and provided weapons and transportation facilities—French officers conducted the ruthless military operations that broke the Commune after only one week of serious combat.[59]

Yet the victory of the army of Versailles, as everyone knew, was tainted. Very likely it could not have been obtained without the active benevolence of the Germans, who literally surrounded the military action and were capable of containing any contingency. Moreover, the brutal suppression of the communards by Thiers's troops hardly proved that a resurrection of the old imperial army was necessary or desirable. In fact, the episode of the Commune did not alter the inescapable lessons of the Franco-Prussian war: that in the future France could rely neither on a small professional army nor on an insubstantial popular militia. The reason for eliminating those two options was the same: by adopting either of them France would be left incapable of competing with Germany—and after 1870 that competition would remain the irreducible criterion of every French military plan.

The False Compromise of Five-Year Conscription

In the summer of 1871 the entire French army probably did not exceed 150,000 men. By expediting the return of prisoners of war from German camps and by adding a class of fresh recruits, that number could be doubled within a year. Yet, more than ever, the most pressing issue was not size but organization. By what principle or formula should the new French army be recruited, staffed, and deployed? To determine an answer to that question and to begin drafting appropriate military legislation, Thiers instituted the so-called Commission of Forty-Five, whose members were charged with presenting a program for recruitment to the Assembly in August. That plan would result in the first in a series of legislative acts intended to reconstitute the army in its entirety. In Thiers's retrospective account, a majority of the commission initially favored the adoption of the Prussian system "in all its details, without omitting anything."[60] Notwithstanding his incorrigible tendency to conceive of himself as a valiant Horatio at the bridge, Thiers's remark was only a slight embellishment of the truth. Throughout his presidency he was to labor mightily to offset a parliamentary majority that desired the French army to adopt a version of the German model of universal conscription.[61] For reasons that we shall examine, the result was a deadlock that fully satisfied neither side and left reform in an administrative quandary. Indeed it is fair to remark in advance that the debilitating effects of this ill-conceived beginning were to hobble French military planning for the succeeding two decades.

Two preliminary observations should be held in view throughout. First, in cutting through the luxuriant thicket of directives, memoranda, articles, brochures, presidential decrees, and parliamentary reports in the 1870s, one must always recall that the basic fact of French helplessness vis-à-vis Germany was perfectly well understood by nearly everyone. The rhetorical bravado and the gossip of revanche could deceive only the most foolish of chauvinists, of which very few sat in positions of authority in France. Apprehension, not revenge, was the dominant mood.[62] The splendid ceremony at Longchamps on 29 June 1871—when about seventy thousand infantrymen paraded by the reviewing stand followed by another twenty thousand mounted cavalry troops—was one of the most impressive but least convincing demonstrations of military prowess ever presented to the Parisian populace. German observers noted that the crowd was curiously quiet and unresponsive, as if attending a wake rather than a celebration.[63] True, there existed a general consensus that the French should prepare for the eventuality of regaining their lost honor and provinces. But one should not imagine an entire nation perpetually straining at the leash nor posit a military mentality that reflected such a singular passion.

Second, it is important to remember that the political context of these first postwar debates was thoroughly conservative: hence the deceptive impression that discussions of military reform were apolitical. In reality they were conducted behind a protective screen of conservatism for the better part of the republic's initial decade. Symptomatic of this ambiance was the arbitration of the troublesome surplus of commissioned officers left from the rash of indiscriminate battlefield promotions in 1870. The task of confirming or rescinding such advancements was administered by a special parliamentary committee, headed by the veteran General Changarnier, whose work effectively resulted in a blanket restoration of the old imperial officer corps.[64] From this process Gambetta was excluded; and when besieged with protests from the demoted or the dismissed who had served under him, he was forced to concede that he was "without influence at this moment and could only demur."[65] Thus the military question during the Thierist presidency cannot be altogether apprehended as a contest among political factions. It can best be judged by another litmus test: the issue of prussification.

The baselines of argument, because they were both predictable and easily perceptible, may be quickly traced. Those who urged adoption of the Prussian system built their case on the indisputable if unpleasant fact that France had just been overwhelmed on the battlefield. Their pronouncements echoed those at the former imperial court immediately after Sadowa in 1866: in a struggle between two military organizations, one had proved to be decisively superior. They stressed the practical advantages of equality of recruitment and rapidity of mobilization, features that had given German units greater coherence and élan than the French.[66] To meet the German military machine was first to match it. As one pamphleteer wrote: "The military condition of our adversaries is the criterion of the magnitude of effort required." Because the identity of the potential foe could not be in doubt, it followed that France must adopt a plan of universal conscription similar to the German.[67]

The other side claimed that the primary blame for France's defeat rested with the Bonapartist regime. If so, salutary political reform and military retrenchment on the basis of the 1832 law would be sufficient to restore French greatness. Quality should not be sacrificed for the sake of quantity.[68] Therefore a large regular army (the figure of four hundred thousand was commonly cited) must be constructed around a solid professional corps, with reserve cadres capable of expansion to a total force of 1.2 million men in case of armed conflict.[69] Such an arrangement was more in accord with French tradition and national character than was the Prussian system. Thiers, who urgently gathered support among French officers for this view, would have preferred the return to a required military service of seven or eight years for recruits, although he grudgingly admitted five years as a feasible minimum. Except for the redesign of a reserve force to replace the defunct *garde nationale mobile*, a measure that would eventually entail a more serious financial investment than before the war, these proposals were not dissimilar to those finally embodied in the modified Niel plan of 1868.[70]

In December 1871 Thiers unveiled his military project. At this early stage, public reaction was mixed and still muted; but police reports indicated a renewal of anti-Thierist hostility in the poorer districts of Paris because of fear that the brunt of new recruitment laws would weigh most heavily on the working class. Professional military analysts were quick to perceive, as one German agent reported back to Berlin, that the Thiers plan was "the absolute opposite of the Prussian."[71] The best informed discussion was conducted in such specialized journals as *Le spectateur militaire*. Although no clear consensus emerged, several general propositions were frequently aired: that France had much to learn from Germany, especially in procedures of mobilization; that the Prussians should not be accorded "the last word"; that any borrowing from Germany must take into account the French character and *esprit frondeur*; that the German system of regional recruitment might be politically harmful to French national unity; and that Thiers's intrepid opposition to the idea of a nation in arms showed, as a critic charged, that "he has not changed one iota."[72] These random assertions indicated a shared conception of the military question—to what extent should France imitate Germany?—without deriving a coherent solution.

The same vagueness was evident in two other influential journals. One, the *Revue militaire de l'étranger*, was founded in late 1871 for the purpose of correlating and disseminating more precise knowledge of European armies. Prepared in the Second Bureau, the intelligence and counterespionage agency of the French Ministry of War, this publication proposed not to resolve issues of military reform but to provide the technical data necessary for informed debate of them. Such a neutral editorial policy inspired scarcely more than the delphic opinion that the French army must henceforward copy as well as conserve.[73] Almost equally enigmatic for the time being was the *Journal des sciences militaires*, which regularly featured articles by the leading military theoretician of postwar France, Colonel (and later General) Jules Lewal.[74] The title of the publication was itself a programmatic statement. Lewal and his fellow contributors were convinced that ignorance of scientific method had sealed the defeat of France; thus the time had obviously arrived to overcome French inertia by rejuvenating and modernizing the army. The example of the Prussians, along with their arrogance, would be "the most useful stimulant" to French military reform.[75] Stated in this elevated and attractive fashion, Lewal's ideas could be favorably construed by either side. Even his advocacy of universal conscription was not totally objectionable to Thiers and his supporters so long as Lewal refrained from descending into the arena of detailed argumentation.

In this regard a pragmatic distinction was proposed by one of Thiers's military advisers, General Bourbaki. Satisfied neither by the 1832 law (too few soldiers, albeit of good quality) nor by the 1868 law (more than enough soldiers, but of poor quality), Bourbaki was still hopeful of finding a viable alternative. Yet he did not hide from Thiers his perception of a "pronounced drift in the direction of Prussian organization." Should public and parliamentary opinion continue to take that course, he observed, the ineluctable result would be "universal and personal conscription" (*service obligatoire et personnel*). To avert such a conclusion, Bourbaki urged the tactic of accepting that military duty become compulsory but that it not be personal: that is, Thiers should simply concede the principle of universal conscription but at the same time deny that every Frenchman "must spend equal time in the barracks." This semantic distinction suggested the arrangement by which the compromise of 1872 was finally to be reached. "To win the essentials," Thiers later confessed, "we had to sacrifice words."[76]

During this time the scrutiny of French military affairs from beyond the Rhine was close and constant. The extensive pamphlet literature appearing in France was systematically collected and summarized by German agents, whose findings were transmitted to Berlin for further evaluation. By July 1871 their conclusion was that, despite all of the proposals and projections, French reform had "still not taken a single step forward."[77] This reading was reconfirmed later in the autumn by additional reports on the condition of the French army and the stubborn position adopted by Thiers in the reform debate.[78] Not until shortly before the end of the year did the first direct evidence of German concern over the reconstitution of the French military organization begin to appear in official dispatches reaching Berlin. Written within a few days after Thiers's military plans had been made public in Versailles on 7 December, these contained explicit cautions about a too rapid French recovery.[79] Presented with the opportunity, Bismarck moved at once to put the Kaiser on notice: "Due to the uncertain circumstances in France, the possibility—I will not designate it as probability—is not excluded that as soon as next year we may confront a crisis in that country which would oblige us to take up arms in self-defense and in execution of our [reparations] demands." Bismarck appended a warning that "unanticipated events abroad" might produce a situation in which Germany "would not have France alone to face." Thereby, for the first of many times, the chancellor conjured before William the threat of an imminent war of revenge to be conducted by France in collusion with an unspecified ally.[80]

This initial commotion may be safely attributed to Bismarck's general misgivings; precise statistical justification for his attitude did not reach Berlin until after the New Year. In an analysis of current and projected military strength, the German military attaché Major von Bülow calculated that the French would raise their troop level in 1872 by sixty-four thousand men and fourteen thousand horses. To that end the Assembly was expected to appropriate an increase in the military budget of 75.5 million francs.[81] With these figures in hand, Bismarck needed nothing more in order to intervene. He immediately recalled General Edwin von Manteuffel to Berlin from his command post with the German occupation force in France. Although no transcript exists of their consultations, the effects were clearly visible in the correspondence from Nancy by Thiers's personal emissary, the Comte de Saint-Vallier. Before his departure to Berlin Manteuffel had reassured the French that their military plans would occasion no alarm in Germany. But after his return the story was changed. Saint-Vallier reported to Thiers that Manteuffel was "quite satisfied" with his voyage, that his contacts with Bismarck and William had been cordial, and that he had seized the opportunity to explicate his own favorable view of the policies of the French government. Yet he had been informed that "a shadow" now lay over Germany because of French "military preparations" and of "alleged projects to increase the military budget beyond the figure attained under the [Second] Empire." These strictures were nonetheless accompanied by renewed expressions of support for the Thierist regime. German confidence in French intentions, Thiers was assured, "rests on you and you *alone*."[82]

One must be struck by the irony of this message. Bismarck's political and financial reasons to encourage Thiers were now buttressed by the motive of delaying or deflecting a reorganization of the French army. Seen in the context of the military question in France, this meant that Germany was actually siding with Thiers *against* the adoption of the Prussian system by the majority in the Assembly, which favored it. In this perspective Thiers was considered useful by the Germans because they thought his military opinions to be superannuated. Thiers suffered from Napoleonic delusions of grandeur and saw himself as the creator and leader of a splendid new professional army.[83] But German military analysts regarded his conception as hopelessly outmoded. It was perhaps understandable that a man lost in senility might entertain such "fabulations" (*Hirngespinste*), one agent remarked, but it was astonishing that so many French officers and military theoreticians took them seriously. When later consulted by Bismarck for an appraisal of French military affairs, General Albrecht von Roon forwarded a General Staff report containing essentially the same judgment and referring to Thiers as "a man of the old school and of routine."[84] Thus the Germans were fully conscious that in supporting Thiers they were attempting to employ him as an instrument to retard French military reform and to discourage the French army from choosing a path of recovery that might closely parallel the Prussian system.

If it was the German intention to strengthen the French president not only in his political position but also in his recalcitrance on the military question, success was soon manifest. In replying to Berlin via Nancy, Thiers first outlined his general intentions: "Above all peace, the restitution of order, the equilibrium of finances, and the reconstitution of the army destroyed by the idiocy of the [Bonapartist] empire." He denied that France held any aggressive ambitions and contended that his military project contained "nothing excessive": "I do not want universal conscription that would inflame every head and put a rifle on the shoulder of every socialist. I want a professional army, firm, disciplined, capable of making us respected at home and abroad, very limited in number but superior in quality. This system is more defensive than offensive, and no one has any reason to object to it." There were those who hoped to raise a mass army "in order to emulate Prussia," Thiers insisted, "but I do not wish to imitate [because] we have different customs and an indocile character that cannot be harnessed except by the discipline of professional armies."[85]

While Thiers thus codified his set of assumptions, the Assembly was preparing its own. On 12 March, after months of deliberation, the parliamentary commission for military affairs released a draft of the new recruitment law, which began with the simple declarative sentence: "Tout français doit le service militaire personnel."[86] Despite the complexities and qualifications of succeeding paragraphs, this document was in potential contradiction with the sentiments that had been expressed by Thiers in his private correspondence and that Saint-Vallier had been instructed to relay to the Germans. The use of the term "personal," after all, might imply a literal uniformity for all recruits in the application of the law. In that event the length of service would necessarily need to be reduced, as in Germany, to accommodate more young men eligible for the draft. Otherwise the principle of universal conscription would remain a dead letter, exactly as Thiers intended and as he had in effect promised. After traveling to Paris in mid-April to confer on the matter, Saint-Vallier reported to Manteuffel that Thiers was standing his ground: "Thiers told me promptly and with the greatest clarity that he would never accept universal conscription such as a part of the Assembly would like to impose on him. . . . The president wants a professional army, an army exercised and disciplined. . . . He wants the law of 1832, resolutely and firmly applied, and he is *certain* to obtain it."[87]

That Thiers would so unequivocally reiterate his position to the Germans, even in face of the rhetorical crescendo in France favoring the concept of a nation in arms, gave some measure of his self-assurance. When his authority was challenged by some deputies in December 1871, he had threatened to resign and soon had his way. If necessary, he would not hesitate to do so again, secure in the knowledge of his indispensability in the negotiations with Germany. For the time being this was the key to the military question in France: as long as the German occupation continued and the existing republican regime had obvious German support, Thiers possessed invincible political clout. He was prepared to use it to obtain the substance, whatever the wording, of the military legislation that he wished and that he had committed himself to deliver.

The Germans were not dictating the military policy of France, but they were deliberately abetting a certain scheme of reform that they deemed to be militarily unsound. During the latter stages of debate in the Assembly, moreover, they contributed to an atmosphere of tension under which the French deputies labored. They did so even though the General Staff advised Bismarck that little danger existed that the French would start "a second German war before 1873, if then."[88] We may therefore conclude that the immediate German concern was not French aggression; that the objective of German pressure in the spring of 1872 was to influence the outcome of the vote on military legislation so as to retard French reorganization; and that the German presence in France weighed for Thiers and against his opponents. French susceptibility to such pressure was illustrated by a boisterous press controversy resulting from a series of articles in the London *Daily Telegraph*, which luridly portrayed German alarm at the enlargement of the French army and the consequent danger to European stability. Parisian newspapers speculated that the story had been inspired from Berlin. Although conclusive evidence was and is lacking to substantiate that charge, French police reports confirmed that such an assumption was widely shared in Paris and that it contributed to a sharp drop in the stock market. In the best Bismarckian style, the official *Norddeutsche Allgemeine Zeitung* then stoked the affair by commenting that, although the *Daily Telegraph* version was exaggerated, projected increases in the French military budget would indeed force Germany to maintain strong occupation forces as a guarantee of orderly procedures.[89]

The message or, more accurately, the menace from Berlin was communicated more directly during the final fortnight before the Assembly's decision. The German military representatives in Nancy, Manteuffel and Tresckow, repeatedly attempted to impress on Saint-Vallier the German mistrust of France's *"arrière-pensées* and secret projects," the growing public appetite for revenge, the fragility of French promises to meet the reparations schedule, and the unsettling plans by the Assembly to create a huge popular army through the adoption of universal conscription. On 27 May Manteuffel confided that he had just received "a *bad letter*" from Moltke, the exact contents of which were secret but which ordered him to take "certain military precautions" in the occupied zone because "the probability of a renewal of hostilities by France appears to be increasing." As the parliamentary balloting in Versailles approached, the German army was thus placed on alert.[90]

The oratory in the Assembly has been often recorded; and the proceedings, in view of all these circumstances, were scarcely surprising.[91] General Trochu's motion that France adopt a conscription plan of three-year service on the Prussian model was handily defeated 455 to 227. A more serious challenge was mounted by General Chareton, but his proposal of a four-year maximum was also rejected after Thiers arose to demand five-year service and to warn that the adoption of anything less would provoke his resignation. One historian has observed that "by threatening to resign, Thiers changed what had been a technical military problem into a political question."[92] Yet the evidence is obvious and overwhelming that the course of French military reform had been a critical political issue ever since 1866. The outcome would prove to be more of a curse than a genuine compromise. The new law saddled the French army with a mode of recruitment that stood in complete contradiction to the simultaneously acclaimed principle of universal military conscription.[93]

Chapter 2

The Reorganization of 1873

The Unresolved Issues of Reform

The recruitment law of June 1872 represented a political accommodation between the executive and legislative branches of the French government. Subsequent months were necessarily devoted to assessing the implications of the arrangement that had just been reached. The French needed both to elaborate the general principles of military organization and to specify the details of their implementation. Such a dual effort unavoidably broadened the debate into areas beyond the technical competence of most deputies in the French Assembly. Another forum of discussion therefore became essential: the Conseil Supérieur de la Guerre (CSG). Yet the military question retained crucial importance for the French public, of course, and its political overtones remained prominent. Indeed, the presidential crisis of 1873, as this chapter should demonstrate, was inextricably linked to persisting differences over the course of military reform.[1]

The primary concern of the 1872 law was technically to establish a procedure of recruitment. It thus prescribed the size of the French army but not its shape. Yet because these two matters were finally inseparable, a longer perspective is useful in order to perceive the likely statistical impact of military reform on the French population. The figures in Table 1 indicate that the regular army would total about 1.25 million men.[2] The territorial army and its reserves, whose composition and deployment were not yet decided in 1872, were eventually to double this pool of available manpower. By the standards of the nineteenth century, such a scheme for placing 2.5 million soldiers under arms was highly ambitious. Even so, this quantity was still below the demographic capacity of the French nation. From a population of 36 million slightly fewer than 300,000 came of military age each year. Of these, well over half were excused for various disabilities (inadequate health or insufficient height), professional exemptions (divinity students or apprentice teachers), and family reasons. The remainder constituted a net annual contingent of approximately 133,000 recruits, a figure that would presumably increase somewhat each year.[3] Here the stipulation of the law for five years of active service became critical. Although well under 50 percent of young Frenchmen in the early 1870s were actually subject to the draft, the army nonetheless had available a greater number of eligible inductees than it could as yet possibly retain for service.[4] There was consequently no alternative to further distribution by means of a lottery in which approximately 83,000 conscripts were selected for five years, with the remaining 50,000 men designated for only a brief tour of duty lasting from six months to a year.[5]

Into this complex paradigm one must place an additional provision in the 1872 law for a system of one-year voluntary service. After nearly a century, the old and often modified procedures of substitution (*remplacement*) were abolished. Their place was taken by regulations, borrowed directly from the Prussian army, under which students beyond the baccalaureate or passing a special examination could enlist for a single year of officer training, provided that they also defray their own costs of maintenance.[6] Ostensibly this new system served the twin functions of facilitating the access of qualified young men to liberal careers by assuring them a minimal interruption of their schooling and of providing a supply of reserve officers. These measures were acclaimed as a democratic advance over the former practice of purchasing an exemption from the draft. In actuality, as numerous commentators then and since have emphasized, this volunteer arrangement perpetuated a convenient refuge for the wealthy and educated bourgeoisie who constituted the principal beneficiaries.[7] Manifestly the French were most inclined to imitate Germany when the advantage of some special interests was thereby secured. Neither political democracy nor military efficiency represented the essential criterion.

If such consequences of military legislation failed to please those who had advocated a more thoroughgoing adaptation of the Prussian system of universal conscription, the proponents of a

Table 1 / Projected Recruitment of the French Army, 1872–1892

Formation	Duration of Service	Projected Manpower	Date of Readiness
Active Army	5 years	719,000	1877
Active Reserve	4 years	520,000	1881
Territorial Army	5 years	594,000	1886
Territorial Reserve	6 years	638,000	1892

Source: Wolseley, "France as a Military Power in 1870 and 1878," pp. 1–21.

more professional army also had reasons for dissatisfaction. Not only was the normal length of service for recruits reduced from seven years to five, but the traditional practice of awarding bonuses for reenlistment was henceforth suppressed. These changes created or, perhaps more accurately, revealed a serious and nagging flaw in the French military structure: a paucity of capable noncommissioned officers (NCO). In the past NCOs had been found mostly among conscripts who had already served a full seven years in the army and who were then induced to remain in uniform rather than to risk a strange career after a long and alienating absence from civilian life. Some French officers such as General Vinoy reflected that "perhaps the reduction in length of service has been pushed too far. The recruitment of noncommissioned officers has already become impossible; it will become even more so with the [increasing] facility of one-year voluntary enlistments. This provision, which is not French but is imitated from abroad, does not appear capable of adaptation in France."[8] There is no question that the number and quality of French NCOs declined drastically in the years after the war of 1870; and the reintroduction of bonuses through later legislation in 1878 and 1881 suggested that a mistake had been made that would require rectification.[9]

Sufficient detail has been examined here to confirm two general impressions: that in practice the 1872 law made a travesty of the principle of universal conscription; and that in theory it raised more fundamental issues than it settled. Both conclusions concerned ordinary Frenchmen, who understandably worried how their personal fate would be affected. But the outcome was impenetrable because President Thiers chose to remove further deliberations of reform from the purview of popular opinion, the press, and the parliament. In any analysis of this period, therefore, the military question can be apprehended only through the secret records of the Conseil Supérieur de la Guerre. Thiers had several reasons for restricting debate to the unpublicized sessions of this body. He was visibly dismayed by the rancor that had accompanied passage of the recruitment bill and was convinced that the remaining technical problems could best be resolved by a selected group of military advisers. Most of all, apparently, he recognized that he would need the allegiance and assistance of the French officer corps if he were to steer successfully through the muddle of reform legislation as well as to maintain his self-appointed status as a peerless authority on military affairs.[10] For the future of the French army it would prove decisive that, in these regards, he soon failed.

The Conseil Supérieur de la Guerre

The CSG was created by executive order on 27 July 1872. A glance at the membership gives a fair indication of its importance. The hard core—meaning those who did most of the talking—was composed of the highest-ranking military personalities of the time. These included the two living marshals of France, MacMahon and Canrobert; the minister of war, General Ernest de Cissey; the military governor of Paris, General Ladmirault; three senior officers from major auxiliary branches of the army, Du Barail (cavalry), Forgeot (artillery), and Chabaud-Latour (fortifications); plus several officers and technicians from various other military services. Also included was one famous gentleman listed simply as a delegate from the French Assembly, the Duc d'Aumale, in addition to three financial advisers from the civilian bureaucracy. When Thiers's name as chairman ex officio was added to this list, twenty-two persons in all were invited to the first five sessions of the CSG held between 9 and 18 October at the Elysée Palace in Paris.[11]

These initial ten days of the CSG's existence were of particular importance because the central issues of reform as well as the pattern of debate were established at that time. Although Thiers obviously held the initiative during the meetings in the Elysée, the counterarguments and the personality of his chief antagonist,

Marshal MacMahon, emerged no less clearly. It is therefore possible to treat the transcripts of these sessions as a whole and to extrapolate from them the contrary views of Thiers and his opposition.

The basic contention upheld by Thiers, and invariably seconded by Cissey, was that France need not, and indeed could not, replicate the German military system. The minutes of the CSG remove any doubt that the heart of the controversy was prussification of the French army. Because the issue of a "nation in arms" had already been debated by the Assembly, in the privacy of Thiers's chambers the military question now took a new and more technical form. It began at once with a dispute concerning the best means to assure rapidity of mobilization, the lack of which was acknowledged by everyone as the immediate cause of the French defeat in 1870. This problem was inseparable, however, from the organization of the army's reserve system. The government proposed to maintain the existing procedure whereby the reservist was called, in case of a national emergency, to report back to the unit with which he had completed his active service. Thiers denied that France would gain any substantial advantage by adopting a regional reserve system, similar to the Prussian, which required that the mobilized reservist report first to the supply depot nearest his residence and then proceed with his local unit to a predetermined assignment. At issue was more than a matter of procedure. In reality the CSG was discussing some of the most fundamental political, economic, and military problems that the republic faced —witness the four mutually supporting arguments constructed by Thiers during the sessions in the Elysée to buttress the government's position.

1. *The social and political structure of France was essentially different from that of Germany.* In pressing this point Thiers was elaborating the rationale of his address to the Assembly in June that Prussia exemplified a unique combination of a "submissive, docile people" and a vigorous aristocracy that "gives tone to all the rest."[12] The regional system, as he now said, had "passed into the mores of Prussia" but would not be appropriate in France and could not be applied "without great inconveniences." Specifically, whereas a high degree of morale and discipline might be expected from the German soldier under any circumstances, it would be "upsetting" (*fâcheux*) to have French reservists serve in a strange

unit, in a corps other than the one with which they had performed their active duty. Thiers was willing to concede that the regional system represented "a considerable advantage" for the Germans, but he insisted that it was nonetheless "impossible" for the French. This was a rhetorically effective argument for the president to make because it granted the indisputable fact of Prussian efficiency and yet denied the conclusion that his opponents wished to draw from it. Thiers's view was, moreover, based on an assumption that none of his interlocutors was likely to challenge: neither individually nor collectively were the Germans as a people comparable to the French.[13]

2. *The restrictions of the French national budget, imposed by the costs of the war and the peace settlement, would not permit the adoption of a regional system like the Prussian.* Prussia's reserve forces had functioned rapidly and effectively in 1870 because they had previously been well trained and were always kept fit. This was possible, Thiers observed, only because the Prussians were able to hold annual maneuvers for all reserve units. Given the current financial situation, the French could not afford this procedure if they were at the same time to maintain a sizable standing army. Thiers evidently wished to place a clear choice before the CSG: either a large peacetime infantry—which he estimated variously between five and six hundred thousand men—or the reserve system advocated by his opponents. The government could not hope to underwrite both. He admitted that a permanent military force of the size he envisaged, composed of four grand armies divided into twelve corps, would require an annual budget of 500 million francs, although "in this matter it is necessary to temporize and not to offend public sentiment. If the government had demanded enormous credits at the outset, there would have been a general outcry; it is preferable to allow the Chamber and the Ministry of Finance to recognize little by little the necessity of a huge budget for the army." The virtue of this proposal, he was confident, would be demonstrated by the military results. "Let us have 500,000 men under arms in peacetime and we will have nothing to fear of Germany." Thiers's conclusion was a paragon of logic: "This strong standing army would be preferable to any system of reserves, because in maintaining it we would always be ready for war." Again, this argument was not easily gainsaid, especially as it was hardly more than a tautology. If the French

could field a standing army large enough to meet any emergency, it followed that they could dispense with a regional system of reserves.[14]

3. *The success of the French army, whatever the form of military organization, depended above all on the quality of political leadership.* Throughout the meetings in the Elysée Thiers returned several times to the assertion that "the difficulties of a prompt mobilization are more political and administrative than military." It was evident to him that the enemy had prepared the war of 1870 "well in advance" and that the astonishingly rapid mobilization of Prussian military forces had been possible primarily because of a prior political decision. The speculations concerning the ability of the German army to mobilize within nine or ten days in a future conflict entailed gross exaggeration: "I repeat, well-calculated preparations for war never require less than six weeks for any government." Therefore, France must possess a regime able to keep its alliances intact and its army on alert. Correct military strategy and its prompt execution, Thiers maintained, always depend on the prescience of political analysis. As for the present, "if one considers the political phenomenon which has occurred these last years in the center of Europe and has substituted a powerful united state for a federation, one cannot hesitate [about] the direction in which our forces ought to be faced." Thiers thought that nearly three-quarters of the French forces should be concentrated on the eastern and northeastern frontiers "because all the political prognostications indicate the possibility of war only from these sectors." He was convinced that the French railway system, which he regarded as superior to the German, would be adequate to assure rapidity of mobilization because the regular troops would already be in frontal position and the vast majority of reservists would be moving from west to east. If one were prepared to grant that France could afford to maintain an army of more than four hundred thousand men stationed permanently on the German frontier, as Thiers now proposed in effect, it would be difficult to contradict his contention that a regional system of reserves—even if it might avoid a brief period of confusion and delay—was unlikely to make an appreciable difference. Except for the emphasis on astute political leadership, presumably his own, this contention was little more than a rephrasing of the preceding argument.[15]

4. *The adoption by France of a regional system of reserves would be "a veritable counterrevolution."* Of all Thiers's assertions, this was the most telling as well as the most revealing. It underscored even more than the others his belief in the primacy of domestic politics. He could not support a plan that would, as he saw it, destroy the "moral unity" of the French nation. It would be detrimental "to copy the Prussian organization, [because] the adoption of a regional system would set us back to an epoch anterior to 1789" and would result in having regiments "animated by a dangerous political spirit." For the good of the nation it would be much better to imitate "the common sense of the English," who were augmenting their army "yet changing so little their system." It had become fashionable to advocate the German system, Thiers admitted, but France should not submit to "la mode prussienne." The implication was obvious that his opponents merely wished, in the name of reform, to restore military authority to the provincial notables. But he was determined to place his personal prestige in the path of such an eventuality. Thiers's position was best summarized by the transcript of the CSG: "He repeats on this subject that what is possible and easy in Prussia is not so for us; that France cannot return to what existed before 1789; that he would never present to the Assembly, nor would it ever adopt, a project which would reestablish armies of Bretons, Provençaux, Picards, etc."[16]

Viewed as a whole, these four arguments demonstrated that Thiers had actually made little or no concession to the idea of universal conscription that had been the theoretical basis of the military reform of 1872. He believed that "obligatory service is rather a principle than a realizable fact"; and he noted that the major advantage of the reform adopted was that it made unnecessary any haggling with the National Assembly over the number of troops to be deployed in an "armée de métier." This term should perhaps not be taken too literally because it might be interpreted simply as a reference to the necessity of maintaining a solid core of troops around which a larger army was to be constructed. Yet the entire debate centered on the choice of certain priorities, and in making that choice the president's feelings were clear. Thiers remained, as he phrased it himself, "the adversary of all changes that are not indispensable."[17]

The opposition to Thiers was led by Marshal MacMahon,

who emerges from the records of the CSG as something more than the inarticulate and insipid figure he is often portrayed to be. So long as Thiers continued to hold the initiative, MacMahon's statements were mostly in the form of extemporaneous counterarguments. The marshal spoke up persistently to contradict Thiers and to contend that the government's proposal would necessarily involve deficiencies and delays in mobilization, "which the German system alone would make it possible to avoid." The substance of that contention may be briefly restated.

MacMahon's case rested, of course, on the indisputable fact that in 1870 the Prussian system had operated successfully and the French had not. The Prussians had been able to place six hundred thousand men on their western frontier within eleven days, whereas the French order to mobilize, issued on 14 July, had still not been fully executed nineteen days later. The marshal estimated, moreover, that in any subsequent conflict the German army would be capable of massing for battle on any given front within a maximum of ten days. He was confident that "many members [of the CSG] wished, as he, to see that system adopted that assures to Germany such a rapid mobilization. . . . The system proposed [by Thiers] appears much too slow." In defending this view MacMahon showed himself to be firm and tenacious. He disputed with Thiers about the relative merits of the French and German railway systems. And he pestered the president with rhetorical questions: what, for example, of the reservist called from Toulon to rejoin his old regiment in Brest? He also made no secret of his skepticism about France's capacity to maintain the standing army proposed by Thiers. About the quality of French political leadership for the present or in the future MacMahon had nothing to say. Yet there was already evidence in these initial sessions of the CSG that he would oppose any political regime that refused "to see imitated the Prussian regional system." From MacMahon's standpoint Thiers represented the reactionaries, the men who had failed to learn the lesson of 1870 and who now seemed bent, for dubious political reasons, on denying to the army the reforms essential for its reconstitution.

MacMahon's assumption that other members of the CSG shared his opinions was not unfounded. Yet the force of Thiers's objections to the political consequences of adopting the German system had an obvious impact as well. Most of the other members were consequently concerned to find some formula that would be mutually acceptable. The Duc d'Aumale proposed that the army at first experiment with a regional system without its being formally passed into law; should it in practice prove inapplicable to French circumstances, it might be possible to arrive at a "système mixte," which would combine the best features of "our present system and the Prussian system, by attempting something analogous to the recruitment by arrondissements, as under the Restoration." This suggestion was supported by General Deligny, who felt that Thiers's political objections could be met by gerrymandering the regions so as to avoid their identification with the traditional provinces. For the majority of military men the overriding consideration was rapidity of mobilization, and for that reason they tended to agree with the regional system in principle. An example was Marshal Canrobert, who concurred with MacMahon that mobilization was slowed because the French system required too many soldiers to report to supply depots located in a direction opposite to that of their regiments. Thus, although he would concede to Thiers that the Prussian regional system "was not applicable in France," he remained convinced that "one could nevertheless approximate it" (s'en rapprocher). This view was balanced by that of Minister of War Cissey, who continued to support the government's proposal although he "did not see any difficulties in experimenting with a mixed system." [18]

On this note the meetings in the Elysée ended, with a disposition to reach some compromise but without any substantive agreement as to the terms or implications. No votes had been taken, and no issues had been settled. One cannot characterize the division as one between civilian and military authorities. Nor would it be accurate to describe the altercation in the CSG as a contest between a political and military rationale of reform. It was, instead, a civil-military controversy among men who recognized that no clear boundary could exist between the two spheres while France remained in the shadow of Bismarck's Germany.

The move of the CSG to Versailles in late October had little noticeable effect on the character of its deliberations. Thiers and MacMahon were still the fixed poles of opinion. The others shifted cautiously between them. Except for Cissey, who was Thiers's man from beginning to end, it is impossible to divide the CSG conveniently into two groups, a government party and a party of opposition. Many of the questions debated—the location of supply depots, the procurement of uniforms and provisions, the arrangements for financial transactions—could be treated strictly as matters of detail. During the first few sessions at Versailles Thiers and MacMahon rarely intervened, as if a tacit agreement had been reached between them not to mention the more fundamental questions that remained unresolved. The first ballot taken in the CSG, on 25 October, was indicative of the deadlock. Whereas Thiers wanted all military financing to be administered through the Banque de France, MacMahon believed that three specialized banks could provide a system more enterprising and more supple. Predictably, one of the other members—Marshal Canrobert—proposed that the CSG compromise on two, thereby retaining sufficient centralization without creating a monopoly. The vote of the CSG on whether to have one bank or several was recorded as eleven against eleven.[19]

The moratorium on discussion of the territorial issue was ended on 8 November. A new round was started by the minister of war's proposal that the CSG prescribe credits for a standing army, which, with all of its supporting units and special services, would total nearly a million men. An immediate response came from MacMahon, who held forth on the important role played in the last war by the Prussian *Landwehr*. Thiers countered at once with the familiar argument about the crucial importance of alert political leadership, then added what he clearly regarded as the clinching point: "But when there are so many sacrifices to demand of the country for the organization of the active army, how can we still speak of the expenses that the formation of a territorial army would necessitate, however important the role of that army might be?" Because the national budget could not be balanced before 1873, it was enough for the moment to present the government's proposal to the National Assembly without asking for more. Thiers added a note of optimism: "A surplus of receipts is probable in 1874; at that time we shall see what it is feasible to do for the territorial army." In the meanwhile it would be possible to prepare "on paper" a territorial force of two to three hundred thousand men and, in fact, a parliamentary committee had already taken the matter under advisement. Thiers's tactic in the CSG could hardly have been made more patent: first to commit the military leaders to his own conception of an *armée de métier*, then to accept whatever else the Assembly and the budget would permit. For the moment the president was not to be faced down, but neither was the government's proposal brought to a final decision.

Attention turned instead to a more technical question. Precisely what would be the distribution of manpower within the total military force? Should there be twelve corps of three divisions each or, as in the newly revised German system, eighteen corps of two divisions each? With little exaggeration one may observe that it sufficed to know which alternative was more similar to the German to be certain how Thiers and MacMahon stood on the matter. It was as if one slight concession by either would result in an immediate polarization of the CSG. In this instance a decision was reached and Thiers emerged the apparent victor. But, by forcing the issue and getting his way, Thiers evidently raised fears among his critics that he would drive through his entire program if he were not soon stopped.

Although the allotment of troops to corps and divisions occupied the CSG through two long meetings, the essential difference of opinion is not hard to define. Thiers favored the greater flexibility permitted by having in each corps three divisions, one of which could be held in reserve and even transferred to another corps if need be. The total number of corps would be less— only twelve as against eighteen if the new German model were adopted—meaning that the French army would require fewer senior officers, fewer special services, and hence a smaller military budget. For these reasons and because "the experience of the past is for three divisions," Thiers opposed an adaptation of the German system.[20]

MacMahon considered the basic unit of modern warfare to be the corps, not the division as in the past. True, the Prussians had fewer divisions in 1870, but for each main army they possessed an additional corps, "and it was almost always with that fourth corps that they were able to turn our positions." The claim to greater flexibility in the French system was an illusion because it was essential that the organization and command in time of war be exactly the same as in peace; a single division was not capable of acting alone, nor could it be simply detached from one corps and added to another at the outset of a campaign. Having fewer and larger divisions would permit greater rapidity of movement and more concentration of artillery. The marshal therefore "prefers the organization of army corps into two divisions, such as it exists in Prussia."

MacMahon was supported most vigorously by the commander of artillery, General Forgeot ("we have much to copy from the Germans"), and by General Lallemand, who argued that "it is the organization by corps which has become the norm." In addition to Cissey, Thiers gained support notably from Canrobert, who thought it better to have twelve excellent commanders than eighteen mediocre ones. The pattern of debate thus remained much as before. The difference was that the government now insisted on a show of hands. At the meeting on 15 November, as the transcript reads, "the Conseil decides by a large majority to form the army corps of *three divisions.*"[21]

For the remaining six weeks of the year the CSG continued to meet and to discuss various questions of general military organization: the future role of the cavalry, the assignment of artillery reserves, the possibility of reforming the officer corps. Whatever the issue, the German example was always relevant and usually central to the debate. Yet throughout it all Thiers continued to insist that the deliberations of the CSG should be guided "less by what is presently practiced in other nations than by the experience of the past." The past to which he referred with increasing frequency was not the disaster of 1870 but the glorious epoch of the Napoleonic campaigns—a period for which Thiers frankly regarded himself to be France's preeminent authority. Although they had made their views clear, the president's opponents were unable to prevail against him. Had a law of general military reorganization been introduced to the Assembly before the end of 1872, it would probably have carried the unmistakable stamp of Thiers's leadership. It would, in other words, have embodied a minimum of concessions to proposals of reform advocated by MacMahon. But the law was not to be enacted until several months later.[22]

The Shift to a German Model

In the issue of the *Journal des sciences militaires* for December 1872, a lieutenant-colonel of the French army by the name of Charles-Alexandre Fay published a proposal for the general military reorganization that was scheduled for public debate during the coming year. In the progress of reform legislation this statement was an event. Fay's article had the effect of bringing discussion of the military bill full circle: "We are dominated, as we shall not cease to repeat, by the question of mobilization. . . . This is, in effect, the capital question." The thesis pronounced by Fay was simply that France could not afford the slightest delay in a military crisis. Anyone who studied the German plan of mobilization (which he had recently published in French translation) and who was acquainted with the facts of 1870 could, he believed, draw no other conclusion. To adopt any system that sacrificed the maximum rapidity of mobilization would be irresponsible. Fay therefore urged the adoption of a military organization based on the division of France into eighteen equal regions.[23]

To someone acquainted solely with the public record of the Thiers regime—that is, lacking detailed knowledge of the closed sessions of the CSG—Fay's plan might seem to be without particular significance. It could be thought just one more proposal among the many that had appeared since the passage of the law of 1872 on recruitment. But the records of the CSG indicate otherwise. Fay's plan had special importance because of its content and its timing. It restored to the forefront of debate the original contention of MacMahon, made at the meetings in the Elysée in October 1872, that the government's proposed mobilization procedure was "much too slow" and would produce delays, "which the German system [of eighteen regions] alone" could prevent. Moreover, Fay's article was printed just as Thiers appeared to have prevailed on the CSG to recommend the government's plan to the National Assembly—and thus, presumably, just as MacMahon and his supporters recognized that the military reforms they desired were unlikely to be legislated so long as Thiers was president of the republic. Political and military considerations remained, as before, inseparable.

The initial two sessions of the CSG during the first week of January 1873 were held in Paris; Thiers did not attend, and the discussion centered on technical details that aroused no dispute. On 9 January the military leaders were convened once more in the presidential residence at Versailles. As the meeting opened, with Thiers still absent, the tone was set by a controversy between Cissey and MacMahon. Whereas Cissey wanted the establishment of a permanent board of military advisers under the personal direction of the minister (*Comité d'Etat-major*), MacMahon urged that this body be given a different designation (*Comité de l'Etat-major*) and that it be empowered "to prepare all questions relative to war," including mobilization procedures, troop movements, coordination of transportation and communication, and germane matters. Cissey was quick to "reject completely this proposition" and to maintain that "the authority of the minister must not be destroyed; it is indispensable that he be left his initiative as well as his responsibility." Although MacMahon subsequently denied any intention to remove military planning from the minister's supervision, the disagreement obviously involved more than an article in the committee's title. It would be fair to formulate the marshal's view with little more bluntness than he did himself: war is too important a matter to be left to politicians.

Whereupon, the politician par excellence entered the room. Whether Thiers had deliberately avoided the preceding discussion, which was terminated inconclusively just as he appeared, it is impossible to say. One must conclude, in any case, that the principal item on the agenda so far as the president was concerned was that which followed: "Projet de répartition des troupes devant composer les divers corps d'armée." Cissey reminded his colleagues in his prefacing remarks that the CSG had already determined the total figure of twelve corps. The only question that urgently required their attention now that the German evacuation of the eastern provinces was nearing completion was the geographical location of the corps. Thiers then reviewed the government's proposal and added his personal opinion that it would be "impossible to distribute the military forces of the country more advantageously." At this juncture, Canrobert, hitherto a sometime supporter of Thiers, introduced the "well-conceived" plan for eighteen corps drafted by Lieutenant-Colonel Fay.

To this intervention Thiers responded with a string of categorical negatives. He described Fay's system as a "contresens" that was of "questionable utility" and demonstrated "little practicality." Fay had treated the problem "too geometrically" by attempting to create military regions of equal population and comparable resources. He had ignored "the political situation of Europe . . . in the light of which the distribution of our military forces ought to be made." By such a euphemism, of course, Thiers referred to the unification of Germany and the necessity of massing French troops on the eastern frontier. To this argument he added one further consideration: the supreme military and political importance of Paris required that the capital be "solidly occupied." Consequently, he concluded, "the propositions [of the government] are incontestably better."

They were nonetheless contested. The minutes of the meeting on 9 January are barely distinguishable from those of the sessions three months earlier when the CSG began. MacMahon once again expressed his professional admiration for the German mobilization procedure, which would permit the enemy to be fully prepared within a fortnight. He was now outdone by Canrobert, who predicted that "in twelve or thirteen days the Prussians can be on our frontier." Thiers admitted, as he had often before, that the foe would enjoy certain advantages that the French army must do its utmost to offset. But he returned to the leitmotiv of his government's military planning since its inception: "We cannot, because of the differences in our political and social order, adopt the German system." As for the specific question at hand, he found some consolation in the fact that Berlin was much farther from Metz than was Paris from Nancy and Verdun. Defeat had at least brought the advantage to the French that, even if they were slower to mobilize, they now had a shorter distance to transport their troops.[24]

After the habitual second of the president's remarks by Cissey, the meeting was adjourned. No ballot was taken to terminate the discussion, and there is consequently no indication of how many members of the CSG would have backed Fay's plan in the face of Thiers's insistent appeal for its rejection. Judging from Cissey's closing statement, one might have supposed that the CSG was to meet again within a few days, as was customary, and that a final vote on the government's program was soon to be expected. Such did not prove to be the case. The CSG was not reconvened until seven weeks later, on the last day of March 1873. Although Thiers and MacMahon were present, the discussion never wandered from two uncontroversial problems concerning supplies and logistics. Yet both men must have been under immense strain. For months they had opposed one another on issues that had still not been resolved and that neither evidently thought it opportune to raise. Each probably knew that a decisive test of Thiers's political strength would not be long in coming. But it is uncertain whether they were aware that this would be the last session of the CSG during Thiers's presidency.[25]

Meanwhile the government's plan had been formally presented to the Assembly, which at once submitted it to the parliamentary commission for military reorganization. A comparison of the text of the legislative proposal with the minutes of the CSG leaves very little doubt that it was drafted by Thiers himself. It echoed all of the arguments and many of the rhetorical phrases already employed by the president behind closed doors to defend his conception of a large standing army divided into twelve corps of three divisions each. It conceded that the German mobilization procedure had become "the object of our admiration," an admiration that was "legitimate" but "ill considered." The government's plan, on the other hand, would retain "the ideal of French unity" while leaving for future legislation the issue of the territorial armies. These measures, the text disclosed, had been "examined maturely [and] approved fully by the Conseil Supérieur de la Guerre, which discusses with zeal and profundity all questions relative to the organization" of France's military forces.[26] This formulation was hardly an accurate rendition of the facts. The evidence shows, rather, that the CSG had been and remained deeply divided. The impression of unanimity and the assertion that a blanket endorsement had been obtained for the government's military policy could only be described as deliberately misleading. It is difficult to see anything in this claim but a high-handed parliamentary maneuver by Thiers, an attempt to brush aside the opposition of MacMahon and his supporters by taking the matter out of their hands. As such it failed.

One explanation for the failure was that informed military opinion had begun to swing perceptibly against Thiers. Colonel Jules Lewal followed Fay in contending that logic as well as experience demonstrated the inferiority of having three divisions per army corps. The sensible solution, he emphasized, was to adopt the German arrangement of two divisions per corps; in fact, Lewal said, it was "scarcely possible these days to do otherwise."[27] Similarly, the anonymous lead editorialist of *Le spectateur militaire* portrayed Thiers as an armchair commander and observed that "the ideal of military organization at the beginning of this century can no longer be ours. . . . Germany early seized this truth." The writer went on to extol the advantages of the German organization over the Thierist conception and to express his dismay "in seeing the government launched in the latter path."[28] As the arguments of the opposition thus sharpened and came to a head, the same analyst summarized the case against Thiers as an onerous but unavoidable reality: "It is truly regrettable always to have to cite the Prussians when one wants to speak either of progress accomplished in military theory or of useful innovations in the practice of military affairs; and yet we are reduced to that."[29]

The narration of Thiers's enforced resignation belongs elsewhere. On the morning of 24 May 1873 he defended himself in the Assembly; during the afternoon he was outvoted; and in the evening he was replaced by MacMahon.[30] It is evident that the continuation of Thiers's term of office had become intolerable to his opponents for military as well as political reasons. MacMahon was suitable as a successor not only because he might hold the door ajar for a monarchy but because he was likely to help break the impasse in military legislation. The marshal had no compelling political ambition and did not relish being held accountable for the high office of the presidency. Yet he was dedicated to the army and, for that reason, the replacement of Thiers could not have been a matter of indifference to him. Above all MacMahon wanted to keep politics out of military affairs, as Thiers deliberately and ostentatiously had not. Perhaps this best explains the rapidity with which the marshal's often expressed scruples were overcome when he was offered the presidency. He was aware that Thiers was thereby being removed as an impediment not only to an eventual monarchical restoration but also to urgent military reform.[31]

The sequel was not long in coming. On 9 June a new proposal for military reorganization was presented to the Assembly by General Chareton, the same officer who had unsuccessfully opposed Thiers's five-year recruitment scheme in 1872. Now he could speak uncontradicted of the necessity for France to adapt to "new conditions of warfare," and he was free to advocate the adoption of a uniform organization of regular and regional corps "as in the German army."[32] Less than a fortnight later, on 21 June, the next meeting of the CSG was convened. The scene was the residence of the minister of war in Paris where the host was now General Du Barail. Speaking in the name of the government of President MacMahon, Du Barail announced that virtual agreement on the military reform bill had been reached between the new regime and the parliamentary commission. The formal consent of the CSG would be desirable, however, because it "would permit the minister to support the legislative proposal with all the more authority." A reporter for the commission thereupon outlined the provisions of the reform proposal, which included the division of France into eighteen military regions; one army corps would be stationed in each region, with two infantry divisions in each corps. General Du Barail recalled days gone by when the CSG had voted to favor three divisions per corps, observing that this decision "had not prevailed in the spirit of the commission over the advantages that the organization of corps in two divisions gives for rapidity of mobilization." Not a single member of the CSG had an objection to register, and the discussion moved on. One week later the members received a message from MacMahon complimenting them on the soundness of their judgment in approving the new reform plan. Du Barail could conclude ceremoniously that "among the Conseil, the government, and the commission there is thus at present the community of views and the understanding desirable in order for the project to be presented to the National Assembly under the best conditions." As a consequence, the law of general military reorganization was enacted, without further controversy worthy of mention, on 24 July 1873.[33]

France thereby went far toward adopting the Prussian system. Much of the outcome was directly attributable to MacMahon's personal involvement in hammering out the details and principles of reform.[34] He also succeeded in galvanizing those military officers who most closely shared his views, including Chareton, Lebrun, and Du Barail. Not only did their voices predominate, but they became increasingly unapologetic in their advocacy of a German form of organization. Du Barail best summed it up: "We imitated much more than innovated."[35] By declining to adopt a regional procedure for recruitment the Assembly made some concession to the political concerns that had been so avidly expressed by Thiers. But in nearly every other regard the French followed other European nations in recognizing Prussian superiority in military affairs by accepting the principle of universal conscription; precisely the same numerical distribution of regions, corps, and divisions; an identical prescription for the uniformity of territorial armies and reserves; and the device of a one-year volunteer option for reserve officer training.[36]

Here we have examined only some of the more salient features of the Prussian model consciously adopted by France. Were there nothing more to add, we might nod in dutiful agreement that, from a strictly theoretical viewpoint, the German impact had indeed been considerable in French thinking about the military question. But we shall see that the penetration of German influence in fact went much further as the practical problems of reconstructing the army began to accumulate. Once the obstacle of the Thiers presidency had been removed, the path of military reform was opened wide to the emulation of Germany. It was a trail that the French would pursue with an astonishing attention to detail.

Chapter 3

Forts, Rails, and Cannons

The Statistics of Disarray

The disaster of 1870 not only shattered the French army. It also left the nation without any semblance of a defensive line on the eastern border. Strasbourg and Metz were lost and with them the network of fortifications and railways that might otherwise have formed the basis of a reconstructed frontier. France had to begin all over again. Moreover, the military deficit had been compounded by extensive destruction and the capture of French matériel in combat. In view of the demonstrated superiority of German artillery and the steady technological advances of the postwar era, the French were obliged to test, manufacture, and deploy an entire new generation of armament. Otherwise they could not hope to compete.

This circumstance required a vast and expensive undertaking in which the French were forced to question, more or less literally, the caliber of their rearmament. On what scale of magnitude should their efforts be measured? Repeatedly the answer was dictated by the necessity of keeping up with the Hohenzollerns. So long as problems were debated in political generalities and organizational principles, the issue of how far France should imitate the German example could remain somewhat vapid. But when it came to the consideration of military hardware, there was less room for speculation in making practical decisions that could not be indefinitely deferred. Again and again only one calculation mattered: whether a given weapon or construction or formation would enable France to thwart a German attack. After 1870 most French military planners were consequently dazzled by comparative numbers; and only by scrutinizing their statistics can we gain a detailed conception of German influence on the military question in France.[1]

When the Franco-Prussian war opened, the French had been immediately able to activate only 154 batteries of artillery.[2] Most of these were quickly eradicated during the initial battles near the German frontier. Other units were mobilized or created in the months before the conflict was finally terminated. By the summer of 1871 the minister of war estimated that the remnants of nearly 300 artillery batteries were scattered throughout France. But the losses, changes, and irregularities of the war had left them so unequal in strength that regimental commanders were authorized to reduce the number of batteries in order to consolidate them and to assure discipline. "These measures," the ministerial instructions concluded, "would have only a quite transitory character, awaiting a probable reorganization of the army."[3] The actual extent of disarray could not be precisely verified even by those who conscientiously attempted to do so. Questionnaires with more than six hundred queries were sent out to artillery commanders; but the replies, late and sporadic in returning, were never fully tabulated.[4]

The lack of an accurate inventory did not discourage provisional plans for reconstruction. In April 1872 General de Cissey acted on a staff report by requesting the newly formed Comité de l'Artillerie to work out a projection for thirty regiments "in preparation for a complete and definitive reorganization of artillery personnel."[5] Even while these measures were being drafted and submitted for approval to President Thiers, the Comité de l'Artillerie was beginning to plan a further expansion to thirty-six regiments. The committee estimated that this could be accomplished within six years, although the problem of recruiting enough trained artillery officers might prove troublesome.[6] When this problem was referred back to the Ministry of War, the verdict was that qualified senior officers were indeed lacking but even more serious was the shortage of cadres (noncommissioned officers). It would therefore be necessary to proceed "very sensibly, very slowly" with the projected expansion.[7] Yet despite these difficulties and some dissension within his ministry, Cissey continued under constant urging from Thiers to press for higher quotas. The authorized level was raised to thirty regiments of twelve batteries each in January 1873; and a few weeks later General Forgeot, the chief artillery officer, submitted a timetable for reaching forty regiments of thirteen batteries by January 1878.[8]

These projections were temporarily interrupted by Thiers's fall from the presidency in May 1873 and by the resulting reconsideration of a general military organization. But the ultimate sense of all these numbers remained the same. That rationale was made patent at a session of the Conseil Supérieur de la Guerre presided over by Cissey's successor, General Du Barail, in June 1873. It was evident that the decision of the CSG to divide France into eighteen military corps areas accorded closely with Forgeot's latest estimates for the artillery. Now the optimal figure could be set at one brigade—that is, two regiments—per corps stationed in metropolitan France, plus an additional brigade in Algeria. Translated into other terms, Forgeot stated, these 38 regiments would represent about 3.60 pieces of mobile artillery for every thousand men in the French army and thus a firepower (*bouches à feu*) of 108 versus 102 in the German army.[9] The primary motive—to outstrip the Germans—was thereby made obvious. To legislate anything less than a numerical advantage for France made no sense; it would only have condemned the French to an inferior status in perpetuity. Hence Forgeot's projections became the statistical basis of planning for the French artillery and were later ratified in the military reform bill of 13 March 1875. But because this law still lacked any provision for fortress artillery, it actually failed to match overall German strength even on paper.[10] Furthermore, records of the Ministry of War show that the French continued to lag far behind their anticipated quotas. One report after another lamented the shortage of trained manpower, until the First Bureau was forced to conclude in the summer of 1874 that the creation of additional artillery units was "practically impossible under the present circumstances because the officers, the cadres, the men are lacking." Thus the result was much like Achilles chasing Zeno's confounding tortoise through an infinite series of points. The German army always seemed one jump ahead. Staff officers in the rue St. Dominique responded with alarm at every rumor that the Germans might soon increase the numerical strength of their artillery. And so the counting relentlessly continued.[11]

Much the same conclusion could be reached by a study of the military budget. After 1871 the French Ministry of War received steady annual increments: from 431 million francs in 1872 to 440 million in 1873 and 480 million in 1874. By 1875 French appropriations were apparently on a par with those of Germany; and by 1876 both nations reached a military allocation of about 500 million francs.[12] Yet such statistics were often deceptive. They did not necessarily mean that France was closing the gap. First, although the Germans were also obliged to meet massive expenses of new construction and equipment, initially they did not have nearly the quantity of new fortifications or weapons to replace as the French. At the beginning of 1875 the German reconstruction of the forts ringing Strasbourg was virtually completed, and the new defensive strongholds around Mainz were "all very advanced."[13] Meanwhile the French had scarcely begun to rebuild and were still faced with a huge expense, which the chief of the Corps of Engineers, General Raymond Adolphe Séré de Rivières, estimated at a minimum of 400 million francs:

million francs			
North	50	Paris	60
Northeast	112	Seine	15
Southeast	32	Pyrenees	10
Alps	15	Ports	20
Interior	58	Other	28
		Total	400 [14]

Modest as these numbers later proved in reality to be, they suggested the immense and permanent strain that military expenditures would represent for France. Second, official budget figures gave only a very imprecise notion of actual military spending. Much of the real cost of reconstruction was hidden under such budgetary rubrics as public works, transportation, and "extraordinary funds." The German government was ostensibly devoting about 22 percent of its total annual revenue to the military. The French admitted to only 19.5 percent in 1876. Including special credits for fortifications, however, the actual percentage allocated to the French army was probably closer to one-quarter of the national budget. If France had been able to keep pace with the remarkable climb of the German GNP in the latter part of the century, the prospects would not have been too discouraging. But that was not to be the case. Third, as indicated by the above statistics, allowance must be made for differences in bookkeeping procedures. French and German bureaucrats seldom accumulated and tabulated statistical data in an identical manner. At a later juncture the analysis will focus on a characteristic example of calculations that ostensibly suggested a near parity of military expenditures between the two nations but that in fact disguised a significant discrepancy. More often than not, as a result, the historian's pretension to statistical precision has proved to be a fool's gold. Finally, as we shall also follow in detail, the very fact of allocating funds did not guarantee that French resources would be effectively employed. The demonstrable mistakes and misestimations born of confusion in the postwar era made this a virtual truism. As one military writer observed in dismayed reference to the "regrettable inferiority" of the French army: "A considerable increase in expenditures does not at all correspond to a similar increase of military power."[15]

For these reasons the actual cost efficiency of the new French defensive system is difficult to establish numerically. Things were seldom what they seemed, and no projection or plan was immutable. Statistics therefore provided a crude indication rather than a precise description of French military recovery.

The New Defensive System

Of all those who contributed to French military planning in the 1870s, the most important individual was General Séré de Rivières.[16] Indeed it is difficult to think of another military figure of the entire nineteenth century, unless it was Napoleon Bonaparte, who had so much practical impact in France. Literally thousands of workers were occupied in constructing forts designed and located according to his specifications; and hundreds of thousands of French soldiers were eventually trained to defend them. Séré de Rivières's fundamental ideas were set forth in a series of detailed secret memoranda that he prepared for the Comité de Défense. It is fair to say that he dominated this body (as well as several ancillary planning groups) from its inception in 1872 until 1877, the important formative phase of military recovery. Any study of the French defensive system should therefore begin with an examination of his views.[17]

The principal deficiency of the French military defense in 1870, Séré de Rivières contended, had been the lack of a central point. France's first priority must therefore be to construct a defensive "screen" (*rideau*) along the Moselle and Meuse rivers. By erecting an impregnable barrier stretching between the fortresses of Verdun and Toul, the French would be able to divide invading German armies and force them into "corridors" to the north or

Map 1 / France's Eastern Front circa 1890

south. There the incursions could be met by mobile French forces, which would be deployed in accordance with the relative weight of the German thrust. This would be, as Séré de Rivières wrote, "an active defense based on several strong points."[18]

Certain corollaries followed from these axioms. In a war of movement railways would be of utmost importance. The French must therefore extend their rail system and at the same time provide a series of redoubts (*forts d'arrêt*) capable of interdicting enemy traffic along those lines. The construction of an interior defense would also be desirable so that, in case of initial setbacks, the French armies could regroup at some distance from the frontier without retreating all the way to Paris. Moreover, because of the longer range of modern artillery demonstrated by the Prussians in the recent war, the fortifications of the capital would also need to be extended as part of a "défense active éloignée."[19] Whereas urgent priority must be given to the eastern front from Verdun to Belfort, the French could not long afford to neglect the northern border even though it was "sufficiently protected, at this moment, by Belgian neutrality." Although some skepticism about Germany's enduring respect for the international guarantee of Belgium's inviolability was manifest from the beginning, more than two decades would pass before that contingency became an integral part of French military planning.[20]

In analyzing Séré de Rivières's conceptions and the defensive network based on them, it is crucial to distinguish between two separate controversies. The first concerned the location of fortified places. The notion of corridors did not go unchallenged, both because the gaps in the French defense might prove too porous and because the proposed scheme required close coordination between mobile and fortress units rather than permitting them to maintain a separate role.[21] Until 1877, Séré de Rivières was able to have his way as the chief architect of French defense. But on 5 March of that year he was overridden in his objection to the proliferation of small forts located in the intervals between major fortifications. Despite his warnings about the folly of attempting to construct "a kind of wall of China," the contrary opinion prevailed. In the words of the current minister of war: "We must close all our doors." Although the basic plan of the French defensive system thus conformed to Séré de Rivières's original design, the decision to construct or reinforce a large number of small outlying forts was henceforth made over his repeated objection.[22]

A related controversy surrounded the extension of fortifications. From the beginning this issue was as much a problem of politics as of engineering or of military strategy. The question was: granted the longer range and heavier impact of modern artillery pieces, should fortresses be constructed and provisioned as independent units capable of withstanding a prolonged siege by themselves, or should they be integrated with mobile arms in a more fluid defense? Immediately after the war a categorical stance in favor of the former option was assumed by President Thiers, who insisted that the existing ramparts and forts of Paris, which dated from his own premiership in the 1840s, should be refurbished. The capital must be held at all costs.[23] Although no one could well argue with that principle, some doubt persisted about the most viable means of defense. Specifically to address that matter a parliamentary subcommittee was composed of generals Chabaud-Latour, Frossard, Lebrettevillois, and Séré de Rivières. Their report, filed in March 1872, bluntly criticized Thiers's position and outlined the assumptions that were to be operative in the design of French fortifications for the balance of the decade. The experience of the past war, they pointed out, had revealed both the strengths and weaknesses of the Paris walls, which were well suited to resist direct assault by enemy infantry but were unable to protect the populace against prolonged bombardment by heavy artillery. The old ramparts were therefore no longer adequate to meet the need for "an extensive and active defense, the only one that can provide favorable prospects." The truth was, the four officers concluded, that technological progress had "profoundly modified the general conditions of warfare and in particular those of assault on fortresses." Rather than invest heavily in the reinforcement of old structures, then, it would be better to expand considerably the outer perimeter of defense.[24] Not until two years later, in March 1874, did an appropriations bill for the Paris forts come to the floor of the Assembly. Its sponsor, Chabaud-Latour, reiterated the rationale of the subcommittee's 1872 report, while admitting that the estimated cost of the project had in the meanwhile risen from 50 to 60 million francs. The ensuing debate was noteworthy as the first oratorical performance by Thiers in the Palais Bourbon since the termination of his presidency ten months earlier. But his advocacy of a concentrated fortification (*enceinte restreinte*) against Chabaud-Latour's proposal of greater dispersal (*enceinte étendue*) failed to prevent passage of the latter's bill by a vote of 386 to 184.[25]

Even at the time, and all the more so later, the distinction between the issues of location and extension was often blurred by polemicists. According to one version, Thiers had in effect become a champion of the classical Vauban design of compact and independent fortifications. Against this was pitted the theory of an active and coordinated defense made necessary by the demonstrated capability of Prussian weaponry. Thus one supporter of Séré de Rivières urged the French to admit the "brilliant superiority of the German school" and to concede that the "Vauban system ought to be abandoned as no longer adaptable to the progress of modern artillery."[26] To regard the passage of Chabaud-Latour's appropriations bill in the Assembly as a victory for the "German school" was perhaps an oversimplification. Yet for the public and for parliamentarians attempting to grasp the technical complexities of the military question, such a formula provided an easy handle.

All of this discussion, as German agents and attachés repeatedly observed, tended to produce more publication than construction.[27] Little was accomplished before 1875. The international diplomatic alarm of that year caused the French to erect hastily around Verdun what became known as "les forts de la panique."[28] But these were admittedly suspect; and it can scarcely be argued that the French possessed serious defensive fortifications anywhere before 1878, even on the eastern frontier from Verdun to Belfort, to which most of the available funding was devoted. Séré de Rivières also made intensive studies of the northern and Alpine borders, but allocations and construction in those areas lagged.[29] Such unevenness in the defensive system was reflected in formal military planning. By the end of 1878 the Conseil Supérieur de la Guerre had examined three separate hypotheses: a German invasion in which the neutrality of Belgium and Luxembourg would be respected (Plan Three); a German invasion in which the neutrality of Belgium and Luxembourg would be violated (Plan Four); and a joint attack by Germany and Belgium against France and the Netherlands (Plan Five).[30] The last of these was paranoid at worst and fanciful at best; the second was still considered by most military men to be implausible for a combination of political and technical reasons; hence only Plan Three was studied in detail and rehearsed for eventual execution. Both French defensive building and planning thereby pointed to the same conclusion: the likelihood of a German attack departing from Alsace-Lorraine and penetrating just to the north or south of France's central bastions. At this point French military thinking began to oscillate. Before 1885 this was the only war for which the French made preparations; and it was seemingly the only war they could afford to fight.[31]

Never was there serious doubt that any future conflict would begin with "an offensive march by the German armies."[32] Yet the

French had to ask not only where the invasion was most likely to come but also how quickly. Their planned deployment of troops was a model of simplicity: of the five main army groups, two would defend north of the Verdun-Toul barrier and two to the south, while the other would be held in reserve to be committed once the main path of the German assault was evident. On an inspection tour in early 1875, however, General Du Barail became alarmed about the possibility of a sudden enemy attack across the frontier while the armies were still in the process of mobilization. After all, nothing could guarantee that the Germans would conveniently wait until France was altogether prepared. The nightmare of a swift debacle reminiscent of 1870 haunted French planners. Hence, although the fundamental conception of Plan Three remained fixed, they tinkered incessantly with the mechanics of troop concentration and mobilization procedures. At first, in response to Du Barail's warning, their major preoccupation was "protection" (*couverture*): in 1876 it was decided to convene military units well behind the frontier, then move them forward. Two years later, when new French railway lines were being put into service, there was a return to the notion of mobilizing close to the German border and even some consideration of an initial offensive thrust to upset the timing of a German invasion before it could be mounted. But again, much discussion produced remarkably few changes.[33]

In the early 1880s two factors served to reinforce French inertia. One was a recognition of German numerical superiority. A tabulation in 1882 revealed that the Germans had nearly twice as many troops as the French stationed in the immediate vicinity of France's eastern border, and their potential mobilization of reinforcements was known to be at least as efficient. Faced with the mass of the German war machine—superior by an estimated 132 battalions of infantry in 1883—the French were in no situation for derring-do.[34] The other reason for caution was political. By this time the French republic was in a period of diplomatic detente with Germany. Any major new fortifications constructed on the frontier might be regarded as a deliberate provocation and might lead the Germans to retaliate in the form of additional forts or troops in Alsace-Lorraine. This judgment was offered by the ambassador in Berlin, Saint-Vallier, when asked about a possible German reaction to the creation of a stronghold at Nancy, the most conspicuously exposed French city outside of the defensive perimeter. For the sake of detente Saint-Vallier advised "extreme prudence."[35] This soon became a sensitive issue that produced anguished letters and rhetorical duels. General Courcy, commander of the sixth army corps directly opposite Germany, warned that France faced "a difficult, even perilous situation" without strengthened fortifications. His successor at that post, General Chanzy, was similarly worried in 1882 about "a security that does not exist"; he urged that France concede no precious territory, city, or population at the outset of a war and that every effort be made to meet the German invaders on the border. His view was contradicted notably by Marshal Canrobert, who asserted that the French should defend the strategic rather than the political frontier. Finally it was Canrobert who prevailed. Chanzy was confidentially informed by Minister of War Billot that, although his complaints about the "weakness and insufficiency" of the French defense were partially justified, "conditions at this moment are such as to require much prudence and circumspection" in order to avoid "arousing susceptibilities that might create serious difficulties for the government." The Germans, in short, would be displeased.[36]

The French fortifications as they were conceived in the 1870s were never actually tested in combat. Hence it is supererogatory to speculate about the degree of military strength they represented. Yet we can reach two preliminary conclusions. First, it is obvious that the forts were constructed solely to meet a potential threat from Germany, and in this elementary respect Germany's influence on French military planning was paramount. Beyond that, the French defenses were initially designed in anticipation of a form of warfare, including heavy artillery, that had been developed and demonstrated by the Germans. In this fashion, too, French military policy was to a great extent predetermined by the necessities of competition with a neighboring power.[37]

Second, many of the military options chosen in the formative years were to remain compelling for the history of the Third Republic until the First World War. Once the forts were located, they could be either reinforced or abandoned, depending on future decisions, but they could not simply be moved. Whether correct or mistaken, one decision thus led to the next. The same principle, as we shall see, applied to other phases of military planning. Unfore-

seen technological advances would force the French, after the indecision of the mid-1880s, to make drastic changes in their defensive arrangements. In our present perspective it is apparent that
they often expended enormous sums for instant obsolescence. Yet
no matter how the French armies later chose to maneuver, they
continued to do so behind the basic system of fortifications that
Séré de Rivières had built.[38]

The Expansion of Transportation

The greatest innovation of nineteenth-century warfare was
the railroad. Better said, it was the rail network that made the
difference and permitted the indispensable combination of modern strategy: mass and movement. Previously large armies could
travel slowly or small units more swiftly. But the effective mobilization of a "nation in arms" necessarily had to await completion
of a sufficient number of railways to transport quantities of men
and matériel with speed over long distances. These were the veri-
ties first tested by the Prussians in 1866 and then demonstrated by
them with such virtuosity in 1870. Unfortunately for France, a
new day of armed combat had dawned in the East.[39]

The lesson administered by Germany was not lost in France;
and a specialized literature on transportation soon appeared. The
seminal work on French railroads after 1870 was the authoritative
study of logistic operations during the Franco-Prussian war by
François Jacqmin. Professor at the Ecole des Ponts-et-Chaussées as
well as director of the Chemins de Fer de l'Est, Jacqmin was not
unbiased in stressing the military importance of mobility by rail.
But his unsparing account of the confusion and ineptitude of the
French performance in wartime was beyond refutation. Nor could
anyone well deny his unflattering comparison of erratic French
procedures with the more centralized and efficacious German organization. There could be no surprise in his conclusion that
France should adopt regulations similar to those already in practice in Germany. Jacqmin's book, as a reviewer in the prestigious
Journal des sciences militaires observed, immediately created "a
great sensation"; and it also prompted in November 1872 the
formation of a Commission Supérieure des Chemins de Fer. The
purpose of this committee was to coordinate the planning and
construction of French railways in order to realize, as the reviewer

noted, "the favorable results this has permitted the Germans to obtain."[40]

With Jacqmin as the dominant figure among its members, the committee devoted long hours to a detailed study of German techniques in adapting their rail system to military problems, paying special attention to the elaborate train schedules that had enabled the Germans to regulate the movement of troops and supplies during the mobilization of 1870.[41] As in other areas of planning, however, practical measures remained in abeyance until the replacement of Thiers by MacMahon in the presidency had cleared the way for the military reform bill of 1873. An initial parliamentary consultation early that summer allowed a modest preliminary appropriation of funds for construction of some trunk lines on the new eastern frontier. But this still fell short of envisaging a thick network of interior rail connections, and the building program plainly lacked a sense of urgency. As the German military attaché commented, the fact that some of the new rail lines were not scheduled for completion until 1880 would mean "a disproportionately long interval."[42] Meanwhile, French intelligence learned that a revised timetable for the military use of German railways had already been "completely perfected . . . down to the last detail." Once again France trailed.[43]

The magnitude of the railway issue did not begin to emerge until the mid-1870s, when the full implications of the general reorganization of the army became clear. To be sure, there were other reasons—among them potential profit—to hasten rail construction, but the chief motive was military necessity.[44] The division of the French mainland into eighteen military territories hypothetically meant that each army corps would be responsible for quartering an equal number of soldiers. Even allowing for some displacement of troops from one corps area to another, the geographical distribution was such that only by rapid transportation could sufficient manpower be assembled near the German frontier in a time of crisis. Three types of construction were required: more local rail lines and roads to carry soldiers to their mobilization depots; major express railways to enable freshly mobilized units to approach the eastern border; and long platforms for embarkation and debarkation.[45] These needs were to be met by a new program of railway construction begun in 1877 that would occupy the French for a decade thereafter.

Before examining that program in more detail, we should note the continuing impetus provided by the German example. From the outset, the French were aware that a gap existed between the two nations and were fearful that it might gradually be widening. Such was the theme of several French deputies appearing before the Assembly in 1877 who advocated the nationalization of France's entire railway system. One of them even claimed that German railway construction had attained a tempo double that of the French.[46] Although these assertions were challenged, they served to sustain apprehensions about the inadequacy of French reorganization.[47] They also posed a recurrent question: if the standard of size and efficiency was to be the German model, why not literally copy it? Most railway experts favored precisely that answer, but they were often reluctant to injure French pride by making a too brutal admission of the need for imitation. A single example among many may suffice. In October 1877 Charles Baum, an engineer at Ponts-et-Chaussées and a disciple of François Jacqmin, published in the *Journal des sciences militaires* an appeal for the creation, as in Germany, of a special railway department in the French Ministry of War. In the conflict of 1870, he wrote, the Prussians had illustrated how trains could be employed as "powerful instruments of warfare," and since then they had gained "a further lead on the path of innovation." Baum wished to follow the German example, but he carefully resorted to circumlocutions as if to avoid a flagrant admission of French inferiority: "There is nothing in this [German] organization that should deter any other nation that would follow the example of Prussia and enter with equal resolution on the path of military progress."[48]

Not everyone was so squeamish in suggesting that France must adopt German techniques, especially after the *seize mai* crisis of 1877 had undercut French conservatism and consolidated the grip of Gambettist republicans. Most prominent of these was Charles de Freycinet, like Jacqmin and Baum a professional engineer, who was to remain a pivotal figure in government until the 1890s. Already known through his writings on the war of 1870 as a frank admirer of German organization, he welded the plans and projections of the first postwar decade into a coherent program of public works and gained the requisite political support from Gambetta, Léon Say, and the French Assembly to finance it.[49]

On the second day of January 1878 Marshal MacMahon was persuaded by Freycinet and his allies to sign a decree that instituted six regional railway commissions, which, under government supervision, were charged with submitting recommendations for the completion of a French rail network. The measure stopped short of nationalization. Instead, 181 lines were designated by a law of 17 July 1879 to constitute a "réseau d'intérêt général." Ten more lines were so classified in 1881. The euphemism of "general interest" meant in reality that the French were charting a comprehensive plan of rail construction that would meet military requirements. Out of this massive effort, despite subsequent financial and political difficulties, eighteen thousand kilometers of new track were eventually added to the French railway system, bringing the total by the mid-1880s to about forty-three thousand kilometers.[50]

Behind all of this effort and expense was a common rationale: to increase the efficiency of French mobilization in the event of a war with Germany. As early as April 1878 the Conseil Supérieur de la Guerre estimated that France would soon possess at least twelve major rail lines capable of transporting between fifteen and eighteen trains a day to the eastern frontier. These French facilities were supposed to be adequate to permit fifteen army corps to be ready for action on the German border by the twelfth to the fourteenth day of mobilization—that is, in about the same time that would be required for the Germans to place fifteen of their own corps on the Metz-Avricourt-Strasbourg front. This progress led the Commission Supérieure des Chemins de Fer, in turn, to revise the mobilization schedule of 1876 and to issue a new timetable in 1880. Thereafter it became a matter of raising step by step the capacity of the French rail system. In July 1881 the quota for "strategic lines of transport" was elevated from thirty-six daily trains in both directions to forty-eight.[51] By laying new tracks and by doubling the single lines in existence, the French were able to gain hypothetical time in their race against Germany. Thus a secret memorandum circulated in 1886 advised that "the concentration of armies in the Northeast" would be possible "*at least twenty-four hours sooner*" by the next year.[52]

Although the commercial value of many of the French railways built before 1885 remained in dispute, their military importance appears in retrospect beyond question. The true author of the 1914 miracle on the Marne, one might conclude, was not Joffre but Freycinet. At the very least, the evidence indicates that the strategic importance of railways was an instruction acquired at great cost by the French from the Germans in the years after 1870.

The Artillery

The *enfant gaté* of the French army was the artillery. No other military service was so carefully reassessed or so lavishly reappointed after the war; and none was more conspicuously affected by the continuing competition with Germany.

Rebuilding began early, in the midst of confusion. Within a few weeks of the suppression of the Paris Commune the first of the many French planning boards was founded: the Comité de l'Artillerie. Initially its duties were circumscribed. The presiding officer, General Forgeot, was admonished by Minister of War Cissey to abstain from consideration of "complete projects of reorganization" and to confine the committee to a study of the use of cannonry in the recently terminated war. These deliberations produced a dismaying but hardly surprising conclusion: "the inferiority of [French] artillery pieces . . . in range and in accuracy, relative to . . . the Prussian weapons." Tests were meanwhile being carried out at the old firing range near Bourges and at a new site near Calais. But these experiments were conducted mainly with English and Prussian cannons acquired before the war. They consequently had only a retrospective value and were halted by the beginning of 1872. At the same time very little attention was being devoted to the *mitrailleuse*, which had been developed in secret before 1870 but was unsuccessfully deployed in battle and was thereupon allowed to fall into temporary neglect.[53]

Adolphe Thiers was the driving force in the revitalization of the artillery. Of his many military hobbies, this was the pet. Although, practically speaking, much of his indefatigable effort was wasted, he did succeed in dramatizing the importance of artillery and in encouraging support for its financing. The president's well-publicized "vacation" at Trouville in August 1872 was a case in point. The performance of the French artillery weapons which he witnessed there was so disappointing that the minister of war later declared himself to be "very happy that no foreign officers came to view this series of tests"—but this fiasco only led Thiers to redouble his efforts to upgrade French weaponry. He personally patronized Colonel Jean-Baptiste de Reffye, inventor of France's first postwar generation of cannons, confiding that he "could not live with the thought that France is disarmed" and urging that he and Reffye should together restore French artillery "to the level of contemporary science." Thiers also corresponded with Eugène Schneider, the famous director of the Creusot metal works, about the potential application of steel to the design of new cannons. Despite Schneider's expressed caution in April 1873, the president's enthusiasm was overflowing that they had "finally discovered a genuine *acier à canon*" that would soon provide France with "a real superiority over the other European powers in the production of this material."[54]

Such optimism was necessarily tempered by realism, however, because budgetary restrictions and the shortage of trained personnel were no less constraining than the initial lack of weapons. When a proposal reached his desk to increase substantially the number of artillery staff officers, for example, Minister of War Cissey objected that the suggested quotas were beyond France's financial means, and he added dryly: "It is useless to demand the impossible."[55] A statistical survey of staffing needs indicated that the problem was chronic. Of the 3,240 artillery officers required for full strength in 1873, only 2,140 were actually available. Beyond this current deficit of 1,100 it was necessary to anticipate 50 new vacancies a year through resignation and retirement. Before the end of 1877, the date targeted for completion of the first phase of expansion and reorganization, about 1,350 newly trained artillery officers would therefore be needed. Of these the Ecole Polytechnique could provide at most 900; the remainder would have to be recruited from the junior ranks and funneled through the artillery officer training program at Fontainebleau. "This is possible," the report continued, "but it is not absolutely certain." The foreseeable difficulties in reaching a full complement of officers could be avoided if "the artillery would not be pressured to [attain] the very elevated number of 520 batteries and if, furthermore, we could take eight or ten years instead of five for its definitive constitution." The pace was too fast.[56]

This was the first detailed admission of a personnel shortage that would plague the artillery service for years to come. Quotas set in March 1875 proved impossible to fulfill; and indeed the deficit of artillery captains and lieutenants grew by December 1876 from 300 to 450. Consequently, 51 new artillery batteries approved by the Assembly in early 1875 were still lacking throughout most of 1876, and only 29 of them were constituted by the beginning of 1877.[57] Yet, as always, the real drama was not a question of numbers alone. "It would be desirable," the minister of war wrote in a disabused memorandum to the Comité de l'Artillerie, "that these batteries be composed entirely of experienced cannoneers." Because trained men were lacking, however, and because the construction of new fortifications on the frontier was creating an increased need for qualified officers to command artillery positions, he advocated a radical solution: to double the manpower of every field battery at the moment of mobilization. Through this means an active unit would be joined in wartime by a reserve unit under the same staff of officers. The French artillery could thereby remain economical in peacetime and still reach a numerical strength sufficient to rival Germany in case of war.[58] But many professional artillery people considered the principle of *dédoublement* far more brilliant on paper than in reality. Their confidence in reserves was low, and they worried about the practical difficulties of a swift transition from peace to war footing. The records show that the Comité de l'Artillerie therefore opposed the proposal and preferred to admit "the impossibility for the artillery to complete [its] cadres within several years." Thus the matter was temporarily deferred.[59]

An equally sober appraisal of weaponry was forthcoming after the political eclipse of Thiers in 1873. French artillery was at an awkward age. An older generation of bronze cannons was becoming obsolete, but the production of breechloading steel weapons was not yet perfected. Hence, while experimentation with the latter continued at Creusot, tests on several models of the Reffye system were hastened as well.[60] The imminence of a critical choice was signaled in August 1873 by the creation of a Commission Supérieure de l'Artillerie, convened and chaired by Marshal MacMahon himself. Within a few weeks the decision was announced to adopt 144 new batteries of Reffye 75- and 85-millimeter cannons. The order for these weapons was placed despite the staggering expense and the knowledge that, because cast in bronze, they were likely to be superseded in a relatively short time by the development of steel.[61]

There was another problem. Although much of the disorganization in France resulted from such technical reasons, there was also considerable apprehension about what artillery pieces were simultaneously being contemplated in Germany, a subject the French attempted to follow with care.[62] The prognosis was not encouraging. A subcommittee charged with investigating the latest innovations in European weaponry repeated earlier findings about Germany's "incontestable superiority" as of 1870, and its members concluded: "Despite the progress other nations have been able to make in their artillery, we observe that Prussia still occupies first place."[63] The rush to invest heavily in the Reffye cannons may thus correctly be regarded as an urgent attempt to establish some credibility for the French defensive system that otherwise, no matter how many forts and railways were constructed, would lack the slightest capacity to resist a German attack. Yet no sooner were these new weapons placed on order than they were declared to be insufficient. Forgeot's interim successor as chairman of the Comité de l'Artillerie, General de Rochebouët, reported in November 1873 that whereas France had adopted cannons of 75 and 85 millimeters, their German counterparts were of 78 and 88 millimeters. Although the Reffye weapons were of good quality, "the tendency everywhere abroad seems to be toward an increase in caliber." He continued: "The opinion of nearly all the infantry generals is that we cannot have a caliber inferior to that of the Germans, whose smallest is 78 millimeters, and all reports confirm that they are planning to increase it. . . . I consider, with the committee, that the caliber of 75 millimeters should not be accepted for . . . the new mobile artillery."[64]

Rochebouët's replacement in early 1874 by General Canu did nothing to alter the statistics of escalation. Again the Ministry of War was reminded by the Comité de l'Artillerie of the one intractable criterion for judgment: "Since Prussia has adopted the calibers of 78.5 and 88 millimeters," Canu wrote, "it currently seems impossible to retain those of 75 and 85, even with an equivalent weight of shells. To obtain a superiority over the German artillery . . . the committee proposes to adopt the calibers of 80 and 90 millimeters." It followed that the decisions of the past several years had to be reexamined, and the costly Reffye system could henceforth be regarded only as a temporary expedient. A new round of testing, commenced in January 1875, was consequently intensified for the Bange 80- and 90-millimeter cannons. The Commission Supérieure de l'Artillerie was reconvened in July by Marshal MacMahon to give its blessing to the new project, thereby implicitly conceding a previous miscalculation. But not until January 1877, fully two years after its initial tests, was the Bange system sanctioned by the Comité de l'Artillerie and then formally designated by the Ministry of War as the French "canons de campagne, modèle 1877."[65]

The arms race continued without respite into the 1880s. Without an assessment based on an actual confrontation between opposing artilleries in battle, one can only conjecture about their comparative strength. But there is reason to suppose that Germany continued to hold a technological advantage. Perhaps the most conclusive evidence was the impressive record of orders placed by other armies—Russia, Austria, Holland, and Spain among them—at the Krupp metal works in Essen. Estimates of weapons sales varied, of course, but French publications disclosed that for the year 1878 alone Russia had placed an order for more than one thousand German cannons.[66] Commenting on such transactions, one French writer acknowledged that the exertions of the Schneider firm at Creusot offered "a point of hope" for France, but he wondered why in the meantime the French army did not likewise purchase needed artillery pieces from Krupp.[67] The French nonetheless preferred to develop their own arsenal of weapons. Yet to do so was to accept the financially oppressive burden, vis-à-vis Germany, of overcoming an apparent deficit in technology and an obvious lag in time.[68]

To meet concurrent and persisting manpower needs during the second postwar decade, the French artillery finally adopted the principle of *dédoublement* in 1880. Much debated and resisted in the late 1870s, as we have observed, this solution became imperative as the only means to follow the Germans in organizing a fortress artillery to complement the existing field artillery. The necessity for a major expansion so as to incorporate France's increasingly sprawling defensive network had been anticipated years before.[69] But not until 13 December 1880 were practical measures ordered to implement it. Barely twelve months elapsed thereafter, however, before the new presiding officer of the Comité de l'Artillerie, General Berckheim, had to admit that "certain complica- tions" were becoming evident. In no other branch of French mili- tary service and in no foreign army, he noted, was it expected that two units would be provided for one. The resulting insolidity was such that "there is reason to organize the field artillery on new basis."[70] There were other symptoms of reappraisal. In March 1884, for instance, the Ministry of War announced plans for a redistribution of artillery formations on the frontier, with the in- tention of strengthening certain fortifications while abandoning others. This was only the first hint of things to come.[71]

The culminating point of these various developments can be precisely located in the year 1886. Rumors that Germany was developing high-percussion shells had been circulating for more than a decade.[72] By the early 1880s there was no longer any doubt that a technological breakthrough in munitions would be achieved, especially because the French themselves had been mak- ing "notable progress." In a word, the key was melinite, a chemi- cal substance that multiplied remarkably the force of explosives.[73] During the late summer of 1886 a series of tests was conducted on the fort at Malmaison. A typical example of French construction of the 1870s, the ramparts were made of lightly sanded earth reinforced by stonework. A team of French military inspectors convened for the occasion stood by and watched with horror as the new artillery shells smashed the fortress with "an astounding violence." According to an official report prepared for the Minis- try of War, "it must be concluded that in a fortification subjected to such bombardment, any activity would be impossible and, fur- thermore, that the morale of the garrison would be completely destroyed within a few hours."[74] The practical consequences of the Malmaison experiment were almost too discouraging to con- template. They seemed to establish that much of the existing French defensive system would be dangerously vulnerable under serious attack by German artillery. Lest this immediate reaction appear overwrought, it is worthwhile to quote from a much later (1909) confidential staff report that attempted to place the Mal- maison tests in a longer perspective: "In any event they showed that, with the new explosive contained in large missiles, the fortifi- cation of that era, taken altogether, had lost the relative and rather prolonged invulnerability it previously possessed . . . and that it was necessary to proceed to a complete rearrangement of all the structures in our defensive system in order to put them in a condition to resist even for a rather limited time."[75]

We shall subsequently examine the implications of such a drastic conclusion. Here it may suffice to draw an interim balance: despite all the efforts in a decade and a half to emulate, to counter, or to compete with Germany, the French army had nevertheless failed by 1885 to provide the republic with a defense capable of resisting an onslaught by the German Reich.

Chapter 4

Soldiers, Officers, and Steeds

The Infantry

The growth of the French army in the nineteenth century was not a steady progression. France had maintained far more men under arms on the eve of the Crimean war than at the outset of the conflict with Germany fifteen years later. From 340,000 soldiers in 1855, the infantry shrank to 211,000 by 1866—its lowest enrollment since the 1830s—and then expanded only slightly to 235,000 by the end of the Second Empire. Statistics for the other combat services indicated the same pattern: the artillery and the cavalry peaked in the mid-1850s and were then gradually reduced in numerical strength by about one-third.[1] Whether attributable to inertia, overconfidence, or naiveté, these facts undoubtedly reflected to some extent an established military orthodoxy that France would be better served by a small professional army than by a large aggregation of draftees. So it was until 1870. Thereafter the changes in attitude produced by demonstration of Prussian success were codified in the military reform bills of the early Third Republic. If the principle of universal conscription was hedged and qualified in this legislation, the capability of placing larger numbers of infantrymen into uniform nevertheless became a national imperative.[2]

Yet the Germans were no less determined to maintain their superiority in numbers, speed, and equipment. By rapid mobilization and deployment of reserves and *Landwehr* troops, German infantry had outnumbered the French during the critical opening phases of combat in 1870 at a ratio of at least three to two.[3] This advantage had more than offset the fact that the French *chassepot* proved to be a more effective infantry weapon than the so-called needle-gun carried by Prussian troops. At the war's end, however, the German General Staff immediately ordered the introduction of a new rifle (the 1871 Mauser) and the retention of six hundred thousand *chassepots* captured from the French. The former were used to reequip the standing army and the latter were distributed to the *Landwehr*, thereby giving Germany an early lead in the small arms race.[4] The subsequent escalation in rifles was not dissimilar to the competition in cannons; and the ultimate rationale, from Berlin's point of view, was the same. It was perhaps best expressed in a private letter to the Kaiser from the commander of the German occupation forces in France, General von Manteuffel. There was no doubt, he wrote, that the recent Germany victory could have been obtained with far fewer casualties had the needle-gun been at least equal to the *chassepot*. But fortunately now the "better weaponry" of the Germans existed as a deterrent because "if France should succeed in surpassing Germany, this circumstance would probably contribute to hastening a war of revenge."[5] Thus the familiar theme that German supremacy was tantamount to European security was ultimately applicable to the most technical of policy decisions, such as the quantity and caliber of infantry rifles.[6] Likewise, from the first days of the republic, the central objective of the French infantry was to erase the deficit in comparison with Germany. While the French sought by all means to establish parity, then, the Germans strove with equal determination to prevent it. Hence we must define that deficit more precisely and trace French attempts to overcome it.

The plexus of the problem was organization. As of the 1870s the French still had no apparent cause to worry about numbers. Ample recruits were available, if only the infantry could do something with them. Therein lay the real German advantage: a more consistent arrangement for the training and utilization of available manpower. In discussing proposals for reconstituting French infantry companies on the Prussian standard of 250 men, a contemporary writer openly confessed that "a parallel between our modus operandi and that of the Germans does not redound in our favor," so that the French "would certainly gain great advantage by constructing, at least in part, our infantry companies on their model."[7] This suggestion proved to be exactly the case: the French army followed the Germans right up the organizational chart in restoring their companies, battalions, regiments, divisions, and corps. The retrospective comment of one historian that French military planners "looked to see what the Germans did and thus adopted the four-company battalion" may put the matter somewhat too simplistically.[8] But the essential truth remains that the reorganization of the French infantry replicated very closely the German system, evidently on the assumption that no other distribution of manpower would yield a favorable result.

Second, and of course inextricably related, was the budgetary deficit. Already mentioned frequently in this account, the economic legacy of the lost war placed severe restrictions on the French capability of responding to all of their military weaknesses at once. An analysis in the *Journal des sciences militaires* summarized the underlying difficulty. If the military bills of 1872 and 1873 provided a theoretical basis for reforms, they needed in practice to be "strictly limited by the most extreme economy." The danger was that the French would be carried away by the resentment of defeat and would prematurely attempt to mount a complete armed force, thereby overloading their resources.[9] Another writer in the *Spectateur militaire* was more cutting in pointing to the implicit contradiction in the new military legislation between the residue of a professional army and the plans for universal conscription. The national budget, he contended, could not possibly be stretched to support both. In choosing definitively between the two options, therefore, France should follow Germany, which "alone has as yet managed to pursue the consequences of this principle [of universal conscription] to their ultimate limits." Unless a clear choice were made, France would remain inferior, unable to finance an adequate reserve system; and "as for the territorial army, it will only exist on paper and will never be called up."[10] In the closed sessions of the Conseil Supérieur de la Guerre these issues were debated in identical terms. General Ducrot reminded his colleagues that over half of the French budget was automatically appropriated each year to retire the public debt, leaving barely a billion francs annually for all the other functions of government combined. Of this sum about 50 percent was allocated to the Ministry of War, an amount insufficient to sustain the huge military establishment proposed. In opposition General Deligny maintained that the CSG "should not occupy itself with questions of finance. It is convened and consulted in order to determine how the army . . . should be constituted and to inquire what is strictly indispensable for defense, without being preoccupied by the expenses that the nation may or may not support." As of 1874 these brave words generally prevailed among France's top-ranking professional officers, but they could not totally ignore Ducrot's warning against the adoption of "inapplicable" reform measures.[11]

Third, France trailed Germany in the application of infantry tactics. Staff memoranda repeatedly took note of the timidity and irresolution of French infantry units in the past war, whereas the Prussians had been inclined "to take the offensive [and] at all costs not to leave the initiative to the enemy."[12] Furthermore, the Germans had avoided the French mistake of massing infantry troops into serried ranks in order to attempt frontal assaults at great cost, choosing instead to extend their lines and to turn the French flanks.[13] These precedents aside, more rapid and accurate infantry rifles were bound to force a reconsideration of tactical concepts inherited from times past. But in the words of Napoleon Bonaparte (reverentially cited as the true innovator of modern tactics), everything lay in the execution. In this respect the Germans were the envy of every French military analyst without exception. German maneuvers, war games, and field exercises were admired throughout Europe. Yet until the end of the 1870s the French infantry arranged nothing comparable, one critic remarked, as if the supreme object of military training were to cavort on the Champs de Mars.[14] To be sure, maneuvers on a large scale were expensive, time-consuming, and often frustrating; and there was no way to replicate the actual conditions of battle. Until they copied the training procedures of German infantry, however, the French could not hope to field soldiers of equal competence and self-confidence.

A fourth disadvantage was concomitant with the preceding one. Even if France's front-line infantry could be raised to a par with the German, they would be hopelessly outmatched without the effective support of reserve units and territorial armies. Remarkably, the Germans had found a solution to this problem in 1870; and in adopting an equivalent to the German structure of reserves, Landwehr, and Landsturm, the French might hope to produce comparable results. In practice this would require that all French units be recruited, equipped, trained, exercised, and somehow inserted into a general scheme of troop deployment. After surveying that imposing agenda, a German agent assured Berlin in 1873 that a fully integrated French army could "scarcely be complete within twenty years"; and in 1875 a French writer somewhat more generously estimated the gap between planning and reality to be at least a decade.[15] Pessimistic as such random prognostications might have appeared at the time, they only hinted at how intractable this particular military deficit would prove to be.

There was, finally, the seemingly insoluble problem of the "cadres." This term was employed, often indiscriminately, in any one of three ways: either to indicate in general the entire command structure as well as the administrative services (transportation, communication, and logistics) that formed the permanent skeleton of the army; or to designate all junior grade officers beneath the superior staff ranks, thereby including captains and lieutenants; or, more usually, to specify only noncommissioned officers. Even taken in the strictest sense, the cadres were undoubtedly the Achilles heel of the French army. The poor quality and inadequate quantity of NCOs adversely affected both the training of recruits and the procurement of officer candidates from the ranks. A commission formed under Marshal Canrobert in 1872 to make a preliminary survey of the cadres singled out this weakness without equivocation: the further one descended the scale of command, the more problematical the matter became. "As for the noncommissioned officers," Canrobert reported, "I must confess that the greater part are wanting in instruction, education, [or] intellectual quality; and some even [lack] the moral fiber that will be so essential."[16] This deficiency in excellence was compounded by the congenital inability of the French army to retain a sufficient number of NCOs of whatever quality through reenlistment, a discomfort made all the more painful by the comparative success of the Germans in the same endeavor. Shortly we shall measure the magnitude of this disability and gauge its seriousness as a factor of retardation for the infantry.

The foregoing analysis should not create the unqualified impression that French reorganization was a complete botch. A major army was being rebuilt and its morale restored. Commenting in 1874 on recently drafted French plans for mobilization "in the Prussian sense," the German military attaché made note of a new "esprit d'ordre et de détail."[17] Expansion of the infantry nonetheless continued to be hindered by the system of five-year service under which some men spent the full term in uniform while others were discharged after only a few months. Paradoxically, this practice resulted in a shortage of well-trained soldiers and yet a plethora of untrained reserves. "Soyons donc logique!" a battalion commander urged his colleagues: either France must adopt a three-year tour of active duty for every recruit, or the military reform could not be expected to attain "its objective"— an allusion to the rivalry with Germany that did not need to be precisely defined to be perfectly understood.[18] This was another variation on the basic military question during the first years of the republic: in order to vie with the Germans, should the French not copy their method of universal conscription? The initially negative verdict obtained by Thiers in 1872 was thereafter under constant challenge; yet nearly two decades would pass before it was definitively reversed in favor of the Prussian model.[19]

In a few instances French efforts were visibly inhibited by deliberate German influence. Despite the lamentable outcome of their journalistic and diplomatic offensive against France in 1875, Bismarck and his associates could count as a partial success the curtailment of the French military budget adopted for the next year.[20] The Germans may also have had a hand in temporarily delaying production of some of France's new Gras infantry rifles in Austria.[21] There is likewise some evidence that the French postponed their initial attempts to hold maneuvers near the German border because of their fear of further diplomatic complications.[22] But these episodes were tangential to the structural reasons for French retardation. Simply the German presence, not overt German pressure, was the crucial factor in military affairs. Indeed one of the most significant consequences of the "War-in-Sight" incident in 1875 was a recognition that, if anything, the manpower gap between France and Germany might be growing. This disturbing fact explains the origin of the first serious campaign to revise the 1872 recruitment law and to introduce three-year military service.[23] Sensitive to the charge that he merely wished to imitate the German system yet again, a columnist for the *Spectateur militaire* responded curtly that France faced a choice between following the German example or harboring "dangerous illusions." The journal further editorialized: "Time is pressing; years have been lost; we must make them up."[24]

But that sense of urgency was not always shared either among a majority of military officers or in certain political circles where it counted the most. Even the relatively balanced arguments of the highly respected General Berthaut, minister of war during the difficult months of the *seize mai* crisis in 1877, tended to cast doubt: whereas three years might be adequate for the training of infantrymen, that period of service would be insufficient for the artillery and the cavalry. He was convinced, furthermore, that the change from five to three years would probably render even more acute the shortage of NCOs in the entire army, an opinion shared even by the few officers who advocated a reduction of military service.[25] Equally crucial, albeit based on entirely different reasons, was the vacillation of Léon Gambetta. During an acrimonious debate in the Assembly in the spring of 1876, the Laisant proposal for three-year conscription was vigorously opposed by Adolphe Thiers in an undisguised fit of self-vindication. This time the old man knew that he could rely not only on firm support from most military officers but also on Gambetta's ambiguity. Well aware of the political stakes soon to be contested and eager neither to affront Thiers nor to alienate his own moderate supporters, Gambetta equivocated. In principle he favored a reduction to three years, but he considered its implementation not yet opportune. The Laisant motion was thereupon lost 230 to 195.[26] One can only comment that this verdict represented both a setback for the republicanization of the French army and, especially for the infantry, the perpetuation of a numerical deficit in relation to Germany.

The extent to which Gambetta's military policy was subject to direct German manipulation during this period cannot be definitively established. The evidence is circumstantial. We know that in 1876 he made a fortnight's tour of Germany, traveling from Basel down the Rhine to Mainz, moving on to Frankfurt, Leipzig, Dresden, and Merseburg—"where the general headquarters of the emperor are located," he related to Juliette Adam—then visiting Berlin, Hanover, Magdeburg, and finally Karlsruhe. He returned to France "loaded with notes, impressions, information, observations." Above all, he was struck with the strength of the German army, the "scientific" superiority of its officers, and the solidity of its reserves and *Landwehr*: "Unfortunately we possess no force that could be compared with the troops that I have just seen." He was consequently convinced that France's only possible course for the time being was to abstain altogether from the "quarrels of

Europe" and to undertake the long march of military reconstruction.[27] Despite our certain knowledge that the German government was to lend overt support to Gambetta in the French electoral campaign of 1877, we need not posit a crude *quid pro quo* in order to explain Gambetta's conclusion that caution was required. In the military question as in other matters, it seems, he was more the realist and less the firebrand than imagined by some of his political opponents.[28]

A second round of discussion on the Laisant proposal opened in late 1876 and soon produced the same negative result. On this occasion the nineteen corps commanders (including Algeria) were consulted, and the consensus was overwhelming that three years might suffice for the training of a recruit but not for the indoctrination of a soldier. Moreover, as Berthaut admitted, the three-year system would neither furnish adequate training for NCOs nor favor retention of them in the cadres.[29] A special parliamentary commission, with Thiers presiding, predictably restated these identical arguments plus one, articulated by Berthaut: "In the German army . . . social conditions are different. The people are poor, obedient by nature. There is a veritable caste to furnish noncommissioned officers. The soldier arrives under the colors all prepared, whereas here education is bad, healthy traditions are lost."[30] In these words could be detected that mixture of racial bias and social analysis that often underlay the rejection of the German model: the visceral assumption that Teutons were a different people and therefore that their example could not and should not be emulated. However vague or dubious such rationalization may have been, it went virtually unchallenged as the Laisant proposal was bogging down once more. A disheartened editorialist of the *Spectateur militaire* observed sardonically that only two sounds regularly inspired German enthusiasm: French quarreling and Wagner's music. "The year 1876," he added, "has been a year virtually lost for our military reorganization."[31]

From a military point of view the *seize mai* crisis of 1877 was only a repetition of the "war scare" of 1875. France was still unprepared, and both sides realized it. A menacing speech by Moltke, his open irritation with the French press, and the reinforcement of German troops in Alsace-Lorraine were all part of a political ploy to remind French voters that a monarchical restoration was likely to endanger the peace.[32] An ancillary effect was to draw attention again to France's comparative military weakness. The first attempt to assemble territorial troops at battalion strength and to execute some elementary maneuvers was undertaken in the following year.[33] Even then, some essential services were still lacking. According to the records of the Conseil Supérieur de la Guerre, a support system of logistics (*service des approvisionnements*) had "only just begun" in 1878, and the plan for an ambulance corps "similar to the German organization" was not adopted until that same time.[34] Thus in its broad outlines as well as in many of the smallest technical details, the French army continued to be patterned on the German. "We have sought to imitate the victor," one commentator wrote; "everywhere the way has been open to ideas from beyond the Rhine, and all the reforms accomplished have been modeled on Germanic institutions."[35] Yet so long as the five-year recruitment law remained in effect, an essential feature of the German system was absent and many of the manifest faults of the French army would remain.

The first formal revision of France's conscription procedures did not occur until 1880. Commenting in 1879 on yet another reconsideration of the Laisant proposal for three-year service, General Gresley as minister of war reiterated the main arguments against it: that it would leave insufficient time for the complete formation of infantry soldiers; that it would not permit adequate training for the artillery and the cavalry; and that all combat services would be further deprived of badly needed noncommissioned officers. Hence, he maintained, France could not risk a change of the 1872 law "without exposing ourselves to compromising our military organization." Yet he conceded that the ordinary routine of the infantry, because of delayed induction and long furloughs, had come to be a required service of only three and a half years; thus the experiment of a slight reduction seemed feasible and, if successful, it might then be legally ratified.[36] This suggestion soon resulted in the adoption of a forty-month service requirement. Although this new arrangement unquestionably had a certain propaganda appeal in the provincial press—forty months seemed much less devastating to a young draftee than five years—for most soldiers it only confirmed the status quo or, at most, gained them a few additional weeks of freedom. Moreover, of course, the reduction did nothing to alleviate the still acute shortage of NCOs.[37] But beyond technical considerations there was another factor. The republican victory in the senatorial elections of January 1879 and the subsequent resignation of Marshal MacMahon from the presidency had increased political pressure for democratization of the army. When General Gresley finally departed from the Ministry of War at the end of that year, the proponents of three-year service supposed that their opportunity was in sight. An editorial probably written by the new editor of the *Spectateur militaire*, Henri Noirot, spoke harshly of the "sterility" resulting from the compromises of the past decade and charged that "our entire military organization rests on expedients and half-measures. It is only a work of transition and transaction. We must discard its provisional character and adapt it entirely to the political situation of the country and to the principles upon which it is founded. We ardently hope that the year 1880 will open the era of this indispensable and urgent transformation."[38]

Such glowing prose was bound to dim, however, in an arena where tough professional officers still held a grip on military planning. Gresley's successor, General Farre, in fact proved to be a tenacious critic of three-year conscription, basing his opposition to Laisant on the contention that a system suitable for autocratic Prussia was not adaptable to republican France.[39] This view was to turn the ideological tables on those who consciously or unconsciously equated the German model with more democratic reforms. The confusion and the tension were compounded by Gambetta's decision actively to support a three-year system, thereby ending his long neutrality on the question. A solution seemed at hand when General Billot became minister of war in the Freycinet cabinet in January 1882. Billot, who as a corps commander several years before had strongly opposed the Laisant proposal, now appeared as its champion. But the expectations for a shift in policy were soon extinguished. Even before Gambetta's untimely death in December 1882 Billot had begun to encounter resistance within the army's high command. Although conceding to his colleagues on the CSG that three-year conscription "might be dangerous for the recruitment of noncommissioned officers," Billot urged that there was no other means to recoup an estimated deficit of two hundred thousand men left untrained in the 1870s because of France's outmoded induction procedures. This contention was challenged in turn by Marshal Canrobert and Generals Chanzy, Galliffet, and Gresley, all of whom found serious fault with attempting to imitate the Germans. When it became clear that the membership of the CSG was nearly unanimous in rejecting a reduction of military service, the matter was abruptly dropped.[40]

The French infantry was thereby allowed to reach the mid-1880s with the same deficiencies that had been created by the military laws of the previous decade, the self-contradictory nature of which had been so often identified in the press and professional journals as well as analyzed by foreign attachés and French military critics. A parliamentary committee formed to steer reform legislation could only lament the exaggerated optimism of earlier numerical projections, which had claimed that France was gradually reaching parity with Germany. Instead, the "deficit of trained men" was becoming "a truly enormous figure": many reserve infantrymen and territorial troops were receiving only "rudimentary instruction," which was "absolutely insufficient" to fit them for combat. "That is the brutal reality," concluded the committee's report, "which is aggravated by comparison with the resources that our neighbors have been able to assure themselves, whereas we do not have the means to do as they."[41]

To obtain a clearer sense of the magnitude of French inferiority to Germany, it may be well to select a fixed point at which military leaders attempted to take inventory of the relative progress of the two armies. In April 1883 the best available estimates were presented to the Conseil Supérieur de la Guerre. They showed that France was supposedly maintaining 641 infantry battalions in peacetime to only 502 for Germany, a positive balance of 139. But the shocking and dismaying news was that Germany's fully mobilized infantry force in wartime could reach 838 battalions against only 706 for France, a debit of 132. The explanation of this apparent anomaly was no deep mystery to the military men present. The French had simply failed to fashion the requisite infantry reserves or territorial armies to match those of Germany; and as General Billot admitted, "We absolutely have need of them." General Thibaudin concurred: "If we do not proceed to [create] new formations, we will necessarily be inferior to the Germans." For his part, General Gresley attributed the inadequate quality as well as deficient quantity of infantrymen to the fact that "the officers of the reserve and the territorial armies are worth nothing, absolutely nothing." But the most sobering analysis derived from statistics gathered in General Farre's recent book: whereas 90 percent of German NCOs regularly joined their infantry cadres through reenlistment, the comparable figure for France was incredibly only 13 percent. "These results," Farre commented, "make the head spin."[42]

French military planning was thus left in suspended animation. The "brutal reality" was that fifteen years of sporadic effort had not achieved the one goal that mattered and by which success or failure had to be measured: parity with Germany. It was symptomatic of a lingering malaise that the CSG was adjourned from April 1883 until 1885; and after convening inconclusively during the first two months of that year, it was disbanded once more until 1887. Thus, as the republic's second decade neared its end, the reform of the French infantry remained at an impasse.

The Etat-Major

Whereas France's army after 1870 was fashioned in many details like the German, it remained conspicuously different in one essential regard: the Prussian General Staff was rejected as an appropriate model for the French Etat-Major. One explanation ordinarily offered has been that France simply possessed no Helmuth von Moltke, the man who conceived, implemented, and personified the German high command. But the reasons for not emulating his example were various and complex. To unravel them, we must attempt to pursue three separate strands of analysis before reaching the snarls and knots of the mid-1880s.

The need to reform the structure and training of the French officer corps had been apparent to some critics well before the Franco-Prussian war. From his post in Berlin the French military attaché, Colonel Stoffel, had more than once warned of the discrepancy in quality between the two armies: "But in a future war, of all the elements of superiority that Prussia would possess, undoubtedly the greatest, the most incontestable, would be the composition of the corps of staff officers. . . . The Prussian general staff is paramount in Europe; ours cannot be compared to it."[43] In the waning months of the Second Empire Marshal Niel was perfectly aware of these admonitions but was unable to respond to them in time. Besides, too little was actually known about

Moltke's procedures.[44] One concrete proposal submitted by the talented and ambitious General Ducrot, who was stationed in Strasbourg during the spring of 1870, would have required graduates of Saint-Cyr and the Ecole Polytechnique to perform a three-year tour of active duty before entering the Ecole d'Etat-Major for further instruction. This scheme would have imitated the Prussian procedure of integrating staff and field work for all officers. What the French required, Ducrot argued, was good warriors rather than expert mathematicians.[45] But the military conflict with Germany cut short such suggestions and left them as one more troublesome item on the crowded postwar agenda of reform.

Within a few weeks of the signing of the treaty of Frankfurt a new set of proposals, nearly identical to those of Ducrot, was published by Captain Derrécagaix. He could now buttress the case for reform by attributing Prussian success to the "well-conducted efforts of their staff officers." By comparison, he wrote, the French high command had been ill prepared for combat, mired as it was in the routine of administrative practices dating back to 1818. By contrast, "the advantages of the system imposed in Prussia for the constitution of a general staff are evident." Nevertheless, Derrécagaix admitted that one feature of the German army would be unsuitable for France: the concentration of supreme military authority "in the hands of a single man."[46]

In an imprecise manner this article suggested several of the main elements of the ensuing debate concerning the French officer corps that began in 1872 and endured for the balance of the century. The parliamentary history of that development has already been capably reconstructed and need not be recapitulated.[47] What must be followed instead—the first of the three strands—is the internal struggle within the French army and, particularly, the several ways in which it revolved around the German example.[48]

Certainly there was no shortage of advice. A single dossier assembled in the First Bureau of the Ministry of War contained more than thirty different reform plans submitted by military men. To study these and to derive from them a coherent legislative project, Minister of War Cissey created in February 1872 a military panel chaired by General Lebrun. After four months of deliberation the Lebrun committee produced two documents: a majority report that urged maintenance of the French "closed" officer corps; and a minority report, signed by Lebrun and three other generals, that advocated a plan much closer to the "open" Prussian model. These statements deserve some elaboration.[49]

The majority report did not attempt to hide the serious differences that had erupted between those who wished to preserve the traditional Etat-Major ("a creation consecrated by time") and those who preferred "to assimilate the institutions of our neighbors despite the situation so different of the two peoples and the two armies." The practice of an "open" system—by which officers could be recruited for the general staff from the three regular combat services rather than always being selected and retained separately—was widely credited for the Prussian success in 1870, the report conceded; and undeniably "there is in the human spirit a tendency to copy, down to the details, the institutions of the victor." But the French must take care that imported ideas not bear a "germ of destruction." The reasons for rejecting the "*radical* solution" of the German system were essentially threefold. First, certain technical features, such as procedures for military promotion, were inapplicable to the French command structure. Second, the moral constitution of France was incompatible with such a reform because "we have neither the same social state, nor the same character, nor the same spirit, nor the same military institutions as the Germans." Third, there was a political reason: the enormous prestige and virtual autonomy of the German general staff gave it prerogatives as extensive as those of the war ministry, a feature that would be unacceptable for the French republican government. Hence the army would do better to modify its command system so as to gain some advantages of the German system without suffering its inconveniences.[50]

The minority found these arguments evasive and unconvincing. But to dissent was a delicate task because it meant criticizing the existing officer corps, disavowing the fabled name of Marshal Gouvion-Saint-Cyr, and appearing to advocate prussification of the French army.[51] To avoid "being accused of wishing to imitate the Prussian system," the minority report went to lengths to demonstrate that its proposals had actually originated in France before 1818 but had been unfortunately deflected thereafter. Now the French would only be returning to their own roots by adopting an "open" system that would restore the close contact between the general staff and combat troops, an indispensable prerequisite for modern warfare. As a concrete step to that end, the minority proposed that the existing separate school for the Etat-Major be disbanded in favor of an Ecole Supérieure de Guerre, which, as General Lebrun did not shy from saying, should be designed to resemble the famous Prussian Kriegsakademie in Berlin.[52]

These contending opinions revealed two aspects of the military debate: that those who initially joined in it tended to see the issues as a question of copying Germany or not; and that the altercation was not strictly a political issue to be categorized in conventional parliamentary terms of left and right.

The foregoing observations are crucial if one is to comprehend the erratic progress of military reform legislation in the early Third Republic. A professional officer such as General de Cissey, although politically faithful to President Thiers when serving as his minister of war, was far from uncritical of an Etat-Major whose members, as he observed, were prone to become "eternalized in sedentary positions." He felt that there were too many incompetent staff officers, that they were out of touch with the realities of warfare, and that their training needed to be improved. True, in the CSG he continued to oppose adoption of an "open" corps; but like most military officers he had mixed feelings, and he maintained a healthy admiration for Germany. Hence his delphic conclusion that "the best [solution] appears to be to maintain what exists while modifying whatever is defective." We have seen how Cissey and Thiers were often contradicted by Marshal Mac-Mahon and others for military rather than political reasons. Here was another instance. Although he felt that severe criticism of the Etat-Major was unjustified, MacMahon believed that French staff officers should gather much more practical experience in the combat services: "They would thus do as does the Prussian general staff." In addition, French officers should be required to leave their desks and to conduct research trips and reconnaissances on the frontier. "In this regard," the marshal said, "Prussia affords us an example to follow." Thereby, in effect, he placed himself on record in support of Lebrun and the minority report.[53]

An exhaustive narrative of the subsequent contest between proponents of the "open" and "closed" systems is unnecessary. Each side remained sufficiently strong to deadlock the other, thereby creating an equilibrium that even MacMahon's accession to the presidency did not upset. When the question was reviewed again by the CSG in the summer of 1873, Marshal Canrobert grandly suggested that the French should perhaps devise a scheme for a general staff that was "partially open" (corps entr'ouvert). But no one appeared to know what such a term implied, and nothing was settled.[54] Nor was the problem clarified by the military reform bill of 1875, which both failed to stipulate the means of access to the Etat-Major and neglected to regulate the organization of the high command. If growth of the army favored a more open system simply by creating the need for a greater number of staff officers, movement in that direction was still imperceptible. The German military attaché was correct to report in 1876: "The Etat-Major has remained what it was."[55] Not until two years later, after the seize mai affair had forced some French officers to face their army's continuing lack of preparation for combat, did serious pressure begin to mount for a basic change. In an open letter to the Journal des sciences militaires General Favé stressed the superior organization and training of the German General Staff and asserted that "the French army could not, without committing the most inexcusable mistake, fail to follow Prussia in this path of indisputable progress." Otherwise, he wrote, "the French army will be in no condition to fight on equal terms with the Prussian army."[56] After several more months of dispute and delay, the French Senate finally responded by approving the concept of a new law intended to create an "open" Etat-Major.[57] The fact that this action coincided with MacMahon's resignation from the presidency only demonstrated once more that the military question was not closely regulated by a political clock. The emergence of Jules Grévy as the next president had little or nothing to do with final passage of the legislation in 1880.

Appropriate as this conclusion might appear, three qualifications must be quickly added: that the reform came only after a full decade had already been lost to indecision; that the principle of an "open" system remained to be converted into reality; and that the introduction of this one feature still failed to guarantee that France would adopt in its entirety a replica of the German General Staff.[58] That involved other matters.

The second strand we must examine concerns the innovation of a modern French military academy. Under the traditional procedures still in effect in 1870, aspiring staff officers graduated from the cadet school of Saint-Cyr or from the Ecole Polytechnique and proceeded at once to two years of further preparation at a special Ecole d'Etat-Major in the rue de Grenelle in Paris. From there it was literally only a few steps to the Ministry of War in the rue St. Dominique, where staff officers were promptly ushered into the labyrinth of bureaucratic tasks necessary to maintain a peacetime army.[59] Thus the French staff officer actually shared little in common, either in training or in function, with his German counterpart, who had practical experience in at least one military service, had received excellent theoretical instruction in Berlin, was ordinarily shuttled between staff duties and field work, and was constantly engaged at some level in the preparation for war. Whereas the French staff officer was likely to become a competent functionary, the German was prepared to command a combat force.[60]

Rendered here with only slight stylization, such was the contrast often drawn in the postwar years by those military writers who favored a thoroughgoing reform of the French system. Of these one of the earliest and by far the most influential was Colonel (after 1874 General) Jules Lewal. As author of several widely discussed books, chief contributor to the *Journal des sciences militaires*, and eventual guiding spirit of the new French officer training school, Lewal undoubtedly had more theoretical impact on French military thinking than any other single personality of the early Third Republic. This fact proved to be of significance because Lewal was an outspoken proponent of German military procedures, which he generally equated with "science," even when he was at pains to avoid a charge of advocating prussification of the army: "It is not a matter of foreign imitation," he assured his readers; "it is a return to sound French doctrines."[61] But he went on to assert that Germany undeniably had been far more successful in applying those concepts than France. "In the past the [French] system has been gravely defective; it must be radically transformed."[62] The agent of such transformation would be a new military academy dedicated to the study of the methods and principles of modern warfare, said Lewal as if reciting from Auguste Comte, because "war is today a positive science." Humiliating as it might be for the French to admit their inferiority, they had no reasonable alternative but to abandon their "radically false" conception of an Etat-Major and to search for more precision and efficiency in military staff work. "The Germans have entered upon this path, the only one that can yield assured results." Therefore,

Lewal concluded, the French must begin by surmounting the "specious objection" that they would be compromising their national honor by introducing similar measures.[63]

Even those for whom any copying of the Prussian system was repugnant were dazzled by the prospect of a new military academy. But there was initial confusion as to the proper nomenclature, something that betrayed ambiguity about the intended function of the general staff as a whole. During one meeting of the CSG Thiers managed within a single sentence to refer to a "Grande Ecole Militaire," an "Ecole d'Etat-Major," and an "Ecole Supérieure de la Guerre." Clearly he favored a new academy of some sort, but he continued to side with those officers, as he so aptly said himself, who thought it better "not to innovate too much."[64] So long as the French army hesitated to shift from a "closed" to an "open" Etat-Major, there was no compelling reason to revise the staff officers' training program, and consequently the old Ecole d'Etat-Major could continue to function.

The creation of a new academy finally occurred in the late 1870s by administrative rather than legislative channels, through the Ministry of War. The evidence permits no doubt that the principal motivation for the change was a desire to provide French officers with a professional training comparable to that of the Germans. In a preparatory survey of the question conducted by the Ministry's Third Bureau, it was the Prussian Kriegsakademie that was cited first and studied most. When the Second Bureau gathered information on other European military schools, Germany headed the list.[65] In the *Revue militaire de l'étranger*, the official publication of the Second Bureau, the number of articles devoted to Germany far exceeded that of any other nation; and the journal was unstinting in praise of the Berlin school as "a veritable military university."[66] French cadets at Saint-Cyr, the Ecole Polytechnique, Fontainebleau, and Saumur had German as their first and only required foreign language.[67] The obsession with German military training gathered such momentum that the decision to found a military academy "open to all" (the words of General Du Barail while minister of war in 1874) both anticipated and precipitated the formal adoption of legislation creating an "open" Etat-Major. Ironically, it was Thiers's earlier subaltern Cissey, during a second term in the rue St. Dominique in 1876, who signed the ministerial decree that brought the academy into existence. In September 1877 General Lewal was appointed as commandant of the new Ecole Supérieure de Guerre; and a few months later the superannuated Ecole d'Etat-Major was closed. All of which was ratified by a military bill adopted by the French parliament in 1880.[68]

This general reorganization of the Etat-Major serves to draw the first two strands of our analysis together and to expose the third. So long as Marshal MacMahon held onto the presidency of the republic, the question of who was commander in chief of the French army was unambiguous. But once he had been replaced by a lawyer and politician, Jules Grévy, the always latent issue of civil-military relations appeared more obviously than at any time since Adolphe Thiers had presumed to be a latter-day Napoleon Bonaparte. In early 1873, it may be recalled, MacMahon had challenged the domination of the Ministry of War in military affairs and had advocated a more comprehensive role for the Etat-Major.[69] What began as a technical military question eventually bifurcated into two related political problems that required a solution: to what extent should the Etat-Major be autonomous from the Ministry of War? And what should be the relationship between the military high command and the republican heads of government?

Without any doubt, most senior officers in the French army were politically conservative. In its sociological composition the higher reaches of the officer corps probably tended to become more of an upper-class domain in the years after 1870 than before because the Etat-Major provided one of the few remaining avenues for professional and social attainment still sheltered, to some extent, from the encroachment of republicanism.[70] A host of reports from both French and German observers in the 1870s testified to this reactionary bias. Yet the same reports usually noted as well that French officers were nonetheless disposed to favor law and order—republican law and republican order—rather than to risk the adventure of a coup d'état.[71] Incidents of military indiscipline from political motives were extremely rare; and the potentially volatile episode of insubordination during the brief Rochebouët ministry in 1877 was a highly exceptional confirmation of the custom: the army was largely apolitical. Several ranking officers were known to retain strong Bonapartist sympathies. A few were avowedly pro-republican.[72] But the majority kept their political predilections, if any, to themselves and were prepared to uphold the constitution. This attitude had the effect both of bolstering MacMahon in office for the duration of his term and of nullifying the possibility that he might suddenly exploit the presidency to overrule the verdict of *seize mai*.

Once MacMahon finally stepped aside, however, the long-pending questions about the military high command were thrust into full view. Perhaps unduly nervous about *seize mai*, the Germans became concerned that Jules Grévy would be unable to exercise any authority over the army and that a resurgence of Bonapartism might occur.[73] French republican politicians were eager to insist that such an eventuality was unlikely and that Germany had no cause to be apprehensive. Thus Gambetta expressed himself with some bravado to the young Bernhard von Bülow at a private soirée in Paris: "All of France wants peace. Don't listen to what the military people say. Power is in the hands of civilians, and it will remain there." Despite the obviously intended reassurance, such a statement was hardly likely to conceal the tension that was developing between the army and the government.[74]

It cannot be surprising, then, to uncover the unpublicized patronage offered by some republican leaders to certain officers whose political inclinations might help to offset the army's prevailing conservatism. One example was General Billot, who effusively thanked Gambetta in a personal letter for his military promotion in 1880. Another, ironically, was Georges Boulanger, boosted at first by Gambetta and later by Charles de Freycinet and Georges Clemenceau because of his avowed republican sympathies.[75] But such men were only Trojan horses in an alien camp; and therein lay the peculiar circumstance that dictated why the French Etat-Major would remain distinctively different from the Prussian model. In Germany the political and military regimes were organically united in the person of the Kaiser. Despite his sometime disputes with Bismarck, Moltke enjoyed a direct and usually harmonious relationship to his titular ruler, who returned that confidence by granting considerable autonomy to his general staff in matters of military organization and planning. The conservative character of the German high command thereby reflected the political tone set by the imperial court in Berlin.[76]

For these cozy arrangements there was not and could not be a literal equivalent in republican France. President Grévy possessed neither William's clear constitutional authority nor his autocratic prerogatives. Not only was there no French general who could parallel Moltke in prestige or preeminence, but such a personage would have been incompatible with the procedures of a republican parliamentary system. Political logic required that the French commander in chief be subject to direct civilian control exercised through the cabinet system.[77] When compared with the German example, however, this had three serious disadvantages: the Etat-Major was subject to constant political instability; it was suspended in ambiguity between its peacetime and wartime assignments; and it was left to function primarily as a bureaucratic adjunct of the Ministry of War rather than as an independent agency with the task—as in Germany—to prepare the nation for the eventuality of war. The first of these three handicaps was a chronic ailment of the Third Republic, with the debilitating effect that the French army changed ministerial leadership on the average of once a year until 1890. The second problem was dramatized by the proposal to designate some officer other than the minister of war to serve as generalissimo and to take charge of French mobilization at the outbreak of hostilities; but this was not specified in the 1880 reform and confusion remained as to the role that staff officers would be expected to perform in case of an abrupt transition from desk job to field command. The third difficulty followed from the first two because the Etat-Major could not be expected to play a vigorous part in military planning unless it was totally reconceived and reconstituted; and that the French could not agree to do.

Some changes were accomplished, to be sure, and the record of reform was not altogether bleak. Yet one can scarcely conclude that after the war of 1870 the French general staff represented a dynamic element of military regeneration. No doubt the French army possessed an abundance of intelligent and capable officers. But they found themselves locked into a system that encouraged routine and that was slow to draw consequences from defeat. The officers tended to measure their progress by that of Germany. As one historian has noted: "Moltke's achievement was always before the eyes of the French as they wrestled with the problem of how best to organize their own high command."[78] If we rigorously apply that standard to the French military leadership, we can ascertain that a number of fundamental issues were only hesitatingly or incompletely resolved by 1885. In the Etat-Major imagination had not yet come to power.

The Cavalry

The loss of prestige suffered by the entire French army in the war of 1870 affected no branch of military service more profoundly than the cavalry. The rousing charges of mounted troops across open terrain, so often effective in European conflicts and colonial wars of the past, only brought disaster when opposed by determined Prussian infantry and artillery. In one skirmish after another the *furia francese* on horseback was expended to little advantage. Within a few weeks the French cavalry, for all of its ancient and proud tradition, had been virtually routed.[79]

As a consequence, the history of the French cavalry after 1870 deserves to be treated as a postscript, albeit a very revealing one, to the history of military reform. Thoroughly humiliated, the cavalry could not hope to retain its former prominence in the postwar years. It needed not only to be rebuilt but reconceived; for, as one of its critics wrote: "It is beyond discussion that the infantry is the basis of the army, that the other branches are only its auxiliaries." Yet this sensible conclusion nevertheless came hard to those who had devoted their professional careers to equitation, who relished the panache and splendor of it all, and who foresaw a greater role for mounted firepower on the vast battlefields of the future.[80]

After all, the capacity of the cavalry for harassment, probing, and reconnaissance presumably remained undiminished. Indeed, the Prussians had convincingly demonstrated in 1870 that with proper organization the service could be successfully employed in these tasks. Nothing was therefore more natural than for the French to repeat an accustomed pattern. The Second Bureau was assigned to gather relevant information about the training, maintenance, and tactical methods of the German cavalry. These findings were evaluated by a military committee specially designated for that purpose. The issues were meanwhile discussed at length in military journals in which, notably, Lewal made his familiar plea that the French adopt "scientific" techniques, which, as usual, happened to be those used by the Germans. Finally, in September 1874 there appeared the first new set of cavalry regulations. This document, according to one German analyst, was in many of its details "an almost literal translation" of the Prussian ordinance of 1870: "One can be virtually certain that the French cavalry will pursue the same goal as the German cavalry, and by the same means."[81]

Yet this evaluation was sanguine, or at least premature, because the French had yet to change the entire organizational basis of their cavalry to conform to German procedures. In the previous war the Germans had deployed a regiment of cavalry with each division of infantry, thereby placing mounted troops directly under the divisional commander. The French had instead attached a division of cavalry to each corps of infantry, thus depriving divisional generals of immediate control over cavalry units. There was no question that the French system had proved less responsive to the hectic conditions of combat. In battle, moreover, French horsemanship had also been found wanting. General Galliffet was particularly keen to remedy that deficiency, and he proceeded to stage the first postwar field exercises for French cavalry troops at Coulommiers in September 1874. A British observer, although flattering Galliffet himself, thought that the performance of his men and horses was frankly disappointing: "Several methods have been attempted in an effort to give the French cavalry the qualities of the German cavalry, but these methods have generally failed." Despite some evident progress in rebuilding, the French cavalry still suffered visibly from the uneven ability of its officers, the poor conditioning of its mounts, and an overall lack of stamina.[82]

As always the French were concerned about relative numbers, and once more they found the inevitable comparison with Germany to be discouraging. France had entered the war of 1870 with 63 regiments of cavalry constituted in 348 squadrons. Combat left ranks decimated and stables vacant. By 1875, after much exertion, the French could boast of 78 cavalry regiments; but of these 406 squadrons, 40 were stationed in Algeria and 70 were assigned to interior depots. Hence the available combat force was actually 296 squadrons of 120 steeds each: a total of less than 36,000. Their strength contrasted disadvantageously with that of the German cavalry, composed of 372 combat squadrons of 150 horses each: a total of nearly 56,000.[83]

These bare statistics relate only part of the story. Documents show that the personnel of the French cavalry was top-heavy with officers and yet short of cadres, symptomatic of an organization more expensive but less efficient than the German.[84] There were also serious and still unresolved differences about the proper deployment of the admittedly outmatched cavalry units: should they be risked at once in battle to cover the mobilization of the infantry or held behind fortified lines at the sacrifice of frontier territory to the invading Germans?[85] Although hidden from public view, these were questions that troubled those whose decisions might suddenly affect the safety of thousands of French citizens.

From such considerations it should be evident that the infamous horse embargo imposed on France by Germany in 1875 was something more than a convenient excuse for a diplomatic charade. Whatever personnel measures were adopted or strategy devised, the ultimate criteria of comparison remained the quantity and quality of horses. Both sides knew that the French were facing a deficit in the magnitude of at least twenty thousand mounts and that obtaining superior animals from abroad was likely to be cumbersome. If so, French rearmament plans would be set back by several years.[86] Besides monitoring rail and sea traffic for French importation of horses, mainly from Russia and Hungary, the Germans also watched for any unusual increments in French grain purchases from eastern Europe.[87] Indications were that French expansion would be steady but slow. Although budgetary allocations for the cavalry doubled during the decade of the 1870s, the bulk of that increase went to fill lacunae left from the war. Thus the progress of the cavalry, despite the augmented expenditures and importations, was not regarded by the Germans with undue alarm.[88]

German confidence was well founded. This conclusion was reached in a comparative study of French and German cavalry conducted on special assignment for the Second Bureau in 1879 by Captain Bronislaw Koszutski, a staff officer of the Etat-Major. His calculations demonstrated that after a full decade the French had failed to reduce the German preponderance. By 1880 the Germans would have a cavalry force of ninety-three regiments of five squadrons each; and they were capable of mobilizing from their reserves another thirty-six regiments of four squadrons. Against this "colossal force" the French would be able to muster only seventy-four regiments of five squadrons; and it was unfortunately useless, Koszutski noted, to add either the three regiments of native cavalry troops (*spahis*) in North Africa or the projected fifteen cavalry regiments of the French territorial armies, "which we currently possess on paper." Even assuming that the French could actually field 150 horses per squadron, obviously the Germans still maintained a "crushing superiority"—all the more so because, in addition to sheer numbers, "they also have quality." Not only were the Germans generally better equestrians, their steeds were more sturdy: "It is with a genuine discouragement that I cast my eyes on the cavalry horses of our army." If the French intended to measure their military strength against that of Germany, the report warned, they must "immediately effect a radical reform in the acquisition of horses for the army." Otherwise the German cavalry could be expected to give an important and perhaps decisive advantage to France's enemy in a future conflict.[89]

Whether such penetrating pessimism was altogether warranted is impossible to document beyond the slightest ambiguity, even though the available evidence suggests that Koszutski was correct. When analyzing official memoranda one must always make allowance for the special pleading of those who wished to promote reform or to gain a larger financial allocation for their own branch of the army by striking a note of alarm. For this purpose a disobliging contrast between French weakness and German prowess was always convenient. One must also keep in mind that the centrality of the cavalry's role in modern warfare was already in doubt; hence a numerical debit in cavalry squadrons would probably weigh less heavily than a deficit in artillery batteries. Yet Koszutski's negative tabulations could not be gainsaid, and, more important, they could not be easily rectified. For French morale it was bound to be depressing to run so hard and still to lag so far behind the pace set by Germany.

If frustration is not precisely quantifiable, it is nonetheless indicative to consider the count of horses as a rough measure of France's continuing inferiority. Estimates from the early 1880s varied according to which factors were evaluated: 150 steeds per squadron or 120; territorial reserves or not; peacetime strength or wartime potential. One comparison prepared by the Second Bureau in 1881 placed the German advantage as high as 70,000 horses; another presented to the CSG in 1883 calculated the figure at only 22,000, an arrearage nearly identical with that of a decade earlier. Whichever sum was more accurate, we must conclude that the French had actually slipped somewhat or, at best, were barely holding their own.[90]

Especially in light of France's increase in the domestic production of horses by about 50 percent from 1876 to 1885, this arithmetic may appear not only disappointing but anomalous. One important and heretofore overlooked explanation of it can be gained, however, by piecing together scattered reports of the exportation of horses from France to Germany.[91] During the period of the embargo in the mid-1870s commerce in cavalry steeds between the two nations had of course ceased. But customs records show that by the early 1880s private traders in France began to acquire horses in large quantity for shipment to Germany, either directly via Nancy or else through Belgium. By 1885 these transfers attained disturbing proportions. Fortnightly shipments of 300 or more horses were recorded by border officials: an annual rate of better than 15,000. A single agent, the horsetrading firm of Kahn in Paris, was responsible for sending as many as 1,000 animals a month to Germany. A summary prepared for the Ministry of War in 1888 estimated that in the previous five years a minimum of 70,000 horses had been secured in France by private merchants and shipped to Germany. This extraordinary phenomenon, the report charged, was apparently following "a plan arranged in advance."[92]

Proof that a conscious and nefarious German government design was behind this activity, or indeed financed it, is lacking.[93] But the German military interest was well served by skimming off the surplus of France's equestrian production and constantly adding it to already well-stocked pastures east of the Rhine. Certainly this must be included among the reasons for "the serious crisis through which the French cavalry is passing and which requires a solution."[94] In light of the evidence examined here, it is fitting that these words could be written in 1887 by the same senior officer who had chaired the original military committee convened in 1872 to guide the reorganization of the French cavalry. The effort of fifteen years had not been entirely in vain. But neither had it brought the French republic markedly closer to military parity with the German Reich.

Chapter 5

A Condition of Unacceptable Inferiority

The Moment of Truth

Was the French army greater than the sum of its battalions? Was it, despite the lingering inadequacies already detailed, nonetheless prepared at last to defend against a German invasion? Was France ready? These were the vital military questions posed from 1885 to the turn of the century and indeed until the summer of 1914. Without an actual test of arms, of course, no definitive answer was possible. Yet all policy decisions must finally rest on estimates of reality, and by the mid-1880s the time had obviously come to make such global judgments in an effort to determine the future of military preparations. If France was approaching combat fitness, then it would be only rational to prescribe more of the same and to follow what optimistic French editorialists preferred to call "la bonne voie" of postwar reform. But if not, French military planners would need to reconsider a number of their basic assumptions.

Whatever option was chosen, the decisive criterion would be the same: a comparison between the military capabilities of the French republic and the German Reich. This was true despite the increasing uncertainty of diplomatic alignments, the apparent atrophy of the Three Emperors' League, and the tantalizing prospect that France might soon emerge from political isolation. A staff report by General Ferron, chief of the Etat-Major in 1883, outlined three hypotheses in the event of a major European conflict: (1) France alone would oppose Germany, Italy, and Spain; (2) France and Russia would meet Germany and Austria; or (3) France, Russia, and Italy would fight Germany and Austria. Many years before its formal conception, Ferron correctly anticipated the underlying logic of the Schlieffen plan: no matter what the configuration, even if faced with a two-front war, Germany would strike France first and with virtually the full force of its military might. Only after achieving their initial objective of "defeating and disorganizing the French armies" would the Germans turn to face their more ponderous foe in the East.[1] This view was acknowledged among most French military men; and it is remarkable how nearly, in this regard, they already perceived the shape of events in 1914. An 1887 editorial in the *Journal des sciences militaires* described the likely circumstances of the "next war" with extraordinary prescience and counseled that France should concentrate on turning back the opening German thrust in an attempt to extend the conflict for as long as possible. France could afford to be patient; Germany could not.[2]

In one conspicuous respect, however, the majority of competent military opinion in the late 1880s failed to predict accurately the military operations later diagrammed and executed by the German high command. Belgium was still discounted by the French as the main avenue of the German incursion. The further the Germans would commit themselves to a wide flanking maneuver, the more inelastic would become their lines of transportation and the more vulnerable their troops would be to a counterstroke. True, the German attack was likely to be directed around Verdun and to the north, but any push into Belgium would be but a diversion from the principal assault originating between Metz and Sarrebourg.[3] The plausibility of this scenario was strengthened by the thought that the Germans were bound to weigh marginal military advantages against the political liabilities incurred through a violation of Belgian neutrality. Not that many Frenchmen were susceptible to naiveté about the morality of the German imperial government, as this might seem to imply. They merely assumed that the masters of Realpolitik would not gratuitously squander their diplomatic credit. All of which would appear thirty years later in a vastly different light.[4]

Thus the French were guilty of wishful thinking. The weaknesses of their defensive fortifications had become glaring. Construction that had been planned about 1875 was in many cases still uncompleted a decade later. There had once been much talk, for instance, of fortifying Reims and erecting a secondary defensive barrier between the frontier and Paris; but an inspection by

General Février disclosed that the Reims forts were incapable of "any effective resistance."[5] As noted, at the urgent request in 1881 of Ambassador Saint-Vallier, who wrote from Berlin of German sensitivity to a putative offensive threat by the French, the constructions at Nancy had also been left in abeyance.[6] Meanwhile, smaller towns near the northern border were being provisionally reinforced as *forts d'arrêt* in order to block key railways from the East: Hirson, Givet, Montmédy, Longwy, and others. But these, it became clear enough, "could not resist very long."[7] And even the major fortified places on the eastern front were undergarrisoned and considered unable to withstand a serious onslaught by more rapid, accurate, and destructive German artillery. The only possible solution therefore began to emerge: a program of costly improvements of the major defensive positions by the installation of concrete and steel supports. This program would eventually require nothing less than a major transformation of France's system of fortifications, the strengthening of a few major strongholds on the eastern frontier, and concurrently the virtual abandonment of the indefensible positions opposite Belgium. Budgetary considerations thus conveniently confirmed the military and political prognosis that substantial resources need not be devoted to the northern sector.[8]

The growing recognition that important changes in the French defense were imperative naturally steadied the hand of those who argued that France's entire military organization was defective and needed to be drastically altered. One writer for the *Journal des sciences militaires* leveled criticisms, ostensibly against French fortifications, that could easily be construed in a broader sense: "We must completely renounce official errors. Nothing, in effect, [is] more illogical than what has occurred until now."[9] Others explicitly extended such harsh judgments to the entire military structure developed since 1871. Even General Thoumas, at the conclusion of his magistral two-volume study, *Les transformations de l'armée française*, expressed the regret that "there were not, just after the war, some spirits vigorous enough or circumspect enough to construct a new edifice rather than to refurbish the old. The moment was propitious then; it is perhaps no longer so today. In any event, we have lost fifteen years."[10]

A similar appraisal had recently been rendered in a more popular form by the anonymous author (allegedly "a Prussian

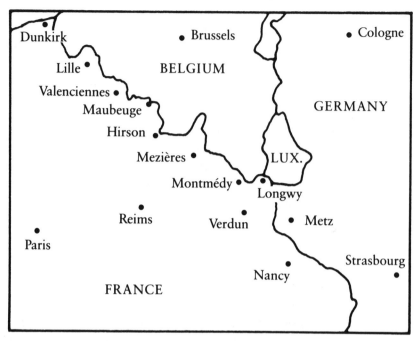

Map 2 / France's Northern Front circa 1890

officer") of a widely discussed book entitled *La France est-elle prête?* After more than a decade of military reform "undertaken on the Prussian model," this writer observed, a discernible pattern of inadequacy had emerged. Each branch of the French army had obvious shortcomings. In its effort to attain numerical parity with Germany, the infantry had sacrificed quality to quantity; the cavalry had insufficient horses and horsemen, whose quality was also "a very large question mark"; and even the artillery, the best of French arms, would require years of further training to be fully effective. The territorial armies, moreover, provided an unreliable reserve force because of their lack of training and organizational coherence. Unable to surmount these defects and plagued by "perpetual changes" of leadership, the French army was manifestly incapable of taking the field against Germany.[11]

Drastic as it was, this assessment was considered tepid by still more radical advocates of new reform legislation. One pamphleteer, while dilating on the theme *Pourquoi la France n'est pas prête*, charged that official estimates of French strength were highly inflated and that large numbers of troops actually existed "only in the cartons of the Ministry of War." The 1872 recruitment law, because it proved inapplicable, had been from the beginning a huge mistake subsequently compounded by "half reforms . . . half measures." The present French military organization was therefore "irregular, incoherent, and inconsistent." Two remedies were urgently required: the immediate adoption of a three-year conscription bill and the appointment of a stable military command. In these regards, this polemicist claimed, far from following the German example too closely, the French army had not gone to sufficient lengths.[12]

Minutes of the Conseil Supérieur de la Guerre establish that such writings, however excessive, did not go unnoticed and that the longstanding reluctance among senior military officers was beginning to yield grudgingly to the demands for reform.[13] At the same time, certain generals dared to discard the camouflage of anonymity behind which much criticism of the army had heretofore been expressed. The most obstreperous of these was General Cosseron de Villenoisy, who chose the professional forum of the *Journal des sciences militaires* to announce: "It is time, it is high time, to call the attention of the country to the constantly growing state of disorganization in which our army finds itself." This confusion, he wrote, was the result of bloating statistics of French troop strength in a vain effort to claim parity with Germany. The consequence was that the French had achieved only a faint copy of the German army. A contemporary (but still anonymous) editorialist in the same journal more temperately analyzed the possibilities for passage of reform legislation, which he regarded as a necessity, and admitted that its adoption would lead to "nothing less than a complete recasting of our institutions."[14] Neither author left much doubt that, in the competition with Germany, France remained well to the rear.

The appearance of this more strident public criticism—illustrated by Thoumas, Cosseron de Villenoisy, and several anonymous writers—has been reviewed here at some length for two reasons: it documents that an honest confession of France's inferiority to Germany was unexceptional by the mid-1880s; and it places in perspective the sudden prominence of General Georges Boulanger as a champion of military reform. The origin of Boulanger's notoriety was not political fantasy but military realism. The truth was that the overmatched French army badly needed some of the measures that he was bold enough to advocate. Boulangism was another matter, a movement of malcontents who hoped to exploit the general's popularity for largely antirepublican purposes of their own. Boulanger's flirtation with them eventually brought him down, a fall he deserved for his disloyalty to those who had earlier furthered his career. Nevertheless, as a reformist minister of war his contribution was important in shaking the army to its senses and, specifically, in gathering support for three-year military service.[15]

His political aspirations aside, Boulanger did not escape severe criticism even from those who shared his devout wish for a new conscription law. Chief among these was General Ferron, whose damning opposition to Boulanger on technical military grounds was formulated in January 1887. The heart of Ferron's complaint was that Boulanger's dramatic demands for an overhaul of the French military structure had only provoked the Germans into increasing their army by 41,000 men and planning further expansion. Germany was recruiting 151,000 new soldiers a year and would soon escalate that to 165,000, whereas France's annual contingent was still less than 135,000. Yet Boulanger proposed to have 200 infantry regiments—a round figure that had excited Bismarck and his press agents—even though the Germans, with their far greater manpower, maintained but 176. Individual French infantry units would thus be inferior, and Boulanger's reform was bound to become "*a fatal abortion.*" The need to bolster the cavalry was also recognized by Boulanger, yet the means he suggested to meet that deficiency were "neither rapid nor economical." As for France's most prized military service, Ferron lamented "the superiority of German artillery in combat" because of the better training afforded Prussian officers. In his view, Boulanger threatened to make matters even worse by imposing a reorganization that would attach more auxiliary troops to the artillery and thereby "paralyze" it. All in all, Ferron believed, the French had been foolish not to accept the Laisant conscription plan a decade sooner. Having failed to do so, however, they would only throw good money after bad by adopting the totality of Boulanger's program.[16]

These criticisms help to explain Boulanger's dismissal from the cabinet and his banishment to the provinces in May 1887. Not only his political ambitions but also his military proposals were suspect. Appropriately, his successor in the rue St. Dominique was Ferron, who aimed to harness the thrust for reform and to silence the polemical fanfare that had accompanied Boulanger's efforts. Ferron took his case directly to the parliament and to the CSG in a series of concrete legislative drafts: to increase the available combat infantry by fifty thousand troops; to recruit from each of the eighteen corps areas in metropolitan France a special new regiment for deployment on the frontier; to provide eleven more regiments of cavalry (in part through transfers from Algeria); and to augment the cadres of NCOs in order to have "as many as in Germany." Within the CSG there was some outspoken skepticism about the projected increases, which, according to General Lewal, "apparently could be accomplished only on paper." Ferron nevertheless won the support he sought, and on 25 July his package was voted into law.[17]

To anyone willing to labor through these bills and the underbrush of accompanying verbiage, it must be obvious that the military legislation of 1887 was a poor compromise. It alarmed those who cherished inherited opinions about the virtues of a smaller professional army and who feared that the entire French military structure was being undermined from within. Yet it also left among reformers an unrequited desire for three-year conscription, a measure that had come to symbolize both modernization and mathematical necessity. The resulting mood of contention and contradiction was best expressed by the most forthright military expert of his generation, Captain Georges Gilbert. In a series of biting articles that appeared in the *Nouvelle revue* beginning in October 1887, Gilbert described the disturbing impasse to which the French army had come. He did so, of course, through a comparison with Germany. By that standard, he wrote, "our infantry is anemic; our cavalry is inadequate"; and even a slight numerical advantage in artillery weapons was nullified by their dispersion. All three combat services were still hampered by an acute shortage of noncommissioned officers: because the French reenlistment ratio was ridiculously low, the number of NCOs was well beneath the 27,250 quota foreseen by law and still further behind the remarkable German figure of 55,000. "The example of Germany," Gilbert added mercilessly, "shows us that the feat is possible." Until this shortage was alleviated, a new three-year conscription law might be premature, however desirable in principle.

Gilbert found a few faint words of praise for both Boulanger and Ferron. At least they comprehended that a substantial increase of French troop strength was essential, an increment that he estimated at about seventy thousand new soldiers. Unfortunately, the recent reform, appearances to the contrary notwithstanding, did nothing to alleviate the situation. It guaranteed "not a single man more," Gilbert wrote, and in fact it seemed to represent the acceptance of a permanent deficit of infantry troops. He added: "The law of 25 July has prepared a better distribution of our peacetime forces; but the forces remain, relative to those of the Germans, in a condition of unacceptable inferiority."[18]

Among his military peers Gilbert scarcely had a rival as a wordsmith. But his most distinguishing characteristic was the utter frankness with which he denounced the "organic vice" of the French army: the instability of its leadership. Small wonder, in view of the incessant ministerial changes, that the armed forces found themselves "in a perpetually provisional state, in a phase of endless transformation." Germany possessed a single hand to plan, train, and inspire the work of the officer corps; but "in France, nothing comparable." To correct this fault and thereby to assure the unity of peacetime preparation and wartime execution, Gilbert proposed that the minister of war be a civilian cabinet member, responsible to the parliament, and that a quasi-permanent commander in chief of the army be appointed by the president of the republic. Whereas Gilbert did not spell out his suggestions in detail, and although he claimed that he favored a solution similar to the British system, the entire context of his criticisms makes it clear that he actually hoped to nudge the French toward adopting a general staff much like the German. While the civilian minister haggled with legislators over military appropriations and procedures, a serene and secure high command would assure the continuity of military planning, whatever might be the vicissitudes of parliamentary life.[19]

The military experts that we have examined—in particular the cluster of Boulanger, Ferron, and Gilbert—must be understood as harbingers of an as yet unfulfilled reform movement for which Germany had set an unattained and perhaps unattainable benchmark. They must also be viewed amidst a setting of political and diplomatic crisis in which Bismarck's exploitation of Boulangism as an alleged threat to German security reached its crescendo in 1888.[20] At an emergency session of the CSG held in the Elysée palace and chaired by the new French president Sadi Carnot in late January, military leaders were informed that recent events had erased "the final doubts about the intention of the German empire to enter war within a short time." This shocking announcement by the then acting chief of the Etat-Major, General Haillot, was followed by a recapitulation of relative troop strength in the "decisive theater" on France's northeastern frontier. Within thirteen days Germany would be able to hurl an army of 1.2 million men and 3,000 mobile cannons against the French, who would be capable in the same period of mustering a mobile force of only 815,000 soldiers and 2,700 heavy weapons. The balance would be far more favorable, the assembled generals were told, if France did not maintain more than 600,000 men stationed in fixed defensive positions. "What a difference," Haillot exclaimed, "if we had a system of fortifications more in relation to our real needs!"[21] But in the event of an imminent German assault, it would be too late to remedy the situation. The truth was that France was not ready.

The Freycinet Reforms

It was especially fitting that the man called upon to culminate the reorganization of the French army was Charles de Freycinet. Ever since 1870, when he served as Gambetta's young aide de camp in the Government of National Defense, Freycinet had remained a keen student of the military question. This interest was evident, as we earlier saw, in the comprehensive plan of public works that bore his name in the late 1870s; and Gambetta came very close to appointing him as minister of war in the *grand ministère* in 1881. At that juncture, however, the precedent of awarding the cabinet post to a military officer still prevailed. But once the proposal to have a civilian minister of war gathered momentum, the selection of Freycinet seemed altogether appropriate. He possessed a number of important qualifications for the position. Trained as an engineer, he had a firm grasp of technical details. He maintained cordial personal relations with several ranking military officers, notably with General Saussier, the military governor of Paris and the man likely to function as generalissimo on the eastern front in wartime. Freycinet had also worked closely with Boulanger in drafting reform proposals in 1886, while yet managing to avoid suspicion of political collaboration. As chair of the Senate's committee on military affairs he had conducted protracted parliamentary negotiations for the new conscription law that still awaited final passage. Finally, and no less fitting, he had long been an avowed admirer of the German military system.[22]

Before accepting his portfolio from the new French premier, Charles Floquet, in April 1888, Freycinet requested and received assurances that the army would remain "absolutely detached from politics" and that he would have "complete liberty" in seeking appropriations for its reorganization.[23] The first promise was an unsubtle disavowal of Boulanger; the second was an indication that, as usual, Freycinet intended to do things in a grand manner. He expected to have the government's full support for a comprehensive program of military reform. For the most part he could count on the cooperation of the army as well. The circumstances were thus propitious as Freycinet entered the cabinet for what was to be an unprecedented five-year term of office in the rue St. Dominique.[24] During that time he was able to bring to a conclusion two essential military reform projects, the need for which was finally admitted by nearly everyone: stabilization of the high command and revision of the conscription requirements. Both deserve some scrutiny.

We need not guess as to Freycinet's motive in reorganizing the Etat-Major. He was frank in advocating a general staff that would be "analogous to the one that had permitted Marshal von Moltke to achieve such great results."[25] Yet to create an exact replica was as much out of the question as ever. For one thing, existing institutions would need to be modified, not abolished outright. For another, France remained without a Moltke. Freycinet's objective was nonetheless analogous, as he said: to produce a secure high command that would be able to prepare in advance for combat and then, without hazardous improvisations, to execute military plans once mobilization was ordered.

From an institutional standpoint, this meant regrouping and upgrading the principal military advisory body, the Conseil Supérieur de la Guerre. The CSG would henceforth function as a de facto general staff, meeting regularly to pass on all critical matters of policy and planning, absorbing the duties of the defunct Comité de Défense, and establishing in the person of the chief of the Etat-Major an administrative liaison with the Ministry of War.[26] To be sure, these provisions suggested a lingering ambiguity about the extent of autonomy from political control that should be granted to the military leadership. But Freycinet's intention was patently to give the high command a vote of confidence and to encourage the sustained effort that he so much admired in Germany. This hope was intentionally reflected in a change of nomenclature: the "Etat-Major du ministère" would thereafter become the "Etat-Major de l'armée."[27]

Naturally such a modification, however uncertain its implications, was welcome to the generals who sat in the CSG. It is far easier to admit error when one stands to benefit from doing so. The members of the CSG did not boggle when General Haillot explained: "The experience of nearly a decade has demonstrated that the law of 20 March 1880 does not satisfactorily assure the functioning of the Etat-Major in peacetime, nor [does it] respond to the exigencies of wartime." As for final passage of legislation through parliamentary channels, Freycinet faced the ticklish problem of gaining adherence for his favorite candidate as France's first chief of staff under the new system. With Saussier's approval he picked General de Miribel, despite the latter's public image as a political reactionary. Once Miribel's reputation had been laundered through a tour of duty as commander of the sixth army corps on the eastern frontier, he was deemed sufficiently acceptable and Freycinet could bring this aspect of his reorganization to a conclusion.[28]

It has been said often and emphatically that the 1890 reform of the Etat-Major in fact stopped well short of adopting Moltke's general staff system.[29] Still, one should not exaggerate the differences, as if to assume that military authorities in Germany were completely independent of any civilian interference, whereas their French counterparts were hamstrung by government control at every turn. Both assumptions are caricatures. But Moltke and his successors did have two a priori qualities that could not be legislated in republican France: a prestige born of military victory and the support of an emperor. The position of a French chief of staff therefore remained necessarily less glorious and more troubled. Despite those irreducible limitations, Freycinet nevertheless largely succeeded in his purpose of stabilizing the French high command by making it more analogous to the German.

Had it not been for its long and bitterly contested history,

Freycinet's other major reform, the new conscription law of 1889, might have been equally uncontroversial. After all, there was total unanimity about France's need for a larger trained military force. Nor was there any disagreement as to why an increase in troop strength was necessary. General de Miribel, already known as Freycinet's protégé, stated the reason frankly to the CSG: "We ought to have forces equivalent to those of the Germans." At the same time, Captain Gilbert, although one of Freycinet's most tenacious critics, also agreed that the criterion must be "the 60,000 [soldiers] we lack in order to be on a par with Germany."[30] Military necessity thus transected partisan lines, and that necessity was defined by the competition between republic and Reich.

By 1888 passage of the three-year reform bill was no longer in doubt. Both the Chamber of Deputies and the Senate favored it. But the former's version foresaw that the military draft would be universal: every able-bodied man should serve a complete tour of duty. The Senate, however, had elaborated a complex scheme of exemptions.[31] The outcome of arbitration between the two houses was the "loi de trois ans" on 15 July 1889, passed on the first day after the republic's centennial celebration. More important, it terminated seventeen years under the five-year recruitment system installed by Adolphe Thiers. Yet the supposedly categorical principle of the new legislation—that military service was to be "*obligatory* and *personal*"—was still undercut by the fine print listing permanent deferments for reasons of health, family, "public interest" (essentially an exemption for the liberal professions), or national budget. Only two-thirds of fit and eligible Frenchmen would actually serve a full term, and the other recruits would be in uniform for but one year. As before, a lottery would decide.[32]

With equal justice it is possible to see this conscription reform in two quite different lights. It was undoubtedly the formal end of a professional army that had been so stoutly defended by certain elements of the officer corps for decades; and to that extent the ideal of a nation in arms had at last prevailed. But the law has also been castigated as "unrealizable" and "absurd" because, with a three-year system, France still possessed more potential inductees than the army could absorb or finance; and it is undeniable that for this reason the new regulations were repeatedly subjected to legislative amendments in the years that followed.[33]

Neither of these two contentions—one emphasizing the long-term progress of a democratic principle; the other, the short-term difficulties of its application—comes adequately to grips with the underlying purpose of the reform in making France competitive with Germany. The measures passed under Freycinet cannot be understood simply as products of a self-generated reform movement. The accumulated evidence shows that both the motive and the measurement of reform derived from the comparison with Germany. When the Germans adopted an army septennate on 11 February 1888, its central provisions were precisely reported to the CSG: the duration of military liability for recruits was raised to forty-five years of age; the total manpower of the German armed forces was set at nearly 2.8 million; after thirteen days of mobilization 1.2 million soldiers and three thousand cannons could be poised on the French frontier. These numbers, and not some purely internal logic, set the standard to which the Freycinet reforms were an attempted response and by which they must finally be judged.[34]

Did France thereby succeed in meeting the German challenge? To read some accounts one might suppose that the answer was affirmative. One historian has written: "In the 1890s France and Germany were spending about the same amounts on their peacetime armies, each of which then numbered somewhat less than half a million men."[35] A search of the documentation of that decade proves, however, that such a balanced comparison is seriously misleading. The familiar lamentation of knowledgeable officers about France's military insufficiencies continued. The "defective situation" of the cavalry was described by General Galliffet to Freycinet, who in turn made no secret to others of the "serious lacunae" that still persisted.[36] A slight numerical edge of the French artillery probably still existed in 1890; but ministerial papers reveal that the chronic lack of cadres to operate heavy weapons was "a very great source of weakness." Moreover, recent German expenditures for mobile cannons and fortresses threatened to wipe out the advantage and to leave the French "in a condition of notable inferiority." This prognostication later proved to be accurate, and it has been reliably estimated that between 1890 and 1914 special German appropriations for such military equipment were double those of the French.[37] As for the infantry, the often admitted numerical deficit led to the adoption of a system of *dédoublement* in 1889, by which the territorial armies were to be amalgamated in wartime with the active army and its reserves. An inspection team reported in 1890, however, that the infantry was the "least prepared" of the combat services, that the territorial troops were "without value," and that the attempted integration of them with the regulars would only bring "disaster."[38] The pressure of German escalation, in short, remained as unyielding as ever. Freycinet was well apprised of these facts, and he confided to Miribel in 1891 that Germany's "considerable augmentations" had placed the French "in a situation of inferiority too dangerous for us to resign ourselves to it. . . . We cannot remain faced with such an increase of forces without taking similar measures."[39]

A detailed statistical comparison of military units was prepared by the Second Bureau at the end of 1892, a few months before Freycinet's withdrawal from the Ministry of War:[40]

	Germany	Metropolitan France
Army corps	20	18
Infantry brigades	86	79
Cavalry brigades	46	34
Artillery brigades (mobile)	20	19
Artillery brigades (fortress)	17	16

These unequal figures might not have appeared so disturbing were it not for a concurrent analysis of military budgets showing that Germany's total military appropriations for 1893 would be more than 730 million francs, whereas the French sum, when adjusted to make the calculations strictly comparable, would reach only 560 million.[41] Such totals reflected the intractable reality of the 1890s: France still trailed behind Germany in military strength, and the distance between them threatened to widen. This truth was known to many informed commentators and staff officers. Yet lulled by the Russian alliance, distracted by the Dreyfus Affair, amused by the Belle Epoque, the French allowed matters to drift. No wonder that in the summer of 1914 a special military appropriations bill of one billion francs was pending in parliament for the purpose of reducing the German preponderance.[42]

After all due credit is awarded to Freycinet, therefore, the conclusion is inescapable that the sustained critique of his reform program by Captain Gilbert was both fair and accurate. The new measures seemed to create an equilibrium between France and

Germany, but "the balance is more apparent than real," Gilbert charged, because of the "detestable habit" of inflating estimates of French resources. In fact the Germans possessed "a notable advantage." With their demographic superiority, their huge appropriations, and their superb organization, they were well prepared to maintain military supremacy over France at any cost. Germany, wrote Gilbert with hardly less admiration than despair, "hopes to surpass us forever."[43]

The Strategy of Defense

One conspicuous feature of the Freycinet years can best be described not as a reform but as a belated response to Germany's technological progress in heavy weapons and explosives. The vulnerability of isolated and inadequately buttressed fortifications to modern artillery had, of course, been recognized long before.[44] We have already witnessed the appalled French reaction in 1886 to tests demonstrating the potential effects of bombardment on forts constructed during the 1870s. Yet without a firm sense of direction before Freycinet took charge, the army was slow to recognize the consequences. A more urgent mood was introduced in 1888 not only by Freycinet's insistence but also by news of Germany's extraordinary military appropriations of that year and by the unanticipated accession of Kaiser William II, whose youth and ambition rekindled apprehensions of an armed conflict in the near future. This new tone was evident in an oral presentation to the CSG by General St. Germain: "The progress realized by artillery in recent times imposes the necessity of executing some profound modifications in the organization of defensive fortifications." Behind this statement lay an implied dialectic with which we are already familiar: that France's major strongholds on the eastern front must be significantly reinforced, whereas many lesser outposts along the northern border should be declassified and perhaps dismantled altogether. "Thus," said St. Germain with a sweep, "there is reason to effect a sort of general revision of our defensive system in order to put it in accord with the new conditions of warfare."[45]

The long and tortuous process of this transformation can only be suggested here. Reconstruction of the eastern defenses from Verdun to Belfort was constantly beset by problems of incorporating or at least accounting for technological innovations: new explosives, smokeless powder, rapid-fire cannonry, mortars, machine guns (back in vogue), revolving turrets, concrete supports, laminated steel, and more.[46] So much effort and expense had been wasted in the previous twenty years that the French were fearful again to invest prematurely in fortifications that might soon be outmoded. The chairman of the technical committee of army engineers, General Dressonnet, confessed to the CSG that "incessant advances in metallurgy complicate the question." Experiments with the mechanism of oscillating steel turrets were still inconclusive, he said, and "we must await further progress." After a tour of inspection on the Belgian frontier General Saussier concurred that "onerous" expenditures should be delayed until it was determined what system of defensive positions could best withstand the new German artillery. The high cost of improved technology was also stressed by an officer in charge of the weapons factory at Puteaux: "It would be better," he advised the Ministry of War, "to allow foreigners to take the first step in this direction and to profit from their discoveries."[47]

The need for caution and economy was thus a recurrent theme of those actively involved in directing construction; and yet their pusillanimity had to be balanced by Freycinet against the pleas by field commanders for immediate and extensive reinforcements. The only way to reconcile these conflicting imperatives was to emphasize further the concentration on a few major fortresses to the neglect of others. As General Billot remarked, France would thereby be returning in effect to the original conception developed by Séré de Rivières in the early 1870s. Confronted by four solid French bastions on the frontier, the Germans would be forced to choose a corridor for invasion either between Toul and Epinal or else to the north of Verdun.[48]

On this basis a program of construction was begun under Freycinet that continued until about the time he resigned. Even work on the major forts of Verdun, Toul, Epinal, and Belfort all but ceased after 1893. By 1914, for example, only 7.5 of the 43 kilometers on the defensive perimeter of Epinal had been "modernized," meaning that nine of the sixteen forts in that defensive cluster remained without concrete and steel reinforcement. These facts bear out the contemporary evaluation of General Berthier that, despite special expenditures of 50 million francs after Freycinet's entrance into the cabinet in 1888, the eastern fortresses still had "numerous lacunae."[49] Yet one must grant, of course, that the intended objective was nonetheless attained insofar as the strategic concept of the Schlieffen plan did finally dictate a German flanking operation to the north. The first offensive, when it came, did not seriously test the positions stretching southward to Switzerland. And in 1916 Verdun held.

The irony was that after 1890 the French began to abandon forts precisely in that region through which a German invasion was thought likely to penetrate. The explanation was partly financial. It was exorbitant to attempt to build and maintain an impervious line on the northern frontier. The French remained convinced, furthermore, that the combination of internationally guaranteed Belgian neutrality and improving Belgian defenses would discourage the Germans from extending their right flank far to the north of Verdun.[50] Logically, then, the weight of the major German thrust would fall on the smaller outposts and *forts d'arrêt* in the Ardennes region opposite Luxembourg. But these positions could be held only briefly, either because they were vulnerable to mobile German artillery or because they could be quickly outflanked on the dense network of railways in the region. Why spend enormous sums on structures that could easily be blasted or bypassed within a few hours? Besides, as General de Miribel noted as if making a virtue of necessity, the French should actually *want* the Germans to attempt an attack between Verdun and the Belgian border because there the invading army could most readily be contained, countered, and finally repulsed. This was to say in other words that France's defensive strategy was not to block the northern route but, having predetermined the most advantageous terrain, to rush mobile forces forward in order to blunt the assault. The Germans were to be lured into an invisible trap.[51]

Such considerations lay behind the French decision to begin a lengthy process of declassification. An inspection by General Mercier in 1888 resulted in a recommendation to Freycinet that many of the smaller or incomplete forts in the north be either reduced to the status of depots or disbanded altogether. Despite his realization that such action would provoke controversy, Freycinet adopted the substance of Mercier's report and forwarded it to the CSG. Throughout the decade that followed, the problem of declassification continued to preoccupy French military planners. The residue of their deliberations in all of that time may be summarized by the observation that, with perhaps one exception, after 1900 no French fortress of any consequence existed between Verdun and the English Channel. Several smaller *forts d'arrêt* on or near the frontier were declared totally unfit and were marked for dismantling: for instance Charlemont, Quesnoy, and Condé. Others were thought indefensible and suitable only to store supplies or for quartering troops: Mezières, Hirson, Curgies (near Valenciennes), Flines, Maulde, and Lille along the border; Reims, Laon, and La Fère in the interior.[52] These positions had once been regarded as essential to withstand a German advance. But as Séré de Rivières was frank enough to admit, the implementation of that concept had proved "very difficult" and resulted in an "excess rather than insufficiency of fortified places in the northern region." He therefore gave his blessing to the sweeping declassification of forts in that area and the preparation of a more mobile defense there.[53]

Only two positions in the northern sector were seriously considered for major improvement, but neither was fully developed. One was Longwy, located strategically but precariously at the intersection of Belgium, Luxembourg, and France. Longwy's importance as a rail junction was crucial. Holding it would prevent the Germans from rapidly slipping an assault into the Ardennes before French mobilization procedures could be completed. When consulted by Freycinet in 1888, the chief of the Etat-Major, General Haillot, favored strengthening Longwy as a *fort d'arrêt*, thereby foreclosing the possibility of an unpleasant surprise. But that objective was unattainable. Isolated and within easy range of German artillery, Longwy could not survive the first impact of invasion. The feasibility of retaining the Longwy garrison was challenged in 1891 by General Jamont, who recommended that the French concentrate instead on the indispensable defense of Verdun. An alternative was to select Montmédy as a fallback position and to make a stand somewhat further from the frontier. But there, too, the risk of a demoralizing early disaster was too great. A staff report approved by the Ministry of War in 1910 declared that both Longwy and Montmédy "had lost much of their value" because they could only be expected "to hinder enemy troops for a very limited time."[54]

For Maubeuge there was more hope. Indeed, with the lowered status or complete declassification of other positions to the West, Maubeuge remained as the only serious fortification from the Sambre to the sea. Inspection teams at the outset of Freycinet's ministry in 1888 encouraged the decision to maintain the six forts at Maubeuge and to strengthen them. A decade later that identical view was reiterated in a thorough summary by the Etat-Major of the reorganization of France's defensive system during the interim. According to the author of this revealing document, General Laurent, only those fortresses capable of being entirely self-sufficient could claim any value; on the northern front, therefore, Maubeuge alone should be further reinforced. This judgment was corroborated by General Mercier's inspection tour in 1898 upon which the Third Bureau based its final recommendations for future construction or declassification. As the only important defensive position between Verdun and Dunkirk, however, Maubeuge had a disturbing flaw: with relatively little difficulty it could be circumvented by rail to the north via Mons or to the south via Anor. Even at its strongest point, therefore, the northern frontier was dangerously porous. Nevertheless, the Third Bureau insisted somewhat weakly that Maubeuge could be expected to retain "a certain importance."[55]

After examining this telling detail gleaned from budgets, maps, and memoranda, we can draw several conclusions with some assurance. First, it is clear that France's entire military posture was defensive. One is struck by the total absence before 1900 of any offensive conception. Lest that observation seem self-evident, let it be recalled that professors of military science at the Ecole Supérieure de Guerre were meanwhile propounding the virtues of offensive warfare.[56] Although such theory served to inspire cadets at the academy, upon graduation they faced the less thrilling realities of geography, finance, inertia, and German superiority. The evolution of France's defensive strategy resembled nothing so much as the story of the Dutch boy attempting to plug a leaking dike. Improvements in transportation and technology dictated that fortresses be extensive, massive, and self-contained. Yet to construct enough such bastions to form an effective barrier along two fronts was far beyond the means of a young republic strug-gling through the effects of an economic depression.[57] To finance elaborate fortifications, moreover, was only half the task. They would also have to be manned. The disadvantage of tying down large garrisons of troops in static positions of defense became increasingly problematical to French planners. The emergence of a more mobile defensive strategy was therefore appropriate. But to pass from that notion to a vision of offensive success, as General Joffre did on the eve of the First World War, was a case of mis-guided enthusiasm. France's best and perhaps only chance to halt a German invasion was a combination of luck and improvised mobile tactics. For that, the wild chase of Parisian taxis to the Marne in 1914 remains a fitting if mythic symbol.[58]

Equally apparent is the fact that the options chosen by the French in the 1890s figured importantly in prescribing the open-ing phase of the war to be fought some years later. If there had been any doubt about where the first blow would fall, it was dissipated. Everyone's attention shifted northward. Whatever defi-ciencies existed in the Verdun-Toul-Epinal-Belfort system, those fortresses were certainly far more imposing than the misbegotten assortment of outposts to the north and west. The French thereby did their part to heighten the temptation for the German army to invade through Belgium, although we have repeatedly established that such was not their original intention. Much discussed even as early as the 1870s, the bold conception of what became the Schlieffen plan continued to be underrated by most French plan-ners until 1900. Not before the first decade of this century did the French high command begin to come to grips with the likeli-hood of the plan. By 1910 there could no longer be a serious question about "strategic ideas openly expounded" in Berlin: "We are obliged," a French staff report in that year read, "to consider as materially feasible and morally possible a German invasion through Belgium."[59] Maybe it is not too much to speak of a cer-tain collusion between the French and the Germans in anticipating the opening military gambit of 1914. At least that was true insofar as the French army chose to construct major fortifications in a region where they expected no attack and to neglect or dismantle others where they all but invited an assault. The only remaining question was how wide the German flanking operation would be.

One final observation is permissible. Among the hundreds of

documents from which this analysis has been reconstructed, there was no mystery concerning the identity of frequent references to "the neighbor," "the foe," or "the foreigner." Thus, in pursuing the theme of German influence, we have unconsciously and yet unavoidably followed the dark thread of xenophobia that twists about French history from the war of 1870, through the Boulanger crisis, and into the entanglements of the Dreyfus Affair. The importance of the affair transcends purely military considerations. But its origins cannot be properly understood apart from the present context of the army's self-perceived inferiority to Germany. To that extent, the onset of the affair was a fitting culmination of the frustrations and apprehensions of the previous decades. The arrest of Alfred Dreyfus in 1894 was a symptom, not an aberration.[60] The timing was also crucial because of the recently concluded alliance with Russia, which was manifestly dictated by a mutual fear of German strength and which betrayed a recognition by French military leaders that they had failed through a quarter of a century to match Germany's vigorous strides. Confidence in the army was shaken; and the competence of the French high command, as well as its loyalty to the republic, were open to doubt.[61] If the political sensations of the Dreyfus Affair had the paradoxical effect of briefly diverting public attention from the issue of military preparedness, the central question nonetheless remained the same as before: how capable was the French republic of meeting the power of imperial Germany? From all that we know, the answer by the close of the nineteenth century was extremely disquieting.

Part Two: The Religious Question

Chapter 6

The Early Republic and the
Roman Church

The Concordat and the Consequences of War

Among the Catholic states of Europe, the textbooks tell us, France long enjoyed a special status as "the eldest daughter of the church." Yet from the Babylonian Captivity of the fourteenth century to the French Revolution, the relationship of the temporal and the spiritual in France was seldom untroubled and often tempestuous. The regicide of 1792 was consequently less than a total aberration, although it posed a new challenge to the notion of theocracy and to the status of French Catholicism. Thus the religious history of the nineteenth century unavoidably began with the question of a viable accommodation between church and state. What forms should it assume or, indeed, was it possible? The initial answer provided by the Napoleonic Concordat of 1801 was a qualified affirmative. If the Concordat stopped short of recognizing a state church, it at least asserted the seemingly undeniable premise that Roman Catholicism was the religion of a large majority of Frenchmen. But the practice of succeeding decades suggested that this formulation was a distinction without much difference. Everyone assumed that France was a Catholic nation, and no one doubted that the Concordat was the legal foundation of French ecclesiastical affairs.[1]

An essential component of the compromise was the financial patronage granted to the Catholic clergy by the French government. In return, the episcopacy was expected to pledge political allegiance to the secular authority. Despite some discernible democratic encrustation, this declaration preserved the tone of centuries past; witness the typical oath of a bishop in 1841: "I swear fidelity to the king of the French [and] obedience to the constitutional charter and to the laws of the realm."[2] The insurrections of 1848 and the testy interim of the Second Republic did little to alter this basic concordatary arrangement. If anything, the Falloux law reinforced it by strengthening the church's role in the administration of public education.[3] Under the Second Empire, accordingly, French prelates continued to offer personal fealty to "His Majesty the Emperor" and to promise explicitly that they would avoid collusion with any foreign or domestic leagues that might threaten public tranquility. Daumier's satirical lithographs are perhaps a sufficient reminder of the overt harmony between church and state that endured until 1870.[4]

Yet if we look behind the imperial panache, it becomes apparent that a latent antagonism was always present. A single episode in 1863 should illustrate the point and also provide background for one of the central religious controversies of the early Third Republic. This matter, which concerned the appointment of a new archbishop of Paris, was explained at length in a memorandum from the current minister of education and religion, Gustave Rouland, to the minister of foreign affairs, Edouard Drouyn de Lhuys. The recent demise of the incumbent archbishop had left vacant the most important ecclesiastical post in France. Therefore, Rouland wrote, "the emperor has just appointed [*nommer*] Monsignor Darboy, bishop of Nancy, to the archbishopric of Paris." But the papal nuncio in Paris, Monsignor Flavio Chigi, suddenly intervened to insist that "a bishop cannot accept a transfer of venue without the consent of the Holy Pontiff." The French government was urged by Chigi not to make Darboy's selection known until an official sanction was forthcoming from the Vatican. To this plea Rouland responded negatively: even if such a delay were considered nothing more than a formality, "the pretension of the papal nuncio seems to me inadmissible [and] contrary to the right of appointment [*droit de nomination*] which, in France, the Concordat assures to the sovereign." Public notification of Darboy's transfer was thus to be published at once, and Chigi was reminded that authority to make episcopal appointments was legally guaranteed to "the French government" by the Concordat of 1801. The incident was thereby closed.[5]

For the balance of the Second Empire, such was the prevailing interpretation in questions of competence. A personal oath of loyalty to the emperor remained a formality for prelates as-

signed to a French bishopric, and the Napoleonic regime continued to exercise the right to designate members of the episcopacy.
As late as May 1870, Napoleon III, "Emperor of the French by
the grace of God and the national will," made official announcement in the *Moniteur* that "Abbé Fournier, vicar of St. Nicholas in
Nantes, is appointed to the bishopric of Nantes."[6] We shall subsequently follow the issue of episcopal investiture and observe how
it was affected by the war, the collapse of the Second Empire, and
the emergence of a republican government whose claim to em-
body the grace of God and the national will was somewhat more
dubious.

In the summer of 1870 the most dramatic news of the church
emanated from Rome, where the Vatican Council, convened by
Pope Pius IX, proclaimed the doctrine of papal infallibility. Two
effects were at once apparent. First, the spiritual authority of the
papacy was strengthened at the expense of internal opposition
scattered throughout the episcopacies of Europe. Pius's intention
to convoke the council, announced in 1867, had sparked intensive
international negotiations among Catholic churchmen who feared
an encroachment of ultramontane autocracy and who sought to
preserve a measure of national autonomy in religious affairs—in
its French form, in other words, to guard the tradition of Gallicanism. Notable among such efforts was the contact between Monsignor Félix Dupanloup, bishop of Orléans, and Ignaz von Döllinger, professor of church history at the University of Munich. Each
in his own manner, the two of them attempted to awaken some
resistance and to forge a Franco-German ecclesiastical alliance
that could deter the pronouncement of infallibility. But their project, always hampered by theological and temperamental differences, quickly collapsed once the council met, and from that failure soon followed disillusionment and mutual estrangement.[7] The
second effect of the Vatican Council, as a necessary consequence,
was that the political options in the relationship between church
and state were drastically narrowed. Just as the opposition had
anticipated, the ultramontane tendency became everywhere ascen-
dant in Europe during the ensuing decades. Any who demurred,
such as the minority of Old Catholics in Germany and a few
intractable Gallicans in France, were either denounced as heretics
or displaced to the periphery of church affairs. Henceforth it
was indeed *Roman* Catholicism with which European statesmen

would need to reckon. For the time being, however, the threat of war crowded out such political and theological considerations.

The opening of hostilities with Germany had a discernible impact on the relationship between the French church and state, which became closely allied in the national defense. In the last week of July, Emile Ollivier, serving as Napoleon III's minister of justice and religion, instructed all French bishops to offer public prayers for "a glorious peace," thereby placing the nation and the imperial dynasty "under the protection of Him who holds in His hands the outcome of battles and the destiny of peoples."[8] Replies to Ollivier's directive showed that the prelates hardly required such prompting. Some had already conducted public prayers in their dioceses at the outset of the war, and others were more than willing to comply at once. Several also volunteered the use of church buildings near the eastern frontier, to be placed at the disposal of military authorities and used as emergency hospitals. Priests and nuns meanwhile expressed their willingness to serve as chaplains or nurses. For good reason and with obvious sincerity, Ollivier responded that "the government is touched by these offers." Thus in 1870 the Roman Catholics of France were not pressed into service by the state. In the face of German invasions they spontaneously came forward with a sense of loyalty and solidarity.[9]

As the war continued, so did the church's participation in the national cause. The declaration of a republic on 4 September did not immediately change that fact. The French clergy responded unhesitatingly to the new regime's appeal for assistance in caring for war orphans.[10] Bishop Dupanloup, with perhaps more than a touch of local pride, went so far as to offer the government his advice on the proper military strategy: "Everything will be decided on the walls of Orléans."[11] When the siege of Paris tightened and Gambetta's resistance to the German armies grew more feeble, some possibility arose that certain bishops might act as intermediaries in armistice negotiations. Most notable among these was the pro-Bonapartist archbishop of Rouen, Cardinal Bonnechose, who advocated that the imperial Corps législatif be reconvened to consider the terms of a peace. Bismarck thought this suggestion "well founded" and expressed a wish to confer with Bonnechose in person. This brief titillation led to nothing, however, partly because events soon swept the republicans into their own negotiations with Bismarck and also, probably, because the church had no interest in bearing responsibility for an unpopular settlement.[12]

The rightist majority of the Assembly elected to Bordeaux in January 1871 was reassuring to the Vatican, although the emergence of Adolphe Thiers as the first chief executive of the republic was more problematical. The Vatican watched carefully for clues provided by Thiers's first appointments. His ambassadorial selections were appraised by the papal nuncio as properly conservative; but the nomination of the veteran liberal Jules Simon as minister of education and religion aroused "lively opposition" among Catholic deputies, who regarded his acquisition of that portfolio as "a scandal." On the whole, nonetheless, Monsignor Chigi assessed the situation positively and reassured Rome that the Bordeaux Assembly would be well disposed toward the church and would uphold "a traditional and conciliatory policy in all questions relating to the Catholic religion." We need not dwell on the daily political uncertainties of the time, except to note that the Vatican continued to pin its hopes on a divinely inspired fusion of the monarchist parties in order to attain "the salvation of France and the liberation of the Holy See from the oppression of its enemies." For his part, Thiers was determined to proceed cautiously in his dealings with the church and to avoid any step that might revive "the Roman question, which we have no means of resolving satisfactorily."[13] Hence, all concerned were initially willing to temporize. In doing so they were consciously or unconsciously acting in a spirit altogether appropriate to the Concordat.

Nothing could have better served to confirm the harmony between the republican state and the Roman church than the eruption of the Paris Commune. One of the regime's first actions after the insurrection was to issue from Versailles an emphatic warning to all French prefects, generals, judges, and bishops that Adolphe Thiers represented the sole legitimate government and that any sign of disobedience to him would result in "a state of forfeiture." Such admonitions were unnecessary for the Catholic clergy, who had no inclination to defect to a cause they regarded as a godless evil. In that same spirit Chigi reported to Rome that he was at once joining the diplomatic community in Versailles at the side of the "legally constituted government."[14] Thiers meanwhile dispatched Bernard d'Harcourt as the French envoy to the

Vatican. There was in these formalities a clear recognition of mutual interests that took precedence in a moment of crisis over any underlying political or theological differences. This sentiment was well expressed by the first republican foreign minister, Jules Favre, in thanking Pius IX for a charitable donation to assist French war victims: the pope had thereby provided further reason for France to maintain its "traditional respect" for the spiritual authority of the "chief of the church."[15] If there was nothing binding in such polite language, the net effect of gesture and response was again to bolster the Concordat.

This general context is important to explain the relative ease with which a crucial issue was broached: the offering of public prayers for the survival of the republic. Before 1870 it had not been uncommon for Catholic bishops to intone a Te Deum or to implore Divine benevolence for a king or emperor. But now the embattled Thierist regime might be thought a far less appropriate vicar of the Almighty. Nonetheless, in mid-May 1871, just a few days before the final assault by the army of Versailles against the Paris Commune, public prayers were ordered in all French dioceses by a vote of the Assembly. When Jules Simon conveyed specific instructions to the episcopacy for prayers "to calm our civil strife and to end the ills that afflict us," no contradiction was audible.[16] We cannot suppose that either priests or public officials were totally unaware of the issues at stake. As the prefect of the Somme wrote from Amiens, "this somewhat delicate circumstance" left him uncertain whether his office bound him to attend religious ceremonies. He was advised from Versailles that the government did not require attendance at public prayers, but in view of the Assembly's action, the participation of prefects was certainly permissible.[17] This unobtrusive exchange was characteristic of the moment and afforded only the faintest premonition of the excruciating problems of future years, when aggressively secular republican officials were to assume a more rigid stance and to force the church into an awkward defensive posture. But in May 1871, while the twin specters of religious atheism and political rebellion still haunted Paris, an alliance of Roman church and Thierist republic was effortlessly consummated.

One episode can provide adequate illustration of how the German military occupation further encouraged the mutual dependence of ecclesiastical and governmental officials in France. In April 1871, in the frontier department of the Meurthe, where a lengthy residence of foreign troops was expected, the mayor of Pont-à-Mousson complained to Jules Simon that the Germans were requesting appropriate space in which to hold Protestant religious services. When the mayor suggested that they use a nearby Catholic seminary, the bishop of Nancy intervened in opposition. Simon felt constrained to support the bishop on grounds that seminary property belonged neither to the town nor to the central government but to the Catholic diocese.[18] Unwilling to tolerate such procrastination by the French, however, German troops began to confiscate church property. Inevitably, on occasion, the seizure of Catholic sanctuaries resulted in the desecration of holy altars. Protests from Catholic bishops in the occupied eastern provinces consequently began to flood Simon's office in Paris. The German requisitions and intrusions were "a veritable blow against the liberty of the Catholic denomination," wrote the archbishop of Reims, who demanded "aid and protection" from the government.[19] Despite efforts to negotiate with German military authorities, there was in fact little that the French regime could do to prevent the occurrence of untoward incidents—except to expedite the complete withdrawal of German occupation forces by hastening the acquittal of reparations. This was among the reasons for which Thiers adopted a policy of accelerated payments. Not until the occupation was finally terminated in early 1873 did the bishops cease their urgent requests for government assistance.[20]

The foregoing fragments of evidence form a collage from which we can perceive how, at all levels of public life, representatives of church and state in France found themselves drawn into mutual support because of the conflict with Germany. Both were vulnerable, and both faced a potentially devastating loss of strength and prestige. Just as the French government was momentarily overwhelmed by German military superiority, so the Roman church felt surrounded by hostile forces of liberalism and secularism. As Bernard d'Harcourt observed to Thiers, the common denominator between Versailles and the Vatican was a fear of isolation. Why should the French risk the loss of their oldest and only remaining diplomatic ally? "If the pope has need of us," Harcourt wrote from Rome, "we also have need of him."[21] That statement expressed one of the most basic realities of French religious life as the Third Republic began.

The Investiture Controversy

Although the struggle over the investiture of bishops is known to every student of medieval history, that issue may seem anomalous in the modern era. Yet the opening years of the Third Republic witnessed such a controversy, and the religious question in France during the 1870s cannot be comprehended without accounting for it. The Napoleonic Concordat had stipulated in effect that the responsibility for filling episcopal vacancies be divided: the secular authority should nominate and the ecclesiastical should confirm. But this formula, as noted above, was never free of an ambiguity that was political as well as semantic. Even though the problem was eventually to become extremely complex, it can be posed simply enough: what did it actually mean for the French government to exercise the right of nomination? Did state officials have the *power to appoint* or merely the *option to present* a candidate for the Catholic episcopacy? From the outset we may be certain that far more than a technicality was in dispute, despite the sometimes tediously legalistic form of the debate. In its contemporary guise, in fact, the investiture struggle involved some of the most fundamental principles of the relationship between church and state.

We have observed how a latent conflict of interests became apparent during the Second Empire when Napoleon III appointed Monsignor Darboy to the archbishopric of Paris without awaiting papal confirmation. The intervention of the nuncio at that time was in vain, and the government successfully upheld its "right of nomination."[22] But the double impact of the Vatican Council and the Franco-Prussian war created a temporary state of anomie, the full political ramifications of which were still impossible to foresee. Understandably cautious, the Roman church at first withheld any official commentary on the conflict of 1870 or the character of the provisional French regime. Not until after the national elections in January 1871 and the convocation of the Bordeaux Assembly did regular contacts resume between the new French president and the papal nuncio. Through Monsignor Chigi the Vatican was kept closely advised about the consolidation of the Thierist government and the subsequent progress of French affairs. We have also noted the Vatican's initial apprehensions about republicanism in France and the fondly nurtured hopes for a fusion of royalist forces. So far as the church was concerned, then, Thiers was to be tolerated more than supported; and once the war was ended, even that toleration was both qualified and provisional.

The first test of the truce between the French republic and the Roman church occurred in the summer of 1871. At issue again, tragically, was the archbishopric of Paris, left vacant after the execution of Monsignor Darboy during the final days of the Commune in May. The choice of a successor quickly became involved with questions of procedure and personality. The problem centered once more on the term "nomination." As early as April, Thiers had attempted to reclaim the role formerly assumed by kings and emperors by notifying the pope that he had "appointed" (*nommé*) the vicar general of Montauban, Abbé Legain, to become the bishop of that diocese. Thiers expressed the expectation that "Your Holiness will give his approbation to the selection that we have made."[23] This careful use of the past tense was in accordance with precedents established in the prewar years. But now, confronted with the pretensions of what seemed only a transient regime in France, and one for which in any case Rome had limited sympathy, the Vatican decided to launch a challenge to the new republic's claim to choose ecclesiastical appointees without prior consultation with church authorities. To Jules Simon, the cabinet official directly responsible for religious affairs, Chigi advocated an alternative procedure: he, the nuncio, would present to the French government a list of prelates considered suitable for advancement and already deemed acceptable by the papacy. Thiers and Simon would thus receive prior assurance that their nominations were satisfactory to the Vatican. Chigi added, as if anticipating an objection, that old political quarrels need not be a complicating factor because "the distinction of ultramontane and Gallican among members of the French clergy was always absurd" and it had become all the more so after the Vatican Council: "Every Catholic is obliged to submit."[24]

At least to Jules Simon, such was not precisely the view of the French government. Instead, he claimed that Thiers was temporarily too preoccupied with the Commune to consider specific decisions about episcopal vacancies. Moreover, Simon preferred not to commit any explanation for his own choices to writing. By doing so, he would permit their relative positions to become too unequal, Simon wrote to the nuncio with a slight trace of sarcasm:

"You propose and I discuss."[25] An agreement was thus stalled. Manifestly, both parties were self-conscious about protecting their prerogatives and determined to approach volatile questions of precedent with all the precaution of demolition experts.

No less significant to the outcome than these procedural matters were the personalities involved. The archbishopric of Paris was not an episcopal seat like any other. Its occupant would in some sense become the primate of France, or so Jules Simon intended, privately hoping to call an outstanding Gallican to the Paris diocese to offset the weight of ultramontanism. Therefore the proper choice, he thought, would be none other than Bishop Dupanloup of Orléans. Simon clung to that preference despite a pointed warning from Rome, transmitted by the bishop of Nevers, Monsignor Forcade, that the Vatican was certain to refuse confirmation of any prelate who had resisted papal infallibility in 1870—hence "Monsignor Dupanloup would not be considered."[26] The same categorical message was soon conveyed to Simon directly by Chigi. Simon nevertheless persisted, and he was encouraged to do so by the Gallican bishop of Lyon, Monsignor Ginoulhiac, who had been another opponent of infallibility in 1870. In a long memorandum to Thiers in early July 1871, Simon thus renewed his advocacy of Dupanloup for the post in Paris. To balance that admittedly controversial appointment, he suggested that two simultaneously vacant bishoprics at Ajaccio and Rodez be filled with moderate ultramontanes. Simon argued that a failure to support Dupanloup would seriously discourage the clerical faction of which he was the acknowledged leader, thereby conceding the definitive triumph of ultramontanism in France. Simon urged Thiers to realize that "a great bishop in Paris is virtually a transformation of the church in France."[27]

Either Thiers did not share Jules Simon's lofty appraisal of Dupanloup's ability or he did not think it prudent to bait the papacy at a time when France was militarily devastated and diplomatically isolated. In any event, his personal choice fell on the amiable and aging archbishop of Tours, Monsignor Joseph Guibert. As one who had dutifully supported the infallibility doctrine at the Vatican Council, Guibert was acceptable to Rome. Yet as a somewhat sickly and seemingly undynamic prelate, he could also be thought relatively unobjectionable to Gallicans. When confronted with this selection, Simon reluctantly withdrew his support of Dupanloup and agreed to make a personal visit to Tours to invite Guibert to accept "the designation of the government."[28] Meanwhile, Foreign Minister Jules Favre notified the French ambassador to the Vatican of the decision by Thiers in favor of Guibert. He assured Harcourt that "this choice, confirmed by the cabinet, . . . offers the Holy Father a proof of [Thiers's] respect and his desire to avoid an altercation."[29] Therewith Thiers deliberately held the French republic on a course of conciliation with the Roman church. The documentation cited here proves that such a policy was not adopted for lack of an alternative. It appears, rather, that Thiers was fully cognizant, in rejecting Jules Simon's advice, of the political cost that France was likely to incur in provoking the papacy by insisting on the nomination of Dupanloup. Under the circumstances of the defeat inflicted by Germany, he had obviously concluded, the fledgling French republic could not afford to squander one of its few remaining resources.

As if by some inexorable dialectic, every solution brought a new problem. Even before the issue of the Paris archbishopric had been settled, another complex legal question was presented with the Vatican's substitution of the term "*présentation*" for "*nomination*" when confirming appointments to the episcopacies of Montauban and Martinique. Jules Simon promptly charged that such "innovations" were inadmissible and that the government should insist that "nothing be altered in the anterior relations between France and the Holy See." If the Vatican had gained a practical victory in matters of personnel through the choice of Guibert over Dupanloup, he contended, the republican regime must stand all the more firm in principle.[30] One may wonder that a slight semantic variation in a text could generate such intense controversy. But this legalism is less baffling if we recall that the Concordat remained the basis of the republic's entire religious policy and that any tampering with a single provision or precedent could place everything in jeopardy of revision. Later we shall have occasion to observe how the roles of church and state were to be diametrically reversed and how the thesis of the Concordat's inviolability would be turned on its head. For the time being, however, it was the government that wished to appear as the defender of traditional practices against possible encroachment by the church.[31]

The current disposition of the Vatican was explained by the

papal secretary of state, Monsignor Giacomo Antonelli. The selection of the bishops of Montauban and Martinique had occurred while France still had a provisional government. A precedent had been set in 1848, when General Eugène Cavaignac employed the word *présentation* as well as *nomination* in reference to Monsignor Sibour, who was then to be invested with the archbishopric of Paris. Antonelli proposed that this dual formula be henceforth maintained. Thus the result would be, just as the French government wished, to continue the use of *nomination*. But, of course, it would also alter the customary formula of the Second Empire and would therefore perhaps imply a modified procedure of investiture.[32] Jules Simon was quick to grasp that implication and to send a "very urgent" memorandum to his personal friend, Ferdinand de Jouvencel, who was presiding officer of a judicial committee temporarily replacing the Conseil d'Etat. Simon requested that the committee render a legal opinion in the matter. At the same time, Simon did not neglect to reiterate his personal opinion to Jouvencel that "nothing should be altered in the relationships and reciprocal usages between France and the Holy See." Not surprisingly, the committee at once ruled that recent papal procedures were "contrary to all precedents" and that they ignored "the rights which devolve to the French government from the terms of the Concordat and the consistent traditions of the church of France." If that pronouncement were not categorical enough, Thiers agreed to take the rostrum of the Assembly in Versailles two days later to deliver an emphatic statement: "The government does not present—it is useful that I state it clearly today—the government does not present, it appoints [*il nomme*] bishops and archbishops."[33] Simon had decidedly scored a point.

For all of its theatricality, this effort by the French government to remove ambiguity failed, and the reason for that failure is simple to identify. The church wished no clarification, certainly not one that awarded primacy of investiture to the state. The controversy therefore continued, albeit in yet another semantic guise. After the summer of 1871 the legal dispute began to center on the Latin phrase "*nobis nominavit*." The subtle use by the Vatican of the ablative in the first person plural was far too conspicuous to escape the learned and distrustful eye of Jules Simon, who persisted in contending that the papacy should be obliged, whether in Latin or French, to employ the word *nomina-*

tion alone. He therefore repeated his tactic of submitting the case to Jouvencel's legal committee for a ruling. Simon was convinced that the inclusion of *nobis* in a papal bull or encyclical, like the addition of the French term *présenter*, was a juristic subterfuge intended to weaken the government's right to appoint bishops.[34] In mid-November 1871 the Jouvencel committee again upheld the language and legal position advocated by Simon—without, however, ordering the invalidation of any investiture proceedings already accomplished.[35]

Sufficient detail has been presented here to establish the polemical character of the investiture controversy by the end of 1871. We may therefore review in more general terms the religious question during the balance of the Thiers presidency with the assurance that the prevailing attitudes of the time were already well defined in the minds of those directly engaged in dispute. The great abundance of evidence need not blur three clear lines of development that became perceptible before May 1873.

The most obvious of these was the defensive stance of the new republican government. The highest aspiration of the Thierist regime in religious affairs was to maintain the status quo and to preserve the prerogatives guaranteed to the government by the Concordat. Although hard-pressed in Italy and surrounded by a volatile citizenry in Rome, the papacy unquestionably held the initiative in dealing with secular French representatives. The church's advantages could be attributed to a nexus of factors: the enfeebling effects on France of the disastrous war with Germany; the loss of prestige and to some extent of legitimacy by the French state in its uncertain transition from an imperial to a republican form of government; and the fact that Gallicanism was adrift in the sea of ultramontanism now inundating the French church. The Vatican was able to exploit these weaknesses and to persist in harassing the French about semantic and procedural issues. Whenever Versailles attempted to regulate matters so as to establish its own precedence, Rome would clutter another portion of the legal landscape with obstacles. In May 1872, for example, papal Secretary of State Antonelli chose to employ the elaborate legalistic formula of *quem nobis nominavit et praesentavit*, thereby provoking another acrimonious round of dispute with Versailles. This complication caused further consternation in Jules Simon's ministry and led Adolphe Tardif, chief of the bureau of religious affairs, to assert that Antonelli's stated justifications for such a change were "without value." This "byzantine controversy," Tardif added, would be inexplicable if there were not certain "monsignori de bas étage" who had "sold out to the Quirinal and to Prussia" and who were attempting to split the French government apart from the papacy. In lodging his rebuttal with Antonelli, Simon refrained from repeating these darkest innuendos expressed by his staff; but he employed verbatim Tardif's argument that the papacy had in effect reverted to the Concordat of 1516, whereas the French case properly rested on that of 1801. This parry was met in turn by Antonelli's "absolute resistance."[36] And so it went, with the French state trying to defend an incontestable legal basis for the right to make ecclesiastical appointments without prior consent of the church and the Vatican on an offensive to restrict that right.

A second development followed from the first. As the French government was repeatedly thwarted by the Vatican, serious differences began to emerge among republican leaders, some of whom were devout Roman Catholics. Thus the hard line advocated by Jules Simon and his colleagues at the Ministry for Education and Religion was increasingly contested by Charles de Rémusat at the Quai d'Orsay. Because communications concerning the investiture struggle were usually transmitted through the French Ministry of Foreign Affairs, all of Simon's messages were filtered through diplomatic agents—meaning Rémusat in Paris and Ambassador Harcourt or his chargé in Rome—before they reached Cardinal Antonelli and Pius IX. Understandably worried about France's isolated position in Europe, the diplomats were far more interested in maintaining cordial relations with the Vatican than in quibbling about a vacant bishopric in a provincial French capital. Initially Rémusat remained impartial in mediating the Simon-Antonelli debate, but he gradually became impatient with what he regarded as Simon's excessive pedantry, such as the demand to eradicate *nobis* from all papal pronouncements containing the word *nominavit*. Rémusat's annoyance grew noticeably when Simon directly challenged Antonelli to show precedent for *nobis* and the Vatican was able to respond with more than two hundred examples. Because the Quai d'Orsay's own records had been destroyed by fire during the Paris Commune, no effective rejoinder was possible. Yet Simon still refused to accept the *nobis* formula and claimed that "many bishops" supported his position.[37] The way finally seemed open to a compromise in September 1872, when the newly reconstituted Conseil d'Etat ruled that, although *nominavit* alone was consonant with the Concordat of 1801, the inclusion of *nobis* "does not diminish the rights of the civil authority." Simon and Rémusat nevertheless continued to quarrel. Simon insisted on the use of *nominavit* alone, whatever the Vatican wished to contend. Rémusat urged that the government be more supple, partly as a simple diplomatic courtesy and also to reflect the "reciprocal situation" of the republic and the Roman church. Simon finally washed his hands of the matter by announcing sarcastically that he would no longer become involved in "a question of diplomatic relations." But in reality, of course, Simon thereby admitted that his strict constructionism had bogged down in the sands of ecclesiastical legality and that his support within the government had eroded.[38]

The third development was the emergence of Adolphe Thiers as an active participant in stabilizing the relationship of church and state. Much more fascinated by financial and military issues, the president had initially been inclined to leave the religious question to Simon's ministry. This insouciance had extended even to his careless use of *présenter* at a time when Simon was adamantly attempting to prevent the slightest semantic alteration.[39] We have seen evidence of Thiers's desire to avoid controversy with the church in his choice of Guibert over Dupanloup for the archbishopric of Paris. Thereafter Simon's persistence, coupled with the papal nuncio's own stridency, unavoidably nudged Thiers closer to involvement in religious issues. In part this tendency could be ascribed to the urging of his close friend Rémusat, who persuaded him that Simon's undue scrupulousness about the Concordat was becoming harmful to French diplomacy. As Thiers admitted to Chigi: "These semantic questions only lead to disputes [that are] very often quite useless."[40] Guibert also sensed the drift and gloated that, after unsuccessfully raising a "puerile question" about the precise Latin phrasing of papal decrees, the French government was finally being taught a "little lesson." By the beginning of 1873 Simon's opposition was thus neutralized and the progovernment *Journal des débats* could announce that a "happy resolution" had been reached and that the controversy was "definitively closed."[41]

By entering into the private correspondence of the principals involved, we have been able to establish a far more intimate account of the investiture struggle at the outset of the Third Republic than was available to the public at that time. We also enjoy the luxury of a longer perspective, enabling us to see that the decisions reached in the early 1870s, although formative for the balance of that decade, would not determine the subsequent pattern of religious affairs in France. Like General von Blücher at Waterloo, Jules Simon had lost an early skirmish, but he would return in the late afternoon with reinforcements.

German Kulturkampf and French Quiescence

A brief *tour d'horizon* is now in order. The Roman Catholic church had reached a critical juncture by 1870. The unification and belligerence of a new Italian state had brought pressing doubt about the temporal power of the papacy to the gates of the Vatican. The spiritual authority of the Holy See, although formally reconfirmed by the Council of 1870, remained under stress. Meanwhile, the wars of 1866 and 1870 had pitted some Catholics against others in nationalistic struggles, during which the papacy could only anguish on the sidelines while opposing sides simultaneously professed the Christian faith.

Within France the Roman Catholic clergy was spontaneously forthcoming in aid of the war effort against Germany: public prayers for victory, offers of service by priests and nuns, temporary conversion of church property into depots and field hospitals. The advent of the Government of National Defense complicated but did not fundamentally alter the favorable disposition of the religious hierarchy toward the French war effort. One primary reason for that easy adjustment was the conspicuously conservative and proclerical composition of the Bordeaux Assembly. Emblematic of the moment was the position of Monsignor Dupanloup, who offered belated obeisance to the Vatican on the question of papal infallibility while taking his place as an elected deputy in the new French parliament.[42] Thus the Roman curia had grounds to conclude that political power in France would reside in a well-disposed National Assembly in which the possibility of a prompt restoration of a Catholic monarchy was by no means precluded.

An additional explanation for continued cooperation between the Roman church and the French republic was the wave of
popular insurrections that engulfed Paris and threatened many of
the principal cities in dioceses throughout France. Under such circumstances, it was natural for the clergy to view the Paris Commune and other local outbursts as the work of atheistic instiga-
tors and agents of the International. The incarceration and execution of Archbishop Darboy confirmed their worst fears. Mutual
diplomatic recognition between the Vatican and Versailles logically followed. Likewise, the German occupation encouraged reci-
procity between civil and ecclesiastical authorities in France. German officers were often contemptuous of French officials and
sometimes demanded that Catholic sanctuaries be opened or confiscated. The same pattern was frequently repeated: preemptive
German orders, protests of a local priest or abbot to his bishop,
appeals from the bishop to the government to intercede, attempts
to placate the Germans and to arrange a satisfactory solution. It is
well to recall that such conditions existed for more than two years
and that they grew more troublesome in the latter stages of the
occupation when the remaining German garrisons were crowded
into fewer and fewer eastern departments. Throughout that time
the passions of revanche and religion were scarcely separable for
many French Catholics who were daily confronted with the German presence.[43]

A visible sign of accommodation between church and state
after 1870 was the continuation of public prayers. It became customary for prayer services to be held in all French churches whenever the Assembly reconvened for its autumn session. On such
occasions the clergy was expected to invoke a blessing for the
work of the legislature. In 1875 this obligation became part of
the republican constitution.[44] But harmony did not exclude ambiguity. Indicative was the activity of the papal nuncio, who followed the prospects of royalists and eagerly reported to Rome
whenever their stock appeared to rise. Monsignor Chigi remained
convinced that the long saga of fusionism would finally have a
"happy ending," despite public indifference, repeated setbacks in
by-elections, and the confounding recalcitrance of the Comte de
Chambord.[45] Because the nuncio was the main conduit of information between the French episcopacy and the Vatican, we may
accept his confidential messages to Rome as a fair record of the

reservations held by the Catholic hierarchy toward the Thierist republic. Any trace of political instability was immediately investigated by Chigi, and his dispatches were both candid and generally accurate. By early 1873 he correctly perceived that the exploratory negotiations between Dupanloup and Chambord were doomed to fail and that fusionism was "largely compromised, . . . sterile, and ineffectual."[46] The papacy thus remained well informed on French affairs and was fully sensitive to the "precarious state" of the Thierist regime at the time of its fall in May. The hypothesis that the Roman Catholic church may have actually conspired to bring down Thiers, however, does not rest on a firm documentary base. True, some of the conspirators—the Duc de Broglie chief among them—were ardent Catholics. But the available evidence does not reveal a papist plot. It indicates, rather, that the French episcopacy had learned to live with Thiers without ever completely trusting him or deeply committing the church to support his regime.[47]

The secular side of the coin displayed a pattern somewhat more complex. A general tendency of the early republic, as we have established, was to collaborate with the church and ordinarily to acquiesce in a modus vivendi. But several factors, both domestic and foreign, served to qualify such a policy. Within France there existed not merely the objections of a few influential figures such as Jules Simon. At various levels of government across the nation appeared functionaries who held firm and sometimes vehement secular views. It was becoming abundantly clear that the anticlericalism of the Paris Commune had not been a complete aberration. Many French townships were soon to be dominated by mayors and municipal councils whose prevailing ethic was anticlerical. All leftist political factions would increasingly draw strength from this phenomenon. The prefectoral corps generally reflected a more moderate stance of the national administration in religious affairs; but there, too, the tendency of the decade was toward secularization. The internal correspondence of the bureaucracy already betrayed these growing undercurrents, and no student of the period should be so dazzled by the surface of cooperation between church and state as to overlook what lay beneath.[48]

Diplomatic considerations were no less symptomatic of the limits of republican complicity with the church. In this regard, the most delicate problem of the early 1870s was the war of nerves between the papacy and the Italian government. Thiers's emissary to the Vatican, Bernard d'Harcourt, was emphatically propapal, and hence he encouraged his regime to cultivate a close alliance with the Holy See. By tilting in that direction, Harcourt contended, France could offer Pius IX protection and receive in return from him valuable moral support. But Thiers was simultaneously exposed to pressure from Florence in the form of strong hints that France's embrace of the papacy would drive Italy into the waiting arms of Germany. French foreign policy, explained to the nuncio by Jules Favre, was therefore a model of caution: Versailles would need to act in concert with other Catholic powers, especially Austria, and to support the Vatican "to such an extent as permitted by its duty to preserve good relations with the kingdom of Italy." This restrained formulation was reiterated by Thiers before the Assembly, and it was to remain a fundamental tenet of French diplomacy thereafter.[49]

So much for a general reconnaissance. In order to pull the various elements of this analysis together, and also to introduce an additional factor without which a treatment of the religious question in France would be incomplete, it is now necessary to take some measure of the initial impact of the German Kulturkampf within the French republic. Although often dated from 1873, the anti-Catholic controversy in Germany actually produced its first repercussions in midsummer 1871. From Rome Harcourt reported three disturbing omens beyond the Rhine: the public stir over the excommunication of Ignaz von Döllinger, the imminent fall of the ultramontane Bray cabinet in Munich, and the publication of a letter from Bismarck to the Vatican's secretary of state, Cardinal Antonelli, in which Berlin's gathering antagonism toward the papacy was plainly expressed.[50] These complexities were confirmed in Munich by the nuncio to Germany, Monsignor Pier Francesco Meglia, who warned that a "malicious war against the church" might soon erupt. The resulting escalation of alarm in Rome was rapid and was at once communicated back to France by Antonelli, who deplored "a state of things that becomes each day more intolerable for the vital interests of the church and its august leader." Although still nameless, the German Kulturkampf was beginning.[51]

Frenchmen directly charged with articulating religious policy did not respond in unison. Harcourt remained in character by arguing that the papacy was "more and more threatened" by an Italo-German rapprochement, that France would consequently come under pressure to remove support from the pope, and that the Thierist republic should therefore compensate for the conflict in Germany by adopting a more forthright ultramontane posture.[52] But Thiers and Charles de Rémusat preferred to retain a balanced stance and to remind the papacy, at a moment when "passions are being unleashed against it," of the value of French patronage. The government reassured Pius IX that "the gates of France are open to him" should he be forced to flee Rome: the French frigate *Orénoque* was being kept moored near Cività Vecchia in case of such an eventuality.[53] These lines of policy were already traced well before Bismarck sent a formal request to Kaiser William in January 1872 that Adalbert Falk be appointed as the Prussian minister of religion (*Kultusminister*), an action that foreshadowed the intensification of danger for Catholicism in Germany.[54]

A discernible pattern thus began to emerge: the more overtly the German Reich moved toward conflict with the Roman church, the more obviously the French republic was inclined to caution. Both civil and ecclesiastical leaders in France were conscious of this triangulation, and they acted accordingly. In January 1872 John Acton visited the Quai d'Orsay in Paris for the purpose of gauging the French reaction. Although his interlocutors there evinced no undue interest in the religious question, Acton observed, Rémusat did confide to him that Bishop Dupanloup had specifically requested that he not be nominated as Darboy's successor to the archbishopric "because the pope would commit some stupidity"—presumably by resuscitating the problem of Dupanloup's doctrinal infidelity at the Vatican Council of 1870. If so, a conflict might ensue that would diminish the pope's trust in France and perhaps drive him toward Germany.[55] A similar remark was meanwhile made by Harcourt, who first spread word that the Thierist government intended to react vigorously to the darkening international scene and who then sought to fulfill that prophecy by advising Versailles to counterbalance Berlin. He reported that relations between the Reich and Rome were growing "more and more difficult" because Bismarck was becoming "frankly hostile" to the papacy and because Germany was "on the verge of an open rupture with Catholicism." Fortunately, however, the Vatican was a "natural ally" of France. Harcourt's repeated recommendation was therefore that the Thierist regime should strengthen its ties with the Holy See in order to thwart the Germans: "The more our adversaries desire that our good relations [with Rome] be terminated, the more we should attempt to maintain them."[56]

The religious question would increasingly conform to this isosceles configuration. In Germany the Kulturkampf acquired its ugly name and face, while Bismarck made no effort to hide "the obvious fact that we find ourselves at war."[57] Pius IX retaliated in kind, venting his hostility against the chancellor before a group of German pilgrims in Rome and thereby making what one French observer could only describe as "a declaration of war."[58] The virulence of these mutual imprecations persuaded Thiers to respond with prudence. Because of "the gravity assumed by the religious question," he said in obvious reference to the Kulturkampf, "we must guard extreme reserve in our actions."[59] In practice this meant that France would keep its gates open to the pope but not encourage him to enter them; France would maintain the *Orénoque* in readiness but hope not to use it; and France would conduct a benevolent policy toward the Vatican but seek to avoid alienating the Italian government.

It should be reemphasized that Thiers's favorable disposition toward the Roman church, though firm, had distinct limits. When Archbishop Guibert of Paris personally warned the president of "grave injustices" being committed in Italy against the Jesuits and other religious corporations and asked that the French government attempt to defend them, Thiers replied vaguely that his regime would "watch over the great moral and religious interests of the country with constant concern" but that "such a delicate and serious matter" required him to adopt an attitude of tactful reserve.[60] These elevated phrases, which were exchanged in effect between the titular heads of the French church and state, can be translated into less evasive language. Guibert wanted the government to espouse an ultramontane policy at home and abroad by offering Roman Catholicism active protection. Thiers refused to do so, recognizing that any show of zeal in support of the papacy would further alienate the Italian monarchy and encourage it to ally with a Germany already sworn to oppose the Vatican. At the highest level, then, the Kulturkampf had a direct bearing on the orientation of the early Third Republic. Given the rupture between Berlin and Rome, a studied restraint was the appropriate French response to the religious question for two reasons: both because French diplomacy stood to gain, especially among Catholic nations, from a favorable contrast with Germany's militant antipapism; and because increased German pressure on France to become involved in the Kulturkampf would surely threaten the nation's inner tranquility. Because the ramifications of these foreign and domestic themes were not yet fully apparent, they will require our subsequent attention. Hence the following very general and provisional conclusion must for the moment suffice.

The Kulturkampf came to dominate the religious affairs of continental western Europe in the decade of the 1870s. Every European nation was obliged to adjust to the struggle taking place, and France was no exception. About the origins of the conflict there could be sharp disagreement. Bismarck did not cease to vilify the reactionary and disruptive policies of Pius IX, contending that, "through decisions of the Vatican Council, changes in the constitution of the Catholic church have occurred."[61] This version was disdainfully rejected by the Vatican, which maintained that the conclave in Rome had in reality met "to sustain and preserve the integrity and the purity of the Catholic faith."[62] By the spring of 1873 these positions had already become petrified at the extreme poles of religious opinion. Henceforth they would define the terms of a European religious controversy in which French Catholicism could not avoid becoming embroiled.

Chapter 7

The Frustration of Educational Reform

The Duruy Program

A realization that the French educational system was in need of reform antedated the war of 1870 by several years. In the closing decade of the Second Empire, educators were fully conscious that France was slipping, especially in the realm of what was vaguely acknowledged as "science." They recognized that the French system possessed three distinctive features: it was elitist, it was centralized, and it was heavily influenced by the Roman Catholic church. Of these characteristics, the first was most seriously challenged in the prewar period; the second was generally accepted, with a certain resignation, as immutably French; and the third assured that educational reform, sooner or later, would become a controversial aspect of the religious question.[1]

Insofar as educational reorganization under Napoleon III took concrete form, it was shaped by his minister of education, the historian Victor Duruy. Because Duruy's career has been so frequently chronicled, we are relieved of any necessity to recapitulate it here.[2] But we do need to document the considerable fascination that Germany exercised in Duruy's planning. It is appropriate, in fact, to portray Duruy as the academic counterpart of Marshal Niel: both enjoyed the patronage of the emperor; both based their original reform proposals essentially on a German model; both saw their efforts stifled by inertia and entrenched conservatism; and both were vindicated belatedly, under circumstances unfortunate for France, by the war with Prussia.

After serving for six years as an inspector of schools in Paris, Duruy accepted a cabinet portfolio at the rue de Grenelle in 1863. There he developed the vision of a vastly expanded pedagogical system based on the Prussian principle of universal and tuition-free primary education. At the secondary level Duruy also hoped to encourage what he termed a "natural bifurcation" between classical and practical curricula, much like the German distinction between the *Gymnasium* and the *Realschule*. And in higher education Duruy admired, although he despaired of ever emulating, the German network of regional universities so beneficial to the variety and quality of scientific research.[3] It is essential to examine this tripartite program in more detail.

The theory, if not always the practice, of costless and compulsory education in the primary grades had long been rejected in France. There were often expressed doubts that the state's function should be to require—and thus inevitably to finance and supervise—universal public instruction. Rather, it could be argued, the responsibility for a child's education properly rested with the family and perhaps, if the parents chose, with the church. It was in that sense only that schools should be "free." Such thinking unquestionably ran deep, particularly among practicing Roman Catholics. The Falloux law of 1850 accurately reflected this educational philosophy by fostering "liberty of instruction" (among others, under Jesuits) and by continuing to allow local schools to contract with various religious orders to supply teachers, a haphazard procedure inherited and perpetuated by the Second Empire.[4] Not all French schools charged tuition, but many did, especially outside urban areas. In Duruy's estimation, these arrangements for primary schooling displayed two serious deficiencies: the French rate of illiteracy remained shockingly high (at least a quarter of the population, compared with less than 10 percent in most parts of Germany); and clerical involvement in the curriculum of public schools was pervasive.[5] After conducting a census of French elementary education and a comparative survey of German and other compulsory systems, Duruy resolved to fight for reform. In doing so, he made little secret that his conception was no less Germanic than French, an admission that proved to be a political liability for his projects, just as it simultaneously retarded those of Marshal Niel in military affairs.[6]

The fundamental problems of secondary education followed from those of the primary level. In the purposely elitist French system, the number of pupils receiving more than a rudimentary instruction was very restrained, all the more so because they were

ordinarily required to pursue a rigorous course of classical training that stressed oral and written exercises in Greek and Latin.
This emphasis was the curricular core of the *lycée*, which provided the only available path to the liberal professions. In addition, France boasted an irregular substructure of secondary *collèges*, which were undeniably of lesser quality and were usually
more permissive in substituting "special" courses more suitable
for youngsters of mediocre academic ability who wished to enter
vocations of lower social status in commerce, trades, and services. Duruy's ambition was to organize and upgrade these *collèges*, thereby formalizing the arrangement of an *enseignement
secondaire spécial* analogous to the German *Realschule*. At the
same time, he hoped to loosen somewhat the grip of the classics in
the *lycées* to make more place in them for science, modern languages, history and geography, and physical education. With these
changes Duruy intended to eliminate the traditional division of
the baccalaureate into classical and scientific branches by integrating them into a broader curriculum. Thereby he touched on what
was to become the most basic difficulty of reform in secondary
education: how was the French school system to maintain the
emphasis on classics and yet simultaneously to prepare pupils in
the modern subjects?[7]

French higher education was of course dominated by Paris.
More than one-fifth of all *lycée* graduates came from the capital, and nearly half of all university students were located there.
Moreover, Paris held a virtual monopoly of the *grandes écoles*,
with all the social clout and professional prestige they represented. Centralization was not without benefits, but it meant
that French provincial institutions of higher learning were condemned to relative inferiority, whereas their counterparts in the
German territories—because Berlin exercised no comparable academic hegemony—were prospering centers of instruction and research. Duruy therefore hoped to encourage "the labor of literary
and historical scholarship, which is so much in evidence on the
other side of the Rhine [but] which is so sadly lacking among us."
He was thus aware of a serious French deficiency, but, seeing no
rapid means to alter the university structure, he made little visible
progress at that level. Indeed, Duruy's one enduring achievement
in higher education, the creation of the Ecole Pratique des Hautes
Etudes in 1868, only enhanced the preeminence of Paris.[8]

The astonishing Prussian victory over the Habsburg monarchy in 1866 gave Duruy's program a renewed sense of urgency. By crushing Austria's professional army within a few weeks, Moltke's soldiers promoted the twin virtues of universal conscription and universal education. Yet the proper conclusion to draw, as Ernest Renan perceived, went beyond a single reform: "It has been said that the victor of Sadowa was the primary schoolmaster. No, what was victorious at Sadowa was German science." Henceforth, in short, nothing less than a fundamental revision of the entire French educational system would suffice.[9]

Despite Duruy's vigorous efforts and Napoleon III's ostensible approbation, the imperial Corps législatif nonetheless rejected a motion in 1867 to establish tuition-free primary education in the public schools by a vote of 199 to 32.[10] The defeated parliamentary minority, however, included such names as Jules Favre, Garnier-Pagès, Glais-Bizoin, Eugène Pelletan, and Jules Simon—virtually a roster of those who were later to sponsor the Government of National Defense and to guide the first tentative steps of the Third Republic. For the time being, French legislation fell short of the most basic changes needed to approach the Prussian model. Yet at least one reform was passed into law that provided for government inspection of any parochial schools (écoles libres) "which substitute for public schools . . . or which receive a subsidy from the commune, the department, or the state." This measure, still only a token, prefigured later demands for secular control of the curriculum, textbooks, and examination procedures of all French schools that were publicly subsidized.[11]

All in all, the church was scarcely moved by the Duruy program, and the clergy's decisive role in education was generally taken as much for granted as their participation in the glittering public displays of the Second Empire. In preparation for an imperial festival in August 1867, for instance, the Catholic priesthood was praised by the Ministry of Justice and Religion for "enlightened patriotism" in helping secure support of the populace for the Bonapartist dynasty. During the climactic evening of the spectacle, held in conjunction with the Paris international exposition of that year, the church was represented in a varied schedule of cultural attractions in the capital city: the celebration of a Te Deum at Notre Dame competed with performances of *Don Juan* at the Paris Opera, *Le misanthrope* at the Théâtre Français, and *Le malade imaginaire* at the Théâtre de l'Odéon.[12] The regime was thus long on glamour and good intentions but short on appropriations for education. Victor Duruy and Marshal Niel were jointly appointed to a special committee to represent the cabinet before the parliament to plead for budgetary increments to finance educational and military reforms. But neither was able to make much headway, and both ended in disappointment.[13]

It is possible to uncover some official documents from the last years of the empire that indicated a continuing dismay within the imperial administration about the retardation of French education in comparison with Germany.[14] For the most part, however, such sentiments were confined to the high-minded articles and editorials of journals like the *Revue des deux mondes*. There one could detect a note of alarm about the "decadence of higher education" in France, the "more flourishing secondary schools" in Prussia, and the growing dominance of German science over the French ("les sciences de la vie elle-mêmes ont une tendance à se germaniser").[15] One commentator, Victor Cherbuliez, claimed that "the war of 1866 and its consequences have changed everything," but he tended to dwell on an intensification of the German challenge rather than to specify a modification of the French response.[16] Perhaps the most outspoken participant in this intellectual forum was Victor Duruy's son Albert, who did not conceal his admiration for the "incontestable superiority of the German universities" because of their greater structural autonomy and scientific freedom. He observed regretfully that the French had recognized a need for reforms but had not proceeded to realize them. Therefore the German lead had only widened. Albert Duruy thus summed up seven years of his father's unrequited effort: "Regarding matters of the intellect, it is impossible not to turn our eyes toward Germany."[17]

Another reformist impulse of the late Second Empire should not go without mention here, both because it suggested that a potential of popular support for Duruy's program existed and because this movement also had an identifiable Germanic component. The Ligue de l'enseignement was organized in 1866 by an Alsatian schoolmaster, Jean Macé, who announced that his purpose was to create a *"Landwehr* of education."[18] By 1870, after spreading his gospel throughout the eastern sections of France and into the Parisian basin, Macé managed to gather three hundred thousand signatures on a petition favoring government sponsorship of a bill for compulsory and tuition-free primary schooling. By then, however, Duruy had already resigned from the cabinet, and a sense of impending crisis paralyzed the imperial regime and parliament alike.[19]

On 18 July 1870 the Conseil Impérial de l'Instruction Publique met in one of its final sessions, as the minister of education solemnly noted, "amidst patriotic emotions that stir every heart."[20] The day's agenda appropriately contained only items of routine—the greater issues of educational reform had been deferred. With the beginning of the war, of course, they were relegated at once to the status of unfinished business. As one qualified observer remarked a decade later, the Duruy program was thereby left by the Second Empire "in a state of mere intention."[21] The ensuing military setbacks at the hands of Germany soon exposed, as nothing else could have done, the inherent flaws of French education. Moreover, the capture and exile of the emperor brought to power precisely those persons who had previously supported the Duruy program and who remained convinced that its implementation was imperative. Shortly after Sedan, Jules Favre spoke for them: "No matter what happens to us, victorious or vanquished, we shall have to reform ourselves radically." France, he added to Adolphe Thiers, was being crushed not by the sheer weight of numbers but by the "moral force" of German science.[22] Just as military defeat overwhelmed the French armies, so would Favre's humiliating logic assail French politicians. Far too late, it seemed, France would finally be disposed to take Victor Duruy's admonitions to heart.[23]

Problems and Plans

During the early Third Republic the cabinet portfolios for education and religion were often combined into a single ministry. If not inevitable, such an arrangement was certainly sensible, as the new government quickly learned. One of the immediate consequences of the war, months before its conclusion and before the Paris Commune, was the frequent allegation that a principal source of French weakness was clerical control of the primary schools. That contention underlay a decision by the municipality of Toulouse in late 1870 to eliminate priests and nuns from public elementary education—ostensibly on the technicality that they lacked the proper teaching credentials (*brevet d'instruction*)—and to replace them with "secular teachers" (*instituteurs laïques*), to begin on the first day of January 1871.[24] This preemptory decree conflated two issues that would be of critical importance in the formative stage of the republic: the balance between municipal autonomy and central administration, and the relationship between church and state.

The specific circumstances of Toulouse are worth our attention as a foreboding of more general problems that subsequently became apparent. At the end of 1870 the city had twelve church-sponsored schools (*écoles congréganistes*) with 4,642 pupils and eight public schools with 1,796 pupils. Municipal officials estimated that they would therefore have to equip and staff twenty public schools in all and that they needed to recruit twelve new principals and eighty-seven new teachers. The obvious question at once arose: where to obtain the necessary funds, buildings, and qualified personnel? Merely to dismiss clerical instructors and to curtail religious appropriations in the municipal budget would not suffice to meet the city's educational needs. Despite these seemingly insuperable difficulties, the new republican prefect of the Haute-Garonne was inclined to support the municipality's intention to enforce instant reform. Firmly opposed, however, was Archbishop Desprez of Toulouse, who apprised the provisional government in Bordeaux of the situation and warned that public agitation by irate Catholic parents was bound to result. Equally perturbed, the inspector of schools in Toulouse also alerted Bordeaux to expect "a demonstration that will very strongly resemble a sedition." When the government responded by advising the prefect that the municipal decree of secularization had "openly violated the law," the latter accused the cabinet in turn of stirring the very crisis that he had been attempting to avert. In hopes of restoring some order, an arbiter from Bordeaux, Charles Zévort, was promptly dispatched to Toulouse, only to be confronted there with another round of bickering.[25] Viewed from the perspective of the provisional government, this elaborate altercation in Toulouse seemed both untidy and ominous, as similar anticlerical contentions were soon reported from other towns in southwestern France.[26] In actuality, the millstones of secularization would grind very slowly. By March 1871 only two new public schools had been opened in the Haute-Garonne, and the surrounding departments showed little or no change.[27] In other sections of France, meanwhile, where the war had created considerable disruption or physical damage, radical reform of the school system was not the most immediate of considerations. Toulouse thus remained largely isolated, although not, as the municipal revolts in Paris and elsewhere soon proved, altogether exceptional.[28]

The Toulouse crisis was but one of the many intractable problems inherited by the new minister of education and religion, Jules Simon. In principle Simon sought what he termed an "amicable arrangement" that would combine tradition and innovation, that would at last realize the reform program of Victor Duruy, and that would reestablish France as an intellectually competitive nation in Europe.[29] Simon consequently favored increased attention to such subjects as history, geography, gymnastics, and modern languages—even if that meant some diminution of the classics. Judging by their inadequate mastery of *langues vivantes*, for instance, the French people were not keeping pace. "In any event," Simon advised all rectors of public schools, "we cannot allow the continuation of the state of inferiority in which we find ourselves in this regard. In commerce, industry, the sciences, and letters, we must become perpetual borrowers from our neighbors" (*nous avons des emprunts perpetuels à faire à nos voisins*). At the very outset of the republic Jules Simon thus identified himself with the substance as well as the rationale of the Duruy reforms, which conspicuously included the emulation of Germany.[30]

But if this theory was lucid enough, its implementation became rapidly muddled. The most immediate reason for disillusionment was a shortage of funds to finance a coherent reform program. The stupendous cost of the war, further compounded by obligations incurred through the sale of public bonds in order to acquit the reparations to Germany, meant that half of the annual French budget was tied up in the national debt, and another quarter was devoted to rebuilding military forces and fortifications to meet the possibility of a sudden German onslaught.[31] Hence only one-quarter of France's yearly revenues was left to be dispersed among the remaining government ministries, including that of education and religion. It was all very well to make ringing speeches in Paris about compulsory instruction for every child in France until one was confronted with the maintenance charges of antiquated school buildings in rural areas, not to calculate the projected cost of new construction. Prefectoral reports were replete with lamentations about the sorry condition of physical plants and with requests for special allocations to repair them. Funds for the provinces were grossly insufficient. "To establish everything in a satisfactory state," commented one prefect haplessly about his department, "it would be necessary to count in the millions."[32] Even in Paris the government's initial efforts were inadequate: in the summer of 1872 President Thiers personally prepared a scheme to finance construction that would create twenty-two thousand new school desks in the capital at a cost of 18 million francs. Yet that measure, he learned, would still leave a need for another thirty thousand places in the city's elementary school system.[33] Furthermore, this effort came before most of the practical consequences of secularization had yet been faced, such as meeting the expense of wages, supplies, and utilities heretofore assumed in many instances by the church. These financial facts of life should be reckoned among the explanations for the reluctance of some republicans to embark precipitously on a course of rabid anticlericalism.

Directly related was the fairly pathetic attempt to inaugurate a more rigorous schedule of physical exercise into the French curriculum. Although earlier advocated by Duruy, such reform gained its most urgent rationale because of the lost war. Prussian soldiers had not only been better trained, they also seemed bigger and stronger; and, again, the unfavorable difference could be ascribed to the slackness of French schools. In addition to a popular mystique about the army becoming the school of the nation (in an effort to stamp out illiteracy), the inverse proposition consequently developed that the schools should prepare pupils for military service. The French high command was eager to encourage the introduction of gymnastics, equitation, and even rifle drills as a regular part of the daily school routine of children throughout the land.[34] Similarly, in the mountainous southeastern regions there was official encouragement for the organization of a Club Alpin Français, the undisguised ulterior purpose of which was to prepare the youth of those areas for the rigors of future warfare.[35] Yet two problems persisted, and no one had a ready answer to either. The first was to find adequate time in an already overcrowded curriculum: was physical training to be gained at the expense of mental gymnastics in Latin? The second was to provide enough space, equipment, and trained instructors to make such activity regular and worthwhile. For years to come material shortages would plague many French schools, most of which continued to lack gymnasiums, with the result that physical education often meant no more than a few minutes of arm-waving and walking led by an ill-suited or infirm schoolmaster. By the late 1870s some progress was evident in the *lycées* and *collèges*, but the primary schools were largely unaffected.[36]

Simon's ministry also emphasized the expansion of geography and history. Ever since the war, stories of befuddled generals and misrouted troops had counted among the usual explanations for French defeat. More often than not the Germans had been much better informed about French rail and road networks than the French themselves. In November 1871 Jules Simon therefore convened a blue-ribbon committee for the study of geography; the group held forty-seven sessions by May 1873. The minutes disclose that Germany was by far the most studied, admired, and imitated of neighboring nations when selecting and preparing new atlases and globes for introduction into the French public schools.[37] As for history, the obviously controversial question was how contemporary events should be presented, if at all. In general, the more conservative the advocate, the less eager he was to expose pupils to the heated political debates and embarrassing military events of the recent past. Simon also worried about the objectivity of instructors as their lessons approached the historical record of the Second Empire, and he concurred that a somewhat earlier terminus would be more appropriate ("Restons dans la science"). Eventually a compromise was reached whereby the bounds of contemporary history were set at 1848, although the unification of Germany and Italy could be mentioned, along with the treaty of Frankfurt, in a class of geography.[38]

Probably the most telling illustration of the motivations and limitations of educational reform in the early years of the republic was offered by the fate of proposals to restructure the study of medicine in France. The first formal motion for a reorganization of the medical curriculum was presented to the Assembly in Versailles at the end of 1871 by Alfred Naquet. Just as Germany had replaced France as the dominant military power on the Continent,

Naquet observed, so was it also becoming the leading nation in science; and just as the French now aspired to reconstitute their army on a new basis, they should likewise strive to regain moral force and intellectual stature.[39] Unfortunately, in medical training the German lead appeared insurmountable. Whereas, after the loss of Strasbourg, France possessed only the two major medical schools of Paris and Montpellier, there were no less than twenty German-speaking medical faculties, a number that included Vienna and Prague along with Berlin, Leipzig, Breslau, and the rest. The creation of new medical schools in France was thus imperative but expensive. It would not suffice, moreover, simply to train medical students to the scientific level of decades past. New facilities were required that could reestablish international contacts and regain a level of preeminence in research. For that purpose the initial choice of the Thiers government for a third medical faculty fell on Nancy, which was to become "a vast atelier" for the assimilation and transmission of German technique. As Jules Simon instructed the new dean of medicine in Nancy, French students would need to learn the language of the Germans and to visit their universities in order "to derive benefit from their theories and their discoveries."[40]

From this rapid survey of the republic's opening phase, we may deduce several preliminary conclusions. Severely jolted by the war, the French were prepared to admit their deficiencies and to revamp their educational system. In most curricular and scientific matters the standard for reform was set by Germany. To observe merely that France had fallen *behind* is to avoid the manifest object of the preposition. It was Germany that France needed to rival in order to recover intellectual as well as military status in Europe. Given their current disadvantage, the French faced the necessity of a massive financial investment—still far beyond the budgetary capacity of a young republic—and above all they had to countenance a provincialism and a spirit of routine that still characterized the nation's educational institutions at all levels.[41] The road to reform was open, but it would unavoidably lead through many repair sites, frequent detours, long stretches of incomplete construction, steep upward grades, and hairpin turns.

The Conseil Supérieur de l'Instruction Publique

The meaning of the term "university," one must bear in mind, was not the same in French as in German or English. Thus the Conseil de l'Université, created by Napoleon Bonaparte and perpetuated by the Restoration and July monarchies, was charged with supervisory responsibility for the entire pedagogical system of France, not merely for higher education. The reformist tendencies of the Second Republic, however, undercut the importance of the Conseil and strengthened political control of public instruction by the cabinet of ministers. This circumstance continued under the Second Empire, when the Conseil Impérial de l'Instruction Publique was largely decorative; more specifically, it deliberated upon, but did not become closely identified with, the legislative reform program of Victor Duruy.[42] After the hiatus of the war of 1870, only a few weeks following the Paris Commune, a motion was introduced to the Assembly by the Duc de Broglie proposing that a new Conseil be established to oversee French education. Yet, for reasons of their own, Adolphe Thiers and Jules Simon allowed this proposal to languish, probably because the list of its Roman Catholic sponsors led them to fear an undue intrusion of ultramontane influence. Whatever the actual explanation, the law establishing a republican Conseil Supérieur de l'Instruction Publique (CSIP) was not passed until 25 March 1873, and the body did not convene until the early days of the MacMahon presidency. This particular incarnation of the Conseil thus began squarely under the conservative and Catholic aegis of the government of moral order.[43]

The pedigree of the CSIP goes far to explain why the reforming impetus of the republic's first years was so ineffectively expended. Under the Thierist regime special parliamentary commissions had been constituted to study the problems of primary and higher education. The reform of secondary education—including the linchpin of the entire system, the baccalaureate—was deferred for the Conseil. Consequently, the task of revising that sector of public instruction fell to a subcommittee, the so-called "Second Commission" of the CSIP, whose chairman was Cardinal Bonnechose of Rouen and whose membership included Archbishop Guibert of Paris, Bishop Dupanloup of Orléans, and soon also Bishop Freppel of Angers. The massive restraining weight of the church was thereby concentrated for maximum effect at the most critical point of potential reform.[44]

From the beginning, the central issue was the role of the classics in French education. All other problems were inevitably related to that question. Dominating the discussions was a consensus that Jules Simon had earlier overstepped permissible limits by yielding to pressures for an increased emphasis in the curriculum for modern languages, history and geography, science, and physical education.[45] Clearly, the more time that was devoted to those subjects, the less would be left for Greek and Latin. In his initial charge to a plenary session of the CSIP, the current minister of education, Anselm Batbie, challenged the wisdom of earlier reform measures: "You should tell us whether they ought to be preferred to traditional methods of instruction." Without mentioning Simon by name, Batbie revealed his feelings toward his predecessor: "If education were left to the caprices of transient ministers, teachers would waste their time and that of their pupils in marches and countermarches. . . . You are the brake that will halt [these] dangerous commotions."[46] The Second Commission picked up its cue at once. Its sessions quickly became forums of complaint about suppression of Latin verse, reduction of classical themes and compositions, overloading of the curriculum, and the resulting confusion and lowered morale in the schools. For these difficulties Dupanloup suggested a simple solution: returning to the curriculum of the July monarchy.[47] He was optimistic that it would be possible therewith "to satisfy at the same time both the needs of classical education and the exigencies of modern society." But at a session of the CSIP during which a preliminary report from the Second Commission was debated, the bishop's argument was criticized as retrogressive. Although the discussion failed to achieve either clarity or unanimity, it did demonstrate that some compromise was desirable and that Dupanloup's rigid stance (which he subsequently sought to relax) was infeasible. The voice of conciliation was that of Bishop Freppel, who stressed the danger of crowding the curriculum and advocated a delay of Latin study until after the first two years of secondary education: "In Germany," he noted, "this system is applied." Moreover, there was general agreement with a proposition that "we must create special commercial colleges for young people who do not wish classical studies."[48] If the CSIP thus displayed a laudable sense of realism and even made certain concessions to the earlier reform programs of Duruy and Simon, its initial deliberations nonetheless indicated that a traditionalist spirit had already blunted the innovative thrust of the immediate postwar years.

It is ironic that the one noteworthy reform approved by the CSIP was a division of the *baccalauréat ès lettres* into two. Along with the *baccalauréat ès sciences*, also maintained in truncated form, more than one path thereby led through the secondary grades to a terminal degree.[49] The irony derives from the recurrent objections expressed in the CSIP against "bifurcation," a term usually uttered as an obscenity. The Second Commission was virtually unanimous that secondary education should ideally have a unified curriculum (allowing for some variety of emphasis) leading to a single baccalaureate. But this vision of a tightly controlled and still more centralized system in France conjured two dilemmas that were closely related and often confused. First was the problem of preparation both in letters and sciences. The preponderance of classics tended to leave secondary pupils inadequately trained in scientific subjects, a result frequently criticized by the faculty of medical and military schools. No member of the CSIP programmatically favored several distinctive curricula leading to separate baccalaureate degrees, and yet to consolidate them into a tight single-track system would place an increasing and perhaps intolerable strain on the classical *lycée*. The second difficulty was in achieving a balance of quality and democracy. As more and more children were admitted to the primary schools, pressure was bound to grow for their further education. Should the rigor of the French *lycée* therefore be lessened to accommodate a lower average of aptitude, or should high standards be maintained in order to separate the academically less gifted pupils from the elite? Such nagging questions arose in one form or another on numerous occasions, and they still remained without a coherent solution. In addition to these basic policy issues, of course, the CSIP also continued to be hamstrung by an awareness of the acute shortage of budgetary appropriations. In any age and in any educational system, innovation appears far less feasible to administrators when funding is restricted. Money alone might not have solved the educational needs of the early Third Republic, but it would surely have helped to embolden those educators who advocated genuine change. Instead, lacking both foresight and finances, members of the CSIP could easily find an excuse to acquiesce in the verdict that institutional reform was less urgent than had previously been assumed.[50]

In the summer of 1874, after months of hearings and negotiations in subcommittees, the CSIP attempted to draft a master plan for French secondary education.[51] The result was predictably uninspiring. No major reforms were to be recommended to the Assembly, the new minister of education Arthur de Cumont explained, because France must submit to "a cruel law" of financial restraint that "paralyzed the best intentions" and required the "most rigorous economy." That apologia, we know, glossed over the absence of unified purpose among members of the Conseil. Perhaps the most indicative debate in this regard concerned examination procedures for the baccalaureate. The French system required pupils to pass a battery of tests controlled by outside examiners, whereas in the German secondary schools the *Abitur* was essentially an internal matter administered by the faculty of the local *Gymnasium*. Thus in France everything depended on the judgment of extramural officials on a single performance by a pupil whom they did not know. German pupils, by contrast, were evaluated primarily on the basis of their aggregate academic record by teachers already familiar with them over a period of several years. Symptomatically, after considering the relative merits and demerits of these two models, the CSIP ended in a temporary deadlock that sired inertia. In this instance, as others, the reasons for inaction were political and pedagogic no less than financial.[52]

Among the closest observers of these developments—or, more precisely, the lack of them—was Jules Simon. His commentary, published in 1874 as *La réforme de l'enseignement secondaire*, contained both a restatement of his program of reform and an admission that its current possibilities were limited. After long years of self-absorption, Simon wrote, the French "had begun to see the world, above all in the conqueror." France's defeat had dramatized the inferiority of an outmoded educational system, "a demonstration that was already apparent to clairvoyants"— doubtless an allusion to Duruy and to himself. The ignorance of geography, history, and foreign languages displayed by French military officers in 1870, in glaring contrast to their German counterparts, had shocked the nation and raised cries of indignation. Yet the exact nature of the reforms required was admittedly difficult to determine, Simon conceded, and he now believed that the main lines of the German system were "incompatible with our needs and ideas." This statement represented a partial retraction of Simon's earlier views and a belated critique of Victor Duruy. To rival Germany was for Simon still a strong motivation for reform; but literally to imitate Germany, he had concluded, was a mistake ("Il faut donc renoncer à nous servir des exemples de nos voisins").[53] The French would therefore be better advised to innovate within their own tradition. Simon suggested, for example, that the classics be maintained at their current level and that only the methods of instruction be altered.[54] He also approved of French examination procedures and admitted that the German classical *Gymnasium* could not in that regard serve as a precept for the French *lycée*.[55] Far from delivering a ringing indictment of the CSIP's failure to advocate a thorough restructuring of secondary education, then, Simon's book bowed to the reality of political retrenchment under the government of moral order. At the most, he seemed to urge that the French must continue to tinker.

It is hardly surprising that the history of the CSIP thereafter trailed off into trivia. To be sure, much of the discussion in plenary sessions and subcommittees was related to problems of church and state. Outstanding among these were the growing demands for secularization of public education, especially originating from the Municipal Council of Paris.[56] Yet such agenda items were only an echo of national issues; they did not reflect quarrels within the CSIP nor call its conservative posture into question. The truth was that the CSIP, in its first embodiment under the Third Republic, had already served its primary function, which was negative. It would become altogether superannuated once the government of moral order had run its course. The CSIP thus met for its final session of the decade in late December 1878—appropriately, only a few days after the death of Bishop Dupanloup. It would not be reconstituted until May 1880, when the new minister of education was Jules Ferry.

Chapter 8

The Wind Shifts

Moral Order and German Pressure

In their origins the fall of the Thiers government in May 1873 and the simultaneous passage of anticlerical legislation in Prussia were apparently unconnected. Yet in their consequences they shared a common denominator through the creation of a French regime, clerically inclined under Marshal MacMahon and Albert de Broglie, with which Bismarck's vigorous campaign against the Roman Catholic church was bound to conflict. French "moral order" and German religious persecution were essentially antithetical, and the tension between republic and Reich therefore reached one of its peaks during this period of political transition.

The new French government naturally experienced no difficulty in establishing reciprocal contacts with the Catholic hierarchy. The conclusion of initial diplomatic formalities was altogether free of friction.[1] MacMahon reinforced the spirit of harmony by following Thiers's precedent of extending presidential congratulations to the pope on the anniversary of his pontificate. Pius thus had reason to be pleased; and he was particularly delighted by a passage in one of MacMahon's letters in which the marshal expressed a wish to "associate his prayers with those of the Catholic world."[2] Certainly those were filial sentiments worthy of the eldest daughter of the church.

The overtly cordial tone of exchanges between the Vatican and Versailles did not fail to create an impression in Berlin that "Catholic tendencies" in France were becoming ominous.[3] With votes to gather for a military bill, Bismarck required little urging to adopt the view, suggested by his Paris embassy, that the new French regime doubtless had "a strong clerical coloring."[4] The most damning assessment of the Broglie government came from the commanding general of German occupation forces in France, Edwin von Manteuffel. In his estimation, the various political factions that had joined to upset Thiers shared above all "a close connection with the Roman Catholic church." Proclerical members of the French Assembly, "in cooperation with the Jesuits," were therefore certain to exercise considerable influence and to stir "a feeling of revenge against antipapist Prussia." As a consequence, Manteuffel advised, the situation in France was "more uncertain and more dangerous" than before—reason enough, he conveniently concluded, for Bismarck to sponsor an increase in military appropriations.[5]

Circumstantial evidence of an alliance between chauvinism and clericalism in France was indeed abundant. In the 1870s religious revivalism was widespread. To a great extent it was unquestionably spontaneous. Yet the mass pilgrimages to Rome and to religious shrines throughout France were never completely free of patriotic overtones, and neither patrons nor participants were always scrupulous in concealing their conservative political preferences. The pope himself set a belligerent tenor in the early summer of 1873. Europe, as he said in unsubtle reference to the Kulturkampf, had entered "a time when a conflict, each day more formidable, twists all the science of the century and all of human knowledge against the church." He therefore wished to thank the faithful who were courageously defending "Catholic civilization" and to bless those who were "struggling for God, religion, and country." Audible through this emotional rhetoric was a central message, often repeated in one form or another by the church hierarchy, that pilgrimages were the moral equivalent of war. "Multitudes of the French," as one cleric commented, were "hastening not to take up the arms of revenge . . . but, with enthusiastic verve, toward a certain number of sanctuaries dedicated to the Virgin Mary."[6]

Such religiosity had predated the war of 1870. Inauguration of the great religious shrines of the nineteenth century had mostly occurred during the Second Empire. Yet not until years later did they attain the imposing proportions of a popular phenomenon, when contrition born of military defeat and completion of long-distance railways combined to give the mariolatry of the early Third Republic an unprecedented mass appeal. Lourdes was of course the prime example: rail connections to the town were opened in 1867; a formal papal blessing was accorded in 1869; and the site was declared worthy of a "national pilgrimage" by the Assumptionists in 1873. As the plaques that still adorn the walls of its chapels testify, Lourdes began to receive great flocks of believers, most of whom benefited from special excursion rates granted to large groups or to individuals traveling longer distances by rail.[7] Under different national and international circumstances, the religious fervor of the time might have remained without noteworthy consequences. But the tenuousness of the French republic and the proximity of the Kulturkampf lent these pilgrimages the appearance of a deliberate political provocation. For instance, the favorite canticle of voyaging religious groups was

Dieu de clémence,
O Dieu vainqueur,
Sauvez Rome et la France
Au nom du Sacré Coeur.

In a spirit of defiance, however, pilgrims often substituted for the third line, "Donnez-nous un roi," as they waved white handkerchiefs out of open train windows. Piety, tourism, and the prankishness of restless travelers thus mingled with some political calculation and much unbridled patriotism to produce a social phenomenon that no one could ignore.[8]

Conspicuous among the pilgrims were conservative politicians, sometimes members of the Assembly, who thereby made public display of their devotion to the Catholic faith. Their presence drew sharp criticism from antiroyalists, who charged that religious sentiment was being exploited for political advantage. One of the most vigorous of such protests appeared in Léon Gambetta's leftist journal, *La république française*, which managed to elicit from Broglie's newspaper, *Le français*, a public denial of deliberate collusion between the government and the pilgrims. This debate was at once recorded by German diplomatic agents and reported back to Berlin: the pilgrimages were gaining a reputation in France not as "purely religious phenomena" but as demonstrations with "political importance." Even if the Broglie regime avoided total identification with the pilgrims, Bismarck was told, it was nonetheless indisputable that the government of moral order contained dedicated ultramontane elements. The chancellor's subsequent dispatches and marginal comments evinced both his sensitivity to these reports from France and his growing annoyance with Broglie. This personal pique was not totally unjustified, in fact, because the French premier deliberately chose to use the religious question as an instrument of self-advertisement at Bismarck's expense. In a directive to his ambassadors, Broglie underscored the "confessional struggles" elsewhere in Europe and instructed French envoys to "stress the absolute peace that France enjoys in this regard, in contrast to most of the other states."[9] One could not overlook in this statement the conscious allusion to an inverse correlation between Gallic restraint and Teutonic excess. Accordingly, it was no wonder that Bismarck's resulting discomfort soon produced efforts by Germany to pressure the Broglie government into suppressing clerical activity in France.

In another context the influence of this campaign on French politics has already been reviewed.[10] Here our dual purpose must be first to measure the impact on relations between the Vatican and Versailles and then to gauge the effects on French religious affairs. As for the former, so far as the papacy was concerned, everything hinged on the success or failure of royalist fusionism; and that, according to Monsignor Chigi, was seriously complicated by Germany's direct intervention in French internal matters, because Bismarck's wish to combat a monarchical restoration was causing Broglie and his friends to hesitate and would therefore predispose them to perpetuate the status quo. Premature reports of an apparent success of Charles Chesnelong's visit to the Comte de Chambord in Austria briefly raised hopes that "the cause of the restoration of the monarchy is definitively arranged and confirmed."[11] But, not alone, the Vatican was quickly forced to conduct an agonizing reappraisal. The papal secretary of state, Cardinal Antonelli, reluctantly acknowledged the collapse of fusionist efforts, which left France "in a quite difficult position." It would therefore be advisable, he thought, to extend President MacMahon's term of office "in such a fashion as not to compromise a more or less distant future." The Vatican thereby declared its willingness to support the marshal's septennate, to do business with the republic, and, as Antonelli wrote, to await "the arrival of more serene days."[12]

By the end of 1873, then, French political leaders found themselves in an uncomfortable stance. They were unable to boost the conservative and clerical monarchy they wanted, and yet they were vulnerable to charges that they were surreptitiously conspiring to do precisely that. One of Bismarck's most trusted agents in France, Dr. Emil Landsberg, described Broglie's predicament: his regime stood "under the domination of the ultramontane party" and, at the same time, it suffered from "a bad conscience." Consequently, the French would now be most sensitive to severe chastisement by the German chancellor.[13] And Bismarck, we know, was not one to leave such an opportunity neglected.

This was the juncture at which the Duc Louis Decazes entered the French cabinet as foreign minister and began his prolonged diplomatic duel with Berlin. Despite Bismarck's repeated and often irritating exigencies, Decazes was undeterred from his stated objective in religious affairs: "the solidification of our good relations with the Holy See." His imperturbability in the face of German hectoring depended in part on the Vatican's comprehension of his delicate task. True, the pope was encouraging the French government to join in protests against "religious persecutions" in Germany and elsewhere. "Yet," the French ambassador, Corcelle, reported from Rome, "His Holiness understands perfectly that we would compromise his own cause if we provoked external conflicts in an effort to support him." Thus Decazes enjoyed a certain latitude and was initially able, without undue recrimination from the Vatican, to yield somewhat to German demands that the French bishops be silenced. He admitted to Berlin that there had indeed been "episcopal errors," and he promised to have a confidential directive sent to every French diocese—anticipating that it would then be leaked to the press—in which he admonished the bishops to desist from any "attack at which the authority of neighboring governments might be alarmed."[14] Bismarck thereby obtained some satisfaction while Decazes received favorable publicity. This arrangement seemed to please nearly everyone in France except Louis Veuillot, who flogged the French government for "not only combating but abandoning" the papacy. This outburst shortly led to the suspension of *L'Univers* on grounds that Veuillot's newspaper was creating "diplomatic complications."[15]

But Bismarck was not finished. The semiofficial *Norddeutsche Allgemeine Zeitung* claimed to detect rumors of war in the Parisian air and added: "Our current antagonist is clerical Rome.

We are engaged in a difficult struggle against papal ambitions to dominate temporal affairs. . . . And therein lies the danger of our relationship with France." Were the French leadership to become a satellite of the Vatican, the editorial concluded, it would represent "an enemy with which we could not live in peace."[16] Just in case Broglie and Decazes underestimated the seriousness of such a threat, Bismarck delivered it personally to the French ambassador in Berlin. The chancellor served notice to the Vicomte de Gontaut-Biron that he was of no mind to tolerate incessant attacks in France against the religious policy of the German Empire, which was unavoidably locked in battle with Roman Catholicism. It was a question of national security, and should the agitation of French bishops persist, Bismarck threatened, "we would be obliged to make war on you." Germany would naturally prefer to maintain peace, he quickly added, but Berlin must expect the French government to take the necessary steps to constrain its Catholic episcopacy.[17]

The Germans brought further pressure to bear through Italy. Speculation about the withdrawal of the *Orénoque* from Italian waters had circulated for at least two years. Fearing serious objections from the papacy, for whom the ship was a symbol of French protection, Thiers had earlier managed to temporize with the Italian government. But now, at a highly sensitive moment, Florence reopened the question with Versailles.[18] A proposal emerged that the French might replace the *Orénoque* with another vessel stationed on the coast of Corsica. When consulted, Antonelli was willing to leave the decision to Decazes, bearing in mind that "the real cause [of difficulty] should be attributed to the exigencies of Germany."[19] How was Decazes to respond? He could neither ignore German threats nor deny altogether that French bishops were guilty of some impropriety in their Germanophobic statements. He saw the need for "much patience, moderation, and courtesy." Meanwhile, like Broglie, he would attempt to expose Bismarck as the true villain by drawing the sharpest possible contrast between the religious calm in France and the Kulturkampf in Germany: "The chancellor presumes to force us to follow him in his crusade against the church. We will not discuss it. We will stand our ground."[20] If such a reflex was eminently sensible, it was not to be without trying complications. Caught between the conflicting demands of Berlin and Rome, Decazes would need to assuage one contestant without offending the other. French policy thus emerged by mid-decade not as a simple neutrality but as a delicate gambit of double appeasement.

Decazes's first defensive move was to request again that the papacy discreetly assist him in tamping the passions of the French episcopacy. He wished to be responsive "insofar as our laws permit" to the concerns of the German government, he said, and yet he could not hope to control the bishops unless the Vatican agreed to cooperate. Pope Pius and Secretary of State Antonelli were therefore approached directly by Corcelle with a plea to admonish the bishops and to encourage "their abstention in foreign policy." They should be warned that "they can compromise their country." To this request the Vatican's initial response was positive: the nuncio in Paris and the French episcopacy would be instructed to observe the "necessary prudence." But the pope added one restriction. He would not issue any public reprimand to the bishops that could be construed as a concession to Germany. Political gestures by the French to Germany "might be necessary and legitimate" (probably an allusion to the *Orénoque*), but "the situation of the Holy See is not the same." Papal collaboration with France would consequently remain qualified.[21]

The pressure points were several, and in each instance the French sought relief by recoiling under the duress of German demands. The *Orénoque* issue continued to torment Decazes, who personally regarded the vessel as no more than "a legend and a difficulty" and who hoped to have it soon displaced.[22] He was also inclined to agree to the reassignment of the Strasbourg diocese to Germany on Berlin's terms, in accordance with the treaty of Frankfurt.[23] From the German capital Gontaut-Biron, with Decazes's blessing, meanwhile contacted secretly his old friend Chesnelong "to beg him to make every effort that the campaign of pilgrimages not be resumed." In the summer of 1874, under constant prodding from the German ambassador Chlodwig zu Hohenlohe, Decazes also moved to renounce support for the Carlists in Spain and to recognize the Spanish republic.[24] Finally, the French minister of the interior, Arthur de Cumont, in response to an inflammatory pastoral letter released by Archbishop Guibert of Paris, placed a formal disavowal in the *Journal officiel* and implored French bishops henceforth to "avoid anything that might in any way cause new difficulties for the government or paralyze its efforts."[25] This itemized list of French concessions over a period of several months documents the consistent attempts made by Decazes to mitigate the acuteness of the religious question by yielding to German insistence.

French pliability, a result of the manifest earnestness with which Decazes regarded the menace of war with Germany, could not fail to increase concern within the hierarchy of the church. The public renunciation of Guibert's pastoral letter was assessed by the new papal nuncio to France, Monsignor Meglia, as proof of "an extreme weakness of the government." Likewise, Meglia interpreted Cumont's admonition to the French bishops as an obvious attempt to parry both Italian complaints and German hints of preemptive war: "Under the present circumstances France can do nothing and [must] recognize its own debility." In resolving the *Orénoque* dilemma, Meglia continued, the Broglie cabinet found itself troubled at home, isolated abroad, and hence without "the strength or the courage to resist." Yet the Vatican should support Marshal MacMahon's presidential septennate, he contended, because otherwise France would either move backward to an empire or forward to a more radical republic: "God save France from those two scourges that would reduce her to ultimate ruin." Admittedly, the practical effects of accepting the status quo in France were not always in the best interest of the church; witness Decazes's recognition of the Spanish republic. But the Vatican would need to admit the existing reality that, as matters stood, "France can only submit to Berlin's every wish."[26]

In the international sphere, then, there is no question that Germany attempted to exert direct influence on relations between the Vatican and Versailles, nor that such influence was perceived by those involved as crucial to their decisions and their deportment. But we must inquire further to observe some of the ways in which these general circumstances began to impinge on France's internal affairs, thereby setting in motion an evolution of the entire religious question.

One aspect of the problem has already been indicated, although it is well to reiterate the point by a final reference to the *Orénoque* affair. In forcing a French retreat, however symbolic, Bismarck clearly intended not simply to embarrass the French in a single matter of foreign policy regarding Italy but to discredit and to dominate the government of moral order. Predictably, the reaction among Catholics in France was a mixture of dismay and outrage. It was therefore no chronological coincidence that orders to withdraw the *Orénoque* were simultaneous with renewed instructions from the Ministry of the Interior to French prefects that they should contact influential clergymen in their departments and urge "the most absolute silence." This directive was in explicit reference to pastoral letters containing any conservative political content that might give "new nourishment . . . to calumnies and unjust imputations of clericalism of which the government is the object."[27] The frequent repetition of such cautions throughout the mid-1870s cannot be properly understood in only one dimension as merely an expression of the Broglie cabinet's sensitivity to the growing political force of anticlericalism in France. It was also, and perhaps chiefly, a conscious response to Bismarck's campaign of intimidation and an effort to avoid being drawn into the wake of the German Kulturkampf.

Furthermore, we need to recognize that the intricate webbing in the triangle of Rome, Versailles, and Berlin was entangled with the most basic issues of church and state in France. As always, external and internal matters were inextricable. When the pope consented to the departure of the *Orénoque* from Cività Vecchia, for example, he expected in return something more than formal letters and flattering visitations by French cabinet members to the nuncio in Paris. Because we have access to private as well as official correspondence of some of the participants, we can establish that the pontiff's agreement was immediately followed by an audience with French ambassador Corcelle in Rome. During the course of their conversation Pius recalled the most recent attempt by Broglie and Decazes to seek advancement for Bishop Dupanloup by moving him to the archbishopric of Reims. Corcelle had previously asked his government to suspend that question until the *Orénoque* issue had been resolved. But now, he wrote to Decazes in confidence, "the pope believes that the generosity of his approval should not be followed by nominations contrary to his sentiments, especially when he is disposed not to support anyone whose political character would be displeasing." It would be difficult to locate a more egregious instance of outright bartering between two allies faced with a common adversary. Germany, as Corcelle cogently remarked in retrospect, "has everywhere pursued France in the Holy See and the Holy See in France." One demonstrable effect of Bismarck's aggressiveness was thus to promote a truce between Versailles and the Vatican in the investiture controversy. At the same time, Dupanloup's elevation to higher ecclesiastical rank was once again thwarted and the preeminence of French ultramontanism was further reconfirmed by the appointment of Monsignor Langénieux to the diocese of Reims.[28]

The German Kulturkampf meanwhile continued to serve as an ominous precedent. Prussia's blatantly anticlerical legislation evicted priests from teaching positions and sometimes from their parishes, sanctioned civil marriage, banished the Jesuits, brought some Catholic bishops before the courts, and ordered the closing of cloisters and monasteries. These measures were a plague to the Roman church in Germany and a threat to the rest of Europe. The papacy responded with fitting hostility, expressed most forcefully by an encyclical in February 1875 that condemned the May laws and other acts of persecution.[29] Apprehensions were undoubtedly similar in many nations, but French Catholics—well aware of German disapproval of their country's military reorganization—had special reasons to be fearful. Consequently, the Duc Decazes repeated his policy of quiescence and requested that the Vatican support it: "It is essential that no pretext be furnished by our bishops, since the sinister designs of Germany are evident."[30] Indeed they were. Bismarck's retort to the papal encyclical was to escalate his anti-Catholic campaign by enforcing further financial restrictions on the church. The impact of these "new and more odious measures" was evaluated by Monsignor Meglia, who considered them a danger to all Catholic nations of Europe and to those individuals brave enough to "raise their voice against the tyranny of Berlin." To Cardinal Antonelli the nuncio expanded: "The government most menaced by Bismarck's wrath is, as Your Excellency can easily understand, the French." This fact explained the timorous attitude of the Duc Decazes, who had proved to be "too docile and always fearful of Prussian threats." Decazes's views were not universally shared in France, however, Meglia pointed out, and a question therefore remained whether the Vatican might begin to encourage a less conciliatory policy in Versailles.[31]

Thus we can confirm that a gap was already perceptible between secular and religious authorities in their evaluation of a proper response to the Kulturkampf—that is, ultimately, to anticlericalism within France as well. Should the French clergy, and through them millions of faithful Catholics, be advised to accept patiently and silently whatever indignity was inflicted on the church? Or should the episcopacy and the Catholic press set about to arouse an opposition before more unfavorable tendencies had time to develop in France? The tension inherent in these questions, as we shall see, was increasingly to grip the French nation at its religious roots.

The archives provide an infinite number of incidents and episodes to illustrate a growing public concern with these underlying issues of ecclesiastical policy. Thousands of ordinary French men and women continued to participate in the pilgrimages. The more famous Catholic shrines throughout the country were thronged with visitors, most of whom could not have remained totally oblivious to the traditional connection between religion and royalism. But the most volatile, because most obviously political, of circumstances was created by the journey to Rome of French pilgrims eager to manifest support of their beleaguered pontiff. Overcome by fatigue and fervency, the faithful were sometimes given to delivering impassioned declamations that caused deep embarrassment back in Versailles. Lest such rhetorical excess appear to receive a papal blessing and thereby gain an even wider currency, the French government recommended extreme caution and occasional censorship to the Vatican "in order to avoid international complications."[32] Another example of emotional involvement by the populace was the controversy in the summer of 1875 about the cornerstone of the basilica of Sacré Coeur on the crest of Montmartre. Popular opposition in Paris to the beginning of construction and to its patent symbolism was so outspoken that Archbishop Guibert decided to scale down plans for a major public ceremony and to hold a more simple service of dedication. "*L'Univers* naturally finds this not to its taste and complains about German influence," Hohenlohe reported to Berlin. In this instance definitive evidence of direct interference is lacking, but the pervasive ambiance of German intimidation was surely not absent, and both the Vatican and Versailles remained sensitive to what Corcelle called "the perils of the general situation."[33] Without straining the evidence, we may posit a high degree of awareness of that situation among prelates and politicians, as well as a less precise and more visceral perception within the ranks of Roman Catholics throughout France.

Gallicanism and Anticlericalism

The wave of religiosity that broke over France in the early 1870s was certain to stir a strong undertow. Only the dimension of the anticlerical undercurrent, not its composition, was new. After all, a tradition of dechristianization had existed in the French countryside for centuries;[34] and a number of factors during the decades previous to the Franco-Prussian war had given it further impetus. These included the dislocating effects of urbanization, the popular disaffection with absolute monarchy, the growing prestige of positivism, and the political appearance of radicalism and socialism. Although it is impossible here to disaggregate such diverse elements, there is no question that an anticlerical predilection emerged from them and that it ran counter to the stream of pilgrimages and other public displays of religious emotion in the early Third Republic.[35]

French anticlericalism always had a forthright political component. Yet, just as it would be a mistake to attribute the faith of pilgrims to conservative political manipulation, so there is a patent distortion in simply equating republicanism with intolerance of religion. If we cannot hope in a circumscribed space to unravel all the intricacy of anticlerical agitation, it should at least be feasible to suggest its demeanor and to relate it to the general theme of this volume. To begin, one interesting aspect of the problem is chronological. Often obscured or deliberately hidden beneath the surface of public life, hostility to the Roman Catholic church was virulent in France long before it became prominent in national politics. Radical demands for the separation of church and state, prefigured by the Paris Commune, were audible as early as 1872; but because of the central government's reluctance to open the issue, the progress of that campaign was extremely slow.[36] Not until the passage of the Ferry laws in the early 1880s was anticlericalism to have a major legislative impact on the republic. Why was that eventuality so long delayed? In part—but only in part—a satisfactory answer can be offered within the traditional canons of French historiography, an answer derived exclusively from French sources. Yet the religious question of this era, as we shall continue to observe, was not strictly a national phenomenon. Reframed in an international and specifically Franco-German context, the problem may therefore be posed more precisely: what inhibiting effect did the Kulturkampf have on French anticlerical-ism? That is the issue of central concern here.

It is essential, before proceeding, to comprehend what did *not* occur in France during the 1870s: neither was there a wide-spread heresy of Old Catholicism nor did Gallicanism manage to rebound. The fate of both rested largely with the personal for-tunes of Félix Dupanloup, whose career as the bishop of Orléans provides an important clue to the character of the French church in the early years of the republic. The possibility that Dupanloup, in one guise or another, might still lead an opposition within the French episcopacy was not overlooked at the Vatican. A plot was not difficult to imagine. In 1869 a *conférencier* at Notre Dame in Paris, Père Hyacinthe (Charles Loyson), had broken with the hierarchy and founded an independent "*Eglise catholique gal-licane.*" What later made this movement seem potentially danger-ous was the fact that its leader had visited Ignaz von Döllinger in Munich during the early summer of 1869. Once back in Paris, moreover, Hyacinthe reported on his conversations with Döllinger to the noted Gallican scholar at the Sorbonne, Charles Maret, who was meanwhile in close contact with Dupanloup and with Bishop Ginoulhiac of Lyon—all critics of the proclamation of pa-pal infallibility. As we have witnessed, however, a Franco-German ecclesiastical alliance at the Vatican Council of 1870 failed to materialize. Père Hyacinthe consequently remained isolated, and Dupanloup soon began his painful and never completed climb back to respectability within the church hierarchy by formally espousing papal infallibility and offering allegiance to Pius IX.[37]

While the Old Catholic movement was gathering consider-able attention and some support in Germany during the early decade, then, in France it struck no roots. To his old mentor in Germany, Professor von Döllinger, the Gallican abbot Eugène Mi-chaud attempted from Paris to explain why. The French tended to regard Old Catholicism as a purely political phenomenon and to neglect its religious content. Hence, Michaud suggested, it could be dismissed as part of the Kulturkampf against the Roman church, and its supporters were saddled with "the appearance of aping Bismarck" (*nous avons l'air de faire chorus à M. de Bis-marck*). Döllinger would comprehend that in reality such was not the truth, Michaud added, but "it is nonetheless an impediment for us."[38] Michaud's connection with Döllinger and his flirtation with the Old Catholic cause were well known to the papal nuncio, Monsignor Chigi, who assured the Vatican that "this scandal" still lacked a popular following in France but who also warned that this "new form of Protestantism" was directly related to a general European malaise created by the Vatican Council. The infection might spread.[39]

Dupanloup's private papers contain evidence that he charted the progress of Old Catholicism in Germany with interest.[40] There is no proof, however, that he at any time seriously contemplated a rupture with the church or that he ever hoped to establish an autonomous position for himself at the head of a Gallican revival. To the contrary, his efforts after 1870 were mostly dedicated to rehabilitating his reputation as a compliant servant of the Holy See. It is fair to conclude that Dupanloup was an exceedingly ambitious prelate and that his fondest wish was to become a true prince of the church as a member of the College of Cardinals. In that desire he was repeatedly disappointed, which explains much of the gloom that pervaded his personal diary during his declining years. His conspicuous attempts to play a major role in the public arena, such as his protracted negotiations with the Comte de Chambord, were doubtless motivated by his political conviction that only the restoration of a monarchy would save France from republican anticlericalism. But his actions were also intended to reingratiate himself with the papacy, and he passed no opportunity to notify Pius IX directly of his strenuous attempts to prevent "unspeakable calamities" and to enlist the pope's support.[41]

Dupanloup's overtures to the Vatican were nonetheless ineffective. One reason was that the Gallican tradition with which he was associated played little part in the prevailing popular religious enthusiasm, of which ultramontanism appeared the beneficent patron. Gallicanism lacked not leaders but troops. As the German ambassador Harry von Arnim once observed, ungraciously but not altogether inaccurately, as a popular phenomenon Gallicanism was "exterminated" (*ausgerottet*).[42] At the same time, Dupanloup's personal advancement was repeatedly prohibited by a vindictive pope. In the summer of 1874, when the archbishopric of Reims fell vacant, Dupanloup's name was suggested by Decazes to the new nuncio, Monsignor Meglia, who passed the signal on to Rome. But Meglia was immediately reminded by Cardinal Antonelli of Dupanloup's disobliging *non placet* at the Vatican Council: "This attitude has left a painful impression not only in the mind of the Holy Father but also among all good Catholics." The pope's refusal displeased Decazes, but he found it useless to insist.[43] Yet Dupanloup continued to perform good works and to advertise them. He finished a book on Freemasonry, intended as a revelation of its "radical antagonism to religion and society," a copy of which was forwarded to Pius. He proposed to Archbishop Guibert that they join in submitting a protest to the government against the preparation of anticlerical legislation by certain French deputies. And he delivered a major oration to the Assembly in support of the bill on higher education. Copies of his speech were printed and, at Dupanloup's request, sent to the pope, who responded with congratulations.[44]

If a thaw between Pius and Dupanloup occurred, was a Gallican comeback still conceivable? That question was posed and definitively answered at the end of 1875, when crucial parliamentary elections were approaching. Although its origins are obscure, a plan was at that time hatched between Dupanloup and Corcelle (on leave in France from his ambassadorial post at the Vatican) for the bishop to make a personal pilgrimage to Rome. The trip might accomplish two objectives: to persuade the pope to make a public statement in favor of French conservatives that could be quoted or commented upon by bishops and priests on the eve of the balloting; and to strengthen the chance that Pius would at last view with favor the award of a cardinal's hat to Dupanloup. Although he at first professed "an insurmountable disgust" with the project, Dupanloup nevertheless shed his misgivings out of a sense of duty to royalism and to religion. After consulting secretly with Decazes, he set off in the final hours of the year to Rome.[45] From any standpoint, his sojourn in the Holy City was a cruel disappointment. Dupanloup's greatest aspiration remained unrequited. Instead, the most he could realistically contemplate was a transfer to the archbishopric of Lyon. But at his age, Dupanloup was disinclined to move from the diocese of Orléans that he had long dominated merely to accept half a loaf in reward for services rendered. Corcelle thought it just as well because Pius might not have ratified the appointment after all, given the pontiff's "regrettable disposition." Moreover, Dupanloup encountered some reluctance in Rome to identify the papacy too overtly with the cause of French royalism at a time of political confusion. Pius was thus

inclined to adopt the more moderate and discreet course counseled by Guibert, whose refusal to become publicly associated
with Dupanloup's electoral initiative was, in Corcelle's eyes, once
again "regrettable."[46]

In reality Dupanloup's sense of chagrin was far more profound than Corcelle realized. The ambassador perceived his ecclesiastical guest to be "very happy" and to be "satisfied" with contacts at the Vatican.[47] Yet Dupanloup's diary tells a much different
story. From the outset he found Corcelle's efforts "pitiful," noting
that the French ambassador had presented him on arrival with
two memoranda that were "in perfect contradiction with what the
pope had said to him." Moreover, the bishop's first conversation
with Pius at an audience on 18 January 1876 was scarcely the
jovial occasion that Corcelle imagined. Instead, the diary records:
"Then with the pope: not a word about what he had written to
me: not a question on the university, nor on elections, nor on
Marshal [MacMahon], nor on good, nor on evil, nor on future.
Not an idea: neither intelligence nor interest in anything." More
than a week later, commenting on his farewell encounter with
Pius, Dupanloup wrote: "The pope: very amiable, [yet] not an
affectionate word = speaks to me again about the military law.
The pope free! He does not have the liberty to appoint priests, to
have counselors, to leave his quarters." Finally, after his departure
from Rome, Dupanloup registered an afterthought: "As for him
[the pope], he esteems no one . . . he fears me somewhat."[48] These
fragments suggest a personal animosity toward Pius that Dupanloup took pains to keep hidden in public. His own honesty and
self-awareness were surely admirable. But he perhaps failed to
realize adequately that his ambition was not the primary issue.
Better than he, Pius recognized the truth that the papacy no longer
had reason to worry about Dupanloup. His hopes to become a
cardinal were buried forever—a clear sign, no doubt intended, to
those who would dare to contradict the pope—and yet it was far
too late for the bishop to become involved in rebellion, whether
beneath the banner of Gallicanism or of Old Catholicism. Dupanloup had become in more than one way enfeebled. He was now
elderly and ailing, suffering from recurrent migraines and deep fits
of depression. Only partially apparent to others, his infirmities
were confided in excruciating detail to his diary, which is above all
the remarkable record of a dying man.[49] Hence, in the end, Du-

panloup possessed neither the physical strength nor the spiritual independence required to be a rebel. Like the activity of more minor figures, such as Père Hyacinthe and Abbé Michaud, Dupanloup's brand of Gallicanism was bankrupt under the precarious conditions of both church and state in France during the postwar years. Consequently, within the Catholic faith, ultramontanism everywhere prevailed.

The eclipse of the Gallican tradition, of which Dupanloup represented the fading hope, had a specific and far-reaching consequence for the religious question in France: there could be no viable liberal course between ultramontanism and anticlericalism. Henceforward those two mortal enemies stood face to face. As we have already confirmed the ascendancy of the ultramontanes in the French church, it remains now to single out more specifically the anticlerical challenges. The plural is essential because the opposition to Roman Catholicism in France assumed a variety of forms in the 1870s. Of these we can identify principally four: Gambettist republicans, Protestants, Freemasons, and Radicals. It is surely unnecessary to belabor the obvious fact that these major components were neither mutually exclusive nor utterly distinct. Individuals could affiliate with more than one of them. Yet clarity requires brief attention to each.

From the outset of the republic the Gambettist brand of anticlericalism was both highly political and remarkably moderate. With the carrot of a premiership or presidency ever before him, Gambetta needed no stick. His attitude was partly a natural feature of his balanced and humane personality; but those traits were inseparable from political calculation. Gambetta had neither supported nor later closely identified himself with the excesses (as he saw them) of the Paris Commune, which included the immediate separation of church and state. Yet his private thoughts, those shared in intimate discussion with his republican cronies, were resolutely hostile to the political influence of the Catholic hierarchy. In a secret meeting of leaders of the leftist Union républicaine in April 1873, on the eve of an important electoral test in Paris, Gambetta had stated his sentiments emphatically: "The countryside demands that we have done with the republic without republicans. Clericalism is the master of the situation today. It is the bishops who appoint functionaries and generals."[50] To rid the government of such nefarious power of the clergy remained one of Gambetta's foremost objectives. But his innate opportunism—never was a political movement more appropriately named—reinforced his determination to make the long march. Only gradually, under constant pressure from his more impatient supporters, did he raise the level of anticlerical rhetoric until he hurled his most dramatic challenge—"Clericalism? There is the enemy!"—as he plunged into the confrontation of the *seize mai* crisis in 1877. Simultaneous and no less significant was his growing strength as chairman of the budget committee in the Chamber of Deputies, a position from which he was able to cajole, threaten, and often restrict the allocation of funds for religious purposes. His oratorical skills, his dedicated following among parliamentary deputies, and his immense public support across the land made Gambetta the church's most formidable critic. That potential was further amplified when he received increasingly active backing from Bismarckian Germany once the open contest against conservative and clerical forces was joined.[51]

To designate Protestantism within a category of anticlericals might seem paradoxical except for the overwhelming statistical preponderance of Catholicism in France. The loss of Alsace and Lorraine had cut the number of French Protestants by nearly half: there remained only about six hundred thousand, that is, less than 2 percent of the total population. They were widely scattered in rural areas, especially in the Midi Cévenol and in the western regions of Poitou and Normandy. Protestant colonies also existed in cities such as Paris, Marseille, Nîmes, Montpellier, Bordeaux, La Rochelle, and Le Havre—a listing that suggests their importance in business and commerce.[52] Numbers help to explain the embattled temper of Protestants during the early Third Republic and the energy with which they supported efforts to loosen the grip of Catholicism on politics and public education. But statistics alone do not account for the extraordinary impact of Protestants on the formulation and implementation of anticlerical legislation in the 1880s. The ultimate reasons for the emergence of such a dynamic minority can only be a matter of conjecture, but it is clear that these men effectively combined political skill and principles of liberal republicanism with a genuine respect for religious sentiment, whereas such a combination of qualities was usually less well integrated by other public figures whose distaste for Catholicism sprang from a different source. Because of its subsequent importance we should also note one other dimension of this re-markable cluster of talent: an admiration for the achievements of Protestant education in Prussia.[53]

Given its secretive nature, the organization of the Masonic movement in France is more difficult to characterize. Even the exact number of Freemasons was uncertain, although a fair esti-mate is between ten and fifteen thousand members during the 1870s. The lodges were located mainly in urban areas: well over a hundred in Paris alone and several dozen more in Bordeaux, Lyon, and Marseille. Of these the Grand Orient constituted a large ma-jority, between three and four hundred *ateliers* in all of France. The Scottish Rite claimed perhaps a quarter of that total.[54] Add-ing to the aura of intrigue, although the Freemasons were very active after 1870, the precise nature of their deliberations was largely unknown to the press and consequently to the public. The historian is less helpless, fortunately, because police agents fre-quently covered closed sessions in Masonic lodges attended by prominent national politicians. From these records we can gather sufficient information to dispel some of the mystery. The focus of Masonic meetings was invariably a denunciation of alleged machi-nations by the Catholic clergy, who were subjected to the "most vigorous attacks," the police reported, and who were singled out as the "most dangerous enemy of the time."[55] The lodges thus represented an underground Kulturkampf well before open strug-gle against the church was feasible or fashionable for their socially prominent members. They were indoctrinated by their leaders with positivism and drilled to prepare for an inevitable conflict between the Catholic clergy and the Freemasons: "Both consecrate their efforts to rally the people to their side, but one only strives to brutalize and misuse them, whereas the other seeks their emanci-pation. Hence a battle is joined that should be pitiless." Nor, ac-cording to such orations, could the ultimate outcome be in doubt: "The success of Masonry is assured. The clergy will be making their last stand."[56] In the words of another speaker, who delivered essentially the same message to a different lodge: "We must com-bat ignorance. The struggle should be ardent especially against clericalism and its doctrines. There is no compromise; whoever believes that is a fool and a dupe or a traitor to truth and reason. We must . . . march courageously against obscurantism." This par-ticular meeting, it should be added, came to a close with a ceremony of mourning for Alsace and Lorraine, concluding with "a huzza for the inevitable return of these provinces to France."[57] The themes of anticlericalism and revanchism were thereby fused behind locked doors with a rhetoric that, if it became public in the 1870s, could have had embarrassing and perhaps dangerous repercussions for France. The Freemasons accordingly repressed their fire for a more appropriate moment, as their numbers and influence continued to grow.[58]

With less immediate political ambitions on the national level than the Opportunists, and with little to lose in local affairs, the French Radicals were relatively unrestrained. Their anticlerical campaign was hampered neither by a desire for secrecy nor a need for respectability. To the contrary, it was the Radical style in the early days of the republic to be blatantly offensive. Nowhere was that attitude more evident than in the Municipal Council of Paris, where the young Georges Clemenceau, Henri Allain-Targé, and others began vigorous anticlerical campaigning in 1872: "It is time that the question of the separation of church and state be resolved, and the refusal by the Municipal Council of the requested appropriations [for religious affairs] can only hasten that resolution."[59] Such adamance was a particular worry to Archbishop Guibert of Paris, who feared that the project to erect the basilica of Sacré Coeur might be successfully blocked by the Council, "which is hostile to religion."[60] The construction proceeded, but Guibert's estimation of Parisian Radicals was not inaccurate. By 1875 Clemenceau had become president of the Municipal Council, and his inaugural speech was among the frankest public statements of anticlerical intentions in the decade: "The dominant character of our municipal policy—and especially in that we are the true representatives of Paris—is to be profoundly imbued with a secular spirit; that is, in conformance with the traditions of the French Revolution, we want to separate the realm of law, to which everyone owes obedience, from the realm of dogma, which is accepted only by a fraction of the citizens. On this basis a great struggle has been joined. . . . We await the shock."[61] Within another year Clemenceau was elected from the eighteenth arrondissement of Paris to the Chamber of Deputies, where he again began to form a vocal minority of anticlerical opinion. He was also a frequent participant in the scores of public banquets organized by the Radicals at a time when their demands

for "reform"—usually a euphemism for anticlerical legislation—
were still frustrated by a cautious and conservative national regime. The Radical opposition to the government of moral order
was thus symptomatic of a growing anticlerical tendency, as yet
somewhat constrained by the tensions generated from the war
scare of 1875, the Kulturkampf, and the *seize mai* crisis of 1877.
Like the Masonic meetings, the extraparliamentary activity of the
Radicals was carefully monitored by incognito agents, who submitted voluminous reports of political gatherings to the Prefecture
of Police in Paris. These documents itemized both the most frequently cited objects of scorn and the most often mentioned political goals. Chief among the former were the "clerical party," the
Jesuits, the Syllabus of Errors, and the keenly resented construction of Sacré Coeur. Conspicuous among the latter were separation of church and state, elimination of all budgetary allocations
for religious purposes, and abrogation of the Concordat. Larded
into this potpourri of protest was a strong sentiment in favor of a
total amnesty for the communards of 1871, always accompanied
by familiar expressions of patriotism and revanchism.[62] It is impossible to calculate precisely the impact of such agitation. But we
may conclude as a minimum that a latent dissatisfaction with the
existing terms of the religious question was gathering force and
that the surface of cordial relations between church and state in
France could not long remain untroubled.

A Balance of Tension

A symbiosis of diplomatic and domestic affairs has long characterized the major European states. Certainly it did so after
1870 in an era of increasingly interlocking national polities and
economies. Advocates of the primacy of foreign policy or of internal policy have stated their respective cases often enough. But
they have been generally unconvincing in the end, and they have
tended to cover their tracks in retreat by claiming that one-sided
arguments are sometimes useful as a heuristic device.[63] As a case
in point we are confronted here with a specific problem in the
history of the Third Republic that cannot be comprehended apart
from the concurrent international circumstances. To be sure, anticlericalism had roots deeply embedded in French tradition, but its
luxuriant growth in the mid-1870s was a European phenomenon

unconfined to a single national terrain. Inversely, however, one must avoid the excess of attributing dramatic changes in France solely to certain individuals or events abroad. The death of Pius IX and the accession of Leo XIII to the papacy in 1878, for example, have been frequently cited as a watershed for European Catholicism and as the beginning of a new liberal epoch for the church. Yet the matter is demonstrably not so simple, and evidence abounds that a transformation of the religious question in France was already under way well before white smoke was sighted above the chimney of the Sistine Chapel.

Insofar as the French episcopacy was concerned, the parliamentary elections of January 1876 were extremely disquieting. Only months earlier a favorable vote on the law of higher education, which established Catholic universities, had been hailed in the conservative press as a triumph of the faith and a symbol of the republic's renewed dedication to the spirit of the Concordat. But now that legislation might suddenly be thrown into jeopardy by a decisive republican victory at the polls. "God grant," the papal nuncio wrote back to Rome, "that these sad prospects are not realized."[64] In fact, within a few days Monsignor Meglia received a cautionary note from the minister of education and religion, Henri Wallon, who expressed his unhappiness about the pope's apparent vacillation over the appointment of Monsignor Ramadié to be the archbishop of Albi. The church could no longer take the government's complaisance in questions of investiture for granted, Wallon implied: "The Vatican Council has not yet resolved the true difficulties; the calm that we seem to be enjoying is only superficial." Meglia's riposte was quick and sharp. He accused Wallon of "an error" in appraising the pope's attitude and chastised his language as "neither canonical nor Catholic." Although Wallon immediately apologized, and the Duc Decazes begged that the exchange be kept from "exploitation by wicked newspapers," the damage was done and a new tension between church and state was already in the air.[65]

The real difficulty was of course structural and not solely temperamental. The church's most reliable political ally in France was President MacMahon, but he was facing republican majorities—that is, probable anticlerical votes—in both houses of parliament. In analyzing the marshal's political impotence, Meglia could suggest no hopeful course of action by which MacMahon

might stem the tide ("Che cosa farà?").[66] Cardinal Guibert was
equally despondent and agonized in an open letter about the problem of offering public prayers for the Chamber and the Senate at a
time when some of their members harbored "sinister projects"
to advance the separation of church and state.[67] Such apprehension acquired concrete form when a new cabinet under Jules Dufaure was named, in which the portfolio for religious affairs was
assumed by a Protestant, William Henry Waddington, who had
previously voted against the law on higher education. Meglia
found this appointment especially alarming because "a majority of
the Chamber is becoming every day more hostile to the church
and the Holy See."[68] Like vultures, two decidedly threatening mo-
tions perched on the parliamentary docket—one to expunge the
state's annual budget of religious appropriations and another
to curtail the staff of the French embassy at the Vatican—waiting their turn to appear before the Chamber's budget committee
chaired by Léon Gambetta. Understandably, the papacy was "profoundly distressed."[69]

These incipient signs of a deterioration of church-state relations in France were precisely contemporaneous with initial indications of an improvement of religious affairs in Germany. In
itself, the release from prison of the archbishop of Posen, Cardinal
Ledochowski, might be considered only an ambiguous legal maneuver because it was obvious that the Prussian government had
nothing to gain by permitting him to assume the role of a martyr.
But this action was accompanied by the arrival in Rome of Cardinal Gustav Adolf zu Hohenlohe, brother of the German ambassador to France. The French envoy Corcelle immediately inquired
of papal Secretary of State Antonelli whether the German prelate had been deliberately dispatched by his government to offer
"some softening" of Berlin's treatment of Roman Catholics. Although Antonelli rejected the notion that Cardinal Hohenlohe
was on political assignment, the Vatican in fact received confirmation from the papal nuncio in Munich that rumors of Germany's reconciliation with the Vatican were circulating in newspapers "which are more or less official." Yet in reply to Munich,
Antonelli once more denied that the cardinal had an official mission and added that, in any case, the pope had no intention of
summoning him "to negotiate the affairs of Germany."[70]

Admittedly, such premonitions of an impending change in

religious policy on both sides of the Rhine were still no more than circumstantial. Nor is the conundrum of cause and effect necessarily brought nearer to solution by demonstrating that in this instance the two developments were chronologically identical. Was there, then, conscious awareness by those well placed that these tendencies were not only contemporary but also interconnected? The answer is indisputably affirmative. One distinct manifestation of such a sensitivity was the increasing use, henceforth, of the term "Kulturkampf" to describe religious conditions in France. Perhaps the first to employ the term in that sense was a Paris agent of Bismarck's banker, Gerson von Bleichröder. This informant appraised the result of recent French senatorial elections as a "mortal blow" to the Vatican, which would now be hard-pressed to defend the church's position in religious and educational matters. "A storm" would soon break over the law on higher education, he predicted correctly, and France would enter "the first stage of a 'Kulturkampf.'" Germany would be able to witness this struggle in France with some satisfaction: "It seems to me in fact [to be] a genuine triumph of Bismarckian policy, which, as we know from the Arnim papers, has pursued this goal since 1872."[71] One might well criticize Bleichröder's crony for an undue eagerness to ascribe primacy to Bismarck's prowess rather than to French politics. But a liaison, in his perception, undeniably existed between them.

A similar vocabulary, if a somewhat different estimate of German motivations, was meanwhile adopted by the French ambassador in Berlin. Gontaut-Biron, we should recall, had frequently speculated about Bismarck's religious designs in the months past; and in response to him, the Duc Decazes had more than once commented that the chancellor's main purpose was to draw the French into a conflict with the Roman church. But Gontaut still found the signals confusing. He had just had a cordial interview with one of Bismarck's trusted subalterns at the Wilhelmstrasse, Ernst von Bülow, and he wondered whether that conversation was meant to indicate "a sincere interest for us." Or was it not, rather, Germany's intention "to profit from the anticlerical disposition of most republicans [in France] toward the struggle of a Kulturkampf?" In confidence Gontaut offered Decazes his unsurprising opinion that the latter hypothesis was the more plausible.[72]

We can locate another example. In late March 1876 the law

on higher education, passed less than a year earlier with great proclerical fanfare, was amended to require that state examiners be included in at least equal number with church examiners on all academic juries of degree-granting institutions, secular or Catholic. This obvious infringement on the autonomy of "free" (that is, Catholic) universities outraged advocates of ultramontanism, notably Louis Veuillot's *L'Univers*, which saw in the amendment the beginning of a "Diocletian persecution" by the new Protestant cabinet minister of education, Waddington, who was maliciously identified as "virtually a foreigner" (*presqu'un étranger*). While relaying these imputations to Berlin, the German ambassador, Hohenlohe, described the effects of a concurrent parliamentary investigation into "clerical machinations" in the election of the Catholic activist Comte Albert de Mun: such procedures "were arousing in ultramontane circles a fear that the Kulturkampf, which they heretofore ridiculed as a thing possible only in Germany, will now begin also in France."[73] A week later Hohenlohe reinforced his conclusion that "the anticlerical character of the new Chamber of Deputies is becoming every day more apparent, and . . . the struggle of the temporal against the spiritual power is also beginning in France, even though to date only in a few skirmishes." He added that, although the republicans clearly possessed the power to impede the church, they would not find it a simple matter to dislodge the well-entrenched clergy. It would therefore be of great interest for the Germans "to follow the further progress of the French Kulturkampf." One other feature of Hohenlohe's messages should be mentioned: his reiteration of vagrant rumors in France "that instructions for this persecution have come directly to the radical party from Berlin." But this allegation remained unsubstantiated, and no evidence exists that such direct contact occurred before the *seize mai* crisis, fully a year later.[74] For the time being, in the spring of 1876, the novelty was therefore not the creation of a diabolical international conspiracy against the church but the recurrence of the term "Kulturkampf" to characterize the religious question in France.

No one was more sensitive to the evolving conflict between ultramontanism and anticlericalism than Bishop Dupanloup. Although still smarting from the failure of his mission to the Vatican, Dupanloup communicated directly to Pius IX his pessimistic views about the "terrible situation" in France, enumerating for the

184 / *The Religious Question*

pope the accumulation of legislative drafts already proposed by "deputies who command an omnipresent majority against us": separation of church and state; elimination of religious appropriations from the budget; compulsory lay education; expulsion of priests and nuns from all public schools; abrogation of the law on higher education; absolute liberty of cabarets and clubs; and required military service for priests. These were not fanciful suggestions, Dupanloup continued, but potential laws, the passage of which would alter the entire situation of the Catholic church in France.[75] A no less detailed and equally urgent warning came from Cardinal Guibert, who, with the waning influence of Dupanloup, had incontestably become the acknowledged primate of the French episcopacy. In three open letters addressed to the premier, Jules Dufaure, Guibert expressed his "painful reflections" on budgetary restrictions already imposed or threatened by the Chamber. Because of inroads by the "anticlerical movement," the church found itself "treated as a suspect and virtually as an enemy." Political opponents of the Catholic church, the cardinal wrote, were prone to favor a rupture with it and to pretend that it represented a threat to the state. They were thereby exploiting an imaginary danger in order to justify "a declaration of war on the church." The cardinal ended by citing the Concordat of 1801 as the fundamental charter of church-state relations in France and by quoting former President Thiers: "The republic will be conservative or it will not be at all." This bit of nostalgia for the earliest days of the Third Republic was indicative of the church's mounting difficulties; and it is ironic, in the wake of the investiture controversy, that the Catholic hierarchy should now insist on the sanctity of the very Concordat it had so recently challenged.[76]

Because Dufaure was regarded as a faithful Catholic and a friend of the papacy, Guibert's tactic of addressing public missives to him was intended as a gesture of support. The nuncio agreed with Guibert's assessment of the premier: it would be "deplorable," Monsignor Meglia wrote on 29 November 1876, if the Dufaure cabinet were to fall.[77] Five days later it fell. Dufaure's replacement was Jules Simon, no stranger to the Vatican or to Versailles. The problem was, in religious terms, that Simon had become a man without a tradition. His former preference for Gallicanism was now inconsequential. Hence a final vain effort to revive Dupanloup's candidacy for the cardinalate collapsed—after

Simon proposed that France should gain a sixth red hat for him and a seventh for the exceedingly ultramontane Archbishop Pie of Poitiers—because the pope correctly regarded such a bargain as less a compromise than a self-contradiction. At the same time, Simon lacked the political grasp to shake Gambetta from his control of the Chamber's budget committee, which, as Meglia warned, "can do immense harm to the church."[78] Simon was stymied. His premiership thus proved to be a brief and unstable interlude, during which the deterioration of the church's position in France was unarrested.

Contrariwise, evidence continued to corroborate an improvement of the church's position in Prussia. During a visit to Rome, the grand duke of Baden revealed his intention to promote better relations between his north German compatriots and the Roman clergy. Commenting on that possibility, the new French ambassador to the Vatican, Baron Georges de Baude, questioned "whether Bismarck was really disposed to rid himself of the religious question" and, if so, what attitude the French should adopt. To aid the chancellor would only "rescue him from the malady that devours him." But otherwise there was danger of "this affliction becoming singularly contagious." France, in other words, might catch the illness unless it was soon cured in Germany.[79] In Berlin, meanwhile, public discussion erupted for the first time about a probable revision of the infamous May laws. The conciliatory tone of the German newspaper press was such, reported Nuncio Angelo Bianchi from Munich, that "it is possible to deduce some favorable indications."[80] Finally, through a confidential coded dispatch from Baude, Decazes learned with accuracy that a German representative in Vienna was seeking to establish preliminary contacts with the papal nuncio there: "Indications of a tendency of the Berlin government to modify its religious policy are becoming more distinct."[81] There seemed to be no question about it.

A general sense of malaise was thus developing in France during the spring of 1877, of which the unsettled religious controversy elsewhere in Europe was an integral factor. Apprehensions were further increased in early April, when Decazes received an urgent private message from Baude that the pope's health had drastically worsened: "The situation is serious." The ambassador recommended that a French cardinal be stationed in the Vatican to attend any initial deliberations after the pontiff's death. Archbishop Langénieux of Reims, by chance in Rome at the time, confirmed that the pope was ailing and temporarily confined to his quarters.[82] The timing was still uncertain, but the inevitability of a new papacy in the near future added tinder to every decision. Lacking was only a first spark. That was supplied on 4 May by Gambetta's most famous speech, many times quoted, in which he served notice that the time for an open confrontation between anticlericalism and ultramontanism had come. "Thereby," Chlodwig zu Hohenlohe immediately signaled to Bismarck, "France has taken the first step on the way to a Kulturkampf."[83]

A Matter of Time

Although it was of fundamental importance for many other aspects of French public life, the contest in 1877 between MacMahonian conservatives and Gambettist republicans is primarily of concern here for its impact on the religious question.[84] We may begin by concurring with Monsignor Meglia's assumption that among President MacMahon's more pressing reasons for dismissing Jules Simon's cabinet on 16 May was a fear that the French government and administration were gradually succumbing to anticlerical influence. Accordingly, there was "lively satisfaction" at the Vatican with MacMahon's decision to act. The pope was delighted at the abrupt exit of Simon, whom he had long distrusted, and at the reappearance of the Duc de Broglie as a premier who could deflect France from adopting the "disastrous course" advocated by a majority in the Chamber of Deputies. So pleased was Pius, in fact, that he decided to award MacMahon one of the papacy's highest distinctions, the Grand-Croix. The church would thereby display its support for the marshal's cause. "In this supreme moment," the nuncio in Paris wrote back to Rome, it was crucial to help unite all conservative factions, for whom the crisis of *seize mai* was "a question of life or death."[85]

One difficulty with papal support, however, persisted. An all too obvious effusion of clerical backing for French conservatism might resuscitate rumors of an ultramontane conspiracy, thus confirming republican allegations and perhaps provoking another German menace of preventive war. These, we know, were precisely the consequences that ensued—especially after a feeble but still feisty Pius IX imprudently denounced Bismarck as the "new Attila" before a gathering of German pilgrims at the Vatican. According to Bleichröder's sources, French leaders "were, with the greatest nervousness, awaiting a counterstroke" by the chancellor. They had good reason to worry. After establishing direct contacts with Gambetta through the German embassy in Paris, Bismarck gave instructions to open a press campaign in favor of the republicans, the central theme of which was that a victory of ultramontanism in France would induce an inevitable European war.[86]

The initial problem created by the crisis for the Broglie cabinet, then, was not to enlist the church's support but to avoid seeming beholden to it. Decazes therefore expedited a confidential and coded telegram to Rome, asking that the award of the papal decoration for MacMahon be delayed and not divulged for several weeks, lest it seem that "this favor is compensation for the action of 16 May." News of the marshal's award nonetheless leaked out through the porous Italian press. Learning of the disclosure, Decazes was so incensed by Baude's handling of the affair that he recalled the ambassador for a reprimand. Baude needed to comprehend that a papal gesture, which might have been appropriate several months before, was no longer helpful: "I can well see," Decazes told him, "that you are not to any degree aware of our internal and external situation." Others required prompting as well. The bishop of Vannes, for example, was admonished by the prefect of Morbihan, on direct orders from the Ministry of the Interior, to avoid "all public demonstrations possibly giving rise to a troublesome interpretation." The bishop was later thanked for his efforts "to keep the religious manifestations [in his diocese] outside of the political realm." One of the most urgent reasons for encouraging such reticence was expressed by the nuncio, who lamented the occasional insensitivity of French prelates to pressures exerted on their government, "especially in respect to Germany, which seeks every pretext to embarrass France."[87]

German inquiries about the political crisis in France added to suspicions in Berlin of connivance between MacMahon's supporters and the Vatican. Bleichröder supplied Bismarck with a report, submitted by "an entirely objective observer" among his banking friends in Paris, that an electoral triumph by the French conservatives would be "decidedly dangerous" because "their true lord and master, at present merely hiding in the wings, is the papacy and the Society of Jesus."[88] In Paris Hohenlohe interviewed Baude (an old friend) and Decazes, both of whom reassured him that their intentions were to discourage excessive ultramontanism in Rome and to urge restraint within the French episcopacy. Hohenlohe commented to Bismarck that he was inclined to accept these promises at face value because "the French regime views with apprehension . . . the distrust it has aroused in Germany and does not underestimate the dangers that could result."[89] Despite its repeated efforts to assuage the Germans, however, the French cabinet remained vulnerable to charges of fostering some dark intrigue. No sooner had Cardinal Guibert departed on a journey to Rome in late June than the Berlin *Post*—which had touched off the war scare in 1875—accused him of launching a campaign to solicit church support for the conservative French government. An unequivocal denial by Decazes was immediately forthcoming. But stationed in Rome, one of Bismarck's closest personal advisers, Robert von Keudell, judged it "very probable" that Guibert was indeed on political assignment, an opinion of which the chancellor took cognizance with "special interest" before passing it on to Hohenlohe. These soundings thus ratified the German view that the Vatican had promoted the *seize mai* crisis from the beginning and was now "threatening Italy and Germany through France." Such notions may appear in retrospect to be overwrought. But the more one enters into the mentality and the vocabulary of another era, the less implausible they seem. Certainly they were unnerving for a statesman like Decazes, who was unhappily left in private to nourish the vain hope that "this phantom of clericalism and ultramontanism will disappear from our horizon."[90]

In the final weeks of the electoral contest of 1877 the church abandoned restraint. The Vatican had become fearful that MacMahon's own campaign efforts were ineffectual and that the conservative cause was failing. According to Monsignor Meglia, the provincial cities visited by the president seemed "hostile not only to the present government but also to the church."[91] The signal for a more vigorous attempt by the hierarchy to rally its flock against the republicans was given on 11 September by the pope. In an audience with French pilgrims led to Rome by the controversial Father François Picard, Pius granted authority for the Catholic clergy to celebrate special election eve religious services and to dispense plenary indulgences to participating communicants. This stratagem produced "a good result," Meglia boasted, and several French bishops for the first time openly joined the political fray. Predictably, however, that activity also drew renewed accusations of ultramontane conspiracy and gave further credence to them.[92]

The republican victory in October 1877 was not overwhelming, but it was sufficient to guarantee a troubled future for the church, which was bound to encounter "complications and agitations."[93] Even though MacMahon hoped to avert the worst by remaining in the presidency at least through 1878, no one could reasonably doubt that French cabinets would henceforth list in an anticlerical direction. Just how adamant would opponents of the church become? One of Bismarck's contacts in Paris, Count Guido Henckel von Donnersmarck, put that question to Léon Gambetta, whose reply was that "the first assignment of a freethinking regime" in France would be "to relieve the Germans of their leadership in the struggle against Rome."[94] Henckel's desire to broker a direct negotiation between Gambetta and Bismarck in Berlin may have caused him to embellish or exaggerate the sense of such a statement. Yet we may at least accept it as the symptom of a general awareness that a period was beginning in which the religious question in France, rather than in Germany, was likely to be inflamed.

Perhaps the most piquant detail of the *seize mai* crisis was that the French cabinet member in charge of religious affairs at the time of the death of Pius IX was a Protestant. Waddington's policy was ostensibly evenhanded ("the new cabinet acknowledges all the rights of the church, but it will suffer no infringement on those of the state"), and yet it obviously left a large field for facile interpretation.[95] In his instructions to the French cardinals departing for the conclave to elect a papal successor, Waddington compounded that ambiguity ("the true interests of the church . . . are those of France"), letting it be known only that the government favored another Italian pontiff.[96] When Cardinal Joachim Pecci emerged as Pope Leo XIII, Waddington could therefore express his "complete satisfaction." This opinion contrasted notably with Bismarck's private conviction that Pecci had been "the real candidate of the Jesuits."[97] But neither man could be certain whether the new pope would attempt to alter the shifting balance of religious controversy. Only one thing was beyond doubt, and it was best stated by Hohenlohe: if Leo were to follow Pius in openly supporting French proclerical factions, he would surely meet stiff opposition from the recently victorious republicans, and the inevitable sequel would be "the eruption of a Kulturkampf in France."[98]

This prognostication coincided with terse reports from French diplomats in Munich, Berlin, and Rome, all of whom confirmed the resumption of Bismarck's contacts with papal agents "relative to the desire of the prince-chancellor to seek a cessation of religious conflict in Germany."[99] But mutual suspicions of long standing were not quickly dissipated, and exactly one year after the onset of the *seize mai* crisis in France, despite an exchange of greetings between the pope and the Kaiser, no substantive bargaining had yet occurred between them.[100] A new opportunity was unexpectedly created by an attempt on William's life, which elicited an expression of sympathy from the Vatican. Yet the meager results, as Waddington was correctly informed, were further "discussions" (*pourparlers*) rather than actual negotiations.[101] Sweet nothings would not suffice. The real break came in early June 1878 with a second attempt against the Kaiser. Telegrams were once more exchanged between Rome and Berlin, but there was a crucial difference: the nuncio in Munich was told that the papacy now regretted the failure of German Catholics to support Bismarck's proposal of antisocialist legislation in the Reichstag. The prompt passage of such a bill with backing of the Center party—which thus gladly abdicated its role as the chancellor's favorite *Reichsfeind* to the German Social Democratic party (SPD)—provided the solid political basis on which a meaningful resolution of the religious conflict in Germany could be constructed. We do not need to pursue that story except to observe that it was followed with close interest and considerable apprehension by the French.[102] Progress toward rapprochement between Berlin and Rome was sometimes irregular and always incomplete. But Leo XIII remained hopeful that his pontificate would witness "Germany's return to the church." As he told the French envoy at the Vatican, "it is a matter of time."[103]

Evidence of linkage of the religious question in Germany and France remained embedded in the perception of most qualified Germans who watched from a close vantage. Writing to Gerson von Bleichröder from his fashionable apartment at 25 avenue des Champs Elysées, for example, Henckel von Donnersmarck reiterated his conclusion of several months before: "The leadership in the struggle against Rome will be assumed from Germany by France as soon as the senatorial elections have been completed."[104] Once the predicted republican majority in the French upper house was secured in late November, just as the Paris Exposition of 1878 was being concluded, MacMahon's presidency began to crumble. The gradual deterioration of French conservatism suggested a possible explanation for Bismarck's tactics to the German Catholic leader Ludwig Windthorst, who conjectured that "the Prussian government wishes to wait until Gambetta begins the Kulturkampf in France, hoping that Rome will then be more malleable."[105] That Windthorst's assumption was not fatuous, at least in the eyes of Bismarck's advisers, was made clear by frequent dispatches from the Paris embassy. Just a few days before MacMahon's resignation, Hohenlohe signaled that "the situation is serious" and that "an acute crisis" might occur if the marshal were unceremoniously evicted by French leftists. In that event, the German ambassador wrote, "the first consequence in domestic affairs would probably be a Kulturkampf."[106]

Although MacMahon's replacement by Jules Grévy was not the seismographic sensation that Hohenlohe had anticipated, it was still disturbing for the church hierarchy. The immediate reaction of the pope is important to notice because it revealed something of his personal attitude and foreshadowed one of the major diplomatic pronouncements of his reign. Commenting on a private letter received from the new French president, Leo expressed hope that the moderate faction in France would "remain master of the situation and not be overturned by the extreme party." Otherwise, he claimed, the Vatican regarded the successive changes of French government personnel with "relative indifference," at least insofar as they had no deleterious effect on matters of religion. The considerations that motivated the papacy, said Leo, were "too elevated to be attached to a certain form of government." Hence the consolidation of republican institutions "will not be for the Holy See a reason for estrangement from France."[107] Even though recorded here only in the memory of a French diplomat, these words manifestly reflected Leo's general appraisal of a need to modify the Vatican's traditional view of church and state, a redefinition that was later to acquire canonical status in the encyclical *Immortale Dei* of 1885. We may therefore posit a growing willingness of the church to adjust to the political facts of life and to seek an accommodation with moderate French republicanism. Yet the already established momentum of the religious question in France would nevertheless force the Roman Catholic hierarchy to retreat in some disarray before new assaults by the secularizing propellants of the state. For the inexorability of that tendency two explanations can be offered. One has been the theme of the foregoing analysis: the emerging religious pattern of Europe in which the locus of strident anticlericalism was shifting from Germany to France. Another must be the subject to follow: the intractability of republican opposition to clerical influence in the French schools and the renewed campaign to reform the entire educational system.

Chapter 9

The German Model and
the Ferry Reforms

Primary Education

Just as programs of educational reform had earlier been associated with the names of Victor Duruy and Jules Simon, in the
1880s they were invariably linked with that of Jules Ferry. Like so
many prominent figures of the Third Republic, Ferry was a lawyer
by training and a politician by trade. His activity in the initial
decade after 1870 was relatively modest, far overshadowed by the
exploits of the more charismatic Léon Gambetta, whose oratorical skills and personal magnetism Ferry lacked. But he was a born
negotiator, both persuasive and patient in obtaining the objectives
he sought.[1]

Ferry had been one of those concerned about the socially
restrictive character of the French school system before the war of
1870. In a speech delivered at a public gathering in Paris just a few
months before the outbreak of the conflict, he identified inequal-
ity of educational opportunity as "the problem of the century,"
and he charged that the imperial regime of Napoleon III was
appropriating ten times more for the military budget than for
public education.[2] Ferry's prewar stance was thus similar to that
of Gambetta, whose sponsorship of the so-called Belleville program in 1869 had also placed him on record in favor of compulsory primary education and the complete separation of church
and school. After the war and the Paris Commune, Gambetta
reiterated those views as he attempted to stake out his claim to
leadership of the political left.[3] If at that time Ferry cut less of a
public figure and was more cautious in published statements, his
private opinions became equally categorical; and by 1872 he had
articulated the three-point program with which he was later to

become closely identified: compulsory, tuition-free, and secular public education. Accordingly, he supported the reform proposals of Jules Simon, even though he considered them insufficient.[4] But during the Thiers presidency, as we have witnessed, such legislative initiatives foundered on the coral reefs of classicism, and the intrusion of Marshal MacMahon's government of moral order finally swamped the Simon program altogether. Thus, in its beginnings, as one scholar has concluded with slight exaggeration, "the Third Republic was singularly more clerical than the Empire."[5]

A lapsed Catholic, who chose to marry a Protestant spouse in a civil ceremony, Ferry was well connected but not ideally situated for political leadership in the 1870s. As the decade progressed, he was subjected like all others to the polarizing tendencies of those years. Symptomatic of a personal drift was his initiation in 1875 into the Masonic lodge Clémente Amitié, in which he became an active participant (whereas Gambetta remained only an apprentice).[6] When the *seize mai* crisis erupted in 1877, Ferry consequently found himself at complete ease on the republican side in the campaign against conservatism. There is no question that his perceptions were strongly colored by anticlericalism. Yet he deserves to be classified as one of those victorious republican politicians for whom anticlerical sentiments did not obscure the ultimate objective of social reform.[7]

When in 1879 Jules Ferry accepted a portfolio at the French Ministry of Education for the first time, he was thoroughly committed to a renewal of reform attempts unrealized in the past. Yet he discovered that he was already outflanked by radical agitators whose principal forum was the Municipal Council of Paris and whose most conspicuous spokesman was its former president Georges Clemenceau. Soon after passing from the Municipal Council to the Chamber of Deputies in 1876, Clemenceau had presented demands for compulsory, costless, and secular primary education. He also favored such controversial measures as the expulsion of the Jesuits from France, required military service for all eligible Frenchmen (including divinity students), and total amnesty for the exiled communards of 1871. The much more aggressive tone adopted by Clemenceau, for whom any step accomplished by Ferry was always too hesitant and halfhearted, created an emotional resentment between the two men that persisted through the 1880s.[8] Pressure from the municipality of Paris, where Clemenceau continued to exert considerable influence, was perpetually bothersome to Ferry. No sooner had he assumed his ministerial responsibilities than he was forced to respond to a motion, previously passed by the Municipal Council in December 1878, that the public schools in Paris be secularized forthwith by consigning all administrative and instructional positions to lay personnel.[9] Ferry's reply, addressed through the prefect of the Seine, was clear in principle but cautious about implementation. The choice of schoolteachers, he stipulated, was a matter entirely in the jurisdiction of legally appointed prefects and not of municipally elected councils. Moreover, secular control of primary education should be accomplished without any disruption of regular instruction in the lower grades, a transition that would require piecemeal rather than wholesale dismissal of clerical teachers ("on ne supprime que ce qu'on remplace"). Finally, considering that reform was to be effected nationwide and not simply in the unique circumstances of the capital, some latitude must be left for the wishes of Catholic parents in the countryside. The government would therefore avoid any "excessive and precipitant measure" that might create "the character of a violent revolution" or present "the appearance of a persecution." In sum, Ferry would lead but not drag France to secularism.[10]

Statistics gathered by Ferry soon revealed that the impatience of the Municipal Council was not altogether unjustified. True, within the twenty arrondissements of Paris, the number of completely secular schools had risen from 200 in June 1871 to 285 by the beginning of Ferry's ministry in February 1879. But the number of parochial primary schools had declined by only 1, from 143 to 142. The city's second and third arrondissements had each suffered the net loss of a single clerically controlled elementary school, whereas the twelfth arrondissement had gained one.[11] The number of male pupils in secular *écoles de garçons* was more than double the total in similar clerical schools, but the enrollment of females in Parisian *écoles de filles* was distributed almost equally between state-supported and church-sponsored institutions (see Table 2). Thus the employment of clerical teachers in Paris still remained high—nearly 40 percent of the entire teaching force of the primary schools—despite an entire decade of agitation by the Municipal Council for sweeping secularization.[12]

So much for Paris. In the provinces the picture was more

Table 2 / Pupils in Parisian Primary Schools in 1879

	Secular	Clerical	Total
Ecoles de garçons	33,051	19,537	52,588
Ecoles de filles	25,951	20,397	46,348
Salles d'asile	15,515	9,122	24,637
Total	74,517	49,056	123,573

Source: "Nombre des élèves inscrits au 15 janvier 1879," AN Paris, F^{17} 9196.

confused and presumably even more clerical. Attempts to promote secularization, as in the case of Toulouse, were mounted sporadically by some municipal councils during the 1870s but to little apparent effect. It was impossible to be certain, however, because no thorough census of teaching personnel throughout France had been conducted since 1870. Consequently, Ferry needed to begin almost *de novo* in assessing the situation across the land, and he undertook to do so.[13]

Church leaders could only be discomforted by what they were witnessing. Both domestic and foreign developments were drastically altering the entire equation of the religious question in France. The inexorable triumph of republicanism after the *seize mai* crisis of 1877 and the simultaneous relaxation of the Kulturkampf in Germany had combined to create a climate favorable for French anticlericals, who now felt unbound from the restraints of recent years. In the eyes of Cardinal Guibert of Paris, there was precious little to choose between the Municipal Council and the Ministry of Education: the only difference was that the former demanded an immediate secularization of all publicly funded schools, whereas Jules Ferry and his associates favored "a successive elimination" of clerical instructors and a somewhat more gradual conversion to a secular system. Guibert charged that "a large number of schools have been withdrawn from the priests and nuns who directed them, and that not because of inferiority of instruction but in execution of a well-known if not always admitted intention to exclude from the school all religious instruction." Hence to defend the right of French families to "free education" (*enseignement libre*), the cardinal announced the formation of a Comité diocésain des écoles chrétiennes, with the objective of raising funds to finance parochial schools despite budgetary curtailments imposed by the republican government.[14] A distinguished group of sponsors, under the presidency of Charles Chesnelong, pledged support of the committee, which thereupon launched a public solicitation. A form letter from Chesnelong explained: "The Municipal Council of Paris, emboldened by the approbation of the prefect [of the Seine] and the minister [of education], is, as you know, pursuing the destruction of the Christian schools."[15] Within the following five years Guibert's organization was able to allocate 13.5 million francs to sustain 193 clerical schools with an annual enrollment of about 68,500 pupils. The church thus moved with alacrity to preserve its first line of defense, primary education, against the encroachments of an increasingly avaricious state.[16]

Within this broad context of reform and reaction, we need now to define the specific role of Germany. Among the three levels of French education, the system of elementary schools was doubtless the least directly affected by German influence. Yet the immense prestige of compulsory education throughout Europe could properly be dated from the wars of 1866 and 1870; and a high level of consciousness about German superiority and modernity, which had demonstrably motivated earlier reform programs in France, was still evident by 1880. For instance, as the legislative phase of Ferry's program began, his close colleague Paul Bert, serving as parliamentary spokesman for the law on primary education, emphasized that sponsors of the bill wanted to introduce into France a compulsory system "in the same sense as it has existed in Germany, in Sweden, in Switzerland, in the United States."[17] Actual implementation of such a law would be inescapably complicated by the peculiar religious composition of the French people, for which the more Protestant or Anglo-Saxon nations of Europe and America provided no precise parallel. Moreover, because the percentage of Roman Catholic population east of the Rhine varied considerably from region to region, there was in reality not one German example of elementary schooling but several. Such complexity contrasted with Ferry's intention to base French primary education on a unified conception that would be both democratic and secular, as was befitting a republic. The three fundamental principles of the Ferry program—*l'obligation, la gratuité, la laïcité*—were in his view inextricable and were intended to form the basis of public education for the entire French nation.[18]

For these reasons, only in an indirect sense did Germany's practice of universal schooling inspire emulation in France.

The urge to uniformity sometimes posed very serious problems in primary education. An excellent illustration was the protracted debate over the publication of instructional manuals, patterned after the German *Lesebuch*, for use in the elementary grades of public schools. Originally the idea was nothing more than to develop textbooks or anthologies of stories by various notable authors so as to provide a common core of basic learning—and, of course, to promote patriotism. But any attempt to enforce standardization under the aegis of Ferry's legislative program was certain to arouse heated opposition from the church.[19] Once again the poles of opinion were clearly marked: at one extreme by Cardinal Guibert, who denounced the attempt to impose "a school without God"; and at the other by the Municipal Council of Paris, in which councillor Sigismond Lacroix insisted that existing school texts were incompatible with republicanism and demanded that measures be adopted at once "to prevent the spread of [clerical] poison."[20] As usual, Ferry made some effort to appease both sides. In his own words, "the school is not and should not be either a chapel, or a tribune, or a theater; the school must be a school and nothing more."[21] But in practice Ferry found it difficult to hold a pose of neutrality. His freedom to maneuver was restricted by a special parliamentary committee charged with studying the issue, which concluded that a literal imitation of the *Lesebuch* in French schools would be unsuitable: "This would be to ignore our tastes and our customs," and it might "do too much violence to the variety of spirits . . . in France." The committee's report conceded, however, that France was courting "pedagogical anarchy," whereas "Germany, it seems, has been able to achieve [conformity] in part."[22] Not until March 1882 was legislation forthcoming that finally prescribed a basis for standard classroom manuals, and thereafter a more distinct difference began to emerge between reading materials in public and private schools.[23] Yet secularization, not prussification, was manifestly at the heart of this controversy, and the German example served mostly for purposes of contrast.

In a closely related altercation about curricular reform of primary education, a German model proved to be of more direct relevance to the form if not to the substance of the solution adopted by the French. At the center of any curriculum, in addition to what subjects are taught and which authors are read, are of course the ideological assumptions conveyed from teacher to pupil. In the early 1880s that issue became focused on a single phrase, "their duties toward God" (*leurs devoirs envers Dieu*), which appeared in the draft of a new proposal for "moral instruction" in the elementary grades. In the Conseil Supérieur de l'Instruction Publique an objection to the formulation was raised in 1881 by Paul Bert, who moved that the words "*envers Dieu*" be stricken, lest they be construed as a sanction for religious indoctrination in the public schools. Bert's motion initially failed, but the debate was resumed in the following summer by the steering committee (*section permanente*) of the CSIP. In effect, its members soon found themselves locked into a theological discussion from which there seemed to be no exit; and they consequently decided to delegate to a subcommittee of five the task of "composing a compromise formula between the doctrine of a personal God and that of an impersonal God." Understandably, a ready solution was not at once forthcoming, and the bickering continued. As Victor Duruy lamented, the steering committee was attempting to avoid any stance that would offend "either the intransigents of the right or those of the left." A means to break this deadlock was finally suggested by Ferdinand Buisson, a leading Protestant, the director of the primary school system under Jules Ferry, and the man whose opinions henceforth weighed most heavily on the curriculum of elementary public education. Buisson argued that belief in God was universal but need not be confessional; hence, whether or not the controversial phrase was literally retained in the law, public instruction should stress respect for all religions and tolerance of various theological doctrines. Otherwise, he warned, the French would end in "a veritable chaos." Buisson also favored a structured program of moral and civic instruction based on the German and Swiss examples, which displayed, he said, "a much more pedagogical character than our own."[24] The curriculum, according to this scheme, would be divided into three parts (physical, intellectual, and moral) and each of these subdivided into three sections (goal, method, and program). Buisson's elaborate proposals, the form of which was Germanic in origin, were promptly adopted by the CSIP and subsequently became the law of the land.[25]

The evidence is thus ample that the French were selective in their borrowing of ideas from Germany's system of primary education. The reason for reticence was twofold: because there existed a fundamental difference in the religious composition of the two countries and because the impetus toward secularization of public education was much stronger and more urgent in France during the 1880s than in Germany. Nevertheless, one must be struck by the detailed attention and marked deference accorded by the French to the principles of German organization.[26] Buisson's curricular model, as accepted by the CSIP, recalled in its structural complexity the military regulations earlier adopted by the Conseil Supérieur de la Guerre, which established the skeleton of the French army precisely along German lines (eighteen corps areas of two divisions each and so on). The importance of this German influence on the form of French institutions was repeatedly stressed by the central journal devoted to problems of public education, the *Revue internationale de l'enseignement*, published in Paris after 1881. One of its contributors, Gabriel Séailles, commented at length on the recent reforms in primary instruction: "What should be imitated from Germany is the constant preoccupation with schools of every kind. . . . Modern pedagogy, born in France, has become an entirely German science. . . . It is this spirit that ought to be imitated and not the letter of scholastic regulations. . . . The men who currently lead Germany are quite conscious of what they want to accomplish. In its preoccupations, Prussia has never separated the two great forces that constitute the power of a people: education and the army. . . . It is urgent [and] it is absolutely essential to create in all the classes of our *lycées*, in all our schools, a moral instruction which has the importance of religious instruction in the German schools."[27]

Such hortatory prose was hardly necessary to convince the already persuaded republican leadership of France. By the 1880s Ferry, Buisson, and most of their reformist colleagues were fully prepared to acknowledge Germany's preeminence in matters scientific and to admit the corollary that competition with Germany must begin in the primary grades. Henceforward the lives of millions of French schoolchildren were daily touched by decisions made in their behalf by men who were responding to an ethos of national rivalry as well as to an ethic of class interest. The form and the content of French elementary education were not entirely separable, nor were the spirit and the letter of the laws adopted by the French parliament at the urging of Jules Ferry. Thus, although France did not closely imitate Germany at the primary level of public education, the Third Republic did significantly modify its structure by adopting a system of universal instruction in a conscious attempt to cope with the altered political and social realities of Europe after the defeat of 1870.

Secondary Education

In spite of earlier reform efforts, the elitism of French secondary education remained largely unaffected before 1880. For a metropolis of more than two million inhabitants, Paris had only five public *lycées* and one municipal *collège* (see Table 3). Proportionately, the city of Vienna provided three times and Berlin seven times the number of such institutions for their populations.[28] In eight adjacent departments outside of the Seine, too, the public secondary student population was nearly stationary, whereas parochial schooling was becoming increasingly popular among middle-class families.[29] Beyond the immediate vicinity of the capital city, the situation was more difficult to assess statistically, but it was certainly far from satisfactory for a new republican regime that vaunted the progress of democracy and modernity. A report from Nancy, for example, documented a decline in *lycée* enrollments in Lorraine, attributable in part to the excessive demands of the classical curriculum: "It is very difficult to house encyclopedic programs in these young heads."[30] Meanwhile, in the southwest, despite some radical agitation there in the early 1870s, the secondary enrollment of parochial schools in Toulouse remained virtually double that of the public schools; and, moreover, "in this region the Jesuits have a tenth of the total number of pupils in secondary education."[31] With such memoranda accumulating on his desk in the rue de Grenelle, Jules Ferry had cause to conclude that another round of reform was imperative if French education were truly to reflect a spirit of republicanism.

As a vehicle for his efforts, Ferry chose to reconvene the Conseil Supérieur de l'Instruction Publique, which had been moribund since 1878 but could now be constituted without the clerical control that had weighed so heavily on its previous deliberations. This "new" CSIP, as Ferry was careful to designate it in his opening

Table 3 / Enrollment of Public Secondary Schools in Paris, 1865–1878

	1865	1871	1876	1877	1878
Louis le Grand	1,212	1,137	1,150	1,178	1,195
Henry IV	681	700	759	752	682
St. Louis	716	622	896	927	901
Charlemagne	938	792	784	815	833
Fontanes	1,118	1,319	1,488	1,478	1,450
Collège Rollin	372	311	529	630	687
Total	5,037	4,881	5,606	5,780	5,748

Source: "Lycées du ressort et collèges de Paris, situations numériques . . . ," 17 Oct. 1878, AN Paris, F[17] 6852.

statement in May 1880, was thus convoked in order to realize at last "that reform of secondary studies so often attempted, so long awaited." Its assignment was to replace traditional routine with *"l'esprit moderne"*—which Ferry tended to equate with increased attention to science, history, geography, and French, largely at the expense of Greek and the "sterile exercise" of Latin composition.[32] To many of his auditors Ferry's statements must have sounded altogether familiar. Appropriately, the man named to preside over a special committee assigned to draft reform legislation (*commission des réformes*) was Jules Simon. If a deliberate continuity of reformist intentions was thereby indicated, Simon's appointment also represented an inadvertent admission that more than one longstanding question still remained without a satisfactory resolution. Soundings by the CSIP immediately relocated the intractable dilemma of attempting to strengthen "modern" subjects in the *lycée* without at the same time weakening the classics or overcrowding the curriculum. Ferry nonetheless brimmed with confidence that the CSIP, in approving his suggestions, would be initiating "one of those serious, profound, durable reforms that will permit us to forego a revolution."[33]

Ferry's sanguinity was shared by many French educators, for whom the *Revue internationale de l'enseignement* provided a convenient rostrum. The journal's editor, Edmond Dreyfus-Brisac, began its inaugural issue in early 1881 with a paean to Ferry's culmination of the Duruy and Simon reform programs. The result, he wrote, was that "classical education is dethroned" and that "sciences and modern languages occupy a place nearly equal to that of classical languages." Dreyfus-Brisac, who had visited Bonn in 1878 to launch an investigation of German education, drew a detailed comparison between the curricula of the French *lycée* and the German *Gymnasium*. The latter had actually retained a relatively stronger emphasis on the classics, he observed, and yet the Germans were also remarkably successful in fostering modern subjects by employing techniques that the French would do well to copy. "Precisely of what do these new methods borrowed from Germany consist?" he asked. The answer was essentially to emphasize inductive rather than deductive procedures in the classroom. "We are entirely partisan to these methods," he added, "from which we expect excellent results." Obviously anticipating an objection that the Ferry reforms of secondary education might be too abrupt, Dreyfus-Brisac pointed out that they bore striking resemblance to measures adopted by the Prussian government during the Napoleonic period, and he put the rhetorical question: "Is Jules Ferry rash to introduce in 1880 a reform that August Wolf conceived in 1811?"[34]

The facile contention that amelioration of French secondary education lay in appropriating German instructional methods, apart from the organization or content of the curriculum, could not survive the careful scrutiny to which it was soon subjected. But the initial assumption of Ferry and his supporters was that the fundamental reform of the French *lycée* was finally being accomplished and that their only remaining task was to regroup the rest of the system accordingly. The most crucial other component was the so-called *enseignement spécial*, which had been an emphasis of the original Duruy plan before the war of 1870. If the modified *lycée* were to be designed to train elites, then a complementary program in preparation for business, trades, and services would also be desirable for the majority of the population. When the Conseil Supérieur de l'Instruction Publique debated the issue in the summer of 1881, a consensus emerged that the *enseignement spécial* needed to be consolidated and upgraded. France would thereby acquire at the secondary stage a separate curricular track parallel to the *lycée*. For this purpose Germany seemed to afford an obvious dual analogue: the *Gymnasium* and the *Realschule*. Ferry invited Victor Duruy to participate with a subcommittee of the CSIP in reviewing the matter and making a recommendation.

The result was a resolution adopted by the CSIP in late July 1881 in favor of a greatly expanded system of *enseignement secondaire spécial*. Both the unpublished minutes of the CSIP and the well-informed commentaries printed in the *Revue internationale de l'enseignement* provided irrefutable evidence that French reformers were purposefully acting in imitation of the German example. True, the subcommittee's report stressed that Duruy's intention had always been to revive "a truly French tradition," but it continued to place *enseignement spécial* into a comparative perspective: "If we want it to thrive rather than to vegetate, is it not logical to give it independent schools, its *Realschulen*, alongside our *Gymnasia?*"[35] A summary of the summer session of the CSIP reinforced the same theme: "In order to mark its intention to constitute [in France] an education analogous to that of the *Realschulen*, the Conseil has proposed that model institutions of *enseignement secondaire spécial* be created as soon as possible, distinct and separate from *lycées* and *collèges*, beginning in the large cities."[36]

Much of the resulting public discussion dwelled not so much on the desirability of the proposed reform but on its feasibility in light of France's severe budgetary restrictions. The vice-rector of the Paris schools, Octave Gréard, noted that the *Realschulen* were a conspicuous factor in German secondary education because they were ordinarily housed in buildings separate from the *Gymnasia* and could thus maintain autonomy from them: "What a difference from our *enseignement secondaire spécial!*"[37] Thereby the more abstract issues of educational philosophy were at once complicated by material questions. Among those to criticize the advocates of "secondary education corresponding to the German *Realschulen* and *Gymnasia*" was Theodore Ferneuil, author of a widely discussed book on educational reform. Ferneuil argued that a separation of classical and "modern" schools would be harmful to the quality of both. The French would therefore be foolish to expend enormous sums for the construction of new buildings that would be required to emulate literally a foreign model.[38] But others, such as Gabriel Séailles, countered that "it could only be useful to profit from the experience of Germany."[39]

Further citations would only reinforce the conclusion that both private and public discussions about French secondary education tended to focus on the merits of a German model. Even the hypercritical Ferneuil had to concede that the Conseil Supérieur de l'Instruction Publique was inclined "to follow the example of Germany and to introduce in France the parallelism of *Gymnasia* and *Realschulen*."[40] This admission, with its imported vocabulary, was characteristic of a certain reasoning among French educational reformers. They, no less than military planners, were aware of the shadow of a superior neighboring power and were anxious to compete with it. Curricular innovation was thus motivated by much the same logic as fortress construction insofar as the ultimate objective of closing the gap with Germany was identical. When the steering committee of the CSIP met in February 1884 to consider the future of secondary education, these were exactly the terms in which the deliberations were framed. The principal reporter, Albert Dumont, stated the majority view that France needed to strengthen its *enseignement secondaire spécial* and "to constitute it on foundations analogous to those of the *Realschulen* in Germany." Thereby, he concluded, the government of the Third Republic would achieve what Victor Duruy had envisaged two decades earlier. By the middle of the 1880s, then, the advisability of a German model for the reform of secondary education in France was generally admitted among most reformers.[41]

Advisability was not yet viability. Criticisms of the Ferry program, as we have gathered, were vocal from the moment of its inception. After his departure from the rue de Grenelle in late 1881, these objections began to coalesce. Prominent among them was the charge, repeatedly expressed by school inspectors, that most French secondary students were unable to bear the punishing load of the revised curriculum. By 1884 some trimming of formal instruction had become imperative, and after much dithering the Conseil Supérieur de l'Instruction Publique consented to limit weekly classroom hours in the *lycée* to twenty. We need not recapitulate the details of that decision, but it is important to record a comment contained in the regular summary of the CSIP's summer session printed by the *Revue internationale de l'enseignement*: "The reform, so modest in appearance, which the Conseil has just passed—this simple reduction in the number of hours—will necessarily lead to placing into question again our entire system of secondary education."[42] The unspoken implications of that statement would require another half-decade to unfold: if the *lycée* were after all to be maintained as a bastion of classical learning, then the place of science and modern languages must inevitably be curtailed. In that event, the only logical recourse would presumably be to raise the *enseignement secondaire spécial* to parity with *enseignement secondaire classique*, thereby creating a true alternative for families who might prefer a more practical education for their children than was afforded by the *lycée*. This strategy, in turn, dictated that French reformers attempt to establish true equality with the classical *lycée* for the new Gallic version of the *Realschule*.[43] Specifically, to render such a duplex structure feasible, the second track must lead to a baccalaureate degree that would provide access to university studies and to the *grandes écoles*. Otherwise it was likely that France would fail to preserve classicism, to attain modernity, or both. This complex vision, with its inherent fear of failure in the competition with Germany, henceforth framed the controversy over secondary education.

Barring the way to such extensive reform, however, was one immense and seemingly insuperable obstacle: the ineradicable social prestige of the classics. In France, no less than in Germany, the distinct notion persisted of an indispensable intellectual format that the truly educated person must possess in order to be an individual of stature. The Germans habitually referred to "*Bildung*"; the French, to "*culture générale*." We must remember that all of those who deliberated on questions of reform had themselves received a classical training and that their own prejudices therefore ran deep. Even one of the staunchest supporters of parity for *enseignement secondaire spécial*, Charles Zévort, could not entirely disguise his condescension when describing it as "an education less elevated, less refined, of a different nature from classical education, but not of a different order."[44] When the new minister of education, René Goblet, sought to bring the reform forward to a formal vote in 1886, he proposed to establish for the second track "a situation parallel and not inferior to classical education." But he was promptly contradicted by several members of the CSIP's steering committee, who pointed out that his conception did not correspond to reality. He would need to face the fact that enrollments in the classical track remained far higher, despite efforts to organize an alternative that would "respond to the new demands of modern society and attract to French secondary studies young people who have neither the taste nor the leisure to devote themselves to the study of dead languages."[45] In an effort to bridge this gap in prestige, the steering committee proposed to baptize the second track as *enseignement secondaire classique français*. That misleading suggestion, however, was abandoned. Hence Goblet was led to reformulate his objectives more modestly and to present his plan as "a new education, if not equal, at least parallel to the first."[46]

The capstone of secondary reform was not to be installed before the beginning of the next decade. That action had to await a tortuous review of the consequences and contradictions of the new system by a special panel, appointed in July 1888, of which the chairman was—yet again—Jules Simon. In December Simon's group divided into four subcommittees, which labored sporadically during the year that followed. Meanwhile, as a member of the CSIP complained, the situation remained "full of ambiguity."[47] Not until December 1889 was a fully revised secondary curriculum presented for the CSIP's approval. In spite of some vigorous objections that the instruction of science would be too constricted, the plan was adopted and subsequently implemented.[48] This outcome, which was in essence a reassertion of the primacy of classical studies in the French *lycée*, might seem surprising after all the talk of far-reaching reform unless one bears in mind the imperatives of a German model. If the French wished to compete in the realm of knowledge, they would need to specialize like the Germans and hence to adopt the double-track system. In the German humanistic *Gymnasium* the place of the classics remained as strong as ever because an option for more modern languages and science was simultaneously available in the *Realgymnasium* or *Oberrealschule*.[49] The French *lycée* could not provide both formations equally well; and therefore the retrenchment of a classical curriculum was considered essential by the Simon panel. This solution, however, underscored the need for a second track, an institution toward which the French had been groping for several years. Throughout this time, as an editorial in the *Revue internationale de l'enseignement* admitted, the effort to upgrade the *enseignement secondaire spécial* had been only "an abortive experiment," and the condition of secondary education outside of the *lycée* was consequently "alarming."[50] The greatest difficulty, as we shall examine more carefully in reference to higher education, was illustrated by the inadequate preparation of French medical students. In conformity with Simon's recommendations, the old bifurcation in the *lycée* between the *baccalauréat ès lettres* and the *baccalauréat ès sciences* was finally abolished. Yet, at the same time, students without a *lycée* degree were still ineligible to study medicine. Thus most *lycée* graduates were scientific illiterates, whereas pupils with some special preparation for medical school were often excluded from entrance.[51]

For this nonsensical circumstance there seemed to be but one rectification, which was to press forward with another type of bifurcation patterned after German secondary education, thereby at last creating a French equivalent of the *Realgymnasium* or *Oberrealschule*. Léon Bourgeois, serving as minister of education in late 1890, described his goal as "elevating the new education in order to place it on the same footing as classical education."[52] Thus after its contemplation in one form or another for fully a quarter of a century, this proposal was finally adopted by the Conseil Supérieur de l'Instruction Publique in June 1891. The innovative curriculum of the second track eliminated classics, emphasized science, and required German as the first modern language. It was fittingly renamed *enseignement secondaire moderne*.[53] On paper, at least, French reformers thereby acknowledged the lessons of the defeat of 1870 and prepared to face a future of further competition with Germany.

Higher Education

No German institution, unless it was the Prussian general staff, elicited more unfettered admiration in France than the university. Better said, it was the extraordinary variety and vitality of the many universities located throughout the German empire that aroused the envy of the French. In the postwar years, testimonials to this effect by those who visited Germany, either on scholarly tours or official assignment, are far too numerous to cite. A few examples must serve for the rest. Edmond Dreyfus-Brisac, editor in chief of the *Revue internationale de l'enseignement*, recalled in its pages his first extended foray into Germany in the 1870s. Although a Strasbourgeois by birth, he had as a boy received only faint impressions of *l'outre Rhin*. Then, "suddenly, I felt myself transported to a new world." He was above all struck by "the superiority of the great German university centers over our Parisian education. . . . In Germany I found higher education in full maturity." That theme was often reflected in Dreyfus-Brisac's journal, which made a concerted effort to establish a comparative perspective, even when it was highly unflattering to the French.[54] Another witness, who had long envisaged in France "a university life analogous to that of Germany," was Gabriel Monod, founder of the *Revue historique* in 1876. More than a decade later, gazing back over the intervening years, he assessed the evolution of higher education: "The political hostility between Germany and France has been, in the scientific realm, transformed into a salutary emulation. We have learned foreign languages, we have gone to study in the German university, we have been penetrated by their spirit and by their methods."[55]

French scholars were especially dazzled by German "science," both in the particular and in the general sense of the term. As for the former, Germany was acknowledged to have moved ahead in technology and the natural sciences by combining the resources of an imperial state with those of the university into one vast research effort. "Germany has perfectly comprehended this point of view," wrote in 1883 the noted chemist Marcellin Berthelot, who praised German laboratories and research institutes as "kinds of intellectual factories." This development was becoming more and more pronounced "for the benefit of Germany and sometimes even to the detriment of France." In evidence, Berthelot offered the fact that production of the German dye industry had increased to ten times that of the French. An equal investment would need to be devoted to scientific as to military equipment, he concluded, if France were to compete.[56]

Likewise, when more broadly defined as systematic erudition about matters cultural and historical, German *Wissenschaft* stood high in the esteem of French educators. Although not, in fact, totally enamored with German historical training, which he considered ponderous and sometimes stultifying, the famous historian Charles Seignobos nonetheless conceded that "France has great need to profit from this example. . . . Withal, we still have much to envy Germany."[57] His illustrious colleague at the Sorbonne, Ernest Lavisse, after several years of study in Germany, was less grudging in his admiration of academic preparation provided by the German universities. "The best method," he wrote categorically, was "that which is practiced in Germany."[58] Such praise of German technique, it should be added, by no means precluded the most ardent French patriotism, of which it was often an inverse expression. That dichotomy was frequently evident among reformist contributors to the *Revue internationale de l'enseignement*, whose views were epitomized by the editor Dreyfus-Brisac: "For a long time higher education, such as it is known abroad, and notably in the Germanophonic countries, has not existed in France," and thus a "veritable revolution" would be necessary to set the French universities aright. The beginnings could be discerned in the budgetary allocations for more scholarships, the construction of additional seminar rooms and library facilities, and the creation of new posts for *maîtres de conférences* in imitation of the German *Privatdozenten*. But further progress would be possible only through a frank and open assessment of French weaknesses, even when that required "confessions painful for our national *amour-propre*."[59]

Beyond the rhetoric, the underlying reasons for reform appear much clearer once we examine some comparative statistics, which also bring into focus many of the special problems with which we are concerned here. Although one must of course keep in view that exactly parallel calculations are elusive, relatively secure generalizations are nonetheless possible. In making a comparison between the total university population in France and Germany, for instance, a pair of qualifications is appropriate (see Tables 4 and 5). First, the inclusion of German theological students accounts for more than half of the absolute difference between the two totals. That factor was very revealing, however, because of the abrogation in 1880 of the French law on higher education (passed five years earlier), which had permitted the creation of Catholic universities. Deprived of equal status and reduced to "institutes," these ceased to thrive, and by 1890 they formally enrolled fewer than a thousand students in all. Thus German theology students—both Protestant and Catholic—participated fully in university life and usually received a broad intellectual training, whereas young men studying for the priesthood in France were confined to separate seminaries.[60] Second, although the number of students preparing for law degrees was virtually identical in the two countries, those enrolled in medical school were more numerous in Germany (even after allowance is made for the German practice of counting dental and veterinary students in the total). As for the humanities and sciences, the difference in structure of the curriculum complicates a comparison. If we disaggregate the German statistics for the philosophical faculty

Table 4 / French University Students, 1890–1891

Faculty	In Paris	In the Provinces	Total
Law	3,571	4,157	7,728
Medicine	3,050	2,141	5,191
Science	583	1,064	1,647
Letters	1,007	1,640	2,647
Pharmacy	973	798	1,771
Theology (Protestant)	31	63	94
Totals	9,215	9,863	19,078

Source: "Statistique des étudiants français durant l'année scolaire 1890–91," RIE 23 (1892):55.

Table 5 / German University Students, 1891 (Summer Session)

Faculty		Total
Theology		
Protestant	4,251	
Catholic	1,301	
	5,552	5,552
Law		7,381
Medicine		8,907
Philosophy		
Philosophy, philology, and history	2,968	
Science and math	2,168	
Pharmacy	1,130	
Agronomy	519	
	6,785	6,785
Total		28,625

Source: "Statistique générale des étudiants allemands, durant le semestre d'été 1891," RIE 23 (1892):65.

and employ the French scheme, the result is fairly similar: France had 2,647 students in letters compared with 2,968 in Germany; 1,647 in science against 2,168; and 1,771 in pharmacy to 1,130. Given the larger German population as a whole, the per capita discrepancy—except in the natural sciences—was not great.[61]

Table 6 / Largest University Student Enrollments, 1892

Paris	9,215	Edinburgh	3,623
Venice	6,220	Munich	3,551
Berlin	5,527	Budapest	3,533
Calcutta	5,257	Athens	3,500
London	5,013	Moscow	3,473
Naples	4,328	Leipzig	3,458

Source: "Statistique générale de l'enseignement supérieur," RIE 23 (1892):495–96.

Table 7 / Doctoral Theses Defended in France and Germany, 1885–1890

	Theology	Law	Medicine	Letters	Science	Total
Aix	–	18	–	3	–	21
Bordeaux	1	19	390	2	–	412
Caen	–	34	–	–	–	34
Clermont	–	–	–	2	–	2
Dijon	–	14	–	–	–	14
Douai (Lille)	–	15	73	–	1	89
Grenoble	–	8	–	–	–	8
Lyon	–	22	245	1	–	268
Montpellier	–	11	474	–	1	486
Nancy	–	21	99	–	–	120
Paris	49	348	1,867	82	150	2,496
Poitiers	–	19	–	1	–	20
Rennes	–	17	–	–	1	18
Toulouse (Montauban)	93	34	–	1	–	128
Totals	143	580	3,148	92	153	4,116

The really significant distinctions must be expressed in other terms. One of these, no surprise, was the location of students: the city of Paris possessed the largest single university population in the world (see Table 6) and contained about half of all the French students enrolled in higher education. German students were far more evenly distributed among twenty-one university centers. The extent of French centralization and the profound difference with Germany in that regard are further magnified by a detailed compilation of the number of doctorates awarded in the late 1880s. The

Table 7 / continued

	Theology	Law	Medicine	Philosophy	Total
Berlin	2	40	707	411	1,160
Bonn	3	7	344	112	466
Breslau	2	14	115	134	265
Erlangen	–	15	208	335	558
Freiburg	–	7	134	290	431
Giessen	1	3	54	69	127
Göttingen	3	75	106	231	415
Greifswald	1	3	320	81	405
Halle	2	11	143	394	550
Heidelberg	–	2	76	50	128
Jena	–	5	160	211	376
Kiel	2	1	208	115	326
Königsberg	3	3	118	117	241
Leipzig	–	1	3	662	666
Marburg	3	7	107	237	354
Munich	12	39	566	146	763
Münster	5	–	–	47	52
Rostock	2	10	17	135	164
Strassburg	1	33	213	200	447
Tübingen	–	36	105	67	208
Würzburg	6	5	881	88	980
Totals	48	317	4,585	4,132	9,082

Source: "Les thèses de doctorat soutenues devant les universités allemandes depuis l'année scolaire 1885–86 jusqu'à l'année 1889–90. Comparaison avec les thèses soutenues devant les facultés françaises durant la même période," RIE 22 (1891):324–25.

conferral of twice as many doctoral degrees in Germany as in France during this period may be partially explained by the normally greater length and difficulty of the French thesis. Yet the data suggested to contemporaries another and equally plausible hypothesis: that nearly all of the twenty-one German universities were viable and vital degree-granting institutions, whereas France boasted four or five at most, of which Paris was incomparably preeminent (see Table 7).[62]

As the French worried about their loss of leadership in matters scientific, it was therefore natural that they should look admiringly toward the German university system. Before leaving the Ministry of Education for the last time in 1883, Jules Ferry urged that a study be undertaken of "questions regarding the creation in France of universities analogous to those of the other countries of Europe." In pursuing that objective, as the director of higher education Louis Liard commented in 1885, the French could not hope to emulate the administrative autonomy of British institutions of higher learning such as Oxford and Cambridge; instead they would need to follow the German example, which allowed for a variety of organization and took regulatory activity by the state for granted.[63] In certain specific ways, moreover, the Conseil Supérieur de l'Instruction Publique deliberately encouraged the emulation of Germany by improving university libraries, creating research seminars, and modifying administrative procedures. To choose one example, a decree in July 1885 established a Conseil Général des Facultés, following Liard's wish for "the equivalent . . . of the academic senate of the German universities."[64] Opening another session of the CSIP in March 1887, the new minister of education, Marcellin Berthelot, reiterated the familiar theme that "the reconstruction of our intellectual and scientific material is not less important for the grandeur of France than the reconstruction of our military material," and he added his hope that France would "someday constitute great provincial universities to rival those that exist elsewhere abroad." Surely none of his listeners could mistake the mixed motives of competition and emulation or fail to detect the allusion to imperial Germany.[65]

It was primarily in the sciences that the French felt they had the most to fear from Germany. The dean of the Paris medical faculty, Dr. Paul Brouardel, put it simply: France must not allow "this scientific glory to pass to the foreigner."[66] That statement was in direct reference to a proposed reform of the medical curriculum, which controlled most of the advanced scientific training in France. Brouardel recognized that the strength of the French system was also its weakness: three-quarters of all doctorates were awarded in medicine, and more than half of those were earned in Paris (see Table 8). In no sector of French education was centralization more pronounced. Outside of the capital France's only reputable medical school was that in Montpellier. The four others—Nancy, Lille, Lyon, and Bordeaux—had all been founded in the 1870s and were still struggling to become established. Thus if the virtual monopoly of Paris was slowly becoming attenuated, the city nonetheless remained both central and supreme. Once trained, moreover, most physicians preferred to practice in urban areas rather than to move into the provinces. The result was a serious social problem: of France's 36,000 communes, about 28,000 lacked a local doctor.[67] Yet this distressing fact caused remarkably little discussion in the CSIP. Among those who favored reform, the primary motive was evidently not a concern for national health care as such. Their attention, rather, was pinned on the relatively poor quality of current medical training in the provincial faculties and the diminishing prestige of scientific research—both of which were frequently contrasted with German success. There is no adequate method to measure the literal accuracy of such assessments, but their repetition both in publications and in confidential discussions was striking. As an example, Dr. Léon Lefort, surgeon at the Hôpital de la Pitié and professor of medicine in Paris, deplored the "profound abyss" between French and German organization of medical studies, which he attributed to a crucial difference in instruction. German professors lectured only to enrolled medical students, whereas French classes were open to the public. "In a word, in Germany the true clients of the professor are the students; in France, they are the sick of the city." Such "detestable" conditions found in France were unknown across the Rhine, wrote Lefort, because in Germany medical practitioners were able "to live in science, by science, and for science."[68]

Such complaints were not uncommon, and by the 1890s they provided additional impetus to reform proposals being simultaneously generated by curricular changes in secondary education. With the maintenance and indeed the reemphasis of classics in the *lycée*, the basic problem was that most French students arrived at medical school, to quote Dr. Brouardel, with "an almost total ignorance" of the natural sciences. As a consequence, much time was wasted in basic instruction, and the general level of achievement was depressed. Brouardel and Louis Liard, who had recently returned from an inspection tour of Germany and Switzerland, therefore advanced a solution: to provide a separate introductory year of science courses, taught at the university, and to require a certificate from that program as well as a baccalaureate degree for entrance into medical school.[69]

Table 8 / *Physicians Accredited in France, 1875–1888*

	1875–76	1876–77	1877–78	1878–79	1879–80	1880–81
Paris	494	552	513	563	507	461
Montpellier	90	85	79	48	64	66
Nancy	17	10	19	26	19	19
Lille	–	–	4	7	13	13
Lyon	–	–	2	24	29	44
Bordeaux	–	–	–	1	7	21
Total	601	647	617	669	639	624

Source: "Rapport sur un projet de création d'une faculté de médicine et de pharmacie dans la ville de Marseille," CSIP (section permanente), 14 May 1890, AN Paris, F^{17} 12983.

To this proposal two specific objections were raised by other members of the Conseil Supérieur de l'Instruction Publique. One was that the new requirement would lengthen medical education by at least a year and thereby bring students into jeopardy of being drafted for military service before they had finished—because, under French recruitment laws, medical students could gain deferment only to the age of twenty-six. But Dr. Brouardel parried this argument by presenting statistical proof that the average duration of medical studies was already well over the prescribed four-year minimum. For a variety of reasons, he contended, many students were deliberately prolonging their stay in medical school rather than finishing in the allotted time. Hence, even with an additional year devoted to the natural sciences, most serious students could complete their doctorate on schedule; only laggards would suffer adverse consequences.[70]

The second objection was of a different order and was directed at the solar plexus of the entire French educational system. Given the classical orientation of the *lycée* and a widespread desire to improve the quality of *enseignement secondaire spécial*, why not simply permit students to pass through the latter track, with its greater emphasis on science, in preparation for medical school? This tactic would immeasurably strengthen the importance of the alternative educational institution, add instant luster to a new baccalaureate degree, and avoid the extra time and ex-

1881–82	1882–83	1883–84	1884–85	1885–86	1886–87	1887–88
411	485	388	383	329	362	373
59	69	70	73	62	64	93
20	21	18	22	17	26	16
25	19	19	13	12	14	17
46	43	53	56	42	47	49
29	44	47	35	77	114	97
590	681	595	582	539	627	645

pense of providing a separate preparatory year at the university. Brouardel met this challenge with emphatic rhetoric and characteristic bias. The study of classics, he contended, gave "an incontestable superiority to those who devote themselves to the practice of medicine." Conversely, "experience demonstrates the inferiority of students who have not completed their classical studies."[71] With very few exceptions, other members of the CSIP echoed the same view; and it seemed altogether appropriate when Jules Simon recalled a statement of years before by the late Bishop Dupanloup: "The dominant classes will remain the dominant classes because they know Latin."[72]

Beyond these rejoinders, the clinching rationale of reform was the necessity to compete with Germany. In medicine France still enjoyed an illustrious international reputation, especially regarding biology. "It is nonetheless certain," Dr. Brouardel admonished, "that for some time medical studies have been following an increasingly scientific direction and that, if today we are in this respect surpassed to a certain extent by Germany, it is in great part because preliminary scientific education has not been sufficiently conveyed to our students." In seconding Brouardel's position, Marcellin Berthelot paid the Germans a more succinct tribute: "They are superior to us in higher education."[73]

These discussions behind the closed doors of the CSIP closely prefigured the public debate of the early 1890s and rendered its outcome totally predictable. Léon Bourgeois's efforts to culminate the reform of secondary education by creating an *enseignement secondaire moderne* was accompanied by his attempt to promote a university system more like that of "the great people of Europe." To be sure, in public he was careful to stipulate that his proposal was not in imitation of others but only a "useful measure of decentralization."[74] Yet from confidential records we have been able to learn more precisely which modifications the government sought and for what motives. By 1893 a formal plan for the reorganization of medical studies in France had been drafted by Dr. Brouardel and Professor Jean-Gaston Darboux, dean of the faculty of science in Paris.[75] It was sponsored by Bourgeois's successor as minister of education and religion, Raymond Poincaré, who joined in advocating that a preparatory year for medical school should be mandated at once. In the steering committee of the CSIP there was little objection, except for one question. Would admission to medical school require, in addition to a certificate of preparation in the natural sciences, solely a baccalaureate in classical studies or might a degree from the alternate track of *enseignement secondaire moderne* also be acceptable? In a plenary session of the CSIP, despite Poincaré's vigorous support of the new French equivalent of the *Realschule*, Brouardel's motion in favor of the exclusivity of a classical background for medical students was victorious.[76]

By the time of Jules Ferry's death in 1893 the momentum of educational reform was nearly expended. Whatever lessons the French might have learned from the defeat of 1870 had been absorbed, digested, and finally legislated.[77] At all levels of France's educational system, the German example had served throughout two full decades as a touchstone of reform. Without that perspective it is impossible to comprehend completely some of the most conspicuous and enduring features of the Ferry era: the introduction of compulsory primary education, the reform of the baccalaureate, the creation of an *enseignement secondaire moderne*, and the attempt to encourage a concentration of research facilities in various provincial university centers. These measures did not assume their legislative form strictly because of a traditional internal dynamic in France. Nor were they conjured by farsighted republican politicians in a burst of progressive enthusiasm for social welfare. They represented, rather, a hesitant and sometimes incoherent response to a national humiliation. They were, furthermore, the expression of a growing fear of France's permanent decline in Europe and of an urgent desire to regain scientific as well as military parity with Germany.[78] Such motivations were neither trivial nor tangential in the minds of those who were actively engaged in the process of drafting educational reforms that ultimately affected the lives of all French children and still affect them. If we are fully to understand the *mentalité* of republican France, this is an aspect of the story that cannot be omitted.

Chapter 10

The French Kulturkampf

Rupture or Ralliement?

The passage and implementation of the Ferry laws could only hasten the deterioration of relations between church and state in France after 1880. Inexorably, it seemed, the religious controversy deepened and darkened. No reader of daily newspapers or diplomatic dispatches could ignore the contrast that French circumstances thereby presented to those of Germany. Although Bismarck had vowed as late as 1877 to press the German Kulturkampf to a bitter end, the death of Pius IX obviously provided him with a convenient rationale to do otherwise; and French reports thereafter presented evidence of a progressive reconciliation between Berlin and the Vatican. The only questions were: How rapidly would this development occur? And to what extent would it be at France's expense?[1] No one was more disturbed by these uncertainties than the French ambassador in Berlin, the Comte de Saint-Vallier, who considered the Kulturkampf in Germany to have been a disaster for Bismarck and who feared that, the chancellor's dubious example not withstanding, "our pitiable republic is going to risk the same gamble."[2]

Well acquainted with the symptoms of a Kulturkampf, the Germans were alert to recognize them in others. At the German embassy in Paris Chlodwig zu Hohenlohe patiently gathered documentation about the preparations of French bishops to enter "the field of battle," a prospect he took as confirmation of his own longstanding predictions. These soundings were amplified in Berlin, where the man most directly responsible for enforcing anti-Catholic measures, Adalbert Falk, was notified of "the beginning Kulturkampf in France." Falk had little time to take satisfaction at the news. His tenure as the Prussian minister of religion was already in jeopardy, and his abrupt dismissal by Bismarck was everywhere interpreted as a signal for Germany's religious rapprochement with Leo XIII. "Rome is obviously gaining ground," the Marquis de Gabriac wrote from the Vatican, and "she will gain it especially if, unfortunately, the Holy See loses it in France." In this remark of the French envoy we glimpse, not for the first time or the last, an assumption that Germany's profit was France's potential debit. The French therefore followed negotiations between the Vatican and Berlin with a certain anxiety. During long talks at Bismarck's country estate at Varzin, Saint-Vallier appraised the chancellor's tactics: the Germans would not seek a formal treaty—*"nothing in writing"*—but would develop a modified relationship between their government and the papacy to serve the interests of both. It would be a long and slow process, Saint-Vallier remarked, because Bismarck tended to view the Vatican as "a woman who gives herself only as a last resort and believes that she makes her defeat more honorable if she delays as long as possible."[3] If the analysis was correct, the quality of humor was strained.

In France the level of rhetoric was meanwhile rising. During much of the 1870s, we recall, open talk of outright religious conflict had usually been confined to the Municipal Council of Paris, which regularly heaped blame and scorn on the church.[4] But by the end of the decade, as the debate over Ferry's legislative proposals became more heated, similar language echoed frequently in the Chamber of Deputies. While denouncing "clerical agitation," for example, the Radical deputy Edouard Lockroy charged that "war has been declared . . . against the government of the republic." This statement drew an angry rebuttal from a member of the conservative opposition: "It was the government that first declared war on the clergy. It was Ferry who began."[5] Thus by 1880 both sides were prepared to admit that an increasingly fierce religious conflict had started, although they disagreed about who had fired the first shot.

In its opening phase the French Kulturkampf assumed three obvious forms. We have already analyzed the first in some detail: the internal dispute over public education. It is worthwhile to add, as a reflection of the dozens of local altercations produced by the campaign to secularize the schools, the interminable diplomatic exchanges that developed between the French government and the Vatican. Paris demanded that the papacy abstain from the appearance of undue meddling in France's domestic affairs. Leo was warned that "the intervention of the Roman curia in the debate would be very upsetting." The pope responded that his public pronouncements were intended to be "more didactical than political" and that he trusted the French episcopacy to resolve any differences with the government. For the more rabid French anticlericals, however, this stance of lofty neutrality was sheer hypocrisy because it left the lower Catholic clergy and laymen free to agitate without rebuke from the church hierarchy. "You cannot open a clerical newspaper," complained Gambetta's *République française*, "nor speak with an ultramontane, without encountering the assertion that Jules Ferry wants to introduce the Kulturkampf into France. The honorable minister of education is assumed to be but an imitator—if not an agent—of Bismarck." These allegations were rejected by the same editorial with righteous indignation. Yet to dwell on them was to concede that they might not appear totally groundless.[6]

At the topmost political level, it should be said, an ostentatious desire to avert hostilities was apparent. In the summer of 1879 the designation of a distinguished new papal nuncio to Paris, Monsignor Vladimir Czacki, was intended by Leo to reaffirm "a policy of conciliation and appeasement."[7] And President Jules Grévy, as he confided to Hohenlohe, likewise fondled hopes for a satisfactory compromise on the Ferry laws that would assuage the worries of the French clergy.[8] But no amount of diplomatic formalities could altogether eliminate recurrent static in the deliberations over educational reform. In his public statements and parliamentary actions Jules Ferry remained consistent in seeking, as he said, a school system in which science and reason would prevail over "the reactionary spirit."[9] Although the government was willing to attenuate strict enforcement of scholastic regulations, it was nonetheless unprepared to abandon "the principle of the separation of church and school."[10] The resulting implications were well understood by Catholic parishioners and parents throughout France, who in 1882 signed hundreds of petitions of protest: "No more illusions! War has been *openly* declared against the conscience. We accept it!"[11] More than one historian has correctly observed that, however genuinely the Vatican may have wished to encourage a reconciliation of church and state in France, the ultimate verdict rested with the village priest and his flock, many of whom never ceased to regard the Third Republic as evil incarnate.[12]

A second manifestation of the French Kulturkampf was an increased repression of the clergy. While Ferry was busy with educational reforms, cabinet responsibility for religious affairs was shifted to the minister of the interior, Charles Lepère, who briefly became Adalbert Falk's French counterpart. In early April 1879 Lepère sent confidential instructions to the prefects to provide him with precise information about any priests who publicly challenged republican institutions; and several weeks later he requested copies of all pastoral letters and diocesan directives (*mandements*).[13] One of Lepère's first victims was the archbishop of Aix, Monsignor Forcade, who dared to attack Gambetta personally and to accuse the government of fomenting atheism and immorality. For that offensive language he was promptly charged with slander (*appel comme d'abus*), a drastic legal action which Bismarck had urged in vain on the Broglie cabinet in 1874.[14] It was this incident that initially ignited acrimonious exchanges in the Chamber—the "first shot" debate—and that revealed just how serious the religious strife in France was likely to become. Lepère intended to leave no doubt in the minds of the prefects: they must maintain "vigilant control" in their departments, exercise "strong and reasonable discipline," and remember the "essentially political character" of their administrative functions. These instructions represented a complete departure from earlier demands by the republicans, when they were still out of power, that the prefectoral corps remain politically neutral. French prefects had of course never been truly impartial, but any such pretense was henceforth dropped.[15]

The Vatican could not suppress its concern about the course of events in France. Alerted that the French government was gathering membership lists of the Society of Jesus and of other "unauthorized" religious orders, the papacy expressed "serious apprehensions about the future." Foreign Minister Charles de Freycinet was advised through diplomatic channels that the pope would not hide his extreme displeasure if the Jesuits were expelled from France: "It is not in a moment when the Holy Father is drawing closer to Germany that he wishes to drift away from France."[16]

Implicit in this admonition was a threat that, should there be an intensification of the religious crisis in France, Leo XIII would be left with no alternative to a closer alignment with the Bismarckian Reich. Yet Freycinet was adamant. He preferred to confine the religious question to the context of French internal affairs, and he reminded Monsignor Czacki, who had personally delivered the papal warning, of the recent past: "We should have no illusions. What is happening today is the inevitable legacy . . . of imprudent political enterprises of the last seven or eight years. It was after the attempts of monarchical restoration in 1873 and 1874, and especially after the reactionary undertaking of 16 May 1877, that the entire republican party found itself embattled and thrown into the fray."[17] Freycinet thus contended that the Jesuits had long plotted against the republic and that the time of retribution had come. In that event, the French Kulturkampf could be seen as just another episode in a concatenation of political crises since 1870. Although such a view may have little merit in retrospect, it served at the time as a convenient device for the government to shift blame onto the church, and it provided a neat rationale for harsh countermeasures yet to be taken.

A government decree dissolving the Society of Jesus in France was issued on 29 March 1880, on the day following Freycinet's apologia. Remarkably, official reaction from the Vatican was restrained.[18] But for the edification of the Comte d'Aunay—who clandestinely reported from Rome directly to Gambetta in a "very confidential" letter—the pope unbuttoned his true feelings. Leo feared not so much Freycinet as his more fanatical colleagues, who were unlikely to stop with merely a rigid enforcement of the Concordat: "Ferry obeys the radicals, who are inclined to destroy religion." Freycinet put that same thought somewhat differently. He advised Leo to abstain from any overt defense of the Jesuits because the government's expulsion of them was in reality the mildest possible response to public pressure. The Holy See should realize that any further struggle would force a change of cabinet, which "could only profit those who secretly pursue a definitive rupture between the republic and religion." Freycinet detected signs of resistance among the French clergy and made clear his unwillingness to tolerate their reaction: "Unless they wish to engage in a *lutte à outrance*, I do not comprehend the attitude that currently seems to prevail." Should there be any concerted opposition or lack of compliance by bishops and priests in France, he wrote to the ambassador in Rome, "you can assure the Holy See that the final stage of the campaign will be *the separation of church and state*. Let there be no illusion in that regard."[19]

Therewith for the first time a government spokesman resorted in official correspondence to a direct threat of complete institutional separation, something which hitherto only Radical orators such as Clemenceau had dared to announce publicly at political rallies, banquets, or municipal council meetings. Freycinet could not possibly have been unaware of the gravity of his language. He was making a deliberate attempt to intimidate the Catholic hierarchy into silence and subservience. He was doing so, moreover, while fully conscious of the papacy's sensitivity and vulnerability in the wake of the German Kulturkampf, concerning which Freycinet had meanwhile remained in constant correspondence with various French emissaries.[20] Despite Leo's recognition that France was on the verge of "a war against clericalism," Freycinet continued to accuse the pope of nurturing "strange illusions" and of encouraging the erroneous notion that clerical intransigence might impede the "irresistible force" of republicanism. He became increasingly aggressive in castigating Leo's pretension to maintain a moderate position without ordering the French episcopate to follow his example. The Vatican, Freycinet wrote, displayed "a mode of reasoning that escapes me completely." The French government should not be satisfied with "vague and platonic declarations" by the pope and should "thus put his back to the wall" (*le mettre ainsi au pied du mur*).[21] When Leo nonetheless refused to counsel the French clergy, choosing instead to count on a mutual spirit of discretion, Freycinet retorted once more by drafting a telegram to Rome: "Do not leave this illusion to the pope. . . . *C'est donc la guerre.*" He then crossed out the final two words and substituted: "*le conflit.*" Later in the day he sent another dispatch that referred to "*la lutte.*" Decidedly the problem had become, in more than one sense, to translate the Kulturkampf into French.[22]

The third form of increased religious tension was a renewal of the investiture controversy. An indication of trouble occurred in the spring of 1879, when the papacy awarded to France two cardinal's hats: one for the aging ultraconservative Archbishop Pie of Poitiers and the other for Archbishop Desprez of Toulouse. The latter, however, had recently made open remonstrance against the government's secularizing policies, and he was consequently notified by the Ministry of the Interior that the cabinet would refuse to approve a budgetary request of 45,000 francs to defray the expenses of his inauguration.[23] Thereupon began a series of incidents during which the French government moved to impose financial restrictions in order to gain compliance from various ranks of the clergy. Successive republican cabinets also began to apply such leverage to challenge the precedent of prior agreement with the papal nuncio in the nomination of bishops. By disregarding invidious distinctions between majority and minority at the Vatican Council of 1870, an exercise that had always favored ultramontane candidates, the government apparently hoped to revive some sort of Gallicanism.[24] But, understandably, the papacy was not prepared to acquiesce in a renewed assertion of secular exclusivity in episcopal appointments. Conflict thus became unavoidable. When Leo annulled the government's nomination of a new bishop at St.-Claude in 1880, Freycinet expressed his "painful surprise" and vowed to defend the power of secular authorities to nominate bishops without restriction.[25] Internal bureaucratic correspondence confirms that Freycinet was far from being the most obdurate of republicans on the subject and that he was under considerable pressure from Ferry's Ministry of Education and Religion, which successfully urged a more aggressive policy on the cabinet. Any official who dissented or demurred when instructed to chastise the church hierarchy, such as the Marquis de Gabriac, was to be relieved from government and diplomatic service.[26] When the papal nuncio, Monsignor Czacki, was formally advised of the regime's intention to nominate bishops henceforth without prior consultation with him, he denounced the procedure as contrary to precedent and warned of "the most regrettable consequences." For his part, the current minister of foreign affairs, Jules Barthélémy Saint-Hilaire, observed that the Vatican thus seemed to be preparing itself for "a rupture, at least for a half-rupture." If so, as always, each side was sure to fix blame on the recalcitrance of the other.[27]

It was in this strained atmosphere that the suggestion of a "*ralliement*" first appeared. The strongest advocate of such a policy was Czacki, who favored papal compliance with French wishes and who supported a consistent effort by the Vatican "to reconcile the republic with the church." In Rome, however, a conservative faction of prelates opposed Czacki's recommendation, demanded his recall from Paris, and urged more categorical opposition to the Ferry laws, to the expulsion of religious orders from France, and to the proposals of legalized civil marriage and divorce. These contrasting poles within the church were identified and analyzed in detail by Vatican Secretary of State Ludovico Jacobini, who advised French cabinet members that Czacki might require their assistance if he were to "rally [the] entire episcopacy definitively to his policy vis-à-vis the government."[28] This conception of a *ralliement* by the Catholic clergy to the French republic was expressed only in a tentative form, still lacking as it did a secure niche on the spectrum of religious attitudes. Yet its emergence hinted that the church might soon have to face stark alternatives in France: either support of the republic or separation from it.

The most extreme possibilities were thus already evident before the onset of Léon Gambetta's *grand ministère* in November 1881. Although greeted with much anticipation or apprehension, depending on one's view, the brief Gambetta government failed to alter perceptibly the course of religious controversy. The enfant terrible of his cabinet was the positivist minister of the interior and of religion, Paul Bert, who promptly ordered that Catholic prayers for the republic be offered every Sunday, that they be chanted alternately by priest and parishioners, and that any infraction by the clergy be punished with suspension of financial support. Because of his strident tone, Bert instantly became the European bogeyman of anticlericalism; indeed, even Bismarck made use of him by cautioning the Vatican that liberal electoral gains in Germany might cause a resuscitation of the Kulturkampf there and hasten the return of a new minister of religion "like Paul Bert."[29] Yet it was doubtless clear to the church hierarchy that the fundamental questions of religion and education did not depend on a single minister or a particular cabinet. Even after the inglorious fall of the Gambetta government, the Catholic cardinals of France remained sufficiently worried to present a list of formal grievances to members of the parliament. In a twenty-page pamphlet the prelates recorded "a profound sentiment of distress" about the scores of legislative proposals that still threatened to disrupt or despoil the Roman church. Unless such bills were blocked, they feared, France would soon fall into complete disarray: "If we cannot stop at its beginning the conflict about to erupt, the nation, divided into two adversarial camps, will be troubled for a long time, and the present generation will not see an end to our dissensions."[30] The French episcopacy did not lack prescience.

Although the Vatican was not officially prepared to encourage open support of the republic by Roman Catholics, its de facto policy was unmistakably permissive. The arrival of Monsignor Camillo di Rende at the nunciate in Paris provided an occasion to reaffirm that the Holy See did not harbor a "marked predilection" for one form of government over another.[31] But the daily reality of what could only be perceived by the clergy as a systematic persecution, deliberately fostered by the French state, was certain to exacerbate serious quarrels between clerical and secular officials. Specific instances of local conflict were at every hand: altercations about the removal of crucifixes from classrooms; refusal by priests of confirmation to children attending communal schools and of communion to parents sending them; bureaucratic retaliation against such acts by sequestering a priest's salary or by forcing his relocation in another parish (*déplacement*); reduction or elimination of budgetary support by communes for the parish church; and so forth.[32] Here in the countryside, and not solely in cabinet meetings or consistories, the ineluctable course of the French Kulturkampf was evident. Hence the church hierarchy repeatedly registered dismay at "the measures that the government of the republic has recently been led to take in regard to many members of the clergy," whereas the French regime continued to deplore the "imprudent zeal" of bishops and priests.[33]

With each unfortunate incident and every harsh measure in France, the contrast with Germany grew more marked. New legislation passed by the Prussian lower house in 1883 permitted further pacification of the religious question there. This action represented, as the French ambassador in Berlin noted, "one more step in the direction of relative moderation and of détente." A reconciliation with Rome meanwhile seemed to be slipping away from the French. After reassuming leadership of the cabinet in February 1883, Jules Ferry expressed a willingness to negotiate the restitution of some clerical salaries that had been suspended for disciplinary reasons; but he added caustically that an accommodation would be impossible in those places where "the struggle has assumed a very marked character of political hostility." That message was transmitted to the Vatican, where Jacobini was provoked into replying with another long list of grievances against the republicans, whom he charged with a "spirit of hostility toward the church." Just as the pope had previously made a gesture of peace toward Kaiser William, he was now willing to extend conciliatory overtures to President Grévy. Yet, Jacobini lamented, the French were instead plunging down "the path of progressive destruction." Accordingly, Leo remained "profoundly distressed."[34]

The famous papal encyclical of February 1884, *Nobilissima Gallorum Gens*, must be read as an expression of that distress and as a sign of the church's growing defensiveness. Leo's statement was framed as a reaffirmation of the Concordat; and as such it was of course greeted by the French episcopacy. But three of its leading members—the archbishops of Paris, Dijon, and Toulouse—spiced their expression of gratitude for papal support with a large measure of pessimism. Despite the "external tranquility" of the moment, they wrote, no one could overlook the disorder created within France by an "imprudent and dangerous modification" of relations between church and state. Leo had done well to encourage "a frank and loyal application of the Concordat," but unfortunately there were politicians who regarded the Concordat simply as "a means for the civil authority to keep the church under control and to restrain its moral influence." The Concordat could therefore no longer be considered as a safe refuge for the church because it had in itself become a source of dispute.[35]

Behind the cheerful congratulations that greeted the encyclical, then, the French episcopacy discerned a dismal present and a disquieting future. Their misgivings were quickly confirmed by another altercation over the investiture of two new French cardinals proposed by the government. When the Vatican refused to award the hats in June 1884 and demanded instead that Jules Ferry accept a compromise in the selection of candidates, Ferry confronted papal Secretary of State Jacobini with a vigorous protest and informed him that a negative attitude "would be fatal to the interests of the Catholic church in France." As such language suggests, Ferry was outraged and convinced that the pope's refusal to appoint more French cardinals was a deliberate provocation. Ferry threatened to leave all vacant bishoprics unfilled in the future and to withdraw the French ambassador permanently from the Vatican, with a resulting curtailment of allocations in the French national budget. These measures, as he fully realized, would force Leo to the brink: "If His Holiness wishes a rupture with the French government, he is on the right track."[36]

Exactly a decade earlier, under similar circumstances, the papacy had condemned the German Kulturkampf. But now the religious question in France was arguably more complex and more subtle. If the reasons for a rupture seemed somewhat less acute, they were likely to be more enduring. Talk of an impending separation of church and state had become endemic, and a growing number of republican politicians frankly favored it.[37] Should the worst occur, the Vatican naturally wished to accept as little of the onus as possible. In the question of investing new cardinals, therefore, the pope decided to temporize by reassuring the French that he expected only to postpone rather than to deny their request altogether ("una dilazione, non un rifiuto").[38] Therewith a new rhetorical formula was devised, and later often repeated, that permitted the Vatican to keep a line open to Paris. Yet the deleterious effects of the preceding half-decade were everywhere apparent, and the condition of French Catholicism was visibly worsening.

The Impact of Imperialism

In the standard diplomatic histories of the nineteenth century, accounts of the period immediately following the triumph of French republicanism in the late 1870s have invariably recorded a Franco-German rapprochement. There is doubtless much validity to that characterization because the German government had long exercised its influence in support of a moderate republican regime in France and was therefore eager to display satisfaction with its establishment. At the very least, a new tone of cordiality was evident for a time in the formal exchanges between the two nations, in spite of their underlying disagreements and differences.[39] Yet in two ways the spirit of conciliation was always qualified and incomplete. The first was of course the ineradicable French bitterness about the recently lost provinces of Alsace and Lorraine, a feeling of resentment that sometimes receded but never totally disappeared. The other, less specific but also forever latent, was an ancient tradition of ethnic or national rivalry, a residue of territorial conflicts in centuries past that could surge to the surface in a variety of forms at any moment. In the Bismarckian vision of Europe, needless to insist, such atavism had no place. Germany had a right and a responsibility to be the superior power and thereby to assure that international harmony would not be threatened by French adventurism or revanchism. The chancellor, in short, was a firm believer in *Pax Germania*. No wonder, then, that the French chaffed at their relegation to a second-class status and desired to regain their reputation as *la grande nation*. Their ambition after 1870 was not necessarily irredentist in essence, but it did connote a readiness to participate in great national endeavors, including imperialism. Indeed, no French regime in modern times was more dedicated to expansion abroad than the governments of the early Third Republic; and no name became more automatically associated with French imperialism than that of Jules Ferry.[40]

It was not coincidental that the espousal of educational reform and of colonial venture should be epitomized by the career of the same public figure. Both were enterprises to rescue the faltering prestige of the French nation. Moreover, each was closely related to the Catholic church's primary duties of spreading the Christian gospel and dispensing the holy sacraments. Thus no one had a keener—if often contradictory—interest in Ferry's policies, at home or abroad, than the priests and missionaries of the Roman faith. Imperialism, too, was part of the religious question.

Such reckoning did not altogether elude church leaders in the decade of the 1880s. For their own reasons, in fact, they occasionally found it useful to promote a public awareness of the French government's dual interest in the reform of schools and the acquisition of colonies. The hierarchy soon discovered that bargaining with Jules Ferry in the latter sphere might serve to restrain him in the former. The church thus stood to gain some leverage, both because successive French cabinets sought the cooperation of the papacy in their imperialistic projects and because the French episcopacy came in turn to recognize that consorting with the government outside of France was one of the few effective means of exercising some constraint within.

It is impossible to determine when the realization of a certain mutual interest in imperialism dawned—probably, in a general way, it was always obvious—but we can certainly assign a date no later than 1881. The death early in that year of French prelates Régnier and Pie left two vacancies in the College of Cardinals.

Acting on a suggestion from his embassy at the Vatican, Foreign Minister Barthélémy Saint-Hilaire proposed to fill one of them with the appointment of Archbishop Charles Lavigerie of Algiers, who would thereby be encouraged to offer greater assistance to colonial administration in North Africa and the Near East.[41] The possible repercussions of this nomination became more evident as the French Kulturkampf sharpened. In May 1883, when Leo XIII and Cardinal Jacobini made vigorous protests in person to the French ambassador in Rome about his government's recent treatment of the Catholic clergy, they pointed out that "the concerns of France and those of the papacy are, in many regards, closely allied." As to the Near East, for example, "the pope indicated that he had been solicited by other powers to consign to them a part of the religious protectorate that has for a long time belonged to France." Fortunately for the French, however, Leo had thus far resisted such requests, indicating an awareness that "the placement of Catholic interests in other hands would mark for the church the opening of a period of difficulties."[42] This observation neglected to mention the obvious corollary: such action would also compromise the colonial interests of the French state. Nor, we can note, was one further matter specified: what "other hands" were implied?

The troubled circumstances of the religious question in France placed enormous stress on diplomatic contacts with the Vatican, and the strain was beginning to show. When, after a prolonged absence, French Ambassador Edouard Lefebvre de Béhaine returned to his post in Rome in January 1885, he could report to Jules Ferry an apparently renewed spirit of reconciliation toward France.[43] But in March the French Chamber of Deputies reaffirmed a tighter restriction of budgetary allocations to the church, causing Cardinal Jacobini to lodge another formal protest in Paris. At the behest of the pope, he expressed his "profound bitterness" at the decision of the French parliament. Leo could only hope that some means would be found to deny "to the enemies of the church their sinister intention, which is to achieve the abolition of the Concordat and the separation of church and state." The French cabinet was taken aback by the Vatican's unsqueamish projection of the ultimate consequences of continued religious strife. Although Jacobini's statement represented "apprehensions rather than realities," remarked the new minister of education and religion, René Goblet, it suggested that any further monetary restrictions would only serve to justify papal complaints. Consequently, the government would soon need to choose whether to renegotiate the Concordat or to renounce it altogether.[44] Neither policy was likely to find approbation at the Vatican, where a sense of gloom prevailed. Leo became more inaccessible and irritable. When Monsignor Lavigerie attempted to arbitrate the question of episcopal vacancies, he was confronted at the Vatican with strenuous complaints about the financial restrictions and the "general tendency of [France's] internal policies in religious matters." And when Lavigerie persisted, Leo abruptly cut him off with uncharacteristic impatience ("Non parliamo di questo.").[45]

More than ever, from a papal point of view, the contrasting trajectories of France and Germany were striking. Meeting at Fulda, the German bishops ceremoniously pledged their unity and fidelity to the Roman pontiff, thereby in effect celebrating the end of the Kulturkampf in Prussia. The principal francophone journal on Vatican affairs, the *Moniteur de Rome*, editorialized: "The Prussian Catholics are thus as great in armistice as in battle. May this example and these lessons not be lost!" But such sanguine homilies were to little effect as long as French educational reform and religious persecution went unchecked, as the *Moniteur de Rome* recognized in deploring the "administrative razzia" in France and the "unjust and illegal war" being conducted there against the Catholic church.[46] A clear sense of this perceived contrast between France and Germany is essential to interpret two important papal encyclicals of the period: *Immortale Dei* (1 November 1885) and *Jampridem Nobis* (6 January 1886). Their juxtaposition is no simple convenience for this analysis but was recognized by some politically alert observers at the time. The former became well known as Leo's sanction of Catholic cooperation with French republicanism: "This, then, is the teaching of the Catholic church concerning the constitution and government of the state. By the words and decrees just cited, if judged dispassionately, no one of several forms of government is in itself condemned, inasmuch as none of them contains anything contrary to Catholic doctrine, and all of them are capable, if wisely and justly managed, to ensure the welfare of the state. Neither is it blameworthy in itself, in any manner, for the people to have a share greater or less in the government: for at certain times, and under certain laws, such participation may not only be of benefit to the citizens, but may even be of obligation."[47] Here the operative phrase was "under certain laws." Leo's unmistakable purpose was to barter cooperation between Rome and Paris for a halt to further anticlerical legislation or financial restrictions by the Chamber of Deputies. What if that offer, however, were declined? An answer to this delicate question was suggested by the second encyclical, which was addressed to the Prussian episcopacy in response to the recent declaration of solidarity at Fulda. *Jampridem Nobis* mentioned, namely, that one of the practical benefits of appeasement would be the assurance of the church's invaluable assistance in colonial areas where missionary work was in progress.[48] This unusually frank association of religious proselytism and imperial venture was simultaneously an explicit gesture to Germany and an implicit threat to France. In Rome the French ambassador Lefebvre de Béhaine instantly comprehended the intended message and attempted to impress his government with the danger of the "increasingly substantial expansion of the German element in the Catholic missions of the Far East." If this trend continued, France's global expansion would be dealt a "serious blow." It was consequently crucial that "the number of our missionaries remain quite considerable in order that we might fight against these new influences." Strongly partisan to a French rapprochement with the Vatican, Lefebvre de Béhaine went so far as to recommend that France sponsor "under colonial aegis" (*au titre colonial*) the founding of Catholic seminaries and *collèges* for special missionary training: "Therein, I believe, is the last resort that remains to us to maintain the preponderance of our secular action in the Near East and in Indo-China."[49]

We cannot infer from such correspondence that republican leaders suddenly found reason in the late 1880s to stop dead in the tracks of anticlericalism. But we can document a moment of hesitation and a heightened awareness that, in religious affairs as otherwise, competition with Germany was still one of France's first priorities—a recognition meanwhile stirred by the growing popularity of the new minister of war, General Georges Boulanger. As chief of the cabinet for a third time, Charles de Freycinet was inclined to treat the colonial problem with all due earnestness and yet to concede little or nothing to the church. Without recommending a change of course in domestic affairs, he alerted the Ministry of Education and Religion about Lefebvre de Béhaine's confidential ambassadorial reports from Rome concerning possible German expansionism and the "dangers that might result from this general movement."[50]

With so much talk among republican officials, who cultivated a well-established and deserved reputation for indiscretion, it was no miracle that the same issue soon became aired in the press. Predictably enough, *L'Univers* proved most eager to embarrass the cabinet by printing an anonymous letter from Rome about the Vatican's threat to rescind France's exclusive claims in China: "Once again a glorious prerogative of the eldest daughter of the church, the protectorate of Catholics in the Orient, is going to disappear." The allegation was that the same republican politicians who were guilty of consorting with "communards and strikers" at home were also forfeiting the "last vestiges of France's prestige abroad."[51] Whether in this vulgar form, or in the bureaucratic prose of cabinet officials, or in the elegant style of diplomatic dispatches, there was thus a common assumption that France's internal and external interests were mutually at stake. If so, any action by the Vatican that might be construed as favorable to German imperialism was certain to increase the strain between church and state in France. Papal collusion with Berlin, Charles de Freycinet warned, would be regarded "as a malevolent gesture toward the government of the republic. Passions, already quite animated, would receive added sustenance."[52]

In the months that followed, as the thunderheads of the Boulanger crisis began to tower over French politics, the tension reached a new peak. In early 1887 Bismarck exploited rumors of increased French military preparations inspired by Boulanger to stage new Reichstag elections, to strengthen his ruling coalition, and to obtain a military septennate.[53] In the midst of this maneuvering the chancellor received a cordial letter from Cardinal Jacobini, which was widely publicized in the newspaper press as an official endorsement of Bismarck's policies by the Vatican. French editorialists were universally indignant, although the quality of their exasperation varied according to their political persuasion. Despite their sense of alarm, leftist republicans had to concede a grudging admiration for Germany. "Bismarck has just obtained a powerful electoral ally: the pope," commented Auguste

Vacquérie. Likewise, Eugène Spuller found it ironic that Leo XIII should achieve "his most significant success" in the land of the original Kulturkampf.[54] Rightists saw less reason for irony and worried that the French government, misguided in domestic and foreign affairs alike, was simply incompetent to match Bismarck: "The great chancellor could teach us . . . that it is always beneficial to live at peace with the church," wrote the conservative parliamentarian Robert Mitchell, but "will Mr. Goblet and his cronies profit from this great example?" The danger was that Freycinet, Ferry, and Goblet were unalterably committed to a French Kulturkampf, of which the apparent armistice between Leo and Bismarck was a mirror image.[55] In turn, this version was vehemently disputed by some republican editorialists, who denied the parallel with German anticlericalism in the 1870s (expulsion of the Jesuits duly excepted) and who claimed that the French cabinet actually sought nothing more than a correct application of the Concordat.[56] When the moderate Le Temps advocated a moratorium on religious controversy and the creation of a "république conciliante," neither side was placated. Ridiculing such a proposal as premature at the least, the Moniteur de Rome blamed the unyielding republican anticlericalism of the past decade for France's misfortunes: since 1885, with one brief exception, "there has not been a single cabinet that has not continued and accentuated the policy of a Kulturkampf."[57]

Although this sampling of contemporary newspaper editorials may establish little about the deeper motives of French public policy, it suggests a widespread awareness—beginning with the inner circle of decision makers and extending well beyond—that religious altercations after 1870 were not conducted within an isolated national context but were thoroughly enmeshed in a network of international relationships. The religious question was not separable from the nationalism and imperialism of the time. By its nature, of course, the Roman Catholic church was an institution with a broader horizon than the gaze of national history is able to scan. Yet even with our eyes fixed firmly on the French church, we cannot hope to comprehend internal affairs without taking extraterritorial considerations into account. Studies of French education, the political activities of bishops, and the relationship between church and state in France are all valuable for an understanding of the religious question. But they can benefit from the added perspective that is provided by regarding French and German Catholicism as reciprocal parts in the same West European comity of nations, whose mutuality derived from a shared rhythm of experience. After 1870 the Catholic church in France did not sway to a separate tune.

Separation

For more than a decade after the republican victory in the *seize mai* crisis of 1877, the Catholic church in France was forced to accommodate itself to the persistent secularizing tendencies of successive republican governments. Inescapably, it was a time for brave rhetoric and small compromises, as the religious hierarchy attempted to avoid the extremes of capitulation or conflict. But by the early 1890s those poles loomed more visible than ever.

The most notable ecclesiastical event of the period was the public announcement of Cardinal Lavigerie's *ralliement* to the republic. That action, as we have witnessed, was actually the culmination of a longstanding development within the French church and was not as sudden or unprecedented as it may have seemed. Nor was it totally unwelcome to Leo XIII, who had in several previous papal encyclicals and pronouncements implicitly sanctioned Lavigerie's more ostentatious embrace of republican principles. Thus the Vatican could hardly have been devastated by the novelty of it all. Yet the question conspicuously remained: just how far would the rest of the French clergy move in the direction of Lavigerie's lead?[58]

At the opposite end of the political spectrum, meanwhile, there was equally intense activity. In the Chamber of Deputies a socialist representative, Paul Lafargue, presented in December 1891 a formal motion for the separation of church and state. The fact that Lafargue was a close associate of the socialist leader Jules Guesde and a son-in-law of Karl Marx naturally brought his bill special attention. But we can easily recall that this proposal, too, had a dense history since 1870, starting with the Paris Commune, stretching through Georges Clemenceau's career as a Radical in the Municipal Council of Paris and in the Chamber of Deputies, and more recently including such militants as Edouard Vaillant.[59] In strictly orthodox Marxist terms, of course, an intellectual and religious emancipation must necessarily follow from economic

238 / The Religious Question

emancipation. Yet Lafargue was willing to admit a certain impatience with the process of historical materialism and to urge that the church be disestablished forthwith. He proposed that the Concordat be immediately abrogated, clerical property confiscated, and the religious budget devoted at once to the working class. Thus France would at last witness a "real war against clericalism," such as Gambetta had long ago anticipated. Lafargue's motion thereby expressed the ultimate logic of the French Kulturkampf, from which more moderate men still recoiled.[60]

On the eve of the Dreyfus Affair, then, the religious question in France stood unresolved somewhere between Lavigerie and Lafargue. Many problems faced by the clergy remained unchanged or had changed for the worse. The slow secularization of public schools continued.[61] So, too, did the sporadic incidents of repressive action by government officials against recalcitrant priests, who could be either deprived of remuneration or expelled from their dioceses.[62] Leading members of the episcopacy were also not immune from the threat of retaliation, as Bishop Freppel of Angers learned after writing a pastoral letter in which he urged Catholics to vote against political candidates who were avowedly hostile to the interests of the church. A sharp objection from Paris was lodged at the Vatican and the pope was persuaded to order his nuncio in France to silence Freppel.[63] Such episodes could still be contained within mutually tolerable bounds, but they were frequent enough to indicate that many French clergymen were sweltering inside their republican muzzles.

There were simultaneous signs of religious agitation originating outside of the regular hierarchy. Celebration of the centennial of the Great Revolution in 1889 provoked organized counterdemonstrations that were hailed by *L'Univers* as the true expression of the French nation. But in alerting the Ministry of Justice, the director of the government's bureau of religion, Charles Dumay, charged that the "political and reactionary character of this movement is undeniable," and he contended that France was in reality being infected by a "royalist movement whose goal is to return us to a social condition anterior to the Revolution."[64] Prominently implicated by Dumay in this allegation was the Comte de Mun, who was also identified by Jules Ferry's newspaper *L'Estafette* as the guiding spirit of a new flurry of Catholic pilgrimages to Rome—a phenomenon classified by that paper under the head-ing of "illusions and vanities." In truth de Mun's new movement of Catholic Action was neither, as it proved by striking a responsive chord among French Catholics, including some workers. Although Christian Socialism at first seemed a novelty, if not indeed a self-contradiction, it quickly prospered.[65] Therewith, once again, a popular enthusiasm prefigured a papal encyclical, *Rerum Novarum* of 1891, the most famous pronouncement of Leo's entire reign: "Hereby, then, it lies in the power of a ruler to benefit every class in the state, and amongst the rest to promote to the utmost the interests of the poor, . . . since it is the province of the state to consult the common good. . . . The richer class have many ways of shielding themselves, and stand less in need of help from the state; whereas the mass of the poor have no resources of their own to fall back upon, and must chiefly depend upon the assistance of the state. And it is for this reason that wage-earners, since they mostly belong to that class, should be specially cared for and protected by the government."[66]

There was more to this formulation than was at first obvious. It could be variously interpreted as a benevolent expression of the papacy's concern for the condition of the laboring population, as the endorsement of a renovated social gospel, as a rejection of economic liberalism along with atheistic socialism, as a demand for officially sponsored public welfare programs, or simply as an admonition that responsibility for charity should be shared by secular as well as religious institutions. Whatever one's preferred emphasis, Leo's message seemed to point toward a possible reconciliation of church and state based on their mutual concern for the mass of humanity who were both children of God and citizens of the republic. For all the reasons that have been previously recounted, however, such noble sentiments were compromised by the already badly deteriorated circumstances of the French church. That unpleasant reality was underscored only a few months later, in January 1892, by the five cardinals of France, who drafted a manifesto that gained the adherence of eighty other archbishops and bishops. Even while asserting that they did not favor one form of government over another—and thus denying again the imputation of royalism—the French prelates deplored the fact that "practical atheism" had become the true law of the land. The ramifications were everywhere at hand: abolition of prayers and crucifixes in the schools, dismissal of military chaplains, sanction of civil marriages and funerals, restrictions on the liberty of the clergy, control of episcopal nominations by the government, curtailment of religious allocations in the national budget, harassment of priests in their parishes, and more. This baleful *cahier de doléances* concluded with a demand that the republican regime promptly restore the rights of the church under the Concordat and thus reverse the existing tendency toward a total separation from the state.[67]

Withal, the rich hopes of *Rerum Novarum* were, insofar as Roman Catholicism in France was concerned, to be virtually thwarted from the outset. The unfolding of the French Kulturkampf was so advanced, in fact, that one must wonder in retrospect why the separation of church and state did not occur much sooner than it did. The reasons for that retardation were several, but paramount among them was the eruption of the Dreyfus Affair in the mid-1890s. Until then the French episcopacy and the conservative press had been forced to adopt a manner that was defensive and usually apologetic.[68] Once the affair exploded, however, that tone changed and the church again—for a time—took the offensive. To pursue the details of these events would carry us well beyond the bounds of this volume. Yet it should be useful in conclusion to refocus attention specifically on Germany's role during the period when the religious question in France reached its climax.

In what ways was the German influence manifest? First, for better or worse, Germany served as an example. For every right-thinking Roman Catholic, of course, Bismarck was the incarnation of villainy. His persecution of the German clergy in the 1870s had been reprehensible in the extreme; and the subsequent relaxation of the German Kulturkampf had become possible only after his wickedness was exposed and defied. Bismarck had been brought to his knees by the steadfastness of the papacy and, above all, by the heroic resistance of ordinary German Catholics. They had persevered, emerged victorious, and thereby regained freedom from persecution. This idealization by French Catholics of their intrepid German coreligionists and of the Catholic Center party was in some ways similar to the widespread, if vague, adulation among French workers of their German labor counterparts and of the Social Democratic party. Exemplary and formidable organization was the indispensable key to success in Germany, whereas the efforts of the French too often seemed uncoordinated and consequently ineffectual. Such self-flagellation was not, to be sure, always distinguished by careful analysis of national differences, which might have revealed that literal emulation of the German example was infeasible. Still, the prestige of German Catholicism unquestionably stood high, and the dazzling precedent of a triumph over the state in the Kulturkampf exercised great fascination for the faithful in France. Abundant evidence of this interest, some of it already cited, frequently appeared in the form of newspaper editorials that invoked the German example. Their gist was generally one of two: either that French republicans should realize the fruitlessness of their anticlerical pursuits or that Catholic clergy and laymen should learn to endure adversity in the confidence of ultimate victory.[69] Thus the defiance and defensive strategy of the church in France were to some extent determined by an awareness of what had previously transpired in Germany. If sheer stubbornness had succeeded on one side of the Rhine, why not on the other? The frequency with which the term "French Kulturkampf" was mentioned both in official documents and in Catholic journals was symptomatic of the awareness that a European precedent had already been set. The German analogy, however unsoundly it may have been based, was too proximate to be ignored by bishops or believers, that is, by all who sought a rationale to stiffen their resolve.[70]

Another index of German influence concerned the continuation of national rivalry. The diplomatic alliances and imperialistic ventures that had begun to impinge on church politics in the late 1880s were even more troubling thereafter. As before, the central axis of Germany, Austria, and Italy threatened to isolate France from any allies, including the papacy. Control of the College of Cardinals was particularly crucial, especially in view of Leo's advanced age, and the French therefore lobbied to have their vacancies filled with alacrity. But, reported Ambassador Lefebvre de Béhaine from Rome, "it is certain that the diplomacy of the Triple Alliance is making continuous efforts at the Vatican to separate us from the Holy See." The grounds for this fear were confirmed by papal Secretary of State Mariano Rampolla. Starting with complaints that Leo's policies had become "too French," he said, the Germans "had recently made great efforts to detach [the Vatican] from the republic." Precisely for that reason, however, Rampolla assured Paris in 1893, the pope desired to name replacements for Cardinals Lavigerie and Foulon (both recently deceased) in order to assist the French "to act with sufficient effectiveness to offset the efforts of the enemies of your country." In that declaration we may recognize the restatement of an unsubtle hint to the French that the Vatican's cooperation in foreign affairs—more specifically, the pope's aid in France's rivalry with Germany—could be assured only by a greater leniency by republican officials in the enforcement of secularization. An informal bargain to that effect was indeed struck between Paris and Rome in June 1893. Yet, it should be added, the French government nonetheless remained firm in extracting compliance from the episcopacy and in seeking advancement for those prelates who were favorable to the republic.[71]

Finally, Germany was prominent in the recurrent waves of xenophobia that periodically broke over France after 1870 and that finally swept the entire nation into the Dreyfus Affair. Although the militant revanchism of the immediate postwar years had noticeably slackened by the early 1880s, the phenomenal public success of Georges Boulanger later in that decade had a distinctly anti-German component.[72] Moreover, Boulanger's intense concern about the problem of security leaks to foreign agents led to a secret campaign within the army and the government to draft aliens-and-enemies lists—the infamous *Carnet A* and *Carnet B*—on which the names of Germans and German-speaking Alsatians were conspicuously numerous. This nefarious project eventually resulted in detailed plans to incarcerate one hundred thousand foreigners and suspected spies in camps, to be located in southwestern France, whenever a signal from Paris indicated that a military crisis was imminent. Although such intentions were never implemented under the Third Republic, their sinister character is heightened by our knowledge that the same officials who plotted these mass arrests were also responsible for apprehending Alfred Dreyfus in October 1894.[73] Once the affair was detonated, it touched off another and still uglier explosion of anti-Semitism. This incredibly complex chapter of French history is of course a subject in its own right. But from the dense documentation of the period there is no difficulty in recovering substantial evidence of defamation that linked European Jews—especially those with Germanic surnames—with French Freemasons and Protestants.[74]

One facet of the Dreyfus Affair was thus a conservative counterattack against an alleged conspiracy of anticlericals. The total effect was to shift attention away from Catholicism and to reduce pressure on the hierarchy and the clergy, in other words, to permit a temporary truce in the French Kulturkampf. In the hailstorm of innuendoes about foreign infiltration of France, the issue of the separation of church and state was suspended.

Yet paradoxically, as the xenophobic excesses of the late 1890s momentarily lessened the likelihood of a break between church and state, they also helped to undermine the spirit of *ralliement*. Across France the attitude of the clergy hardened toward the representatives of republicanism, who seemed to be compromised by the affair. The awful dilemma of the French Kulturkampf—either to grant to the state a series of humiliating concessions or else to mount an intractable resistance that would eventually provoke a total rupture—appeared to threaten the Catholic church no longer. By the turn of the century, this illusion of security was abruptly shattered.[75] Once the prevailing sentiment about the affair was reversed and the dreyfusards took the offensive, the momentum toward a separation of church and state was again escalated. In the end, the Dreyfus Affair therefore served only to delay until 1905 the culmination of the French Kulturkampf.

Conclusion

Just as wars differ in scope and character, so do the settlements that follow them. Sometimes, after a bitter struggle, the outcome is decisive and the peace is accordingly harsh, as our language suggests by the adjective "Carthaginian." But in other cases the conquerors are magnanimous—for whatever motives of their own—and the losers are enabled within a brief span to recover and even to prosper, as each of the two parts of Germany has done in separate ways since the Second World War. The French nation after 1870 appears to occupy an intermediate position on such a spectrum. The German terms of peace, dictated by Otto von Bismarck in the treaty of Frankfurt, were severe but scarcely ruinous for the Third Republic. The loss of Alsace-Lorraine and the imposition of reparations, to name only the most obvious conditions, were a rude shock to the French that exacerbated their sense of humiliation. Yet in hindsight it is clear that the German extractions were not in themselves crippling for France. Moreover, we can be fairly certain that the advance of Germany to the first rank of European nations was already gathering momentum and would likely have occurred in any event, even if the war of 1870 had never been fought. The German victory thus hastened, but did not create, a Teutonic hegemony of continental Europe at the end of the nineteenth century.

Can we therefore speak of a French "decline" after 1870? This question, very complex and often debated, is not subject to a simple affirmative or negative response. There are various criteria of progress, of course, and by some of them the French continued to thrive. If certain sectors of the economy remained lethargic, others were more resilient, and France was not bereft of innovative vitality in the decades before 1914. Still, on a comparative scale, France undeniably lost ground to Germany. Economically and demographically the Second Empire of Napoleon III had been at virtual parity with the North German Confederation between the wars of 1866 and 1870. Thereafter Germany vaulted to a decisive statistical lead. By 1914 Germany had nearly lapped France, attaining a population and an industrial capacity almost double that of the French. It should be kept in mind that the chronological limitations of this volume place France in an unflattering light. Before 1870 and after 1900 the picture seemed less bleak. Yet the fact remains that in the three decades following Sedan, France's performance as a nation was mediocre at best; and during that time France virtually resigned from the military and scientific leadership of Europe. Specifically, France failed to match the hectic tempo of German development, and to that relative extent it is unquestionably true that France did decline, or at least stagnate. That truth is somewhat offset, to be sure, by the retrospective realization that the French lag was not totally irretrievable. The demographic and technological recovery of France in the mid-twentieth century provided posterior proof that all was not lost.

When discussion is confined solely to the nineteenth century, however, the effort of the French has sometimes been defended on the grounds that their per capita growth rate was not much inferior to that of the Germans. Expenditures for scientific research and laboratory facilities around the turn of the century, we are led to believe, were almost identical for the two nations, although only if the figures are adjusted for differences in population and income. This curious formulation is essentially obfuscating. The compelling reality was that France had dropped far behind Germany both demographically and industrially. The necessity of regulating the numbers for purposes of comparison is in effect a concession that the French research capacity was likewise weak. No amount of statistical legerdemain can compensate for the absolute difference. It is not generally advisable to wager on a welterweight boxer against a heavyweight on the premise that both are, pound for pound, capable fighters. Hence the antideclinist argument is difficult to sustain.

The foregoing comments lead directly to another cluster of problems concerning the notion of "modernity." Surely by now everyone recognizes that there are inherent flaws in the application of modernization theory to historical analysis. Those imperfections become especially glaring in the light of a comparative approach because it is impossible—short of some flagrant national or ethnic bias—to determine what the normative standards of progress should be. From a theoretical point of view, it is inadmissible and indeed preposterous to posit that whatever conformed to a putative German model was somehow "modern" and that whatever deviated from it was retrogressive. That said, it must nevertheless be conceded that we have been confronted here with a specific historical situation in which such an assumption was often made, notably by the French themselves. More precisely, many of the military and educational reformers of France, whose moment had come after 1870, were so convinced. For them, time and again, French tradition and Teutonic superiority were opposite and mutually exclusive poles, and they tended to regard the German example as the inexorable wave of the European future. Theoretical considerations notwithstanding, therefore, it is important in studying the institutional history of late nineteenth-century France to grasp that the conceptions of modern and German were, to a remarkable degree, synonymous.

Another question is thereby posed: was the German system of education more "democratic" than the French? That term is of course difficult to define or to document. No absolute measurement of democracy exists, and a solid basis of comparison has yet to be established in the relevant historiography. Controversy still abounds. With all due caution, then, we can at least observe that in some regards the Germans did take the lead. They were the first to adopt universal requirements for primary education, to create the secondary *Realschule* as a viable alternative to classical instruction, and to develop a broad range of regional universities. Before 1900 literacy in Germany was higher than in France and learning was probably more widespread. But we need to make a number of qualifications. Germany never quite lived up to its principles—one thinks of the Polish population in eastern Prussia and Silesia—whereas France made important strides in eliminating illiteracy even before the Ferry laws and certainly thereafter. In secondary education, moreover, both nations remained fundamentally elitist, emphasizing the cultural superiority of the classics and allowing only a small minority, mostly students of already secure social status, to pass through to the university. If there was a real difference in this regard, it probably resided in the stronger regional and civic traditions of Germany, and thus it had little to do with national unification or power politics. The *Realschule*, although much admired by the French, was never altogether imitated by them, and the provincial trade schools in Germany were doubtless better developed there than in France. These finer distinctions are not negligible, but neither do they make an irrefutable case for a much higher degree of democratization in German education. If anything, one might surmise that Germany was especially more successful than France in preserving a strong artisanal tradition and in adapting it to the needs of modern industry. But such speculation clearly transcends the boundaries of this volume and must await firmer support.

A comparison of French and German universities after 1870 is particularly instructive. The balance of any historical ledger must pay tribute to the remarkable efflorescence of German science, technology, and industry at the end of the nineteenth century—all of which were sustained by the intellectual vigor of the German universities. The French were fully aware of their unfavorable contrast. Hence they were usually willing to admit the preeminence of Germany in this realm and to make a gigantic effort to emulate the German example. Yet here the weight of tradition was uniquely heavy, and it is arguable that this attempt after 1870 constituted one of France's most notable and enduring failures. In paradoxical fashion French reformers sought both to develop a system of strong provincial universities but also to maintain, and indeed to augment, the prestige of the *grandes écoles*. As a consequence, the overwhelming dominance of Paris in higher education was barely lessened by all the reforms of the Third Republic, and one is tempted to conclude that, in facilitating scientific research and humanistic learning, the large investment in provincial laboratories and classrooms added little to France's capacity to compete with Germany.

It is pleasant to end on a theme that now elicits near unanimity among historians, an agreement that this account could only reinforce. Once upon a time it was thought by every French patriot worth his salt that after 1870 the nation was strongly and perpetually agitated by a spirit of revenge, that it heroically arose from the ashes of defeat, and that it finally achieved its most cherished objective—the recovery of the lost provinces—in 1918.

The evidence makes clear that there is precious little to be said for this monomaniacal scenario of French history. Despite some brilliant flashes of chauvinism from time to time, the truly remarkable fact is the extent to which the results of defeat were absorbed and accepted by the French after 1870. Irredentism was only episodic in the postwar decades, during which the Boulanger crisis was an exception that clinched the rule. The prevailing emotions of the French were apprehension, fear of war, and reluctance to risk honor and fortune against an intimidating opponent. We have confirmed that the military balance remained sharply tilted in Germany's favor, primarily because French reforms of the army were confused and self-contradictory. With the long Freycinet ministry about 1890, France at last turned a corner and set on a more realistic military course. It was also, however, a more dangerous one insofar as the Franco-Russian entente fed the German phobia of encirclement. Still, in retrospect it is hard to avoid a sense of fatalism about Germany's two-front circumstance, which was always the *cauchemar* of Bismarckian diplomacy and which seemed logically predestined by geography. France was drawn into the arms race above all by a dread of Germany and by a desire to catch up, not by a compulsion for revenge. If the French generally perceived Germany to be militarily and scientifically superior, most of them were also prepared to live with that fact of life, perhaps in the faint and distant hope of gradually overcoming it. Granted, there was a revival of nationalism in France shortly before 1914. Yet it is well to recall, after all, that the immediate cause of the Great War was located in the Balkans and not on the Franco-German frontier.

Notes

Abbreviations to the Notes

UNPUBLISHED SOURCES
AA / Auswärtiges Amt, Bonn
AAP / Archives de l'archevêché, Paris
AN / Archives nationales, Paris
APP / Archives de la Préfecture de Police, Paris
AS / Archives de la Seine, Paris
ASS / Archives du seminaire de Saint-Sulpice, Paris
ASV / Archivio Segreto Vaticano, Rome
BA / Bundesarchiv, Koblenz
BL / Baker Library, Harvard Business School, Cambridge, Mass.
BN / Bibliothèque nationale, Paris
BStB / Bayerische Staatsbibliothek, Munich
BT / Bibliothèque Thiers, Paris
MAE / Ministère des affaires étrangères, Paris
SF / Schloss Friedrichsruh, near Hamburg
SHAT / Service historique de l'armée de terre, Vincennes

PUBLISHED SOURCES
DDF / *Documents diplomatiques français*
GP / *Die Grosse Politik der europäischen Kabinette*
GW / *Bismarck: die gesammelten Werke*
JORF / *Journal officiel de la république française*
RIE / *Revue internationale de l'enseignement*

Chapter 1

1. For a general orientation see the remarkable study by Monteilhet, *Les institutions militaires*. For the period before 1870 consult especially Casevitz, *Une loi manquée*, and the superb sociological analysis by Serman, *Les origines des officiers français*. For a highly condensed version of some of my own findings, see Mitchell, " 'A Situation of Inferiority.' "

2. This view was attributed to Marshal Randon by an essay among ministerial papers, "De la réorganisation de l'armée," *Etudes d'Etat-Major 1874–1875 et années antérieures* (n.d.), SHAT Vincennes, MR 1999.

3. Forcade, "Chronique de la quinzaine," *Revue des deux mondes* 65 (1866):237–48.

4. "After 1814 the example of Prussia was constantly presented in the course of deliberations about military laws. . . . [But] it was not until 1868 and 1872 that France, diminished by Prussian victories, borrowed its military institutions from Germany (Monteilhet, *Les institutions militaires*, pp. 40–44). Also see Choisel, "Du tirage au sort au service universel."

5. The opinions of Louis Bonaparte first appeared in a series of articles in the *Progrès du Pas-de-Calais* in 1843; they were later reprinted as "Projet de loi sur le recrutement de l'armée," *Oeuvres de Napoléon III*, 2:301–23. He remained convinced that Prussia possessed "a system that will be inexorably adopted by all the powers on the continent" (ibid., 1:423–34). See Casevitz, *Une loi manquée*, pp. 11–15.

6. Report of 8 Sept. 1866 by Stoffel, *Rapports militaires*, pp. 1–14.

7. See Kitchen, *Military History of Germany*, p. 124. French misunderstanding of the German system is a recurrent theme of Carrias, *Le danger allemand* and *La pensée militaire française*. A concise and balanced comparison of Prussian and French military reforms before 1870 is given by Howard, *Franco-Prussian War*, pp. 18–39. A useful survey of recent German military historiography is Messerschmidt, *Militär und Politik*.

8. Directive by acting Foreign Minister La Valette, *Le moniteur universel*, 17 Sept. 1866.

9. Randon to Napoleon III, 24 Oct. 1866, SHAT Vincennes, MR 2021; Randon to Napoleon III, *Le moniteur universel*, 30 Oct. 1866.

10. Forcade, "Chronique de la quinzaine," *Revue des deux mondes* 66 (1866):242–53.

11. Prefectoral reports suggested that popular opposition to ending the lottery system was strong. See Wright, "Public Opinion and Conscription"; Case, *French Opinion*, pp. 233–40; and Armengaud, *L'opinion publique en France*, pp. 91–93.

12. Support of the *"population aisée"* for this procedure is expertly documented by Schnapper, *Le remplacement militaire en France*, pp. 218–29, 243–49.

13. See Casevitz, *La loi manquée*, pp. 16–20.

14. "Projet sur l'organisation de l'armée," *Le moniteur universel*, 12 Dec. 1866. Note that reservists in the so-called *"second ban"* of reserves were to be mobilized only in case of war and would thus have little or no training, at least none that incorporated the latest technological or tactical developments.

15. Prussia had long made provision for a system of one-year volunteers, who were generally university students interested in continuing their professional careers without prolonged interruption and who were thereby accorded the coveted status of a commissioned reserve officer. The texts of German military laws in the nineteenth century have been conveniently collected by Frauenholz, *Das Heerwesen*.

16. "Projet sur l'organisation de l'armée," *Le moniteur universel*, 12 Dec. 1866. It was decided that reservists should train for no more than two weeks a year, one day at a time, twelve hours a day. Thus no sustained training or conditioning was possible.

17. Napoleon III's statement on 13 Nov. 1866 is quoted by Casevitz, *La loi manquée*, p. 26. By the end of the year, however, he had relented and decided only "to do something for the press" (Ollivier, *Journal*, 2:263).

18. The precise chronology has been worked out by Casevitz, *La loi manquée*, pp. 33–39.

19. *Le moniteur universel*, 15 Feb. 1867.

20. "Projet de loi relatif à l'armée et à la garde nationale mobile," ibid., 8 Mar. 1867.

21. Adolphe Thiers to the Corps législatif: "Remember, gentlemen, what happened in Bohemia last year. . . . One side was ready, the other was not; there is the secret of what occurred" (*Le moniteur universel*, 1 Jan. 1868).

22. General Changarnier, "Un mot sur le projet de réorganisation militaire," *Revue des deux mondes* 68 (1867):874–90. This piece was also published as a pamphlet.

23. Thiers was not opposed to an increase of military service to eight years, according to *Le moniteur universel*, 1 Jan. 1868. Marshal Randon favored a term of nine years of active service (*Mémoires*, 2:221–22).

24. Changarnier, "Un mot sur le projet de réorganisation militaire," *Revue des deux mondes* 68 (1867):881.

25. *Le moniteur universel*, 1 Jan. 1868.

26. Ibid., 19 Nov. 1867.

27. "Annexe au procès-verbal de la séance du 12 décembre 1867," ibid., 17 Dec. 1867.

28. See Casevitz (*La loi manquée*, pp. 94–133), who describes the final bill as "a series of concessions and forfeits" that were "but a caricature of the project drafted by Marshal Niel."

29. See Niel's rebuttal to Thiers, *Le moniteur universel*, 1 Jan. 1868.

30. Niel consented to have his remarks stricken from the minutes of the Corps législatif, but they were quoted by Du Barail, *Mes souvenirs*, 3:86. See Kovacs, "French Military Institutions."

31. Du Barail, *Mes souvenirs*, 3:80.

32. Forcade, "Chronique de la quinzaine," *Revue des deux mondes* 68 (1867):515–25, and ibid. 69 (1867):502–12. Forcade's disillusionment with the final version of the law was later apparent: ibid. 73 (1868):525–36.

33. For example, the report of 2 Dec. 1867 by Stoffel, *Rapports militaires*, pp. 64–77.

34. *Le moniteur universel*, 25 Dec. 1867. One writer who favored a litcral adoption of the Prussian system, including three-year military service, was André Cochut, "Le problème de l'armée. Réorganisation de la force militaire en France," *Revue des deux mondes* 67 (1867):645–77.

35. General Trochu quoted with derision an 1864 manual from the French artillery school at Metz, which commented as follows on the Prussian system: "It is a magnificent organization on paper but a dubious instrument for defense, and it will be seriously defective during the initial period of an offensive war" (*L'armée française en 1867*, pp. 6–7).

36. Ibid., p. 278 and passim. Similar opinions were expressed in the Corps législatif by Emile Ollivier (*Le moniteur universel*, 24 Dec. 1867). For an overview of this tendency, see Challener, *French Theory*, pp. 10–45.

37. *Le moniteur universel*, 3 July 1867. Simon also made a forceful summary of his position in the closing debate (ibid., 20 Dec. 1867).

38. Ibid., 22 Dec. 1867.

39. Besides Picard and Simon, signers of this motion included Jules Favre, Garnier-Pagès, Glais-Bizoin, and Magnin. The link between this faction and the later Government of National Defense in 1870 could not be more obvious.

40. *Le moniteur universel*, 20 June, 24 Dec. 1867.

41. Cluseret, *Armée et démocratie*, pp. 13, 54–55, and passim.

42. Report of 12 Aug. 1869 by Stoffel, *Rapports militaires*, pp. 289–327. See Schnapper, *Le remplacement militaire en France*, pp. 251–60.

43. This development was well expressed by Forcade's successor as editor of the *Revue des deux mondes*: "Without any doubt the nation

responded emotionally to the events of 1866. . . . Yet whereas the government proceeded on this costly path, the nation ended by cooling down" (Charles de Mazade, "Chronique de la quinzaine," *Revue des deux mondes* 76 [1868]:497–509). See Chabanier, "La garde mobile."

44. "It was the tragedy of the French army, and of the French nation, that they did not realize in time that military organisation had entered an entirely new age" (Howard, *Franco-Prussian War*, p. 39).

45. Ibid., pp. 77–82.

46. Two examples were Mazade, "Chronique de la quinzaine," *Revue des deux mondes* 88 (1870):738–52; and Paul Leroy-Beaulieu, "Les ressources de la France et de la Prusse," ibid. 89 (1870):135–55.

47. The incisive contemporary analysis of Marshal Canrobert, "Causes générales de nos défaites," has been reprinted by Martin, *Le maréchal Canrobert*, pp. 326–28. Statistics vary, but the French probably mobilized about 250,000 troops in 1870 against a German force of 400,000 regulars and 100,000 reservists. Canrobert inflates these estimates, respectively, to 300,000 and 1,000,000. See Ralston, *Army of the Republic*, pp. 21–25.

48. "France was vanquished because she was the weaker. This inferiority was manifested in three ways: by numbers, by armaments, and by organization" (Freycinet, *La guerre en province*, p. 331). The "désarroi éclatant" of the French army was lamented by Mazade, "Chronique de la quinzaine," *Revue des deux mondes* 89 (1870):361–75. See Howard, *Franco-Prussian War*, pp. 203–23, and Porch, *March to the Marne*, pp. 32–33. The latter comments: "The trauma of the Franco-Prussian War convinced most Frenchmen that a thorough reform of the army was vital. . . . The year 1871 found most of French society, in a moment of rare lucidity, staring into the mirror to discover that it was middle-aged and unhealthy, easy pickings for a young and confident Germany."

49. "Discours . . . concernant l'armament de la garde nationale et la formation d'un comité de défense," in Reinach, ed., *Gambetta*, 1:311. See Monteilhet, *Les institutions militaires*, p. 97.

50. Documents concerning the legal controversy about his role as commander of the Paris garrison were collected by Trochu, *L'empire et la défense de Paris*; decree by Gambetta, Freycinet, et al., [10] Oct. 1870, MAE Paris, Papiers Gambetta, 48. See Bury, *Gambetta and the National Defence*, pp. 125–39.

51. "Recueil des principaux actes administratifs du ministère de la guerre à Tours et à Bordeaux du 10 octobre au 9 février 1871," in Freycinet, *La guerre en province*, pp. 369–438. See the summary in Bury, *Gambetta and the National Defence*, pp. 140–58.

52. Freycinet, *Souvenirs, 1848–1878*, pp. 135–50. Gambetta's militia units "never stood a chance against the Prussians in the open field.

... Whenever German troops appeared in any quantity local defence measures crumbled away" (Howard, *Franco-Prussian War*, pp. 250–56). Gambetta quoted in Reinach, ed., *Gambetta*, 1:59–64.

53. See Baumont, *L'échiquier de Metz*, pp. 7–10, 341–45.

54. Véronique to Le Flô, 5 Feb. 1871, SHAT Vincennes, G^8 177; Véronique, "Note sur l'avancement dans l'armée du 15 septembre 1870 au 8 février 1871," ibid.; decree by Thiers, 7 Mar. 1871, ibid.; Véronique, "Nécessité d'une révision générale de tous les avancements accordés pendant la guerre," 5 Mar. 1871, ibid.; "Le ministre de la guerre [Le Flô] à MM. les chefs d'état-major des troupes actives et les généraux commandant les divisions territoriales," 12 Mar. 1871, ibid. The Assembly also resolved to undertake an inventory of "forces and resources" of France, with the military as the first item on the agenda ("Annexe au procès-verbal du 19 janvier 1871," JORF, 25 Mar. 1871).

55. See Mitchell, *German Influence*, pp. 15–20. An effort to revive the military debate during the period of the Commune failed to gain sufficient backing. See "Annexe No. 96 (séance du 31 mars 1871): Proposition tendant à nommer une commission chargée de déterminer les bases d'un projet de réorganisation de l'armée presentée par M. Margaine, membre de l'Assemblée," JORF, 10 Apr. 1871.

56. Cluseret, *Mémoires*, 1:21. He added: "So much ignorance, pretensions, and presumptuousness virtually attained the level of a crime. ... That there was any military organization whatever worthy of a name, I deny" (ibid., pp. 41, 49).

57. Ibid., p. 115; Dessal, *Charles Delescluze*, p. 365. Also see the brief account of "betrayed hopes" written from prison shortly before his execution by Rossel, *Papiers posthumes*, pp. 85–152.

58. "In other respects the national guard had been incapable of fighting against the Germans but was an active element of the Commune; its action revealed that it was only an instrument of civil war" (Carrias, *La pensée militaire française*, p. 268). Also see Girard, *La garde nationale*, pp. 341–60.

59. JORF, 31 Mar. 1871; proclamation signed by Thiers and Le Flô at Versailles, ibid., 8 Apr. 1871. See Edwards, *Paris Commune, 1871*, pp. 313–50.

60. Thiers, *Notes et souvenirs*, p. 282. One recent analysis is not far from the same conclusion: "Post-1870 reformers were faced with the task of creating a defence machine capable of meeting the Prussians on equal terms. By their very success, the enemy had largely dictated the military model. The republicans basically sought to apply, with minor modifications, a system developed and perfected by an autocratic monarchy" (Porch, *March to the Marne*, p. 24). Another commentator says:

"France after her defeat set herself to copy the institutions of the victor as closely as possible" (Howard, "Armed Forces," p. 211).

61. "The Assembly attributed the victories of Germany to the numerical superiority resulting from universal conscription. This explanation was in large measure correct, and above all it was the least humiliating" (Monteilhet, *Les institutions militaires*, p. 115).

62. See Mitchell, *German Influence*, p. 143.

63. Waldersee to Bismarck, 1 July 1871, AA Bonn, I.A.B.c. 71, Bd. 2. From the south of France came similar evaluations of the public calm and the virtual political indifference of the French population, which seemed stunned by defeat (agent's report sent to the Wilhelmstrasse by Major von Brandt, 3 July 1871, ibid., II.B.10, Bd. 4).

64. See Ralston, *Army of the Republic*, pp. 32–33; and Porch, *March to the Marne*, pp. 2–4. Porch notes that Changarnier's committee reduced fourteen of Gambetta's generals in rank and retired four others; but, he argues, "competence . . . weighed more heavily than politics in the naming of generals to top commands" (ibid., p. 3).

65. Marginal notes on a letter from A. Clauzel to Gambetta, 19 Sept. 1871, MAE Paris, Papiers Gambetta, 55. In protest against the Assembly's reactionary policies, General Faidherbe, Gambetta's closest military adviser, made an ostentatious withdrawal from political affairs (Faidherbe to Gambetta, 29 Sept. 1871, BN Paris, NAF 24900).

66. "Let us say above all that this [German] organization was devised precisely with a view to mobilization and that it should be the same for every rational military organization" (anonymous editorial, "La mobilisation," in *Bulletin militaire de l'étranger*, no. 5 [21 Nov. 1871], pp. 49–50). The same argument was advanced by a staff officer in the Second Bureau of the French Ministry of War (Lemoyne, *La mobilisation*, pp. 154–57).

67. *L'armée nouvelle*, pp. 22–23. An identical view was expressed by Ferron, *Etude sur l'armée nouvelle*, pp. 3–12.

68. The chief advocate of this position was Thiers, *Notes et souvenirs*, pp. 275–84. Freycinet recorded the following scene with Thiers in December 1871: "He offered several observations on military reorganization, the basis of which preoccupies him very much. 'Come back to see me,' he concluded; 'we will chat about it. You must have some ideas on the subject. We will not be of the same opinion because I am of the old school, and I see from your book that you favor the Prussian system. You can explain your reasons to me.'" But when they next met, Thiers failed to listen and insisted that if the French had been properly commanded in 1870, they would have been victorious (*Souvenirs, 1848–1878*, pp. 291–92).

69. General Bourbaki to Thiers, 15 Nov. 1871, SHAT Vincennes, 7 N 33. In this forty-four-page document, solicited by Thiers, Bourbaki spelled out the rationale for many of the opinions later conveyed in the president's public statements on the military question.

70. But the real basis of Thiers's military ideas probably lay even further in the past, as is suggested by an unsigned and undated memorandum among his private papers, "De la supériorité de la loi de 1832 sur les lois imitées du système prussien," BN Paris, Papiers Thiers, NAF 20642.

71. Daily police reports of 11–13 Dec. 1871, APP Paris, B A/86; report of agent Kodolitsch to Brandt, 8 Dec. 1871, AA Bonn, II.B.10, Bd. 4.

72. P.F., "Sur quelques points de l'organisation militaire," and "De la réorganisation du corps d'état-major," *Le spectateur militaire* 26 (1872):5–26; 29 (1872):460–77; R. de Coynart, "Réorganisation militaire," ibid. 27 (1872):233–50; L. Adé, "Réorganisation de l'armée," ibid. 251–62; A.P., "Encore quelques réflexions à propos de la réorganisation de l'armée," ibid. 28 (1872):385–417; T.X., "Observations sur la division de la France en régions militaires," ibid. 26 (1872):446–51; A.D., "Réorganisation militaire," ibid. 28 (1872):337–84. Many such articles, because of their frank criticisms of the army, were signed only with initials or pseudonyms.

73. "After all, France will do nothing more than imitate other nations, [which are] virtually all led, to protect their existence or their interests, to follow the example of Prussia in the militarization of all the vital forces of their population" (New Year's editorial, "1872," *Revue militaire de l'étranger* 1 [1872]:1).

74. Lewal became well known for his critique of past French negligence in *La réforme de l'armée*. But his indications for the future were sometimes less precise. See the criticism of him by Carrias, *La pensée militaire française*, pp. 272–74.

75. Lewal, "Etudes de guerre," *Journal des sciences militaires*, 8th ser., 1 (1872):7–39. Many years later another famous military analyst commented: "The example of the victor seems decisive. Although many judge Renan's humility to be excessive in affirming that 'the victory of Germany is that of science and reason,' the fact remains that, in military affairs as in others, the French spirit would submit for a long time to the influence of German thought" (De Gaulle, *La France et son armée*, p. 195).

76. Bourbaki to Thiers, 6 Jan. 1872, BN Paris, Papiers Thiers, NAF 20624; Thiers, *Notes et souvenirs*, p. 283.

77. For example, copies of agents' reports forwarded to the Wilhelmstrasse by Brandt, 2 June, 22 July 1871, AA Bonn, II.B.10, Bd. 4.

These reports contained a review of eight recent French pamphlets on the military question. Among them was one by a writer whose opinions were soon to prove crucial in the presidential crisis of 1873: Lt.-Colonel Charles-Alexandre Fay. Brandt commented on Fay: "Of all the authors he is the most inclined to the Prussian or German system" (ibid., report of 22 July 1871).

78. E.g., copy of an agent's report to Brandt, 11 Oct. 1871, ibid.

79. Manteuffel to William, 24 Nov. 1871, ibid., I.D.44; Arnim to Bismarck, 7 Dec. 1871, ibid., I.A.B.c 71, Bd. 3.

80. The Kaiser was, however, assured by his generals that in a test of arms the French would once again be defeated (Bismarck to William, 13 Dec. 1871, ibid., I.D.44; Roon to William, 16 Dec. 1871, ibid.). The parallel between Bismarck's repeated use of the specter of war with France in the 1870s and the threat of a coup d'état in the 1880s has been pointed out by Stürmer, "Staatsstreichgedanken im Bismarckreich," pp. 570–71.

81. Military report from the attaché Captain von Bülow, 12 Jan. 1872, AA Bonn, I.A.B.c 75, Bd. 1.

82. Saint-Vallier to Thiers, 12, 25 Jan. 1872, BN Paris, Papiers Thiers, NAF 20630.

83. A telling portrait of Thiers's puerile delight with military affairs was given by his close friend Rémusat, *Mémoires de ma vie*, 5:337–38. A strikingly similar description was sent from a Paris agent by Bleichröder to Bismarck, 26 Apr. 1872, AA Bonn, I.A.B.c 75, Bd. 1.

84. Report by agent Kodolitsch, 8 Dec. 1871, ibid., II.B.10, Bd. 4; Roon to Bismarck, 3 May 1872, ibid. I.A.B.c 70, Bd. 132.

85. Thiers to Saint-Vallier, 29 Jan. 1872, BN Paris, Papiers Thiers, NAF 20630. Yet a few weeks later Thiers revealed less modest ambitions to Rémusat: "I will confide it only to you: in two years France will have an army and I will seek revenge." This passage was expurgated from the published version of Rémusat's memoirs, of which the original manuscript is to be found in BN Paris, Papiers Rémusat, NAF 14468.

86. The final draft of the law was published in JORF, 16–17 Aug. 1872. Texts of all major legislative bills and executive decrees concerning the military question in 1872 were collected by an anonymous editor, *Lois annotées*.

87. This twenty-two-page letter from Saint-Vallier to Manteuffel, 21 Apr. 1872, although marked "*particulière et confidentielle*," can be found both in BN Paris, Papiers Thiers, NAF 20630, and AA Bonn, I.A.B.c 70, Bd. 132. The latter copy was annotated by Bismarck, who indicated his willingness to continue cooperation with Thiers.

88. Roon to Bismarck, 3 May 1872, ibid.

89. Detailed account in daily police reports of 18, 22 Apr. 1872,

APP Paris, B A/86; Wesdehlen to Bismarck, 26 Apr. 1872, AA Bonn, I.A.B.c 75, Bd. 1.

90. Saint-Vallier to Thiers, 27 May 1872, BN Paris, Papiers Thiers, NAF 20630; Thiers to Saint-Vallier, 29 May 1872, ibid. Similar admonitions were also transmitted via Gontaut-Biron to Rémusat, 8 June 1872, MAE Paris, Allemagne 6.

91. This was the occasion of Thiers's famous speech that began: "Do not tell us that the Prussian system vanquished France" (JORF, 9 June 1872). See Hanotaux, Histoire de la France contemporaine, 1:431–37. The Germans were delighted by Thiers's performance in the Assembly. Manteuffel and Tresckow spoke of a "chef d'oeuvre" and a "triumph," and they assured the French that the results marked "a very decisive step toward the liberation of [French] territory" (Saint-Vallier to Thiers, 12 June 1872, BN Paris, Papiers Thiers, NAF 20631).

92. Ralston, Army of the Republic, pp. 44–45. Ralston follows, almost verbatim, the observations of Simon, Le gouvernement de M. Thiers, 2:65–66.

93. It is consequently far too sanguine to conclude that the 1872 law represented "a definite step towards the achievement of the nation in arms," as does Challener, French Theory, p. 42. It has been more appropriately described as the "mutilation of universal conscription" by Monteilhet, Les institutions militaires, p. 125. The enduring lack of enthusiasm for military service among Frenchmen is emphasized by Weber, Peasants into Frenchmen, pp. 292–97. He adds: "But it is likely that the war with Prussia, which mobilized unusually great numbers while focusing attention on their fate, a war also in which the connection between local and national interests became more evident to large numbers of people, marked the beginning of change. . . . By the 1890s there is persuasive evidence that the army was no longer 'theirs' but 'ours' " (ibid., p. 298).

Chapter 2

1. This argument is based on an earlier version of my findings: Mitchell, "Thiers, MacMahon, and the Conseil Supérieur de la Guerre."

2. The projections given in Table 1 were originally prepared from official French statistics gathered in the British War Office and then reiterated in the analysis of Wolseley, "France as a Military Power in 1870 and 1878." For further data see "Recrutement de l'armée" and "Situation de l'armée" in the Annuaire statistique de la France:1878, pp. 297–323. Besides conscripts, noncommissioned officers were also included in these totals. To the 719,000 soldiers in the standing army must be added about 76,500 officers to gain an accurate estimate of troop strength.

3. Wolseley, "France as a Military Power in 1870 and 1878," pp. 10–13. Slightly different calculations, but similar conclusions, are advanced by Monteilhet, *Les institutions militaires*, p. 125.

4. The growing difficulty of keeping demographic pace with Germany was later reflected in the fact that by 1911 France was forced to draft nearly 83 percent of its annual contingent whereas Germany needed to induct only 53 percent. See Vagts, *History of Militarism*, p. 217.

5. In actual practice the five years of active service were sometimes reduced to four because recruits usually reported for duty six months after their formal induction procedures and were, in addition, often awarded six months of furlough.

6. One authority has commented on the abolition of the old system: "It disappeared not only under the influence of democratic ideas but because of the convincing example of Germany" (Schnapper, *Le remplacement militaire*, p. 278). See Porch, *March to the Marne*, p. 25.

7. See Schnapper, *Le remplacement militaire*, p. 281; and Ralston, *Army of the Republic*, pp. 47–48.

8. Vinoy, *L'armée française*, pp. 98–114. The number of reenlistments by NCOs fell by nearly 50 percent between 1874 and 1880. See Monteilhet, *Les institutions militaires*, p. 171.

9. See Thoumas, *Les transformations*, 1:27–28.

10. There is, characteristically, no mention of the CSG in the self-glorifying account by Thiers, *Notes et souvenirs*, pp. 280–81.

11. "Historique de l'organisation du Conseil Supérieur de la Guerre depuis 1870," SHAT Vincennes, 7 N 36. See the sketch of the CSG by Ornano, *Gouvernement et haut-commandement*, pp. 138–46. The minutes of the CSG have been ignored by such reputable French military historians as Carrias, Girardet, and La Gorce; they have been examined by Ralston, but he disregards their significance for the presidential crisis of 1873.

12. JORF, 9 June 1872.

13. Conseil Supérieur de la Guerre (CSG), *Registre des délibérations*, 9–18 Oct. 1872, SHAT Vincennes, 1 N 2.

14. Ibid.

15. Ibid.

16. Ibid.

17. Ibid.

18. Ibid.

19. Ibid., 22–25 Oct. 1872.

20. Ibid., 8 Nov. 1872.

21. Ibid., 15 Nov. 1872.

22. Ibid., 17–26 Dec. 1872.

23. Fay, "Projet d'organisation et de mobilisation de l'armée fran-

çaise, *Journal des sciences militaires* 3 (1872):449–77; "Note explicative du projet d'organisation du Lt.-Colonel Fay," 20 Jan. 1873, SHAT Vincennes, 7 N 33.

24. CSG, *Registre des déliberations*, 9 Jan. 1873, SHAT Vincennes, 1 N 2.

25. Ibid., 31 Mar. 1873.

26. "Projet de loi sur l'organisation de l'armée active . . . ," Annexe no. 1578 (séance du 30 janvier 1873), JORF, 19 Mar. 1873. At least one historian has been deceived by a superficial reading of the *Journal officiel*: "The discussion of this law was an example of the close collaboration between government, parliament, and military circles," contends La Gorce, *La république et son armée*, p. 17.

27. Lewal, "Etudes de guerre," *Journal des sciences militaires* 4 (1873):5–40.

28. X.V., "Chronique mensuelle," *Le spectateur militaire* 31 (1873):120–38.

29. Ibid. 32 (1873):454–66. To contradict this view Thiers had his supporters as well: e.g., Ducrot, *De l'état-major et des différentes armes*; and Gillon, *Le nouveau soldat du service obligatoire*.

30. See Hanotaux, *Histoire de la France contemporaine*, 1:571–632.

31. The politicians who conspired against Thiers correctly calculated that MacMahon "would accept the command . . . like a battle station" (Broglie, *Mémoires*, 2:158). The timing may have surprised the marshal, but it is not true that he was "innocent of all these intrigues," as claims Chapman, *Third Republic*, p. 44. In fact, Thiers had abruptly faced him with the question: "Do you realize, monsieur le maréchal, that several persons are planning to put you in my place?" (Silvestre de Sacy, *Le maréchal de MacMahon*, pp. 266–71). See Mitchell, *German Influence*, pp. 76–84.

32. "Rapport fait au nom de la commission de la réorganisation de l'armée sur le projet de loi relatif à l'organisation générale de l'armée, par M. le général Chareton, membre de l'Assemblée nationale," Annexe no. 1800 (séance du 9 juin 1873), JORF, 8 July 1873. After national unification Germany had been divided into eighteen corps areas: thirteen from the former North German Confederation (including Saxony), two from Bavaria, and one each from Württemberg, Baden, and Alsace-Lorraine. See Rüdt von Collenberg, *Die deutsche Armee*, pp. 8–11. The French counterpart scheme is traced in the "Tableau de la répartition de la France en 18 corps d'armée," SHAT Vincennes, MR 2032. See Monteilhet, *Les institutions militaires*, pp. 195–96.

33. CSG, *Registre des déliberations*, 21–28 June 1873, SHAT Vincennes, 1 N 2; Du Barail, *Mes souvenirs*, 3:489–92. Some, of course,

argued that parity with Germany could not be achieved by adopting the same regional system: e.g., Chabaud-Latour, *Etude militaire*, pp. 134–36.

34. Ducrot, "Division du territoire en 18 régions de corps d'armée," 1871, SHAT Vincennes, 7 N 33; "Comparaison entre le projet conçu d'après les idées du Maréchal de MacMahon et celui de Général Ducrot"; and "Projet de M. le général Lebrun: note sur la division de la France en 18 corps d'armée," ibid., MR 2032.

35. Du Barail, *Mes souvenirs*, 3:459. With some exaggeration a French expert has concluded: "The military institutions of France, in all that was not conserved from a professional army, became the servile copy of the military institutions of Germany.... Thus from 1871 to 1914, in its institutions, in its doctrine, in its regulations, the entire French army lived, thought, acted in the wake of the Prussian army" (Monteilhet, *Les institutions militaires*, pp. 158–59). Similarly, see De Gaulle, *La France et son armée*, pp. 196–97.

36. Consult the summary by Ralston, *Army of the Republic*, pp. 49–57.

Chapter 3

1. For a general statement of the problem, see Contamine, *La revanche*, pp. 25–37.

2. France had some additional forces stationed in Algeria and in Rome. See Thoumas, *Les transformations*, 1:135–40.

3. Directive from Cissey, 24 July 1871, SHAT Vincennes, G^8 178.

4. Directive from Cissey (signed in his stead by General Susane), 16 Oct. 1871, ibid.; "Enquête sur le matériel d'artillerie employé pendant la guerre de 1870–1871," 16 Dec. 1871, ibid.

5. "Rapport au ministre sur les mesures à prendre pour amener les régiments d'artillerie à 30 régiments mixtes ayant la même composition," 29 Mar. 1872, ibid., XS 163; "Extrait du registre des déliberations du Comité de l'Artillerie," 8 Apr. 1872, ibid.

6. Cissey, "Instruction sur la marche à suivre pour l'exécution du décret du 20 avril 1872, relatif à l'organisation provisoire à donner aux régiments d'artillerie," 22 Apr. 1872, ibid.; "Extrait du registre des déliberations du Comité de l'Artillerie: avis sur les mesures à prendre pour l'organisation complète de l'artillerie à 36 régiments," 29 Apr. 1872, ibid., 164.

7. Fourth Bureau, "Note," 31 Aug. 1872, ibid.; Forgeot to Cissey, 4 Oct. 1872, ibid.

8. "Analyse au sujet de la formation d'une nouvelle batterie dans les 29 régiments d'artillerie stationnés en France," 13 Nov. 1872, ibid.; di-

rective from Cissey to commanding generals, 25 Nov. 1872, ibid.; For-geot to Cissey, 3 Mar. 1873, ibid.

9. CSG, *Registre des délibérations*, 21 June 1873, ibid., 1 N 2. See Mitchell, "Thiers, MacMahon, and the Conseil Supérieur de la Guerre," pp. 250–51.

10. See Thoumas, *Les transformations*, 1:146–48.

11. "Note au sujet de la création de batteries à pied destinées aux places fortes de la frontière de l'est," 12 Apr. 1874, SHAT Vincennes, XS 164; "Note relative à la création de batteries aux places fortes de la frontière nord-est, est et sud-est," 19 June 1874, ibid.; Fay to the Second Bureau, 6 July 1875, ibid., 7 N 1116.

12. "Tableau général du budget," 1873 and 1874, BN Paris, Papiers Thiers, NAF 20641.

13. Lt.-Colonel Haillot (chief of the Third Bureau), "Renseigne-ments sur l'Alsace-Lorraine," 10 Oct. 1874, SHAT Vincennes, 7 N 1106; Charles de Hell to Gontaut-Biron, 13 Jan. 1875, ibid., 7 N 1120; De-cazes to Cissey, 19 Jan. 1875, ibid.

14. Séré de Rivières, "Exposé du système défensif de la France," 20 May 1874, ibid., MR 2136.

15. See the analysis by A. Simouneau, "Les dépenses et les trésors de guerre," *Journal des sciences militaires* 13 (1876):33–56, 321–56.

16. No adequate study of Séré de Rivières has yet been written. Astonishingly, his name is not even mentioned by Carrias, *La pensée militaire française*, pp. 266–72. The best brief critique is by Doise, "La deuxième ligne."

17. The extraordinary number of committees and subcommittees spawned by the Assembly and the Ministry of War resulted in overlap-ping functions and confusions of nomenclature. The Comité de Défense met less and less frequently after 1877 until it was finally fused in 1888 with the Conseil Supérieur de la Guerre ("Note indiquant les composi-tions successives du Comité de Défense, 1872–88," SHAT Vincennes, 7 N 1803). See Jauffret, "Monsieur Thiers et le Comité de Défense."

18. "Réorganisation des frontières entre la Mer du Nord et la Médi-terranée: rapport de la sous-commission de défense," July 1873, ibid., MR 2146. The presiding officer was Marshal Canrobert, but it was Séré de Rivières who principally authored this document and who counter-signed it.

19. Ibid.; "Observations présentées par M. le général de Rivières au sujet du classement, par ordre d'urgence, des défenses intérieures entre la Meuse et Paris," 11 July 1873, ibid., 2150. The same views were elabo-rated by two close collaborators of Séré de Rivières: General Forgeot, "Note sur l'emploi des places fortes pour la défense du pays," 24 June 1873, ibid., 7 N 1786; and General Frossard, "Note rédigée par M. le

général Frossard concernant l'organisation du système défensif de la Champagne," 30 July 1873, ibid., 1821.

20. Séré de Rivières, "Considerations sur la reconstitution de la frontière de l'Est," 15 Nov. 1873, ibid., MR 2150; "Exposé du système défensif de la France," 20 May 1874, ibid., 2136; and "Organisation du nouveau système défensif," 10 Nov. 1875, ibid., 7 N 1787. Authorship is uncertain of a "Note sur le rassemblement d'une armée sur la frontière du Nord dans le cas de la violation de la neutralité de la Belgique par l'Allemagne," 8 Feb. 1876, ibid., 1812.

21. Among the papers of Marshal Canrobert is a memo by Séré de Rivières in favor of an "intimate alliance" between mobile and static defense, "Considérations générales sur l'organisation défensive de la France," 1876, ibid., 1803. Among his strongest critics was General Ducrot, "Coup d'oeil général sur la frontière de l'Est," 1874, ibid., 1821. This internal debate was reported from Paris by a German agent to Brandt, 13 July 1875, AA Bonn, I.A.B.c 81, Bd. 1. Séré de Rivières, who favored investing the military governors of major fortresses with considerable authority, had to settle for a vague compromise (Commission des places fortes, procès-verbal, 15 Mar. 1877, SHAT Vincennes, 7 N 1803).

22. Third Bureau, "Note faisant ressortir les opinions émises au sujet de la création et du développement des places d'Epinal, Toul et Verdun dans la sein de la Sous-Commission de Défense présidée par le Maréchal de Canrobert, du Comité de Défense et du Conseil Supérieur de la Guerre," Dec. 1893, ibid., 1826.

23. Thiers, Notes et souvenirs, pp. 327–29. See O'Brien, "L'Embastillement de Paris."

24. "Mémoire sur l'avant-projet des améliorations à introduire dans le système de défense de Paris," 20 Mar. 1874, BN Paris, Papiers Thiers, NAF 20645.

25. "Rapport fait au nom de la commission de l'armée chargée d'examiner le projet de loi relatif aux nouveaux forts à construire autour de Paris," JORF, 21 Mar. 1874; ibid., 28 Mar. 1874. See Saint-Marc Girardin, Chabaud-La-Tour, pp. 16–17; and Carrias, La pensée militaire française, p. 272.

26. Vauban (i.e., Thiers) was defended by Prévost, Des fortresses françaises pendant la guerre de 1870–1871, and attacked by P. Poulet, "Etude sur le système de défense de la France," Le spectateur militaire 37 (1874):5–28, 337–52.

27. An analysis of the French fortification system ("Befestigungswesen") from a German agent to Brandt, 9 Dec. 1873, AA Bonn, II.B.10, Bd. 5; and a report from the German military attaché Major von Bülow to the Auswärtiges Amt, 20 Feb. 1874, ibid., I.A.B.c 79, Bd. 1.

28. Canini, "Géographie militaire."

29. Séré de Rivières, "Rapport sur l'organisation de la frontière du Nord," Apr. 1876, SHAT Vincennes, MR 2150; and "Considérations sur les attaques qui pourraient être dirigées contre la frontière de Jura," July 1877, ibid.; General Melchior, "Etat des moyens défensifs du 5eme groupe," 18 June 1879, ibid., 7 N 1826; Duc d'Aumale to Gresley, 30 Aug. 1879, ibid. 1810.

30. "Historique des plans I (1874) à XVI (variante no. 2), 1874–1913," ibid., 1737.

31. Speaking of the third revised plan of defense in 1882, Minister of War Billot confirmed that "in the present state of affairs, a single plan of concentration has been fully studied and could perhaps be implemented if we were to have war with Germany tomorrow" (CSG, *Registre des délibérations*, 21 June 1882, ibid., 1 N 3).

32. General Frossard, "Note sur les ouvrages de fortification à établir pour reconstituer la défense de la frontière nord-est de la France et pour la défensive intérieure entre cette frontière et Paris," 7 Apr. 1872, BN Paris, Papiers Thiers, NAF 20644.

33. "Historique des plans I (1874) à XVI (variante no. 2), 1874–1913," SHAT Vincennes, 7 N 1737; General Ferron, "Examen critique du plan de concentration contre l'Allemagne," 20 Feb. 1883, ibid., 1789.

34. "Table comparative des forces françaises et allemandes dans une zone de 100 kilomètres de chaque côté de la frontière de l'Est," 16 Mar. 1882, ibid., 1825; "Rapport sur les plans de concentration en 1883," in CSG, *Registre des délibérations*, 7 Apr. 1883, ibid., 1 N 3. A week later the current minister of war, General Thibaudin, concluded that "if we do not create new formations, we will necessarily be inferior to the Germans solely with our front-line troops" (14 Apr. 1883, ibid.).

35. Saint-Vallier to Barthélémy Saint-Hilaire, 8 July 1881, ibid., 5 N 1. The Nancy fortifications remained, as they had been earlier described, "altogether hypothetical" despite many years of discussion (Lt.-Colonel Antoine, "Rapport du chef du génie sur la fixation de l'armement et des garnisons des ouvrages projetés autour de Nancy," 30 Dec. 1875, ibid., 7 N 1825).

36. Courcy to Campenon, 9 Jan. 1882, ibid.; Chanzy to Billot, 5 Mar. 1882, ibid.; Billot to Chanzy, 4 Apr. 1882, ibid.; CSG, *Registre des délibérations*, 22 June 1882, ibid., 1 N 3.

37. See Monteilhet, *Les institutions militaires*, p. 196.

38. See Grasser, "Un exemple de fortifications"; and Ralston, *Army of the Republic*, pp. 353–55.

39. "Emploi des chemins de fer pour la concentration de l'armée prussienne en 1870–1871," *Bulletin militaire de l'étranger*, no. 2 (6 Nov. 1871). In 1872 this journal was retitled *Revue militaire de l'étranger* and adopted as the official organ of the Second Bureau in the Ministry of War. See Thomas, "Armies and the Railway Revolution."

40. Jacqmin, *Les chemins de fer*, pp. 241–78 and passim; *Journal des sciences militaires* 4 (1873):147–49. Another anonymous author, noting that many ideas put into practice by the Germans in 1870 had earlier been expounded but not adopted in France, recalled the fable of the hare and the tortoise: "La nouvelle instruction prussienne sur le service des étapes et des chemins de fer en temps de guerre," *Revue militaire de l'étranger*, no. 66 (26 Nov. 1872).

41. Captain Noix, "De l'emploi des chemins de fer pour les mouvements stratégiques," *Journal des sciences militaires* 4 (1873):167–96.

42. JORF, 28 May–18 June 1873; report by Major von Bülow to the Auswärtiges Amt, 15 June 1873, AA Bonn, I.A.B.c 78, Bd. 2.

43. French agent's report from Hamburg, 9 Sept. 1873, APP Paris, B A/311.

44. Another aspect of the question—the political confrontation between financial "oligarchs" (e.g., Léon Say) and bourgeois republicans (e.g., Eugène Spuller)—is discussed by Elwitt, *Making of the Third Republic*, pp. 103–35.

45. This agenda was first outlined in a proposal by General Lebrun, who thought it necessary to construct "for *each* territorial region a major railway permitting the rapid transportation of its troops to the frontier most seriously threatened." He also echoed Jacqmin in urging a standardization of procedures for rolling stock to ensure "unity, method, order" and to avoid the improvisations that had disrupted French logistics in 1870 ("Projet de M. le général Lebrun: note sur la division de la France en 18 corps d'armée," [Aug. 1873], SHAT Vincennes, MR 2032).

46. JORF, 18–23 Mar. 1877. The debate was accurately summarized in a report from Wesdehlen to Bülow, 27 Mar. 1877, AA Bonn, I.A.B.c 79, Bd. 13.

47. For example, an article under the pseudonym Major X, "Les chemins de fer allemands et les chemins de fer français au point de vue de la concentration des armées," *Journal des sciences militaires* 23 (1879):5–16; and Captain Samion, "De la nécessité d'un régiment des chemins de fer," *Le spectateur militaire* 11 (1880):5–32.

48. Baum, "Un chemin de fer militaire en Prusse," *Journal des sciences militaires* 18 (1877):231–40. In the same vein, the retired inspector-general of the school of Ponts-et-Chaussées, Pierre Gustave Charié-Marsaines, wrote: "France has paid dearly enough for its lack of organization. . . . [Our] rivals have provided, in this regard, examples that it would be inexcusable not to follow" (Charié-Marsaines, "Mémoire sur les chemins de fer considérés au point de vue militaire," *Le spectateur militaire* 4 [1879]:161–88).

49. See Mitchell, *German Influence*, pp. 190–92. The military significance of the Freycinet plan was explained in an attaché's report forwarded from Hohenlohe to Bülow, 25 Nov. 1878, AA Bonn, I.A.B.c 79,

Bd. 27. This facet of the problem is ignored by Gonjo, "Le 'Plan Freycinet' "; Elwitt, *Making of the Third Republic*, pp. 136–69; and Weber, *Peasants into Frenchmen*, pp. 209–11.

50. Fourth Bureau, "Rapport fait au ministre. Analyse: nouvelles lignes de chemins de fer à classer dans le réseau d'intérêt général," 12 May 1881, SHAT Vincennes, 7 N 2016; Freycinet, *Souvenirs, 1878-1893*, pp. 11–18.

51. "Des zones de rassemblement de nos armées en cas de guerre avec l'Allemagne, dans l'hypothèse où l'Italie resterait neutre et où les neutralités de la Suisse et de la Belgique seraient respectées," CSG, *Registre des délibérations*, 29 Apr. 1878, SHAT Vincennes, 1 N 3; "Very confidential" directive from Minister of War Farre to all corps commanders, 20 May 1880, ibid., 7 N 2016; directive from Farre to the directors of engineering (*génie*), 2 July 1881, ibid., 37.

52. These developments may be followed in various memoranda from the Fourth Bureau of the Ministry of War, e.g., "Liste des travaux de chemins de fer à exécuter d'urgence dans l'intérêt de la défense du pays," 27 Jan. 1882, ibid., 2016; "Envoi des demi-fiches du nouveau plan de transport," 24 Apr. 1883, ibid.; and "Bases de préparation du plan de concentration de 1887," 13 Aug. 1886, ibid.

53. "Rapport fait au ministre au sujet du Comité de l'Artillerie," 15 June 1871, ibid., 9 N 4; Cissey to Forgeot, 14 Aug. 1871, ibid.; Lt.-Colonel Allan, "Effets du tir de l'artillerie contre l'enceinte et les forts de Paris," 21 Aug. 1871, ibid. A military subcommittee met in Versailles to consider the deployment of artillery weapons and concluded as follows: "We think that the machine gun is a good weapon and capable of giving excellent results, on the condition that it is properly employed. It is a weapon of opportunity. . . . We will not count it in the artillery, and it will have a role apart and completely distinct" ("Conférence sur l'organisation de l'artillerie de campagne," 14 Mar. 1873, ibid., MR 1903). See Hutchison, *Machine Guns*, pp. 9–27; and Ellis, *Social History of the Machine Gun*, pp. 63–65.

54. Cissey to Thiers, 23 Jan. 1873, BN Paris, Papiers Thiers, NAF 20627; Thiers to Reffye, 16 Feb. 1873, ibid., 20628; Schneider to Thiers, 15 Apr. 1873, ibid.; Thiers to Schneider, 20 Apr. 1873, ibid. See Challéat, *Histoire technique*, pp. 272–78.

55. Cissey's remarks were appended to the "Rapport fait au ministre: analyse au sujet de l'Etat-Major général et de l'Etat-major particulier de l'Artillerie," 1 Feb. 1873, SHAT Vincennes, 9 N 4.

56. "Note sur le recrutement des officiers nécessaires à l'arme de l'artillerie," 29 Apr. 1873, ibid., XS 164.

57. Service de l'Artillerie, "Note: personnel de l'Artillerie," 15 Apr. 1875, ibid., 9 N 4; "Instruction faisant suite à celles du 15 avril 1875 et du 2 janvier 1876 . . . en ce qui concerne l'artillerie," 2 Nov. 1876, ibid.;

"Notes et observations relatives . . . au service des places fortes," 7 Dec. 1876, ibid.

58. Berthaut to Canu, 6 Dec. 1876, ibid. The policy of *dédoublement* had already been favored by Berthaut's predecessor General de Cissey.

59. "Extraits du Registre des déliberations du Comité de l'Artillerie," 13 Mar. 1877, ibid., 40; General Chappe, "Etude d'un projet de modification de l'organisation de l'Artillerie," 1 Oct. 1877, ibid., 4.

60. A special committee headed by General Schnéegans found the Reffye cannon to be "excellent." ("Commission d'expériences exécutées avec des canons de 5 en bronze, système de Reffye," 1 Oct. 1873, ibid., MR 2130).

61. Langlois, *Les artilleries de campagne*, pp. 8–16. See Challéat, *Histoire technique*, pp. 272–78; and Thoumas, *Les transformations*, 2:135–37.

62. For instance, the article by P. Guzman and A. Roswag, "Déscriptions du matériel d'artillerie prussien," *Journal des sciences militaires* 3 (1872):382–421. Meanwhile, of course, the Germans also kept watch on the French: military report by Major von Bülow, 25 Oct. 1872, AA Bonn, I.A.B.c 75, Bd. 2.

63. "Mémoire: armée de Versailles, 4e corps, 2e division, artillerie," 12 Mar. 1873, SHAT Vincennes, MR 1983.

64. Rochebouët to Du Barail, 29 Nov. 1873, quoted by Challéat, *Histoire technique*, p. 290.

65. Canu to Cissey, 25 May 1875, ibid., pp. 305–11.

66. "Fabrication de canons Krupp pour la Russie," *Revue d'artillerie*, 11 (1877–78):576–78; "Renseignements statistiques sur l'usine Krupp à Essen," *Revue militaire de l'étranger*, no. 387 (26 Jan. 1878); "Fabrication de bouches à feu à l'usine Krupp," ibid., no. 393 (9 Mar. 1878).

67. Thomas Anquetil, "Etude sur l'artillerie," *Le spectateur militaire* 14 (1876):408–27.

68. Not until 1885 was the Thomas-Gilchrist process described in detail by a French military publication, which noted that little use had as yet been made of steel by the French artillery: "Nevertheless, everything leads one to expect that, as in all other branches, it will soon be constrained to make use of it" (A. Aubanel, "Nouveaux progrès de la déphosphoration des fontes et des aciers," *Revue d'artillerie* 25 [1885]:521–38; 26 [1885]:6–21, 201–25).

69. "Commission de revision des lois militaires, 4e sous-commission: projet d'organisation de l'artillerie à pied et exposé des motifs," 13 Mar. 1879, SHAT Vincennes, MR 1983; "Réorganisation de l'artillerie," 7 July 1879, ibid., 7 N 46.

70. "Extrait du Registre des déliberations du Comité de l'Artillerie,"

ibid., 9 N 40. Some changes were effected on 24 July 1883 by the creation of ninety-six new batteries of fortress artillery and the suppression of forty-five field batteries plus fifty-seven supply companies ("Note faisant ressortir la nécessité d'une augmentation des batteries de campagne," 1888, ibid. 7 N 46).

71. Campenon to Grévy, Mar. 1884, ibid., 9 N 26.

72. Report by French agent "A. no. 1" to the Prefecture of Police, 18 Jan. 1874, APP Paris, B A/311.

73. "Influence de la constitution des projectiles sur les effets qu'ils peuvent produire dans diverses circonstances de guerre," *Revue d'artillerie* 27 (1885–86):211–26, 297–314. Made from picric acid, melinite was discovered in the early 1880s by a young chemist named Eugène Turpin.

74. "Rapport sommaire sur les expériences faites du 11 aôut au 22 septembre 1886 au fort de Malmaison," 22 Sept. 1886, SHAT Vincennes, 7 N 46.

75. "Rapport aux comités techniques de l'artillerie et du génie," 1 Mar. 1909, ibid., 11. See Doise, "La deuxième ligne," pp. 143–44.

Chapter 4

1. "Tableau présentant pour chaque année, depuis 1830 jusqu'en 1870, la composition des divers corps de l'armée," SHAT Vincennes, MR 2121. In the mid-1850s the cavalry had reached 85,000 men and the artillery 50,000; but by 1870 those numbers had diminished respectively to 50,000 and 35,000.

2. See Ralston, *Army of the Republic*, pp. 34–35.

3. General de Miribel, "Note sur l'organisation des corps de réserve," 20 Jan. 1877, SHAT Vincennes, 7 N 33. See Howard, *Franco-Prussian War*, pp. 57–71.

4. Gabriac to Favre, 9 July 1871, MAE Paris, Allemagne 1. See Sor, *Les fusils*, pp. 44–80.

5. Manteuffel to William, 24 Nov. 1871, AA Bonn, I.D.44.

6. The Gras rifle adopted by France in 1874 was similar to the German Mauser in caliber (11 millimeters), rapidity (one shot every four seconds), and weight of bullet (25 grams). Both employed a metal clip. The French weapon was slightly lighter (4.78 kilograms with bayonet) than its German counterpart (5.23). See Thoumas, *Les transformations*, 2:100–108; and Challéat, *Histoire technique*, pp. 323–28.

7. P.F., "Sur quelques points de l'organisation militaire," *Le spectateur militaire* 26 (1872):5–26.

8. Ralston, *Army of the Republic*, pp. 59–60.

9. A. Simouneau, "Etude sur les cadres et le budget de l'armée en France," *Journal des sciences militaires* 6 (1873):368–420.

10. X.V., "Le 1er janvier 1874," *Le spectateur militaire* 34 (1874):5–23.

11. CSG, *Registre des déliberations,* 28 Feb. 1874, SHAT Vincennes, 1 N 3. Deligny received strong support from Marshal Canrobert and General Lallemand.

12. Captain P. Amos, "A propos de la tactique et de l'instruction de l'infantrie: comparaison de l'esprit de la tactique française avec l'esprit de la tactique prussienne," 1873, ibid., MR 2008. With the endorsement of General Berthaut, this report was forwarded from the Second Bureau to Minister of War Cissey, 23 Mar. 1873 (ibid.).

13. An unsigned editorial advocated a compromise between "the inconveniences of the Prussian dispersed formation and . . . the French serried or deep ranks" ("Projet d'étude de la tactique de l'infantrie," *Journal des sciences militaires* 2 [1872]:321–38). But more typical of that journal was this conclusion: "In sum, if we compare the tactics of the French and those of the Germans during the war of 1870–71, we see that there is much more to be copied from the latter than from the former" (Captain E. Poirot, "Etude sur la tactique de détail de l'infantrie," ibid. 7 [1874]:99–134).

14. The "truly practical spirit" of the Germans was praised by the same editorialist in "Les manoeuvres d'automne de l'armée prussienne," *Revue militaire de l'étranger,* no. 16 (16 Mar. 1872).

15. Report of German agent to Brandt, 16 Dec. 1873, AA Bonn, II.B.10, Bd. 5; A. Simouneau, "Les effectifs, les cadres et les budgets des armées européennes," *Journal des sciences militaires* 10 (1875):191–224.

16. Canrobert to Cissey, 5 Mar. 1873, SHAT Vincennes, MR 2134.

17. Report by Major von Bülow, 15 Aug. 1874, AA Bonn, I.A.B.c 79, Bd. 3. The Germans were extremely well informed about French mobilization plans. Copies of all three parts of the December 1875 plan —"Dispositions générales," "Dispositions à prendre en temps de paix pour préparer la mobilisation," and "Dispositions à prendre au moment de la mobilisation"—were somehow obtained and forwarded to Berlin by Major von Bülow, 28 Feb. 1877 (ibid., Bd. 13).

18. J. Moch, "Etude sur l'organisation du régiment d'infantrie," *Journal des sciences militaires* 8 (1874):506–35.

19. For the most part the Germans were content to follow the French military debates from a distance, convinced that the reform legislation was "cancerous" because of "a series of compromises between two basically contradictory principles" ("Militärischer Bericht Nr. 100 des Majors von Bülow, betreffend den Stand der Militärgesetzgebung bei dem gegenwärtigen Schlusse der Nationalversammlung," 4 Jan. 1876, AA Bonn, I.A.B.c 79, Bd. 8).

20. Report by Major von Bülow, 23 Mar. 1875, ibid., 81, Bd. 1;

Wesdehlen to the Auswärtiges Amt, 11, 14 May 1875, ibid., 79, Bd. 6.

21. Kamecke to Bismarck, 3 July 1875, ibid., 83, Bd. 2. In this report General von Kamecke evaluated French hesitations as symptomatic of "the current unreadiness of the French army and the fear of the French government of an imminent war with Germany."

22. Report of French agent to the Prefecture of Police, 21 June 1875, APP Paris, B A/312; report of German agent to Brandt, 3 July 1875, AA Bonn, I.A.B.c 81, Bd. 1. See Defrasne, "L'armée française."

23. See Ralston, *Army of the Republic*, pp. 96–100.

24. Lt.-Colonel Martin de Brettes, "Etudes sur le budget de guerre en 1876," *Le spectateur militaire* 42 (1876):255–80; "Chronique mensuelle," ibid. 43 (1876):276–86.

25. Memorandum by General Berthaut, 1876, SHAT Vincennes, 5 N 1.

26. See Ralston, *Army of the Republic*, pp. 96–101.

27. Gambetta to Juliette Adam, 20 Sept., 17 Oct. 1876, BN Paris, NAF 13815.

28. See Bury, *Gambetta and the Making*, pp. 356–73. Porch comments: "The fact that these demands were not met earlier had less to do with conservative pressure than with Gambetta's fears that an official declaration of three years' service might provoke Bismarck" (*March to the Marne*, pp. 27–29).

29. "Deuxième proposition Laisant," 14 Dec. 1876, SHAT Vincennes, 7 N 33; Lt.-Colonel Haillot (chief of the Third Bureau), "Note pour le ministre," 27 Feb. 1877, ibid., 1954.

30. "Commission d'examen de la proposition Laisant," 1876, ibid., 7 N 33. Berthaut made no bones about "the inferiority of our cadre of noncommissioned officers," and he consequently urged the creation of separate training schools for NCOs "analogous to those that exist in many foreign armies" (Berthaut to General Garnier, 27 Dec. 1876, ibid., 5 N 1). The Comité de l'Artillerie considered the reduction to three years "a grave danger" because the time would be too brief for proper training in that branch of service ("Avis sur les conséquences qui pourraient avoir, en ce qui concerne l'armée de l'artillerie, la réduction à trois ans," 16 Feb. 1877, ibid., 9 N 40. The same negativism generally pervaded the entire Ministry of War. See "Note résumant les divers avis exprimés par les bureaux de la direction du personnel consultés au sujet de la proposition de loi Laisant," 1877, ibid., 7 N 33.

31. "1876," *Le spectateur militaire* 46 (1877):5–24. A police informant described rumors spread by the Bonapartists that Thiers had received letters from Moltke and Manteuffel with congratulations for his success in maintaining five-year military service. Thiers issued a public denial, but it was "too late" to offset the bad impression (report by the agent "Léon," 12 Apr. 1877, APP Paris, B A/1280).

32. See Mitchell, *German Influence*, p. 148.

33. "Chronique mensuelle," *Le spectateur militaire* 50 (1878):440–49. Another editorial made clear the potential importance of the German example for French maneuvers: "Of all the military institutions that we have borrowed or recovered from Prussia, none is more effective when it is seriously implemented" ("1880," *Revue militaire de l'étranger*, no. 488 [3 Jan. 1880]).

34. CSG, *Registre des déliberations*, 3, 7 June 1878, SHAT Vincennes, 1 N 3.

35. "Notes sur l'armée française en 1877," *Le spectateur militaire* 49 (1877):254–67. A British expert made much the same analysis: "In all the great military reforms effected and still being carried out in France, the Prussian army has been the model followed.... In their tactical arrangements, in the distribution of their troops into brigades, divisions, and army corps, the German organization has been carefully copied, and above all things it has been sought to give to their reformed army that power of rapidly passing from a peace to a war footing which has been brought to such a high state of perfection in Germany" (Wolseley, "France as a Military Power").

36. Gresley, "Note sur le service de trois ans," 1879, SHAT Vincennes, 7 N 33; and "Résumé des procès-verbaux de la commission chargée d'étudier la proposition Laisant," 1879, ibid. The new program was implemented by Gresley's successor as minister of war, General Farre, "Note sur le service de 40 mois," 14 Dec. 1880, ibid., 2.

37. Despite the laws of 22 June 1878 and 23 July 1881, which were designed to improve the lot of NCOs (through better housing, personal privileges, more lenient discipline and punishment, wine instead of water at the table, and so on), the shortage remained, and the government's only recourse was to offer handsome bounties for reenlistment ("Chronique mensuelle," *Le spectateur militaire* 7 (1879):141–52; CSG, *Registre des déliberations*, 18 Apr. 1883, SHAT Vincennes, 1 N 3). The problem was reviewed in an anonymous editorial, "Les sous-officiers d'infantrie et le service militaire actif de trois ans," *Journal des sciences militaires* 22 (1879):351–90.

38. "Le programme de 1880," *Le spectateur militaire* 8 (1880):10–19.

39. Farre wrote: "The supporters of three-year service invoke the example of Germany. We are often led to imitate too slavishly what is done by our powerful neighbors without taking into account existing differences in social conditions and customs." Commenting on German discipline, he added: "It is perhaps an aptitude of race" (*Observations*, pp. 11–12).

40. CSG, *Registre des déliberations*, 21 Mar. 1882, SHAT Vincennes, 1 N 3.

41. "Commission temporaire de révision des lois militaires, 2ème sous-commission: rapport spécial sur la révision de l'article 34 (formation de guerre de l'armée territoriale)," 20 Feb. 1882, ibid., 5 N 1.

42. The generals were prodded by the questioning of Jules Ferry: "Would it not be possible to modify our military practices and to pursue the same course as Germany?" (CSG, *Registre des déliberations*, 7–23 Apr. 1883, ibid., 1 N 3; Farre, *Observations*, pp. 19–20).

43. Dispatch of 23 Apr. 1868 by Stoffel, *Rapports militaires*, pp. 111–13.

44. See the critique by Carrias, *La pensée militaire française*, pp. 253–57. A general comparison of the German Generalstab with the French Etat-Major has been attempted by Hittle, *Military Staff*, pp. 50–128. Also see Bond, *Victorian Army*, pp. 30–43.

45. Ducrot, *De l'état-major*, pp. 17–34.

46. Derrécagaix, *Etude sur les états-majors*, pp. 8, 29–30, 49–56.

47. See the informative chapter entitled "The Problem of the High Command: 1871–1897," by Ralston, *Army of the Republic*, pp. 138–200.

48. See Thoumas, *Les transformations*, 1:180–223.

49. The Lebrun committee was composed of eight divisional generals, four brigadier generals, and two nonvoting secretaries (of which Lt.-Colonel Fay was one). The ranking officers split 4 to 4, but the brigadiers unanimously opposed Lebrun.

50. *Projet de réorganisation du corps d'état major*.

51. The most trenchant critic of the French tradition was the director of the First Bureau in the Ministry of War, Lt.-Colonel Fay, who wrote: "Today we know the result of this system. The last war has unfortunately exposed it all too clearly. . . . It permitted us to see how the system imposed by Gouvion St. Cyr, despite his personal convictions [that were] justifiable at the time, was bad for modern armies" (Fay, "Notice sur le corps d'état-major," 1 Mar. 1872, SHAT Vincennes, MR 1999). Fay's personal dossier is available with those of other senior officers, ibid., Gx/3:57.

52. *Réorganisation du corps d'état-major*. This report was augmented by General Lebrun, "Du corps d'état-major, de la nécessité de l'organiser sur les bases nouvelles et de modifier le fonctionnement de ses officiers," 2 Feb. 1872, SHAT Vincennes, MR 1999.

53. Confidential directive by Cissey, 1 July 1872, SHAT Vincennes, G^8 179; CSG, *Registre des déliberations*, 17, 26 Dec. 1872, 9 Jan. 1873, ibid., 1 N 2.

54. CSG, *Registre des déliberations*, 7 July 1873, ibid. The same frame of mind was reflected in a perspicacious editorial by E. Dusaert, "Réorganisation du corps d'état-major," *Journal des sciences militaires* 5 (1873):55–68.

55. "Militärischer Bericht Nr. 102 des Majors von Bülow, betreffend die höheren Führer der heutigen französischen Armee," 25 Feb. 1876, AA Bonn, I.A.B.c 79, Bd. 8.

56. Favé, "La stratégie et le corps d'état-major," *Journal des sciences militaires* 20 (1878):135–40.

57. An anonymous editorialist of the *Journal des sciences militaire* commented on the proposed legislation: "One cannot deny that it rests on a new principle adopted before us by all other modern armies: an open general staff" (22 [1879]:5–28).

58. "Note à l'appui du tableau comparatif des états-majors français et prussien," 1880, SHAT Vincennes, MR 1999. See Kuntz, *L'officier français*, pp. 57–64; and Ralston, *Army of the Republic*, pp. 89–92.

59. The background is accessible in such works as Chalmin, *L'officier français*, pp. 295–326; Girardet, *La société militaire*, pp. 48–64; and Serman, *Les officiers français*, pp. 7–20.

60. The standard works on Germany are Ritter, *Staatskunst und Kriegshandwerk*, 1:125–237; Craig, *Politics of the Prussian Army*, pp. 217–54; and Demeter, *Das deutsche Offizierkorps*, pp. 74–115. Also see the comparative suggestion by Barnett, "Education of Military Elites."

61. Lewal, *La réforme de l'armée*, pp. 1–7. Lewal deserves a major biography rather than the cursory treatment by such writers as Caemmerer, *Development of Strategical Science*, pp. 229–39; Carrias, *La pensée militaire française*, pp. 272–74; and Luvaas, "European Military Thought and Doctrine," pp. 69–93.

62. Lewal, "Etudes de guerre," *Journal des sciences militaires* 1 (1872):326–43. A series of articles under this title was gathered into a book the following year.

63. Lewal, *Etudes de guerre*, pp. 3, 342–45; and "Tactiques de combat," *Journal des sciences militaires* 7 (1874):321–57. It is worthwhile to quote further from the latter article: "I sense an objection from many officers: it is a Prussian importation; the French army should not be Germanized. I have already responded often in my writings to this erroneous assertion. . . . Let us admit that the Prussians have made great progress. . . . France has been in turn initiator and imitator. She has that in common with many other armies. If she is today in a period of imitation, that is her fault. She fell behind and is now obliged to recover lost time" (ibid., p. 327).

64. CSG, *Registre des déliberations*, 17, 26 Dec. 1872, SHAT Vincennes, 1 N 2.

65. Lt.-Colonel Maillot (Third Bureau), "Note pour le 2e Bureau de l'état-major général," 2 May 1874, ibid., MR 1998. The French also investigated the Bavarian military academy in Munich (Decazes to Lefebvre de Béhaine, 3 June 1874, MAE Paris, Bavière 254).

66. "L'académie de guerre de Berlin," *Revue militaire de l'étranger*,

no. 13 (1 Mar. 1872); and "L'académie de guerre de Berlin et ses conditions d'admission," ibid., no. 351 (19 May 1877). During 1873 this journal published 119 articles on Germany, 91 on Italy, 75 on Austria-Hungary, and 44 on Russia. A decade later the emphasis was still more marked: 93 articles on Germany (of which one was in twenty installments!), 38 on Italy, 35 on England, and 24 on Austria-Hungary.

67. A small handbook setting forth entrance requirements for prospective cadets in the 1880s announced categorically on the first page of instructions: "It is necessary to know German" (*Préparation à l'école supérieure de guerre*). Unfortunately, most of the pertinent literature on military academies in France is larded with patriotic hagiography: for example, Pesch, *Histoire de l'Ecole de Saint-Cyr*; Pinet, *Histoire de l'Ecole Polytechnique*; Titeux, *Saint-Cyr*; and Durosoy, *Saumur*. See the brief overview by Chalmin, "Les écoles militaires françaises jusqu'en 1914."

68. "Note sur les lois essentielles votées depuis 1832, relatives aux cadres et effectifs de l'armée," SHAT Vincennes, 7 N 33. See Laulan, *L'école militaire*, pp. 96–97.

69. See Mitchell, "Thiers, MacMahon, and the Conseil Supérieur de la Guerre," p. 247.

70. The classic statement of this view is by Girardet, *La société militaire*, pp. 185–92. But it has been challenged and to some extent qualified by Porch, *March to the Marne*, pp. 17–22.

71. Arnim to Bülow, 30 Nov. 1873, AA Bonn, I.A.B.c 78, Bd. 4. Nearly three years later a sixty-page report to Berlin reconfirmed that the political activity of the French generals was negligible: "In fact it has entirely ceased" ("Militärischer Bericht Nr. 102 des Majors von Bülow, betreffend die höheren Führer der heutigen französischen Armee," ibid., 8). See Serman, *Les officiers français*, pp. 45–84.

72. For instance, General Billot to Gambetta, 16 Mar. 1876, BN Paris, NAF 24900. As a rule the Germans were not inclined to overestimate the Bonapartist influence within the French army (Hohenlohe to Bülow, 19 Jan. 1878, AA Bonn, I.A.B.c 79, Bd. 23).

73. Bleichröder to Bismarck, 2 Feb. 1879, SF Hamburg, Bismarck Nachlass, B 15; Hohenlohe to Bismarck, 3 Feb. 1879, AA Bonn, I.A.B.c 87, Bd. 2. An unpublished notation in the German ambassador's diary suggests that the common source of these two dispatches was the journalist Blowitz: entry for 5 Feb. 1879, BA Koblenz, Hohenlohe Nachlass, XX C 7. Yet the German military attaché was confident about the loyalty of the French army to Grévy's regime, at least "until the next political upset" ("Militärischer Bericht Nr. 181 des Oberstleutnants von Bülow, betreffend einige Massregeln politischer Art u. deren Einfluss auf die Armee," 3 Mar. 1879, AA Bonn, I.A.B.c 87, Bd. 2).

74. Bernhard von Bülow to Hohenlohe, 10 Mar. 1879, BA Koblenz, Bülow Nachlass, No. 21.

75. "I am very pleased to owe my general's epaulettes to you. To the devotion that I have pledged to you as a republican, it is satisfying to add the gratitude that I owe you as an officer" (Billot to Gambetta, 29 Feb. 1880, BN Paris, NAF 24900). Among the other generals to enjoy Gambetta's direct support were Galliffet, Farre, Ferron, and surprisingly (given his involvement with the other side in the *seize mai* crisis) Miribel. See Ralston, *Army of the Republic*, pp. 155–59.

76. In addition to the works of Ritter, Craig, and Demeter cited (in note 60 of this chapter), see the biographies by Stadelmann, *Moltke und der Staat*, and Kessel, *Moltke*. These are expertly evaluated by Messerschmidt, *Militär und Politik*, pp. 8–31, 75–98.

77. See Ritter, *Staatskunst und Kriegshandwerk*, 2:33–43.

78. Ralston, *Army of the Republic*, p. 160.

79. The most authoritative account of the war gives a full measure of the disaster. During an initial encounter at Froeschwiller, in early August 1870, "nine squadrons [of French cavalry] were destroyed; it is doubtful whether a single Prussian infantryman lost his life." And later: "It does not appear that a single French horseman got within sabre-reach of any Prussian. All that their courage had done was to prove that there was no place for cavalry on a battlefield dominated by breech-loading rifles. . . . The disaster to the French cavalry emphasized that an epoch in warfare was now ended" (Howard, *Franco-Prussian War*, pp. 111–19).

80. Lt.-Colonel Warnet, "Note," 1 Aug. 1873, SHAT Vincennes, 7 N 45. See Howard, *War in European History*, p. 104.

81. Commission de Saint-Cyr, "Réorganisation de la cavalerie," 1872, SHAT Vincennes, 7 N 45; General Brahaut to Cissey, 15 Mar. 1872, ibid.; Lewal, "Tactiques de combat," *Journal des sciences militaires* 9 (1874):5–36, 175–81; "Etude tactique sur la cavalerie allemande, russe, autrichienne et française d'après un ouvrage allemand," Sept. 1874, SHAT Vincennes, 7 N 657.

82. Second Bureau, "Organisation de la cavalerie en Allemagne au point de vue de l'endivisionnement avant 1866, entre 1866–1870 et depuis 1870," 27 Nov. 1880, SHAT Vincennes, 7 N 657; "Les manoeuvres de la cavalerie française; lettre du correspondant militaire anglais," 19 Sept. 1874, ibid.

83. These estimates are from Thoumas, *Les transformations*, 1:70–73. The French inferiority of seventy-six cavalry squadrons was confirmed by Fay, "Note pour le 2e Bureau de l'Etat-Major Général," 29 Jan. 1877, SHAT Vincennes, 7 N 1116.

84. See Thoumas, *Les transformations*, 1:74.

85. This question was raised by General Du Barail, "Mémoire à

propos du role que la cavalerie indépendante pourrait être appelée à jouer dans le cas de guerre avec l'Allemagne," 12 Feb. 1875, SHAT Vincennes, 7 N 45.

86. The weakness of the French cavalry had been called to Bismarck's attention long before the embargo was imposed: "The most problematical difficulty facing the restitution of the French army is the extraordinary shortage of horses, which cannot be even remotely attenuated within France and Algeria" (Roon to Bismarck, 3 May 1872, AA Bonn, I.A.B.c 70, Bd. 132). The German military attaché in Paris, however, did not believe that the horse embargo would provide more than a temporary delay in French rearmament ("Militärischer Bericht Nr. 82 des Major von Bülows, betreffend das Pferde-Ausfuhr-Verbot in Deutschland," 16 Mar. 1875, ibid. 79, Bd. 5).

87. The extensive correspondence in early 1877 concerning grain shipments to France is contained in ibid., Bd. 12.

88. Military reports by Bülow, 4 Mar. 1877, ibid., Bd. 13; and 1 Feb. 1879, ibid., I.A.B.c 87, Bd. 1.

89. "Rapport sur la cavalerie par le capitaine Koszutski," Oct. 1879, SHAT Vincennes, 7 N 657.

90. Second Bureau, "Effectifs comparés des cavaleries étrangères," Apr. 1881, ibid.; CSG, *Registre des déliberations*, 7 Apr. 1883, ibid., 1 N 3.

91. These fragmentary statistics may be gathered from ibid., 7 N 664 and 1116.

92. "Note relative à l'exportation des chevaux" (countersigned by Charles de Freycinet as minister of war), 18 May 1888, ibid., 7 N 2. Apparently the peak was reached about 1887, when, during a single fortnight in mid-June, 389 horses were shipped directly to Germany and another 142 exported through Belgium ("Relève présentant le nombre et l'age des chevaux exportés pour l'Allemagne," 4 July 1887, ibid., 664).

93. My efforts to investigate this matter at the present German military archives in Freiburg-im-Breisgau were inconclusive. If such evidence once existed, it was presumably destroyed by a bombing raid during the Second World War.

94. General Grandin to Minister of War Ferron, 21 Aug. 1887, SHAT Vincennes, 7 N 45.

Chapter 5

1. Ferron, "Plan de campagne," 2 Apr. 1883, SHAT Vincennes, 7 N 1736.

2. "La prochaine guerre. Aperçu du théâtre des opérations," *Journal des sciences militaires* 28 (1887):20–32. Young cadets at the military academy were meanwhile exposed to a different view: "We insist again

that offense is the true mode of warfare, that it alone leads to victory" (Maillard, *Cours de tactique d'infanterie*, p. 538).

3. On the French side this zone between Verdun and Montmédy was known as the "trouée de Stenay." See Noix, *Géographie militaire*, 3:91–96; Ferron, "Projet d'ordre général dans l'hypothèse où l'ennemi, pour forcer la ligne de la Meuse entre Toul et Verdun, exécuterait un mouvement tournant au nord de la place de Verdun," 25 June 1885, SHAT Vincennes, MR 2137; Third Bureau, "Etude sur la marche possible d'une armée allemande par la Luxembourg et sur les dispositions à prendre," 30 Nov. 1887, ibid., 7 N 1812.

4. A minority view was expressed, however, by the commandant of the Ecole Supérieure de Guerre, who argued that the Germans would probably violate Belgian neutrality "whether Russia is our ally or whether she maintains her independence" (General Schnéegans, "Etude sur les moyens de lutte de la France et de l'Allemagne opposées l'une à l'autre," 15 May 1887, ibid., MR 2137). On the development of Germany's offensive blueprint, see Ritter, *Der Schlieffenplan*, pp. 13–81.

5. Février to the First Bureau, 2 July 1884, SHAT Vincennes, 7 N 1825. This secondary defense "came to be totally botched," concludes Doise, "La deuxième ligne," p. 136.

6. Lewal to Freycinet, 3 Mar. 1885, SHAT Vincennes, 5 N 1.

7. Colonel Grisot, "Note sur la frontière nord-est," 26 July 1885, ibid., 7 N 1826.

8. Captain Guitry, "Etude d'actualité sur les fortresses," *Revue d'artillerie* 29 (1886–87):421–37, 493–516; Février to Ferron, 22 Nov. 1887, SHAT Vincennes, 7 N 1825. Verdun was estimated to have only fourteen of a necessary thirty infantry companies, in "Rapport sur la situation dans laquelle se trouve la place de Verdun par suite de la réduction de la garnison d'infantrie (armée active)," 23 Dec. 1887, ibid. See Truttmann, "La fortification," pp. 55–79.

9. C. de L., "Les erreurs de la fortification actuelle," *Journal des sciences militaires* 27 (1887):64–83. This opinion was seconded by General Cosseron de Villenoisy, "Des critiques formulées contre la fortification et les ingénieurs," ibid., pp. 391–402.

10. Thoumas, *Les transformations*, 2:657.

11. *La France est-elle prête?*, pp. 6, 52–54, 99, 126, and passim. The identity of the author is impossible to establish with certainty. He may have been a German or, as rumored, a French officer who wished both to hide his identity and to lend his critique more weight by attributing it to the enemy.

12. *Pourquoi la France n'est pas prête*, pp. 76, 87, 298, and passim. The debate was continued in a more vulgar polemical style by yet another anonymous essay entitled *La France est prête!*

13. A vote on five-year conscription was deadlocked at 4 to 4 (CSG,

Registre des déliberations, 16 Jan. 1885, SHAT Vincennes, 1 N 3). Presiding at that session as the minister of war, General Lewal made no attempt to hide France's "numerical inferiority vis-à-vis Germany" (ibid., 18 Feb. 1885).

14. Cosseron de Villenoisy, "La désorganisation de l'armée française," *Journal des sciences militaires* 23 (1886):321–39; "Observations sur le projet des nouvelles lois militaires," ibid., 340–82.

15. See Dansette, *Le boulangisme*, pp. 34–44; Ralston, *Army of the Republic*, pp. 167–73; and Seager, *Boulanger Affair*, pp. 203–10.

16. Ferron, "Ce qu'il faudrait faire," [?] Jan. 1887, SHAT Vincennes, MR 2137.

17. CSG, *Registre des déliberations*, 19 June 1887, ibid., 1 N 3.

18. Gilbert, "Les nouvelles lois militaires," *Nouvelle revue*, 15 Oct., 15 Nov. 1887, reprinted in Gilbert, *Lois et institutions militaires*, pp. 3–74. See Strieter, "The French Army's Problem of Numbers."

19. Gilbert, *Lois et institutions militaires*, pp. 77–114. The proposal to have a civilian minister of war had been discussed at least since Gambetta's premiership in 1881. See Ralston, *Army of the Republic*, pp. 178–80.

20. See Mitchell, *Bismarck and the French Nation*, pp. 101–4.

21. CSG, *Registre des déliberations*, 23 Jan. 1888, SHAT Vincennes, 1 N 3.

22. See an earlier version of this section by Mitchell, "Freycinet Reforms." Also see Ralston, *Army of the Republic*, pp. 180–200.

23. Freycinet, *Souvenirs, 1878–1893*, pp. 394–95. On the army's tradition of political neutrality and the resulting inhibition of the Boulangist movement, see Porch, *March to the Marne*, pp. 6–15.

24. Since General de Cissey joined the cabinet under President Thiers in 1871, there had been seventeen executive changes in the Ministry of War.

25. Freycinet, *Souvenirs, 1878–1893*, p. 403.

26. Ibid., pp. 444–46.

27. JORF, 7 May 1890. The relevant documents are collected in an anonymously edited volume, *Recueil des lois, décrets, circulaires et décisions portant organisation du service d'état-major*. See the commentaries by Carrias, *Le danger allemand*, pp. 105–6; Ornano, *Gouvernement et haut-commandement*, pp. 139–46; and Zaniewicki, "L'oeuvre de Freycinet," pp. 55–72.

28. CSG, *Registre des déliberations*, 3 June 1889, SHAT Vincennes, 1 N 4; Freycinet, *Souvenirs, 1878–1893*, pp. 444–48.

29. "That Freycinet did not go further in this direction is understandable, for an independent and virtually irresponsible high command on the German model was too much for a French government to accept

in 1890, even if it was sponsored by a civilian politician of unimpeachably republican sentiments" (Ralston, *Army of the Republic*, p. 192).

30. CSG, *Registre des délibérations*, 6 Aug. 1888, SHAT Vincennes, 1 N 4; Gilbert, *Lois et institutions militaires*, pp. 137–72.

31. Freycinet, *Souvenirs, 1878–1893*, pp. 409–12.

32. The length of obligation for military service was raised from twenty to twenty-five years, thus making the French induction system identical in that respect to the German law of 1888. See Doumer, *Note sur la réorganisation*, pp. 45–54.

33. Challener, *French Theory*, p. 42; Moch, *L'armée d'une démocratie*, pp. 25–33. Moch's severe critique of Freycinet's military reforms was first published in 1900. It followed another by Captain Henri Choppin (Charles Delacour), who wrote in 1890: "Let us leave to the Germans their reorganization, which until now seems to have been our only precept, the undeniable cause of this multitude of changes and innovations so prejudicial to the condition of our military establishment" (*L'armée française*, p. 11).

34. CSG, *Registre des déliberations*, 13 May 1889, SHAT Vincennes, 1 N 4. Germany's standing army was estimated at about five hundred thousand men in "Les effectifs bruts et les effectifs nets de l'armée allemande," *Revue militaire de l'étranger*, no. 758 (Jan. 1891). See Kitchen, *Military History of Germany*, pp. 149–53.

35. Ropp, *War*, p. 180. The same view has been accepted by Poidevin and Bariéty, *Les relations*, pp. 126–27. Likewise, Kennan speaks of "the greatly improved strength and readiness of the French armed forces" by the end of the 1880s, and he even goes so far as to claim that they were "moderately larger than the German ones" (*Decline*, pp. 247, 415). But the archival evidence contradicts such assumptions. See Mitchell, " 'A Situation of Inferiority,' " pp. 49–51.

36. Galliffet to Freycinet, 1 Dec. 1888, SHAT Vincennes, 7 N 45; Freycinet directive to commanding generals of the army corps and to the military governors of Paris and Lyon, 20 Mar. 1889, ibid.

37. "Note: augmentation de l'artillerie de campagne," 19 June 1889, ibid., 46; "Note sur un nouveau projet d'organisation de l'artillerie allemande attribué au général de Waldersee," [?] Jan. 1889, ibid., 665; "Note sur l'organisation de l'artillerie allemande: comparaison avec l'artillerie française," 18 Mar. 1890, ibid. See Ralston, *Army of the Republic*, pp. 134–35.

38. An official summary of military planning prepared in the Ministry of War in 1913 was unambiguous as to the reason for the adoption of a scheme of *dédoublement* by the French infantry: "Given the development of German forces, it was judged necessary to adopt the organizational principle of doubling our regional forces by constituting eighteen

new army corps (corps d'armée *bis*)." This document is entitled "Historique des plans I (1874) à XVI (variante no. 2), 1874–1913," SHAT Vincennes, 7 N 1737. The inspection report was sent by the commander of the seventh army corps General de Négrier to Freycinet, [?] May 1890, ibid., 44.

39. Freycinet to Miribel, 24 Feb. 1891, ibid., 5 N 2.

40. "Situation comparative des armées française et allemande," [?] Dec. 1892, ibid., 7 N 665.

41. A document prepared in the Ministry of War explains: "To compare rationally the German budget to the French budget it is necessary to deduct from the latter expenditures that in Germany are debited to accounts other than the military allocation and that in France are totally drawn from military funding." Because these annual administrative expenses were estimated by the Second Bureau at 75 million francs, the actual discrepancy was far larger than indicated by the unadjusted figures published in the *Journal officiel*, on which military historians have heretofore relied ("Comparaison des budgets de la guerre en France et en Allemagne," [?] Dec. 1892, ibid.).

42. See Ralston, *Army of the Republic*, p. 135.

43. Gilbert, *Lois et institutions militaires*, pp. 137–72, 213–19.

44. As early as 1880 this matter was put succinctly by General Cosseron de Villenoisy to the Comité de Défense: "Isolated forts of modest size cannot withstand alone the effects of the powerful artillery that the enemy will not fail to deploy" (quoted from a document among papers of the Third Bureau, "Note faisant ressortir les opinions émises au sujet de la création et du développement des places d'Epinal, Toul et Verdun," [?] Dec. 1893, SHAT Vincennes, 7 N 1826).

45. Freycinet, *Souvenirs, 1878–1893*, pp. 412–14; CSG, *Registre des délibérations*, 6 Aug. 1888, SHAT Vincennes, 1 N 4. Although this report remained confidential, its substance was publicly restated by an anonymous editorialist who contended that the "inferior condition" of French defenses required a "radical change" and the creation of a "new system" (J.B., "L'artillerie actuelle et la fortification," *Journal des sciences militaires* 31/3 (1888):411–26; 31/4 (1888):67–97, 255–66.

46. The contemporary periodical literature on these topics is far too vast to cite, but as an example of a careful technical discussion, see Moch, "La poudre sans fumée," pp. 297–341, 393–416, 498–522.

47. CSG, *Registre des délibérations*, 7 Jan. 1889, SHAT Vincennes, 1 N 4; Saussier, "Notes sur un voyage d'étude (Hirson-Namur-Liège-Anvers-Bruxelles)," 25–28 June 1889, ibid., 7 N 1812; Ducros, "Note sur les canons à tir rapide," 17 June 1890, ibid., MR 2137.

48. "Rapport de la commission des places fortes sur les projets d'amélioration des places de Verdun, Toul, Epinal et Belfort," 1 June 1890,

ibid., 7 N 1826; Billot, "Inspection de 1894: rapport spécial sur la place de La Fère," 7 Dec. 1894, ibid., 1818.

49. Grasser, "Un exemple de fortifications"; Berthier, "Note sur les travaux de première urgence à exécuter dans les 4 grandes places de la frontière de l'Est," 5 Aug. 1898, SHAT Vincennes, 7 N 1804. This document indicates that the expenditures for the period 1888–97 were: for Verdun and Toul, 14.5 million francs each; Belfort, 11.5 million; and Epinal 9.5 million.

50. Third Bureau, "Note relative au cas de violation par l'Allemagne de la neutralité belge," 19 Oct. 1888, ibid., 1812. The question was vigorously debated among junior staff officers. One of them, Captain Pettelot, accompanied General Saussier on his inspection of Belgian fortresses and recorded the majority view at that time: "For these diverse reasons the eventuality of a major attack on the Belgian frontier may be ruled out. The sole hypothesis worthy of discussion is that of a simple diversion" ("Note relative à la violation de la neutralité belge (degré de probabilité, mesures à prendre)," 20 Mar. 1889, ibid.). But a dissenting opinion by Captain Hamel was forwarded by General Jamot to Freycinet, 26 May 1891, ibid.

51. "[Because] Verdun prevents them from turning our right flank, the enemy will probably attempt to turn our left flank; but the more he emphasizes that movement, the more he will fall into the trap that we have set for him" (Miribel, "Note sur le travail de Grouard," [?] Jan. 1890, ibid.).

52. Third Bureau, "Considérations générales sur le système défensif du Nord," 1899, ibid. Freycinet, who was serving his second term as minister of war, was instrumental in creating a new Haute Commission des Places Fortes on 25 April 1899. This body under General Brugère, who was then the military governor of Paris, had the assignment of executing new construction on the eastern frontier and of supervising the declassification of indefensible fortresses in the north. It is noteworthy that the recording secretary of the committee was a young colonel named Joseph Joffre. See Brugère to Galliffet, 18 Nov. 1899, ibid.

53. "We must be content to prepare the elements of an active defense based on several good installations [that are] virtually invulnerable and very well provisioned," observed—not for the first time—Séré de Rivières ("Réorganisation défensive du territoire," 1898, ibid., 1804).

54. Freycinet to Haillot, 13 Sept. 1888, ibid., 1817; "Rapport: place de Longwy," 6 Oct. 1888, ibid.; Jamont to Freycinet, 3 Mar. 1891, ibid., 1825; First Bureau and Third Bureau, "Organisation défensive des frontières du Nord et de l'Est," 20 May 1910, ibid., 1821.

55. "Note du Colonel Garnier, directeur du génie, sur l'opportunité de déclasser et de démanteler certaines places fortes de la direction de

Maubeuge," 24 Feb. 1888, ibid., MR 2136; Jamont to Freycinet, 14 Nov. 1888, ibid., 7 N 1813; Laurent, "Mémoire sur la réorganisation du système défensif de la France," 26 Sept. 1898, ibid., 1736; Third Bureau, "Considérations générales sur le système défensif du Nord," 1889, ibid., 1812.

56. Copies of lectures delivered at the Ecole Supérieure de Guerre may be found in the library there: e.g., Maillard, *Cours de tactique*, pp. 734–51; and Bonnal, *L'art nouveau en tactique*, pp. 9–17, 43–54. See Bonnal's tribute to Maillard, *Note posthume*, pp. 41–45; and the critique of them both by Carrias, *La pensée militaire française*, pp. 278–84.

57. A secret memorandum circulated by the Third Bureau estimated that an additional allocation of 250 million francs would be necessary to refurbish fortresses on the eastern frontier alone. "Note au sujet du classement des places fortes constituant le système défensif de la France," a document transmitted with his personal approval by Freycinet to Jamont, 30 Jan. 1889, SHAT Vincennes, 7 N 1804.

58. The chief disciple of Maillard and Bonnal, and Joffre's most important mentor, was Ferdinand Foch. See Luvaas, "European Military Thought and Doctrine," pp. 79–81; Contamine, *La victoire de la Marne*, pp. 82–102; and Williamson, *Politics of Grand Strategy*, pp. 205–6.

59. First Bureau and Third Bureau, "Organisation défensive des frontières du Nord et de l'Est," 20 May 1910, SHAT Vincennes, 7 N 1821.

60. See Mitchell, "Xenophobic Style," pp. 414–25. The background is presented in such standard works as Baumont, *Aux sources de l'affaire*; Chapman, *Dreyfus Case*; and Johnson, *France and the Dreyfus Affair*. Also see the more recent account by Wilson, *Ideology and Experience*, pp. 290–300.

61. For the rest see Ralston, *Army of the Republic*, pp. 203–51; Mitchell, " 'A Situation of Inferiority,' " pp. 60–62; and Porch, *March to the Marne*, pp. 54–72.

Chapter 6

1. Three standard surveys are those of Latreille et al., *Histoire du catholicisme en France*; Dansette, *Histoire religieuse de la France contemporaine*; and Coutrot and Dreyfus, *Les forces religieuses dans la société française*. A convenient overview is provided by McManners, *Church and State in France*.

2. "Procès-verbal de la prestation de serment par Mgr. Rossat (Louis), Evêque de Gap," 27 Jan. 1841, AN Paris, F^{19} 5592.

3. See Prost, *Histoire de l'enseignement en France*, pp. 28–30, 172–77.

4. "Dispositions relatives à la remise de la barette aux cardinaux et

à la prestation de serment des archevêques et évêques," 1855, AN Paris, F¹⁹ 5592.

5. Rouland to Drouyn de Lhuys, 11 Jan. 1863, ibid., 1954; Rouland to Chigi, 11 Jan. 1863, ibid.

6. *Le moniteur universel,* 17 May 1870.

7. See Lösch, *Döllinger und Frankreich,* pp. 247–343; Latreille et al., *Histoire du catholicisme en France,* 3:392–99; Aubert, "Das Vatikanische Konzil," pp. 774–91; and Mitchell, "Partners in Failure." Controversy about the pope's personal role in forcing the proclamation of the infallibility dogma has been stirred by the appearance of an extremely critical and massively documented work by Hasler, *Pius IX.* See the appreciation of Hasler by Weitlauff, "Pius IX. und die Dogmatisierung der päpstlichen Unfehlbarkeit."

8. Directive from Ollivier to French bishops, 26 July 1870, AN Paris, F¹⁹ 5608–9.

9. For the period from 27 July to 18 August 1870, see the replies to Ollivier from the archbishops of Rennes, Besançon, Strasbourg, and Rouen, as well as the bishops of Nevers and Dijon (ibid.). The citation is from a letter by Ollivier to the bishop of Gap, 25 Aug. 1870, ibid. See Gadille, *La pensée et l'action,* 1:207–10.

10. For example, "Lettre pastorale de Monseigneur l'évêque de Gap," 12 May 1871, AN Paris, F¹⁹ 5608–9.

11. Dupanloup to Thiers, 19 Nov. 1870, BN Paris, Papiers Thiers, NAF 20620.

12. Bismarck to Edwin von Manteuffel, 24, 28 Dec. 1870, 6 Jan. 1871, GW 14²: 1374, 1378, 1383. Gadille, *La pensée et l'action,* 1:210–11. On the general circumstances, see Geuss, *Bismarck und Napoleon III.,* pp. 294–312; Giesberg, *Treaty of Frankfort,* pp. 67–83; and Mitchell, *Bismarck and the French Nation,* pp. 55–71.

13. Chigi to Antonelli, 22 Feb., 2 Mar. 1871, ASV Rome, SdS 393, rubrica 165; 12 Mar. 1871, ASV Rome, SdS 394, rubrica 242; Thiers to Favre, 10 Mar. 1871, BN Paris, Papiers Thiers, NAF 20623.

14. Directive issued by Thiers, 19 Mar. 1871, AA Bonn, Fasc. 1, Nr. 11, Bd. 1; Chigi to Antonelli, 21 Mar. 1871, ASV Rome, SdS 394, rubrica 242. Accordingly, Chigi presented his diplomatic credentials to the "government of the republic" (JORF, 1 Apr. 1871).

15. Favre to Chigi, 6 Apr. 1871, ASV Rome, SdS 393, rubrica 165. The amount of the contribution was 10,000 francs. Another 30,000 francs were later presented by the pope to help the needy of Paris after the Commune (Favre to Chigi, 5 June 1871, ibid.). See Gadille, *La pensée et l'action,* 1:252–53.

16. Directive from Simon to French bishops, 20 May 1871, AN Paris, F¹⁹ 5580.

17. Prefect of the Somme to Ernest Picard (minister of the interior),

24 May 1871, AN Paris, F⁷ 12389. The reply, undated and unsigned, was drafted on stationery of the Ministry of the Interior (ibid.). Its transmission may have been interrupted by Picard's resignation from the cabinet on 31 May.

18. Mayor of Pont-à-Mousson to Simon, 7 Apr. 1871, ibid., F¹⁹ 5608–9; Simon to the mayor of Pont-à-Mousson, [?] Apr. 1871, ibid.; bishop of Nancy to the mayor of Pont-à-Mousson, 28 May 1871, ibid.

19. Monsignor Landriot to Simon, 30 May 1871, ibid.; Simon to Rémusat, 1 June 1871, ibid. A similar incident near Châlons was described by Monsignor Meignan to Simon, 1 Sept. 1871, 3 Jan. 1872, ibid.

20. For further details see Mitchell, *German Influence*, pp. 43–46.

21. Bernard d'Harcourt to Thiers, 30 May 1871, BN Paris, Papiers Thiers, NAF 20622. In dealing with church officials, Thiers deliberately identified himself with Harcourt's view and frequently reassured the Vatican of his constancy: "Moreover, monsieur Thiers has given me no indication of modifying in any way his political attitude toward the Holy See" (Chigi to Antonelli, 27 Dec. 1871, ASV Rome, SdS 398, rubrica 165).

22. Rouland to Chigi, 11 Jan. 1863, AN Paris, F¹⁹ 1954. On this issue see Gadille, *La pensée et l'action*, 1:282–88.

23. Thiers to Pius IX, 19 Apr. 1871, ASV Rome, SdS 394, rubrica 248.

24. Chigi to Simon, 8 May 1871, AN Paris, Papiers Simon, 87 AP/10. During Simon's ministry an *entente préalable* was reached with Chigi on eight of eleven bishops appointed and on all five archbishops. See Bertocci, *Jules Simon*, pp. 151–80. Although well informed, this account underestimates the severity of the conflict between Simon and the hierarchy.

25. Simon to Chigi, 9 May 1871, AN Paris, Papiers Simon, 87 AP/10. It is therefore dubious that one may properly describe Simon's main purpose from the beginning as a "close collaboration" with the nuncio, as does Gadille, *La pensée et l'action*, 1:285–86.

26. "Extrait d'une lettre particulière écrite par Mgr. Forcade, évêque de Nevers," 25 June 1871, AN Paris, Papiers Simon, 87 AP/10. Rumors about Darboy's successor meanwhile spread: "Mgr. Dupanloup is often mentioned as the future archbishop of Paris; but I think that Thiers fears him" (Michaud to Döllinger, 7 June 1871, BStB Munich, Döllinger Nachlass, 2).

27. Ginoulhiac to Thiers, 4 July 1871, BN Paris, Papiers Thiers, NAF 20622; Simon to Thiers, [?] July 1871, AN Paris, Papiers Simon, 87 AP/10. This draft of Simon's memo is undated, and it may never have reached Thiers. But it leaves no doubt as to Simon's true feelings: "I used

to think, and I still think today, that we should appoint the bishop of Orléans as the archbishop of Paris. I know that you share my opinion on the appropriateness of this choice and that you are deterred solely by a desire not to vex the pope. . . . Are we going to obey and choose for the three vacant seats three candidates absolutely reassuring for the pope? If we do, the faction of the French episcopacy of which Mgr. Dupanloup is the leader will correctly believe that it has been abandoned." For a somewhat different view, see Gadille, *La pensée et l'action*, 1:286.

28. Thiers to Guibert, 14 July 1871, BN Paris, Papiers Thiers, NAF 20623; Guibert to Chigi, 16 July 1871, ASV Rome, SdS 394, rubrica 248. Later the interview with Simon was recalled by Guibert to Thiers, 13 Apr. 1872, AAP Paris, 1 D IX-1. Privately Simon nonetheless maintained his pressure on Thiers to bolster the Gallican wing; he wrote regarding recent choices for bishoprics: "I persist in believing that it would be a wise policy to demonstrate . . . that we do not intend to exclude the faction of the French clergy that recognizes Mgr. Dupanloup as its leader and that remains attached to the principles of the Gallican church" (Simon to Thiers, 21 Sept. 1871, BN Paris, Papiers Thiers, NAF 20623). See Bertocci, *Jules Simon*, pp. 155–60.

29. Favre to Harcourt, 14 July 1871, MAE Paris, Rome 1052. Thiers soon reinforced the point himself by reassuring that he wished "to avoid any measure, any nomination, that might add to the sorrows of the Holy Father" (Thiers to Harcourt, 11 Aug. 1871, BN Paris, Papiers Thiers, NAF 20623).

30. Simon to Favre, 15 July 1871, AN Paris, F¹⁹ 1955. Simon also objected that notification from the Vatican came in the form of writs (*brefs*) rather than papal bulls. See Gadille, *La pensée et l'action*, 1:283–84.

31. Thiers had a message conveyed to Antonelli: "We are determined to change nothing that is established in our reciprocal relations regulated according to the Concordat" (Favre to Harcourt, 14 July 1871, AN Paris, F¹⁹ 1955).

32. Harcourt to Favre, 17 July 1871, MAE Paris, Rome 1052.

33. Simon to Jouvencel, 18 July 1871, AN Paris, F¹⁹ 1955; "Extrait du registre des délibérations de la Commission (provisoire chargée de remplacer le Conseil d'Etat)," 20 July 1871, ibid.; JORF, 23 July 1871. Yet records at the Vatican show that on at least two subsequent occasions Thiers carelessly used the formula "nous le nommons et présentons" (Thiers to Pius IX, 8, 10 Aug. 1871, ASV Rome, SdS 394, rubrica 248).

34. On a memo received from Rémusat, Simon wrote: "My advice is to demand the word 'nomination' alone—and always in bulls" (Rémusat to Simon, 12 Aug. 1871, AN Paris, F¹⁹ 1955). *Nobis nominavit* could be translated as "has suggested to us," whereas *nominavit* clearly

implied "has appointed." For a careful examination of the semantic implications, see Feine, *Kirchliche Rechtsgeschichte*, pp. 691–92.

35. Simon to Rémusat, [?] Aug. 1871, AN Paris, F¹⁹ 1955; "Commission provisoire chargée de remplacer le Conseil d'Etat: extrait du registre des déliberations," 16 Nov. 1871, ibid. The Vatican was informed that any papal bull that by "inadvertence" employed *praesentare* rather than *nominare* could not be registered by the Conseil d'Etat before the "error" had been officially acknowledged by the Holy See (Rémusat to Harcourt, 3 Jan. 1872, ASV Rome, SdS 399, rubrica 248). The point was conceded by the Vatican—a temporary victory for Simon. See Antonelli to Harcourt, 7 Jan. 1872, AN Paris, F¹⁹ 1955; Harcourt to Rémusat, 5, 11 Jan. 1872, MAE Paris, Rome 1054.

36. Tardif to Simon, 6 June 1872, AN Paris, F¹⁹ 1955; Simon to Rémusat, 12 June 1872, ibid.; Bourgoing to Rémusat, 26 June 1872, MAE Paris, Rome 1055. The basis of Simon's personal opinion was well stated in a single sentence: "It is purely a formality, but it constitutes an alteration of the Concordat and a diminution at least in appearance of our rights, to which I am unable to consent" (Simon to Rémusat, 22 May 1872, AN Paris, Papiers Simon, 87 AP/10).

37. Michels to Rémusat, 9 July 1872, MAE Paris, Rome 1055; Antonelli to Michels, 30 July 1872, AN Paris, F¹⁹ 1955; Simon to the bishop of Nevers, 30 July 1872, ASV Rome, SdS 399, rubrica 248.

38. "Conseil d'Etat: extrait du registre des déliberations," 19 Sept. 1872, AN Paris, F¹⁹ 1955; Simon to Rémusat, 12 Nov. 1872, ibid.; Rémusat to Simon, 29 Nov. 1872, ibid.; Simon to Rémusat, 7 Dec. 1872, ibid. Simon conducted his own survey of French diocesonal archives: of the 202 bulls reported to him, 169 employed *nobis* whereas 33 did not. Thus his legal case was weakened by his own contradictory statistics, which he thereupon suppressed ("Situation du Nobis," 11 Nov. 1872, ibid., 1956). In view of all this evidence, to conclude that "Simon worked to lay the foundations for a reconciliation between the French Church and the Republic" is simply not an accurate description of his objectives or activities, despite that characterization by Bertocci, *Jules Simon*, p. 154. See Gadille, *La pensée et l'action*, 1:282–85.

39. See above, note 33. For this reason, the French ambassador to the Vatican tended to blame Thiers for the entire controversy (Harcourt to Rémusat, 12 May 1872, MAE Paris, Rome 1054).

40. Some caution is necessary here because the only source for Thiers's statement is a letter from Chigi to Simon, 4 Aug. 1872, AN Paris, Papiers Simon, 87 AP/10.

41. Guibert to Richard, 14 Aug. 1872, AAP Paris, 1 D IX-1; *Journal des débats*, 3 Feb. 1873.

42. Dupanloup to Pius IX, 18 Feb. 1871, cited by Lösch, *Döllinger und Frankreich*, p. 315.

43. "Des actes de brutalité et de violence" in the Haute-Saône, for example, were reported by Simon to Rémusat, 1 Sept. 1871, AN Paris, F¹⁹ 5608–9. The persistence of such incidents was described and lamented in turn by Rémusat to Simon, 19 Dec. 1872, ibid.

44. Directive from Simon to French bishops, 26 Oct. 1872, ibid., 1882; directive from Guibert to Parisian *curés*, 11 Nov. 1872, AAP Paris, 3 B-10. But a directive issued on 16 Oct. 1875, stipulating that *Domine salvam fac Rempublicam* should be chanted each Sunday, did not go without challenge from some of the clergy. See Gadille, *La pensée et l'action*, 1:317–19.

45. Reports from Chigi to Antonelli, 19 Apr., 17 May, 12 June, 22 Oct. 1871, ASV Rome, SdS 394, rubrica 242.

46. Reports from Chigi to Antonelli, 24 Jan., 21 Feb., 14 Nov. 1872, ASV Rome, SdS 399, rubrica 248; also reports from Chigi to Antonelli, 30 Jan., 26 Feb., 3 Mar., 6 May 1873, ASV Rome, SdS 405, rubrica 248.

47. Chigi to Antonelli, 23 May 1873, ibid. There is, for example, no hint of conspiracy in Dupanloup's personal diary, although he saw Broglie the day before Thiers's fall. Instead, he records some bare facts after the event and comments without apparent irony: "pauvre M. Thiers" (Dupanloup, "Journal intime," entry for 24 May 1873, ASS Paris, Fonds Dupanloup).

48. This theme is properly stressed by Mayeur, *Les débuts de la troisième république*, pp. 48–54, 111–19, 135–45.

49. Harcourt to Thiers, 30 May 1871, BN Paris, Papiers Thiers, NAF 20622; Favre to Choiseul, 10 June 1871, DDF 1:7. The quotation is from a dispatch by Favre to Chigi, 1 July 1871, ASV Rome, SdS 393, rubrica 165. Thiers's speech to the Assembly on the religious question (JORF, 23 July 1871) was reported in full by Waldersee to Bismarck (23 July 1871, AA Bonn, I.A.B.c 71, Bd. 2).

50. Harcourt to Favre, 17 July 1871, MAE Paris, Rome 1052. See McManners, *Church and State in France*, pp. 36–37; and Acomb, *French Laic Laws*, pp. 82–93.

51. Meglia to Antonelli, 26 July 1871, ASV Rome, SdS 443, rubrica 255; Meglia to Antonelli, 4 Aug. 1871, ibid., rubrica 248; Antonelli to Chigi, 16 Aug. 1871, ibid. In a later dispatch, the nuncio in Munich wrote of the "tempests" unleashed from Berlin against the church and predicted "the worst of tyrannies" (Meglia to Antonelli, 22 Nov. 1871, ibid., rubrica 255). The best available studies of the religious controversy in Germany are by Franz, *Kulturkampf*; Schmidt-Volkmar, *Der Kulturkampf in Deutschland*; and Becker, *Liberaler Staat und Kirche*. For a brief description, see Feine, *Kirchliche Rechtsgeschichte*, pp. 676–88.

52. Harcourt to Rémusat, 25 Sept. 1871, MAE Paris, Rome 1052; Harcourt to Thiers, 18 Jan. 1872, BN Paris, Papiers Thiers, NAF 20624.

53. Rémusat to Michels, 2 Oct. 1871, MAE Paris, Rome 1053; Casimir-Périer to Harcourt, 24 Nov. 1871, ibid.; Thiers to Harcourt, 25 Jan. 1872, BN Paris, Papiers Thiers, NAF 20626.

54. "Immediatbericht," 20 Jan. 1872, GW 6^c:14.

55. Acton to Döllinger, [?] Jan. 1872, cited in Conzemius, ed., *Briefwechsel*, 3:43. Reporting from Rome, Harcourt left no doubt that German intentions were "to exploit the matters of discontent that may exist here against us. Bismarck hopes to use Italy to harm both France and the papacy" (Harcourt to Rémusat, 27 Feb. 1872, MAE Paris, Rome 1054).

56. Harcourt to Rémusat, 17 Feb., 4 Apr. 1872, ibid.

57. Bismarck to Delbrück, 3 June 1872, GW 14^2:1455. See Fuchs, ed., *Staat und Kirche*, pp. 184–200.

58. Bourgoing to Rémusat, 25 June 1872, MAE Paris, Rome 1055.

59. "It is becoming less improbable than before that the pope may leave Rome; I therefore believe, given the seriousness that the religious question has assumed, that we must maintain an extreme reserve in our measures. . . . In view of the open war undertaken by Prussia, the withdrawal of the pope to France would be a grave incident" (Thiers to Rémusat, 2 Sept. 1872, BN Paris, Papiers Thiers, NAF 20626). Diplomatic orders were issued accordingly (Rémusat to Michels, 4 Sept. 1872, MAE Paris, Rome 1056). Pius himself asked about the *Orénoque* and was assured of its readiness (Bourgoing to Rémusat, 22 Sept. 1872, ibid.). That assurance was later renewed by Thiers to the nuncio, who reported back to Rome (Chigi to Antonelli, 4 Jan. 1873, ASV Rome, SdS 404, rubrica 165).

60. Guibert to Thiers, 12 Jan. 1873, AAP Paris, 1 D IX-1; Barthélemy Saint-Hilaire to Guibert, 17 Jan. 1873, ibid.

61. Bismarck to Antonelli, 12 Feb. 1873, ASV Rome, SdS 443, rubrica 255.

62. Antonelli to Bismarck, 9 Mar. 1873, ibid.

Chapter 7

1. The recent literature is vast, but it is best to begin with the survey by Prost, *Histoire de l'enseignement en France*. Other general guides are provided by Ponteil, *Histoire de l'enseignement en France*; more concisely by Léon, *Histoire de l'enseignement en France*; and by Chevallier et al., *L'enseignement français*. Especially useful as background for this chapter are the works of Anderson, *Education in France*; Moody, *French Education*; and Harrigan, *Mobility, Elites, and Education*.

2. A self-appraisal is contained in Duruy, *Notes et souvenirs*. The first appreciation of his work was by Lavisse, *Un ministre*. Notable among more recent studies are Rohr, *Victor Duruy*; the concise chap-

ter entitled "Prelude to Reform, 1866–1870," by Keylor, *Academy and Community*, pp. 19–35; and Moody, *French Education*, pp. 72–85. The latest biographical study is by Horvath-Peterson, *Victor Duruy and French Education*. For the rest, see the extensive bibliographical annotations by Prost, *Histoire de l'enseignement en France*, pp. 68–69; and the commentary by Harrigan, "Historians and Compilers Joined," pp. 3–21.

3. Duruy, "Projet de programmes pour l'enseignement professionel," 2 Oct. 1863, AN Paris, F¹⁷ 6806. See Duveau, *La pensée ouvrière*, pp. 38–41. Although university systems of other countries were also compared, "there was not the same sense of urgency. . . . Frequently, the developments in Germany seemed to have more serious economic and political implications" (Paul, *Sorcerer's Apprentice*, p. 12).

4. "Loi relative à l'enseignement dite loi Falloux du 15 mars 1850," reprinted by Chevallier et al., *L'enseignement français*, 2:160–78. The standard commentary remains Michel, *La loi Falloux*, which has been updated by Hébert and Carnec, *La loi Falloux*. Also see Prost, *Histoire de l'enseignement en France*, pp. 173–82; and Anderson, *Education in France*, pp. 45–50.

5. On the question of literacy in France, see Furet and Ozouf, *Lire et écrire*, 1:349–69. Comparative statistics are conveniently assembled by Cipolla, *Literacy and Development*, pp. 62–99, 113–30. As for the role of the church, two qualifications are necessary: (1) clerical domination was much more prominent in schools for girls than for boys; and (2) there was a notable expansion of separate Catholic parochial schools throughout the Second Empire. On the first theme see Mayeur, *L'éducation des filles en France*, pp. 34–56, 113–47; and for the second see Anderson, *Education in France*, pp. 103–12.

6. Duruy, *Notes et souvenirs*, 1:209–14. "It was clear that the University was unsympathetic, and the fact that some of Duruy's ideas were borrowed from abroad did not help—'it smells too much of Germanism, and it thus is condemned in advance in France' was one inspector's comment" (Anderson, *Education in France*, p. 182).

7. Duruy, "Note pour le conseil impérial: projet d'arrêté contenant quelques modifications à l'organisation de l'enseignement du grec dans les lycées," [?] Nov. 1863, AN Paris, F¹⁷ 6806; "Conseil impérial de l'instruction publique: projet d'arrêté relatif aux nouveaux programmes de l'enseignement scientifique des lycées," [?] Nov. 1863, ibid. The French *lycée* under Duruy is described by Isambert-Jamati, *Crises de la société*, pp. 69–104. On the social composition of the secondary schools, see Gerbod, *La vie quotidienne*, pp. 108–11.

8. Duruy, *Administration de l'instruction publique*, p. 546. See Anderson, *Education in France*, pp. 225–39; Zeldin, *France*, 2:342–43; and Keylor, *Academy and Community*, pp. 19–35. Keylor (ibid., p. 39)

describes the Ecole Pratique des Hautes Etudes as "an experimental institution grafted onto the regular university structure whose faculty was given free rein to introduce the pedagogical and scholarly methods developed in Germany." Graduates of the *grandes écoles* enjoyed "a de facto monopoly on the top brackets of the civil service, the universities, and medicine, and decisive advantages in entering most professions and many industrial organizations," writes Crozier, *Bureaucratic Phenomenon*, p. 243. In this regard see also Suleiman, *Politics, Power, and Bureaucracy*, pp. 75–85; Ringer, *Education and Society*, pp. 124–27, 170–80; and Harrigan, "Secondary Education and the Professions," pp. 349–71.

9. Quoted by Prost, *Histoire de l'enseignement en France*, pp. 228–29. The thesis that France's educational system was already in decline, relative to that of Germany, well before the war of 1870 has been often repeated since Irsay, *Histoire des universités françaises et étrangères*, 2:290–97. It is argued with particular vigor in a chapter entitled "The Rise and Decline of the French Scientific Center in a Regime of Centralized Liberalism" by Ben-David, *The Scientist's Role in Society*, pp. 88–107.

10. *Le moniteur universel*, 8 Mar. 1867. Although the emperor claimed to be a champion of more socially progressive schooling, he did not always have the courage of his implications. His failure to give Duruy emphatic support helps to explain the outcome. See Duveau, *La pensée ouvrière*, pp. 38–41.

11. "Loi sur l'enseignement primaire" of 10 April 1867, published in *Le moniteur universel*, 17 Apr. 1867.

12. Ibid., 4 Aug. 1867.

13. Ibid., 7 May 1867. A tireless campaigner for greater state funding for education, Jules Simon claimed that the imperial regime was spending nearly 30 percent of its budget on the military but barely 1 percent on schools (Simon, *L'école*, pp. 209–26). For a detailed record of prewar allocations to public education, see Rohr, *Victor Duruy*, pp. 50–51.

14. For instance, Lipart to Duruy, 5 Oct. 1868, AN Paris, F^{17} 12338; and "Note à l'appui d'un projet de décret portant création d'une section économique à la faculté de droit de Paris," [?] July 1869, ibid., 6806.

15. These remarks are quoted, respectively, from Gaston Boissier, "Les réformes de l'enseignement: l'enseignement supérieur," *Revue des deux mondes* 75 (1868):863–64; H. Blerzy, "De l'enseignement secondaire en Europe," ibid. 80 (1869):96–128; and Georges Pouchet, "L'enseignement supérieur des sciences en Allemagne," ibid. 83 (1869):430–49.

16. Cherbuliez, "La Prusse et l'Allemagne," ibid. 86 (1870):624–50. This essay was the conclusion of a five-part series.

17. Albert Duruy, "La liberté de l'enseignement supérieur," ibid. 85 (1870):736–57.

18. Macé, *La ligue de l'enseignement*, p. 211. See Dessoye, *Jean Macé*, pp. 94–95; Capéran, *Histoire contemporaine de la laïcité*, 1:21–29; Ozouf, *L'école, l'église et la république*, pp. 26–33; and Boivin, "Les origines de la ligue de l'enseignement." The most recent account, which praises the virtues of Macé and of public education, is by Auspitz, *Radical Bourgeoisie*.

19. See Rohr, *Victor Duruy*, pp. 171–75; Anderson, *Education in France*, pp. 137–44; and Zeldin, *France*, 2:151–54. It was the lost war that truly made Macé into a national figure and enabled him to gather more than a million signatures in 1872. See Dessoye, *Jean Macé*, pp. 96–106, 113–18.

20. Conseil Impérial de l'Instruction Publique, *procès-verbaux*, 18 July 1870, AN Paris, F^{17} 12958.

21. Edmond Dreyfus-Brisac, "Les réformes de l'enseignement supérieur en France," RIE 1 (1881):121–36.

22. Favre to Thiers, 16 Sept. 1870, MAE Paris, Papiers Favre, 22. One of the most distinguished republican educators commented regarding higher education: "The war, which adjourned these reforms, emphasized all the more forcefully their urgency and necessity. . . . With a passionate curiosity we inquired everywhere about the German universities, and we gained the conviction that they had created the German spirit and through this spirit the German nation. Thereafter the reform of our faculties was no longer simply a matter of science; it became a question of patriotism" (Liard, *Universités et facultés*, p. 32). See Isambert-Jamati, *Crises de la société*, p. 122.

23. The harshest indictment of France's prewar inferiority in education, compared to Germany, was written in 1871 by the former military attaché in Berlin, Baron Stoffel: "I foresaw an imminent struggle between the [German] people—virile, educated, disciplined, filled with patriotism and faith, governed by venerable and solid institutions respected by all—and our unfortunate nation, ignorant, skeptical, egoistic, and vain" (*Rapports militaires*, p. iv).

24. "Extrait du rapport du M. le président de la commission administrative municipale de Toulouse concernant le budget de 1871 approuvé par ladite commission dans sa séance du 22 novembre 1870," AN Paris, F^{17} 9174. On the general agitation of public opinion, see Ozouf, *L'école, l'église et la république*, pp. 15–23.

25. "Extrait des registres des délibérations de la commission administrative municipale de Toulouse," 22 Nov. 1870, AN Paris, F^{17} 9174;

Desprez to Crémieux, 23 Dec. 1870, ibid., and request that the archbishop of Bordeaux intercede: Desprez to Donnet, 24 Dec. 1870, ibid.; Vidal Lablanche to Crémieux, 26 Dec. 1870, ibid.; telegram from the Bordeaux government (no signature) to Armand Duportal (prefect of the Haute-Garonne), 29 Dec. 1870, ibid., and reply: telegram from Duportal to Crémieux, 30 Dec. 1870, ibid.; "Extrait des registres des délibérations de la commission administrative municipale [of Toulouse]," 6 Jan. 1871, ibid. Zévort achieved a temporary compromise, but the government continued to fear a "dangerous irritation" among the populace of Toulouse, which apparently supported the municipal council (Crémieux to Duportal, 25 Jan. 1871, ibid.).

26. "Pétition pour le maintien des écoles des frères," 15 Jan. 1871, ibid., 9175. This petition opposed a vote by the municipal council of Roanne on 11 January to dismiss all of the priests who were teaching in the city's public schools. But unlike the incident in Toulouse, the prefect of the Loire overruled the council's directive. Not until two years later did the Conseil d'Etat reach a definitive ruling in favor of the prefect. The two cartons F^{17} 9174–75 in the Archives nationales, Paris, contain more evidence of such episodes. Also see Bertocci, *Jules Simon*, pp. 163–70.

27. Sometimes *écoles congréganistes* were converted into *écoles laïques*, with the usual result that Catholic parents withdrew their children from those schools. In the department of Gers such a conversion caused a drop of enrollment from 230 pupils to 35; and in the Tarn-et-Garonne a school with 81 pupils dropped to 14. But in the Haute-Garonne, outside of Toulouse, the 5,010 pupils in nine *écoles congréganistes* all continued when those schools were simply redesignated as *écoles libres* under Catholic authority. In the Hautes-Pyrénées no changes were reported, suggesting that the more rural and remote areas remained largely untouched by municipal controversies (Vidal Lablanche to Simon, 4 Mar. 1871, AN Paris, F^{17} 9174).

28. See Greenberg, *Sisters of Liberty*, pp. 9–10, 140–41, and passim. On the aborted attempt to effect a "radical transformation" of Parisian schools during the Commune in the spring of 1871, see Duveau, *La pensée ouvrière*, pp. 42–46.

29. Simon to the president of the Conseil d'Etat, 20 Dec. 1871, AN Paris, F^{17} 9174. In the same vein was the letter from Simon to Charles Ferry (prefect of the Haute-Garonne), 10 Dec. 1871, cited by Pisani-Ferry, *Monsieur l'instituteur*, p. 82.

30. Directive from Simon to rectors of French public schools, 21 May 1871, AN Paris, Papiers Simon, 87 AP/9. A passage from this document illustrates the matter-of-fact manner in which Simon invoked the

German example: "There are often demands that physical education should have a greater part in our general system of instruction. You know how it was in classical times; you see how it is in Germany. I beg you to assist me in introducing it into our customs." The result, he added, would be "an immediate improvement of our race." Of like mind was the noted linguist, Michel Bréal, who had "gathered notes on the comparative value of education in France and Germany" and who now used them to criticize rote learning, conservatism, and clerical influence in the French schools (*Quelques mots*, p. 1). See Chevallier et al., *L'enseignement français*, 1:113; and Bertocci, *Jules Simon*, pp. 175–79.

31. See Mitchell, *German Influence*, pp. 21–27, 34–40, 46–48.

32. Prefect of the Côtes-du-Nord to Simon, 24 Jan. 1872, AN Paris, F^{17} 9149. Another typical example was a prefect who inquired of his department's educational council about local conditions and then reported back to Paris: "The council insists especially on the poor condition of a great number of school buildings and their insufficiency to receive a greater quantity of students. Considerable expense will be required to improve this situation, and many communes will be unable to countenance such costs if they do not obtain a large subvention from the state" (prefect of the Ain to Simon, 22 Dec. 1871, ibid.). See Weber, *Peasants into Frenchmen*, pp. 303–4.

33. Léon Say to Simon, 19 June 1872, AN Paris, Papiers Simon, 87 AP/7.

34. "The government attaches the greatest importance to physical exercises, including rifle drills and especially equitation, which have been far too neglected until now. [They should] henceforth occupy an important place in the education of our youth" (directive from General de Cissey [minister of war] to commanding officers of the army, 18 Nov. 1871, SHAT Vincennes, G^8 178). The same theme was later adopted by Jules Ferry in his speech to a gathering in Reims of the French gymnastic societies, quoted in "Nouvelles et informations: l'éducation militaire," RIE 3 (1882):626–29. See Girardet, *La société militaire*, pp. 162–71.

35. The military rationale of defending against Germany was undisguised: "France is certainly not disposed to provoke anyone, but if attacked she will repulse the assault in the Vosges, the Juras, and the Alps" (program of the Club Alpin Français, [?] Apr. 1874, AN Paris, F^{17} 2516). A deputy from the Hautes-Alpes later praised Jules Simon for his support of the movement and its organization of hiking expeditions: "This practice, very common in Germany and Switzerland, has not yet become widespread in France despite numerous well intended efforts of this sort" (Cézanne to Wallon, 19 Aug. 1875, ibid.).

36. Académie de Lyon to Wallon, 13 Mar. 1875, ibid., 2625; Acadé-

mie de Clermont to Wallon, 1 March 1875, ibid. In Paris all *lycées* had a gymnasium, but the great majority of primary schools neither had equipment nor offered regular physical education (Académie de Paris to Wallon, 31 Mar. 1875, ibid.).

37. "Procès-verbaux de la Commission de l'Enseignement de la Géographie," 22 Nov. 1871–3 May 1873, AN Paris, F^{17} 2915–16. Among the Levasseur papers is a dossier entitled "Enseignement de la géographie à l'étranger," in which Germany is by far the major subject of inquiry (ibid.). As Gerbod has remarked: "The defeat of 1870 precipitated the movement. History and especially geography appeared to a humiliated nation to be indispensable disciplines" (*La vie quotidienne*, p. 133). See Broc, "La géographie française face à la science allemande."

38. Directive from Simon to rectors of French public schools, 21 May 1871, AN Paris, Papiers Simon, 87 AP/9. See Mitchell, "German History in France."

39. "Proposition de loi tendant à réorganiser l'enseignement de la médicine, présentée par M. Alfred Naquet," *Impressions*, no. 672 (annex of 5 Dec. 1871); JORF, 6 Dec. 1871.

40. Simon to the dean of the faculty of medicine at Nancy, 12 Nov. 1872, AN Paris, Papiers Simon, 87 AP/10.

41. In December 1872 Jules Simon surveyed the effects of curricular changes in the primary schools. Reactions of course varied, but one typical report literally commented that "a spirit of routine prevails" (Académie d'Aix to Simon, 17 June 1873, AN Paris, F^{17} 9154). The continuing domination of French secondary education by the upper middle class at least until the end of the nineteenth century is emphasized by Ringer, *Education and Society*, p. 162. Another historian adds this comment: "Meritocracy in theory but often hereditary in practice, it was a cautious system, designed and supervised by cautious men. . . . Educators of the 1870s and 1880s had more to worry about than fostering mobility. They had to 'modernize' the curriculum so that France could compete against Germany [and] they had to protect themselves from Catholic secondary schools, which were increasing in popularity and quality" (Harrigan, *Mobility, Elites, and Education*, pp. 143–44). On the frustration of Simon's reform efforts, also see Weill, *Histoire de l'enseignement secondaire*, pp. 154–69; Gerbod, *La condition universitaire*, pp. 524–34; and Bertocci, *Jules Simon*, pp. 151–80.

42. Some records of the Conseil Impérial de l'Instruction Publique can be found in AN Paris, F^{17} 12958. On the background, see Prost, *Histoire de l'enseignement en France*, pp. 23–31; and Rohr, *Victor Duruy*, pp. 32–37.

43. "Rapport fait au nom de la commission chargée d'examiner la proposition de MM. le duc de Broglie, Wallon, de Corcelle, Saint-Marc-

Girardin et plusieurs de leurs collègues. . . ," 27 June 1871, BN Paris, Papiers Dupanloup, NAF 24713. In his brief sketch of the CSIP's history, Prost (*Histoire de l'enseignement en France*, p. 31) unfortunately passes over the years from 1873 to 1880.

44. CSIP, *procès-verbaux*, 10 June 1873, AN Paris, F^{17} 12959. These minutes were also inscribed in a bound volume, ibid., F^{17}* 3199. The composition and chairmanship of the CSIP's most important subcommittee were determined on the same day during its initial session: Second Commission of the CSIP, *procès-verbaux*, 10 June 1873, ibid., F^{17}* 3251.

45. The debate concerned the relative proportion of classical studies to other disciplines. In fact, the Second Commission still hoped to maintain a healthy dose of modern languages, "especially German," because of their importance for "scientific, literary, and political considerations" (Second Commission of the CSIP, *procès-verbaux*, 16 June 1873 [morning], ibid.).

46. CSIP, *procès-verbaux*, 10 June 1873, ibid., F^{17} 12959.

47. Second Commission of the CSIP, *procès-verbaux*, 12 June 1873, ibid., F^{17}* 3251. Insofar as primary education was concerned, Dupanloup likewise wanted to maintain the Falloux law of 1850. See Gadille, *La pensée et l'action*, 1:329–39.

48. "Conclusions de la Deuxième Commission sur les dispositions principales de la circulaire ministérielle du 27 septembre 1872" (attached to the CSIP minutes of 24 June 1873), 17 June 1873, AN Paris, F^{17} 12959; CSIP, *procès-verbaux*, 28 June 1873, ibid., F^{17}* 3199. This measure was formally advocated by Bishop Dupanloup and Edouard-René Lefebvre de Laboulaye.

49. But the primacy of classics remained basically intact (Second Commission of the CSIP, *procès-verbaux*, 20 June 1873 [morning], AN Paris, F^{17}* 3251). See Prost, *Histoire de l'enseignement en France*, pp. 61, 249–50.

50. Batbie posed the pivotal question: "Surely the increase in the number of pupils indicates a marked social change. But should the quantity of pupils diminish the quality of secondary education?" (CSIP, *procès-verbaux*, 26 June 1873, AN Paris, F^{17}* 3199).

51. "Plan d'études des lycées. Programmes de l'enseignement secondaire classique et du baccalauréat-ès-lettres. Propositions faites à la commission du plan d'études par la sous-commission," 18 May 1874, AN Paris, F^{17} 6872^2; CSIP, "Révision des programmes de l'enseignement secondaire," 9 June 1874, ibid., 6806. A final version was published as *Nouveau plan d'études des lycées* (Paris, 1874).

52. CSIP, *procès-verbaux*, 10 June 1874, AN Paris, F^{17} 12959; ibid., 16, 17 June, F^{17}* 3199.

53. Simon, *La réforme*, pp. 8–12, 306, 59–60. Simon's revised view was not necessarily the rule for others. In the year following, while discussing the expansion of higher education, the minister of education, Henri Wallon, proposed to locate selected *agrégés* on university campuses: "This will be the first attempt in our establishments [to create] *Privatdozenten*, whose positive influence within the German universities has been vaunted" (CSIP, *procès-verbaux*, 26 Oct. 1875, AN Paris, F^{17} 12960).

54. Simon, *La réforme*, p. 43. This was essentially to adopt a position in the quarrel between *"anciens"* and *"modernes"* in favor of the former. See Prost, *Histoire de l'enseignement en France*, p. 250.

55. Simon, *La réforme*, p. 59. The French Ministry of Education nonetheless continued to seek specific information on the German school system, which was on occasion supplied by the German embassy in Paris, for example, Hohenlohe to Waddington, 10 July 1876, AN Paris, F^{17} 12338.

56. See Mitchell, "Crucible of French Anticlericalism," pp. 148–49. One other issue is of special note for future reference. In 1878 the current minister of education, Agénor Bardoux, wondered "if it would seem useful to place into the hands of our children a single volume that would concentrate the various subjects of study, a *manuel* analogous to the *Lesebuch* of a neighboring country" (Comité consultatif, Section primaire, of the CSIP, *procès-verbaux*, 7 Feb. 1878, AN Paris, F^{17*} 3156). Allowed to languish for the time being, this proposal was revived in 1880 under Jules Ferry. See Chapter 9.

Chapter 8

1. Chigi to Antonelli, 27 May, 1 June 1873, ASV Rome, SdS 405, rubrica 248.

2. Corcelle to Broglie, 11, 15, 18 June 1873, MAE Paris, Rome 1057.

3. Report by a French agent in Berlin, 2 June 1873, APP Paris, B A/320.

4. Arnim to the Auswärtiges Amt, 27 May 1873, AA Bonn, I.A.B.c 78, Bd. 2. Reporting from Marseille, however, the German consul there judged that clerical influence in southern France was too diffuse to be dangerous: "The celebration in the ultramontane camp is thus in any event unjustified" (Tattenborn to the Auswärtiges Amt, 6, 12 June 1873, ibid.).

5. Manteuffel to Bismarck, 16 June 1873, ibid.

6. Pius IX to the Company of Jesus (Lyon), 23 June 1873, AN Paris, Papiers Dupanloup, AB XIX, 524; L'abbé Gustave Materon, "Les pèleri-

nages au XIXe siècle," 1873, AN Paris, F¹⁹ 5562. See Ozouf, *L'école, l'église et la république,* pp. 40–47; and Weber, *Peasants into Frenchmen,* pp. 351–55.

7. Notices and advertisements for group rates and reductions were regularly printed in a new journal begun in 1873, *Le pèlerin.* See Marrus, "Pilger auf dem Weg," pp. 329–51.

8. "Pèlerinage du Mans au Mont-St.-Michel," 1873, AN Paris, F¹⁹ 5562; Ministry of the Interior (directeur de la sureté générale) to Ministry of Education, 16 Oct. 1873, ibid. See Gadille, *La pensée et l'action,* 1:229–37.

9. "It is nonetheless incontestable that the coalition cabinet contains committed ultramontane members" (Wesdehlen to Bismarck, 3, 16 July 1873, AA Bonn, I.A.B.c 78, Bde. 2–3; Bismarck to Wesdehlen, 3 Sept. 1873, GP 1:131; Broglie to Gontaut-Biron, 26 Aug. 1873, MAE Paris, Allemagne 11.

10. See Mitchell, *German Influence,* pp. 99–104.

11. Chigi to Antonelli, 9 Sept. 1873, ASV Rome, SdS 405, rubrica 248; Chigi's analysis was updated and reconfirmed on 3 Oct. 1873, ibid., SdS 420, rubrica 248; Chigi to Antonelli, 20 Oct. 1873, ibid., SdS 405, rubrica 248.

12. "Traduction d'une lettre du Cardinal Antonelli à M. de Corcelle du 8 novembre 1873," BT Paris, Papiers Decazes, 690.

13. "In Versailles they have a bad conscience and are sensitive to having their fingers so mercilessly slapped by Bismarck" (Landsberg to Bleichröder, 24 Nov. 1873, AA Bonn, II.B.10, Bd. 5).

14. Decazes to Chigi, 27 Nov. 1873, MAE Paris, Rome 1057; Corcelle to Decazes, 17 Dec. 1873, ibid.; Decazes to Gontaut-Biron, 2 Jan. 1874, BT Paris, Papiers Decazes, 716. A copy of Decazes's directive was addressed from Fourtou to Guibert, 26 Dec. 1873, AAP Paris, 3 B-3. Thus we know that the episcopacy was cautioned by the government in accordance with Decazes's promise to Bismarck.

15. "France," *L'Univers,* 2–3 Jan. 1874; directive by Ladmirault (military governor of Paris), 19 Jan. 1874, ASV Rome, SdS 413, rubrica 248. The Vatican was meanwhile informed of the action against Veuillot, which the papal nuncio described as "a satisfaction that the [French] government feels obligated to give primarily to the demands of Prince Bismarck" (Chigi to Antonelli, 20 Jan. 1874, ibid.).

16. *Norddeutsche Allgemeine Zeitung,* 16 Jan. 1874.

17. Gontaut-Biron to Decazes, 14 Jan. 1874, MAE Paris, Allemagne 12. The ambassador reinforced his dispatch with a private letter, on which Decazes inscribed a comment about Bismarck: "He wants to associate us in a crusade against Catholicism!" (Gontaut-Biron to Decazes, 15 Jan. 1874, BT Paris, Papiers Decazes, 680).

18. The *Orénoque* issue was first raised by Harcourt to Rémusat, 27 Jan. 1872, MAE Paris, Rome 1054. The resumption of discussions was reported by Chigi to Antonelli, 18 Jan. 1874, ASV Rome, SdS 412, rubrica 165.

19. Corcelle to Decazes, 12, 26 Feb. 1874, MAE Paris, Rome 1058. See Gadille, *La pensée et l'action*, 1:274–78.

20. Decazes to Gontaut-Biron, 18 Jan. 1874, BT Paris, Papiers Decazes, 716. The same message was more than once restated by Decazes in private, for example: "Bismarck intends no less than to sweep us into the wake of his crusade against Catholicism. We shall not follow him" (Decazes to Harcourt, 19 Jan. 1874, MAE Paris, Papiers Hanotaux, 6).

21. Directive from Decazes to French ambassadors, 24 Jan. 1874, MAE Paris, Rome 1058; Corcelle to Decazes, 4, 13 Feb. 1874, ibid. In Paris, meanwhile, the church's expertise about Germany was bolstered by the arrival of Monsignor Meglia as the new papal nuncio, replacing Monsignor Chigi. Meglia had long been the nuncio in Munich.

22. Decazes to Corcelle, 29 Apr. 1874, BT Paris, Papiers Decazes, 716.

23. The Vatican was reluctant to agree, but the Versailles government advocated a quick settlement of the Strasbourg issue because of its "political urgency" (Corcelle to Antonelli, 6 Apr. 1874, ASV Rome, SdS 413, rubrica 248). This request was repeated several weeks later in light of "a situation that could create unexpected difficulties" (Corcelle to Antonelli, 1 June 1874, ibid.). This time the papacy concurred (Corcelle to Decazes, 5 June 1874, MAE Paris, Rome 1058).

24. Gontaut-Biron to Decazes, 21 Apr. 1874, BT Paris, Papiers Decazes, 690. The complex negotiations that led to Decazes's decision concerning Spain can be reconstructed from the following documents: Hohenlohe to Decazes, 17 July 1874, ibid., 691; "Conversation du 26 juillet avec le Pce de Hohenlohe," 1874, ibid.; Decazes to Gontaut-Biron, 4 Aug. 1874, ibid., 717; Bülow to Hohenlohe, 15 Aug. 1874, ibid., 692; and Hohenlohe to Decazes, 18 Aug. 1874, ibid. The news broke in *Le Temps*, 22 Aug. 1874.

25. JORF, 31 July 1874; directive from Cumont to French bishops, 2 Aug. 1874, AAP Paris, 1 D IX-1; a copy of this document was also sent to the Vatican: ASV Rome, SdS 413, rubrica 248.

26. Meglia to Antonelli, 3 Aug. 1874, ibid., 9 Aug. 1874, ibid., SdS 412, rubrica 165; Meglia to Antonelli, 23 Aug. 1874, ibid., SdS 413, rubrica 248.

27. Directive from Cumont to French prefects, 3 Oct. 1874, AN Paris, F[7] 12389.

28. Meglia to Antonelli, 28 July 1874, ASV Rome, SdS 413, rubrica 248; Corcelle to Decazes, 9 Oct. 1874, BT Paris, Papiers Decazes, 692;

Corcelle to Decazes, 9 Nov. 1874, MAE Paris, Rome 1058. The Vatican's veto of Dupanloup and the French cabinet's displeasure with it were described by Meglia to Antonelli, 18 Aug. 1874, ASV Rome, SdS 413, rubrica 248. Thus if ultramontane pressure on the French government was less conspicuous than during the Thiers presidency, it nonetheless persisted. See Gadille, *La pensée et l'action*, 1:150–51, 293–94.

29. See Schmidt-Volkmar, *Kulturkampf*, pp. 128–46.

30. Decazes to Corcelle, 5 Mar. 1875, MAE Paris, Rome 1059.

31. Meglia to Antonelli, 7 Mar. 1875, ASV Rome, SdS 443, rubrica 255. Corcelle conferred with Pius IX and Antonelli about means to withstand "the evil designs of our foreign enemies." German demands that the French government take measures to silence the Catholic clergy and press might create "very grave dangers" unless the pope encouraged prudence. Corcelle also urged efforts by the Vatican to rally support for MacMahon (Corcelle to Decazes, 9 Mar. 1875, MAE Paris, Rome 1059).

32. Such worries were expressed by Decazes to Corcelle, 17 Mar. 1875, MAE Paris, Rome 1059. Led by Père Picard, who was overtly snubbed by the French ambassador and refused lodging by him, a group of fifteen hundred French pilgrims arrived in Rome that spring (Corcelle to Decazes, 29 Apr. 1875, ibid.). Censorship was recommended by Corcelle to Antonelli, 5 May 1875, ASV Rome, SdS 422, rubrica 261.

33. Hohenlohe to Bismarck, 27 May 1875, AA Bonn, I.A.B.c 83, Bd. 1; Corcelle to Decazes, 29 May 1875, MAE Paris, Rome 1059. Much later, in 1883, the Chamber of Deputies actually voted to rescind the land grant for the basilica, but it was of course to no avail. For the circumstances and sequel of the conflict over Sacré Coeur, see Harvey, "Monument and Myth"; and Mitchell, "Crucible of French Anticlericalism," p. 401.

34. See, for example, Vovelle, *Piété baroque*, pp. 593–614; and the brief summary by McManners, *Church and State in France*, pp. 4–19.

35. A satisfactory account of French anticlericalism remains to be written. The overview by Rémond, *L'anticléricalisme en France*, is disappointing. But see the excellent suggestions by Mayeur, *Les débuts*, pp. 111–12, 135–45.

36. See Mitchell, "Crucible of French Anticlericalism," pp. 396–99.

37. Maret to Döllinger, 3 June 1869, BStB Munich, Döllinger Nachlass, 2. See Houtin, *Le père Hyacinthe*; and Mitchell, "Partners in Failure," pp. 387–90. Perhaps two-fifths of French bishops considered the timing of the infallibility proclamation to be inopportune; but of these only eight or nine were identifiably Gallican in doctrine—and all, like Dupanloup, eventually submitted to the pope (McManners, *Church and State in France*, p. 24).

38. Michaud to Döllinger, 7 Nov. 1871, BStB Munich, Döllinger

Nachlass, 2. On Germany see Lill, "Die Entstehung der altkatholischen Kirchengemeinschaft."

39. Chigi to Antonelli, 12 Feb. 1872, ASV Rome, SdS 443, rubrica 255.

40. For instance, one finds a twenty-one-page manuscript of notes entitled "Congrès de vieux catholiques à Cologne, 20–23 septembre 1872," AN Paris, Papiers Dupanloup, AB XIX, 524.

41. Dupanloup to Pius IX, 23 Jan. 1873, ibid., 525.

42. Arnim to Bismarck, 17 Mar. 1874, AA Bonn, I.A.B.c 82, Bd. 2. On the lack of support for Gallicanism among the lower clergy, see McManners, *Church and State in France*, pp. 24–25.

43. Meglia to Antonelli, 28 July 1874, ASV Rome, SdS 413, rubrica 248; Antonelli to Meglia, 1 Aug. 1874, ibid.; Meglia to Antonelli, 18 Aug. 1874, ibid. A similar incident occurred in the following year, when Henri Wallon, then the minister of education and religion, attempted to obtain a cardinal's hat for Dupanloup but was forced to withdraw support of his candidate because of "the resistance that [Dupanloup] earlier encountered in Rome" (Corcelle to Decazes, 13 Aug. 1875, BT Paris, Papiers Decazes, 697; Wallon to Decazes, 16 Aug. 1875, MAE Paris, Rome 1059).

44. Dupanloup to Antonelli, 10 Apr. 1875, ASV Rome, SdS 423, rubrica 283; Dupanloup to Guibert, 25 May 1875, AAP Paris, 4 B I-7; Meglia to Antonelli, 17 June 1875, ASV Rome, SdS 420, rubrica 248; Dupanloup to Antonelli, 21 July 1875, ibid., SdS 423, rubrica 283.

45. Dupanloup to Corcelle, 19 Sept. 1875, BT Paris, Papiers Decazes, 698; Corcelle to Decazes, 29 Sept. 1875, ibid.; Dupanloup to Decazes, 29 Dec. 1875, ibid., 740.

46. Corcelle to Decazes, 9 Jan. 1876, MAE Paris, Rome 1060; 19 Jan. 1876, AN Paris, F[19] 2448; 29 Jan. 1876, BT Paris, Papiers Decazes, 700.

47. Corcelle to Decazes, 29 Jan. 1876, AN Paris, F[19] 2448; telegram from Corcelle to Decazes, 29 Jan. 1876, MAE Paris, Rome 1060.

48. The three quotations are from the entries of 11, 27 Jan., and 15 Feb. 1876, Dupanloup, "Journal intime," ASS Paris, Fonds Dupanloup.

49. It is worthwhile to cite a few instances in the original: "La nuit, très malade . . . vomissements très pénibles . . . J'étais seul, sans feu, loin de tout, sans sonnerie, moment cruel" (entry for 25 July 1875). "Douleur en bouche . . . très vive souffrance . . . le dentiste me délivre" (entry for 25–28 Apr. 1875). "Affreux mal de tête" (entry for 3 May 1875). With time his condition continued to deteriorate: "Très mal à la tête = travail impossible, affreux tems" (entry for 18 Feb. 1877). "Après ma messe, je suis fatigué, accablé de peines, de tristesse et d'impuissance . . . triste vie" (entry for 22 Feb. 1877). While visiting in Venice, as if anticipating Thomas Mann, he wrote: "Je suis triste partout et tout m'attriste.

. . . Tout ici est mort = Je me suis promené au milieu des morts" (entry for 29 Apr. 1877). That summer and fall he added: "L'age et l'infirmité depuis 2 mois . . . des infirmités plus menaçantes encore" (entry for 12 July 1877). "J'y ai été fort souffrant tout l'été, p^{dt} 6 mois" (entry for 25 Oct. 1877). Later: "Très mal à la tête" (entry for 11 Feb. 1878). And so on. Dupanloup's public image of vitality was thus belied by his private discouragement and debility.

50. The principal topic of discussion was a decision to support Désiré Barodet against Charles de Rémusat in a Paris by-election. Notes on the meeting were taken by Auguste Scheurer-Kestner, 21 Apr. 1873, AN Paris, Papiers Scheurer-Kestner, AP 276-1. On the evolution of Gambetta's anticlerical views, see Bury, *Gambetta and the Making*, pp.68–71.

51. JORF, 5 May 1877. See Mitchell, *German Influence*, pp. 69–76, 148–49, 162–64.

52. See Léonard, *Le protestant français*, pp. 83–88; Schram, *Protestantism*, pp. 80–81; Mours and Robert, *Le protestantisme*, pp. 311–45; and, for a survey of recent scholarship, the excellent papers gathered from a colloquium by Encrevé and Richard, eds., *Les protestants*.

53. See Acomb, *French Laic Laws*, pp. 54–58. The other side of the coin has been examined by Thadden, "Les protestants allemands."

54. See Acomb, *French Laic Laws*, pp. 113–22; Ligou, *Dictionnaire universel*, 1:501–10, and "Les protestants et la franc-maçonnerie"; and Chevallier, *Histoire de la franc-maçonnerie française*, 3:28–29.

55. Police report of 25 July 1876, APP Paris, B A/87.

56. From a speech at the lodge of L'union de Belleville by a member named Armand, quoted in a police report of 25 Aug. 1876, ibid.

57. Speech delivered at a lodge of the Scottish Rite, Les Trinitaires, by a member named Arago, quoted in a police report of 2 Nov. 1876, ibid.

58. Chevallier speculates that the number of lodges in the Grand Orient may have declined somewhat in the 1870s, but it certainly increased rapidly thereafter, probably trebling between 1870 and 1914 (*Histoire de la franc-maçonnerie française*, 3:28–29).

59. Statement by Allain-Targé while seconding a speech by Clemenceau in the Conseil Municipal de Paris (CMP), *procès-verbaux*, 12 Dec. 1872, AS Paris. See Mitchell, "Crucible of French Anticlericalism," p. 397.

60. Guibert to Antonelli, 26 July 1873, ASV Rome, SdS 409, rubrica 283.

61. CMP, *procès-verbaux*, 29 Nov. 1875, AS Paris. See Ellis, *Early Life of Georges Clemenceau*, pp. 59–70.

62. Examples may be found in police reports of 29 May, 26 June, 7 Aug., 22–23 Sept., 26 and 30 Oct. 1876, APP Paris, B A/87.

63. Ranke's famous dictum about the primacy of foreign policy has

302 / Notes to Pages 179–84

been challenged notably by Wehler's work, *Bismarck und der Imperialismus*. It is no coincidence that Wehler has also edited the essays of Eckart Kehr under the title *Der Primat der Innenpolitik*. But more recently he has qualified that notion as a "polemischer Gegenbegriff" in two articles: "Moderne Politikgeschichte" and "Die Sozialgeschichte zwischen Wirtschaftsgeschichte und Politikgeschichte." See the sustained but sometimes intemperate attack on Wehler and the "Kehrites" by Blackbourn and Eley, *Mythen deutscher Geschichtsschreibung*. Among the many sharp rejoinders is Wehler's " 'Deutscher Sonderweg' oder allgemeine Probleme." For a balanced summary see Pflanze, "Bismarcks Herrschaftstechnik."

64. Meglia to Antonelli, 2 Feb. 1876, ASV Rome, SdS 428, rubrica 248.

65. Wallon to Meglia, 5 Feb. 1876, ibid.; Meglia to Wallon, 6 Feb. 1876, ibid.; Meglia to Antonelli, 7 Feb. 1876, ibid. Wallon promptly fell from favor with the Vatican, and the French ambassador there had to warn Versailles that "even the hint of a conflict" because of Wallon would be harmful to French interests in Rome (Corcelle to Decazes, 19 Feb. 1876, MAE Paris, Rome 1060).

66. Meglia to Antonelli, 22 Feb. 1876, ASV Rome, SdS 428, rubrica 248.

67. "Lettre circulaire de son Eminence le Cardinal Archevêque de Paris ordonnant des prières publiques pour le Sénat et pour la Chambre des Députés," 28 Feb. 1876, AAP Paris, 3 B-10.

68. Meglia to Antonelli, 10 Mar. 1876, ASV Rome, SdS 428, rubrica 248; Meglia to Antonelli, 2 Apr. 1876, ibid., SdS 426, rubrica 165.

69. Corcelle to Decazes, 30 July 1876, MAE Paris, Rome 1060.

70. Bianchi (nuncio in Munich) to Antonelli, 2 Feb. 1876, ASV Rome, SdS 443, rubrica 255; Corcelle to Decazes, 3 Feb. 1876, MAE Paris, Rome 1060; Bianchi to Antonelli, 5 Feb. 1876, ASV Rome, SdS 443, rubrica 255; Antonelli to Bianchi, 8 Feb. 1876, ibid.

71. "Sch." (probably Schluga-Rastenfeld) to Bleichröder, 23 Feb. 1876, AA Bonn, I.A.B.c 79, Bd. 8.

72. Gontaut-Biron to Decazes, 4 Mar. 1876, BT Paris, Papiers Decazes, 701.

73. Hohenlohe to Bismarck, 28 Mar. 1876, AA Bonn, I.A.B.c 79, Bd. 9. See Martin, *Count Albert de Mun*, pp. 41–46.

74. Hohenlohe to Bismarck, 4 Apr. 1876, AA Bonn, I.A.B.c 79, Bd. 9. This dispatch was sent to Falk as well as to all German embassies. See Mitchell, *German Influence*, pp. 162–63.

75. Dupanloup to Pius IX, 9 Apr. 1876, AN Paris, Papiers Dupanloup, AB XIX, 525.

76. Guibert's messages were dated 24 July, 20 Sept., and 28 Oct.

1876. They were published together as *Les trois lettres de Son Eminence le Cardinal Guibert, Archevêque de Paris, à M. le Garde des Sceaux, Ministre du Conseil et des Cultes, à l'occasion de la discussion du budget pour l'année 1877.* See Gadille, *La pensée et l'action,* 2:50–51.

77. Meglia to Vannutelli, 29 Nov. 1876, ASV Rome, SdS 428, rubrica 248.

78. The negotiations concerning Dupanloup and Pie can be followed in this series of dispatches: Baude to Decazes, 9 Jan. 1877, BT Paris, Papiers Decazes, 709; Decazes to Baude, 11 Jan. 1877, ibid., 718; Baude to Decazes, 5, 13, 14, 16, 19, 26, 29 Jan. 1877, MAE Paris, Rome 1061. The nuncio's commentary on Simon was sent by Meglia to Simeoni, 28 Jan. 1877, ASV Rome, SdS 439, rubrica 248.

79. Baude to Decazes, 28 Feb. 1877, BT Paris, Papiers Decazes, 710. This opinion was buttressed by two further confidential dispatches from Baude to Decazes, 28 Feb. and 8 Mar. 1877, MAE Paris, Rome 1061.

80. Bianchi to Simeoni, 7 Mar. 1877, ASV Rome, SdS 443, rubrica 255.

81. Baude to Decazes, 18 Mar. 1877, MAE Paris, Rome 1061. When Decazes confronted Meglia with a question about the Vienna contacts, claiming to have certain information of them, the nuncio continued to deny the story (Meglia to Simeoni, 28 Mar. 1877, ASV Rome, SdS 443, rubrica 255).

82. Baude to Decazes, 2 Apr. 1877, BT Paris, Papiers Decazes, 711; Langénieux to Decazes, 25 Apr. 1877, ibid.

83. Hohenlohe to Bismarck, 5 May 1877, AA Bonn, I.A.B.c 79, Bd. 14.

84. See Mitchell, *German Influence,* pp. 144–76.

85. Meglia to Simeoni, 17 May 1877, ASV Rome, SdS 439, rubrica 248; Baude to Decazes, 19 May 1877, MAE Paris, Rome 1061; Meglia to Simeoni, 28 May 1877, ASV Rome, SdS 439, rubrica 248.

86. Baude to Decazes, 19 May 1877, MAE Paris, Rome 1061; Bleichröder to Bismarck, 29 May 1877, AA Bonn, I.A.B.c 79, Bd. 15; Hohenlohe to Bülow, 24 May 1877, ibid.; Herbert von Bismarck to Bülow, 29 May 1877, ibid.; Bülow to Hohenlohe, 4 June 1877, ibid. After exchanging views with Gambetta through an intermediary, the German ambassador met him in person for the first time in early July, as reported from Hohenlohe to Bismarck, 3 July 1877, ibid. On the central importance of German propaganda in the electoral campaign, see McManners, *Church and State in France,* pp. 42–43.

87. Decazes to Baude, 2 June 1877, MAE Paris, Rome 1062; Decazes to Baude, 4 June 1877, ibid.; Fourtou to the prefect of Morbihan, 2, 4 June 1877, AN Paris, F[7] 12683; Meglia to Simeoni, 20 June 1877, ASV Rome, SdS 439, rubrica 248. Meglia also complained that the Quai

d'Orsay was unduly influenced by the Marquis de Noailles, French envoy to the Italian government, which was under the "menacing shadow of Bismarck" (ibid.).

88. "Abschrift eines vertraulichen Berichtes aus Banquierskreisen," forwarded by Bleichröder to Bismarck, 8 June 1877, AA Bonn, I.A.B.c 81, Bd. 2.

89. Hohenlohe to Bülow, 25 June 1877, ibid., 79, Bd. 16. Confidential assurances were sent by Decazes directly to Berlin: "He, the Duc Decazes, will never allow himself to become the tool of ultramontane tendencies and would rather resign than permit such influences to extend into foreign policy" (report by Radowitz [to Herbert von Bismarck?], 28 June 1877, ibid., 79 *secr.*, Bd. 2).

90. Tiby to Decazes, 29 June 1877, MAE Paris, Allemagne 21; Decazes to Tiby, 1 July 1877, ibid.; Keudell to Bismarck, 8, 11 July 1877, AA Bonn, I.A.B.c 79, Bde. 16–17; Decazes to Vogüé, 10 Aug. 1877, BT Paris, Papiers Decazes, 719.

91. Meglia to Simeoni, 16 Aug. 1877, ASV Rome, SdS 439, rubrica 248.

92. Father Picard was director of the Association de Notre Dame de Salut. At odds with Guibert, who continued to urge greater discretion by church leaders, he nonetheless gathered support for a more activist policy from other bishops (*Journal des débats*, 30 Sept. 1877; Meglia to Simeoni, 5 Oct. 1877, ASV Rome, SdS 439, rubrica 248). See Mitchell, *German Influence*, pp. 157–58.

93. Meglia to Simeoni, 16 Oct. 1877, ASV Rome, SdS 439, rubrica 248.

94. Henckel von Donnersmarck to Bismarck, [?] Nov. and 23 Dec. 1877, SF Hamburg, Bismarck Nachlass, B 52.

95. Waddington to French ambassadors in London, Vienna, and Rome, 2 Jan. 1878, MAE Paris, Papiers Waddington, 4.

96. Waddington to Baude, 10 Feb. 1878, ibid., Rome 1063; Waddington to Bonnechose (naming him to head the French delegation), 10 Feb. 1878, ibid., Papiers Waddington, 8.

97. Waddington to Baude, 20 Feb. 1878, ibid., Rome 1063; Bülow to Hohenlohe, 28 Feb. 1878, AA Bonn, I.A.B.c 79, Bd. 23.

98. Hohenlohe to Bismarck, 28 Feb. 1878, ibid.

99. Montmarin to Waddington, 6 Mar. 1878, MAE Paris, Bavière 258; Saint-Vallier to Waddington, 12 Apr. 1878, ibid., Allemagne 23; Croy to Waddington, 19, 27 Apr. 1878, ibid., Rome 1063; Lefebvre de Béhaine to Waddington, 6 May 1878, ibid., Bavière 258. The direct quotation is from the last of these dispatches.

100. The absence of concrete discussions was confirmed by Bismarck to Falk, 16 May 1878, GW 6c:120.

101. "I say 'discussions' because until now there have not been negotiations in a literal sense" (Gabriac to Waddington, 19, 28 May 1878, MAE Paris, Rome 1063).

102. For instance, Gabriac to Dufaure, 28 June, 1 July 1878, ibid., 1064; Waddington to Gabriac, 23 July 1878, ibid.; Waddington to Moüy, 25 July 1878, ibid., Allemagne 24; Croy to Waddington, 28 July, 8, 19, 28 Aug., 7, 19 Sept., 9 Oct. 1878, ibid., Rome 1064. See Acomb, *French Laic Laws*, pp. 82–93; and Schmidt-Volkmar, *Kulturkampf*, pp. 219–67.

103. " 'It is a matter of time,' the Sovereign Pontiff said to me, 'but it seems that on every hand an arrangement is desired. As for me, I ardently wish it in the interest of Germany as well as that of the church' " (Gabriac to Waddington, 25 Oct. 1878, MAE Paris, Rome 1064).

104. Henckel von Donnersmarck to Bleichröder, 9 Oct. 1878, BL Harvard, Bleichröder Nachlass, Box 20.

105. Windthorst's statement was reported by Jacobini (papal nuncio in Vienna) to Nina (papal secretary of state), 19 Dec. 1878, reprinted by Lill, ed., *Vatikanische Akten*, 1:169–70.

106. Hohenlohe to Bismarck, 15 Jan. 1879, AA Bonn, I.A.B.c 87, Bd. 1.

107. Gabriac to Waddington, 27 Feb. 1879, MAE Paris, Rome 1065.

Chapter 9

1. Jules Ferry was minister of education on three occasions: from 4 February 1879 to 14 November 1881; 30 January to 7 August 1882; and 21 February to 20 November 1883. He remained premier until his ouster in March 1885. On his character and his career, see Israël, *L'école de la république*; Legrand, *L'influence du positivisme*; Chevallier, *La séparation*, pp. 71–83; and, despite its inappropriate title, the more intimate family portrait by Pisani-Ferry, *Monsieur l'instituteur*, pp. 89–103 and passim.

2. The text of Ferry's speech is reprinted and analyzed by Legrand, *L'influence du positivisme*, pp. 113–37, 217–37.

3. Reinach, ed., *Gambetta*, 2:174–80. See Bury, *Gambetta and the Making*, pp. 68–69.

4. See Israël, *L'école de la république*, pp. 1–2; and Chevallier et al., *L'enseignement français*, 1:108–33.

5. Duveau, *Les instituteurs*, p. 113.

6. See Pisani-Ferry, *Monsieur l'instituteur*, pp. 108–12; Bury, *Gambetta and the Making*, pp. 71–72; and Chevallier, *La séparation*, pp. 83–100.

7. Ferry's collaborator in the 1880s, Ferdinand Buisson, has also been described as one "who seemed more interested in reform of the State educational system than in the battle with Catholic education" (Watson, "Politics of Educational Reform," pp. 81–99).

8. See Watson, *Georges Clemenceau*, pp. 66–67, 81–100.

9. CMP, "Compte rendu sommaire, séance du jeudi 5 décembre 1878," AN Paris, F^{17} 9196.

10. Ferry to Hérold (prefect of the Seine), 25 Feb. 1879, ibid. See Mitchell, "Crucible of French Anticlericalism," pp. 149–51.

11. "Etat comparatif du nombre des écoles primaires et des salles d'asiles en 1871 et 1879," AN Paris, F^{17} 9196.

12. "Nombre des élèves inscrits du 15 janvier 1879," ibid. These statistics listed 1,337 secular and 858 clerical teachers in the primary schools of Paris.

13. Ferry requested a Commission Statistique de l'Enseignement Primaire to amass data both on French schools and the "comparative situation abroad," meaning principally Germany and England (Ministry of Education to Berger [inspecteur primaire de la Seine], 19 Mar. 1879, AN Paris, F^{17} 9172).

14. "Lettre de Son Eminence le Cardinal Archevêque de Paris à MM. les curés de son diocèse sur l'oeuvre des écoles chrétiennes," 1 May 1879, AAP Paris, 1 J-3.

15. Chesnelong to Monsieur ——, 23 June 1879, ibid.

16. "Oeuvre Diocésaine des Ecoles Chrétiennes Libres," 10 Apr. 1884, ibid.

17. "L'instruction primaire obligatoire," *Le Temps*, 29 Sept. 1879.

18. This unity of conception was also stressed by Paul Bert, "Rapport sur l'instruction primaire," 6 Dec. 1879, AN Paris, F^{17} 12560.

19. See Ozouf and Ozouf, "Le thème du patriotisme"; Freyssinet-Dominjon, *Les manuels d'histoire*, pp. 32–37; and Weber, "Comment la Politique Vint aux Paysans," pp. 369–71.

20. "Mandement de Son Eminence le Cardinal Archevêque de Paris pour le Carême de l'an de grâce 1880," 4 Feb. 1880, AAP Paris, 1 J-3; "Les livres au Conseil Municipal de Paris," *La république française*, 27 Mar. 1880.

21. Directive from Ferry to French prefects, 23 Sept. 1880, AN Paris, F^{17} 9162.

22. "Rapport présenté au nom de la commission chargée d'examiner des livres classiques destinés aux écoles primaires publiques," [1880?], ibid., 9208.

23. See Freyssinet-Dominjon, *Les manuels d'histoire*, p. 37; and Pisani-Ferry, *Monsieur l'instituteur*, pp. 216–17.

24. CSIP, *procès-verbaux*, 29 July 1881, AN Paris, F^{17} 12963; CSIP

(section permanente), *procès-verbaux*, 23 June 1882, ibid., 12980; ibid., 24 June 1882. On the intensive public debate, see Ozouf, *L'école, l'église et la république*, pp. 74–81, 113–16. CSIP (section permanente), *procès-verbaux*, 26, 28 June 1882, AN Paris, F¹⁷ 12980. On Buisson's importance for French primary education, see Zeldin, *France*, 2:154–56. In the end, "leurs devoirs envers Dieu" did not appear in the law but nonetheless figured in the printed material used for moral instruction in the schools. See Capéran, *Laïcité française*, 2:123–33, 168–86; Pisani-Ferry, *Monsieur l'instituteur*, pp. 184–88; and Ponteil, *Histoire de l'enseignement*, p. 288.

25. "Règlement d'organisation pédagogique pour les écoles primaires publiques (nouvelle rédaction)," CSIP, *procès-verbaux*, 24 July 1882, AN Paris, F¹⁷ 12964. See Zeldin, *France*, 2:177–85. The parliamentary debates concerning the reform of primary education are summarized by Acomb, *French Laic Laws*, pp. 163–68.

26. This conclusion is not incompatible with the view that Ferry, despite his attempts to reform the structure of education, was basically "content with the existing organization of society" (Watson, "Politics of Educational Reform," p. 85).

27. Gabriel Séailles, "L'enseignement de la philosophie en Allemagne," RIE 6 (1883):956–76.

28. "Académie de Paris: note sur les besoins de l'enseignement secondaire à Paris," 30 Apr. 1879, AN Paris, F¹⁷ 6852. A project to open six new *lycées* in Paris was conceived soon thereafter, but funding was scarce (Henri Marion, "Rapports faits au nom de la commission chargée d'examiner divers projets de transformation de collèges en lycées," 7 June 1880, ibid., 12961). On the elitism of French secondary schooling, see Zeldin, *France*, 2:248–58, 267–74, 291–99.

29. "Rapport sur la situation morale et scolaire des lycées et collèges des départements, présenté par M. Beaujean, inspecteur de l'Académie de Paris," June 1879, AN Paris, F¹⁷ 6852.

30. "Académie de Nancy, conseil académique, session de juillet 1879: rapport sur l'enseignement secondaire," 26 July 1879, ibid., 6851.

31. Choppin (rector of the Académie de Toulouse) to Ferry, 2 Aug. 1879, ibid., 6852. On the complex relationship of public and private education, see Zeldin, *France*, 2:274–91. Also see the detailed statistical account of French secondary enrollments by Ringer, *Education and Society*, pp. 316–29.

32. CSIP, *procès-verbaux*, 31 May 1879, AN Paris, F¹⁹* 3200. On the new era in secondary education inaugurated by Ferry, see Gerbod, *La condition universitaire*, pp. 602–22; and Weisz, *Universities*, pp. 120–25.

33. "Rapport présenté au nom de la commission des réformes," 11

June 1880, AN Paris, F¹⁷ 12961; "Rapport sur les modifications à introduire dans l'enseignement de l'histoire et de la géographie," 11 June 1880, ibid.; "Enseignement des sciences," 11 June 1880, ibid.; Ferry quote from CSIP, *procès-verbaux*, 17 June 1880, ibid.

34. Dreyfus-Brisac, "Les réformes de l'enseignement secondaire en France," RIE 1 (1881):1–24. On the founding and importance of this journal, see Keylor, *Academy and Community*, pp. 60–61.

35. Georges Morel, "Rapport présenté au nom de la commission de l'enseignement spécial," 30 July 1881, AN Paris, F¹⁷ 12963. Note that the French usually preferred to use the Latin plural *Gymnasia* rather than the German form *Gymnasien*.

36. Henri Marion, "La session d'été du Conseil Supérieur de l'Instruction Publique," RIE 2 (1881):171–76.

37. Gréard, "L'enseignement secondaire spéciale: mémoire présenté au conseil académique de Paris dans la séance du 22 juin 1881," ibid., pp. 249–63.

38. Open letter from Ferneuil to Dreyfus-Brisac, 4 May 1882, printed in "Correspondance internationale: les nouveaux programmes d'enseignement secondaire," ibid. 3 (1882):514–15. These views were elaborated by Ferneuil, *La réforme de l'enseignement public en France*, pp. 29–49 and passim.

39. Séailles, "Les Realschulen," RIE 4 (1882):319–45.

40. Ferneuil, "La réforme du plan d'études," ibid. 5 (1883):131–46.

41. CSIP (section permanente), *procès-verbaux*, 13 Feb. 1884, AN Paris, F¹⁷ 12981.

42. A. Couat, "La session d'été du Conseil Supérieur de l'Instruction Publique," RIE 8 (1884):159–65.

43. The same struggle to establish full parity for both secondary tracks was already being waged in Germany. Michel Krück, "De l'état de la question des écoles réales en Allemagne," ibid. 6 (1883):1155–79. A particularly critical issue there was the relationship between the *Abitur* and admission to medical studies (R.B., "Chronique de l'enseignement: Allemagne," ibid., pp. 1287–92.)

44. CSIP (section permanente), *procès-verbaux*, 13 Feb. 1884, AN Paris, F¹⁷ 12981. One historian comments: "Enseignement spécial was not a fully vested partner in the secondary system. Therein lay the inability of the French school system to accommodate itself to the twentieth century. For no logical reason, classical education was deemed necessary for the proper formation of elites and the only appropriate route to the baccalauréat and to the grandes écoles" (Harrigan, *Mobility, Elites, and Education*, p. 153).

45. CSIP (section permanente), *procès-verbaux*, 16, 23 June 1886, AN Paris, F¹⁷ 12982.

46. CSIP, *procès-verbaux*, 22 July 1886, ibid., 12968.

47. Statement by Louis Liard in CSIP (section permanente), *procès-verbaux*, 17 Dec. 1888, ibid., 12982. The work of the Simon committee was reviewed by C. Bayet, "L'enseignement secondaire et la circulaire du 28 mars 1888," RIE 17 (1889):360–77.

48. CSIP, *procès-verbaux*, 23, 28 Dec. 1889, AN Paris, F¹⁷ 12969.

49. For a compact explanation of the complexities of the German secondary system—with its *Realschule, Oberrealschule, Pro-Realgymnasium, Realgymnasium, Pro-Gymnasium,* and *Gymnasium*—see Müller, *Sozialstruktur und Schulsystem*, pp. 37–60. This account can be complemented by Lundgreen, *Sozialgeschichte der deutschen Schule*, 1:70–87; and Albisetti, *Secondary School Reform*. A major attempt to place the matter into a comparative perspective is by Ringer, *Education and Society*, pp. 32–112 (on Germany) and pp. 113–205 (on France). Ringer's suggestion that the German educational system was more "democratic" or "progressive" than the French has drawn criticism from Lundgreen, "Bildung und Besitz," pp. 262–75, and from Harrigan, *Mobility, Elites, and Education*, p. 22.

50. C.D., "A propos de la réforme de l'enseignement secondaire," RIE 19 (1890):73–81. Note that the entire discussion was by and about men. For the impact of the Ferry laws on women, see Mayeur, *L'éducation des filles*, pp. 148–80.

51. CSIP (section permanente), *procès-verbaux*, 10 Dec. 1890, AN Paris, F¹⁷ 12983. A similar problem was posed by the training of engineers. In Germany their initial preparation was usually in the *Realschulen*, which permitted students to move directly into the *Technische Hochschulen* and *Bergakademien*. By contrast, most French engineering students continued to emerge from the classical *lycée* before studying further at the Ecole Polytechnique, the Ecole des Ponts et Chaussées, or the Ecole Supérieure des Mines. See the comparative analysis by Locke, "Industrialisierung und Erziehungssystem." The inherent superiority of the German system, assumed by Locke, is challenged by Lundgreen, "Organization of Science and Technology," pp. 311–32. Further, on technical education in France, see Shinn, "Des corps de l'état au secteur industriel"; and Day, "The Making of Mechanical Engineers in France." The sociological background is also provided in works by Shinn, *Savoir scientifique et pouvoir social*, pp. 65–99; and Weiss, *Technological Man*.

52. CSIP (section permanente), *procès-verbaux*, 12 Dec. 1890, AN Paris, F¹⁷ 12983.

53. "Projet de réorganisation de l'enseignement secondaire spécial," CSIP, *procès-verbaux*, 3 June 1891, ibid., F¹⁷ 12970. See the summary by Day, "Technical and Professional Education in France."

54. Dreyfus-Brisac, "L'enseignement en France et à l'étranger con-

sidéré au point de vue politique et social," RIE 17 (1889):113–26. These views were expanded by Dreyfus-Brisac in *L'université de Bonn* and the three volumes of *L'éducation nouvelle*. His message was simple: "I wish that our young universities would constantly have before them the example of the German universities. That is the best of models" (ibid., 2:xii). For France see Moody, *French Education*, pp. 87–92; and for Germany, McClelland, *State, Society and University*, pp. 239–87.

55. Monod, *Portraits et souvenirs*, p. 316; and "Les études historiques en France," RIE 18 (1889):587–99. In the inaugural issue of the *Revue historique* Monod contrasted French amateurism with the "superiority" and the "rigorously scientific character" of German universities: "It is Germany that has contributed the lion's share to the historical work of our century" ("Du progrès des études historiques en France depuis le XVIe siècle," *Revue historique* 1 [1876]:5–38). See Keylor, *Academy and Community*, pp. 36–45; and Zeldin, *France*, 2:316–45.

56. Marcellin Berthelot, "L'enseignement supérieur et son outillage," RIE 5 (1883):383–93. Germany had demonstrated "a spirit of pragmatism that is evident in military organization as well as in the construction of laboratories," agreed Georges Dumesnil ("L'enquête relative à l'enseignement supérieur," ibid. 11 [1886]:2–19). An inventory of scientific equipment in 1885 revealed that French universities had barely surpassed the level of the July monarchy. See Zeldin, *France*, 2:319–21; Guerlac, "Science and French National Strength"; Gilpin, *France in the Age of the Scientific State*, pp. 82–85; and Ben-David, *The Scientist's Role in Society*, pp. 108–38.

57. Charles Seignobos, "L'enseignement de l'histoire dans les universités allemandes," RIE 1 (1881):563–600. See Keylor, *Academy and Community*, pp. 74–82.

58. Ernest Lavisse, "L'enseignement supérieur et la préparation aux agrégations de l'enseignement supérieur," RIE 5 (1883):371–82. See Nora, "Ernest Lavisse"; Keylor, *Academy and Community*, pp. 90–100; and Mitchell, "German History in France after 1870," pp. 84–86.

59. Dreyfus-Brisac, "Les réformes de l'enseignement supérieur en France," RIE 1 (1881):121–36. See Keylor, *Academy and Community*, pp. 55–65; Zeldin, "Higher Education in France," reprinted in his *France*, 2:316–45; and Weisz, *Universities*, pp. 65–69.

60. "Statistique des étudiants français durant l'année scolaire 1890–91: facultés de l'état et facultés libres," RIE 23 (1892):55. See Chevallier et al., *L'enseignement français*, 1:112; and Acomb, *French Laic Laws*, pp. 130–37.

61. "Statistique des étudiants français durant l'année scolaire 1890–91," and "Statistique générale des étudiants allemands durant le semestre d'été 1891," RIE 23 (1892):55, 65. On the development of the French legal profession, see Gaudemet, *Les juristes et la vie politique*.

62. The emphasis on centralization of the French system is qualified but not really contradicted by Nye, "Scientific Periphery in France." Nye ends by conceding "the failure of the periphery" to advance fundamental science. She also notes that such progress as was made in the provinces was "the result of educational reforms in imitation of the German university model" (ibid., pp. 375–76, 402–3). See Weisz, *Universities*, pp. 22–23.

63. Louis Liard, "Projet de décret sur l'organisation des facultés et des écoles d'enseignement supérieur," in CSIP, *procès-verbaux*, 22 Dec. 1885, AN Paris, F¹⁷ 12967. Liard's predecessor as director of higher education, Albert Dumont, appointed by Ferry in 1879, had been equally impressed by the organization of the German university system, which he described as "a vast *Landwehr*." See Mayeur, "Albert Dumont."

64. CSIP, *procès-verbaux*, 22 Dec. 1885, AN Paris, F¹⁷ 12967. The annual budgetary allocation for French higher education doubled in the first postwar decade from 4,300,000 francs in 1871 to 8,625,330 francs in 1879, and it increased further to 11,391,495 francs by 1889. But it still lagged far behind the financing of Germany's twenty-one faculties. The ten universities of Prussia alone received about 2 million more francs a year than the total of their French counterparts, according to Liard, *Universités et facultés*, pp. 46–49. Put into other terms, Paris could match Berlin, but other German universities received three times as much funding as the provincial faculties in France (Zeldin, *France*, 2:323–24).

65. CSIP, *procès-verbaux*, 21 Mar. 1887, AN Paris, F¹⁷ 12968. A lively debate has developed over the question whether French higher education, especially in the natural sciences, was seriously eclipsed by Germany. The so-called "declinist literature" (which includes such authors, already cited, as Gilpin, Crozier, and Ben-David) has been attacked notably by Paul, *Sorcerer's Apprentice*, pp. 84–86, and "The Issue of Decline." The entire matter is reviewed in the introduction to Fox and Weisz, eds., *Organization of Science and Technology*, pp. 1–28. At the least it is certain that the French generally followed in the wake of the Germans in the latter half of the nineteenth century and not vice versa. See Lundgreen, *Sozialgeschichte der deutschen Schule*, 1:116; and Weisz, *Universities*, pp. 62–64.

66. "Projet de règlement portant révision du régime du concours d'agrégation des facultés de médicine," CSIP, *procès-verbaux*, 28 July 1887, AN Paris, F¹⁷ 12968.

67. Statement by Dr. Brouardel, in CSIP (section permanente), 13 Feb. 1891, ibid., 12984. The crux of the problem was thus not the number of physicians trained in France but the quality of their training and the geographical distribution of their subsequent practice. See Sussman, "Glut of Doctors"; and Weisz, "Reform and Conflict." The latter

essay, an otherwise excellent summary, fails to locate the debate over medical education within the context of reform of the baccalaureate and thus provides an inadequate explanation of the expressed need for a preparatory year of science training for medical students.

68. Lefort, "Le professeur médical en Allemagne et en France," RIE 23 (1892):71–74.

69. CSIP (section permanente), *procès-verbaux*, 11 July 1890, AN Paris, F^{17} 12983–84.

70. Ibid.

71. Ibid., 12 Dec. 1890, 18 Mar. 1891.

72. C.D., "A propos de la réforme de l'enseignement secondaire," RIE 19 (1890):73–81.

73. CSIP (section permanente), *procès-verbaux*, 19 Dec. 1890, AN Paris, F^{17} 12983.

74. "Le projet de loi sur les universités devant le sénat," RIE 23 (1892):385–415.

75. "Réorganisation de l'enseignement médical en France," ibid. 25 (1893):154–74.

76. "Projet de décret relatif au doctorat en médicine," in CSIP (section permanente), *procès-verbaux*, 28 June 1893, AN Paris, F^{17} 12985; CSIP, *procès-verbaux*, 19 July 1893, ibid., 12971. "The apparent failure of educational reforms during the Third Republic" is deplored by Weisz, "Reform and Conflict," pp. 82–94.

77. Of course, the story continued: witness the creation in 1899 of a parliamentary committee, chaired by Alexandre Ribot, to undertake yet another revaluation of secondary education. In theory, Ribot's intention was to place the classical and modern tracks on the same footing; in reality, the result was meager. "Henceforth, there was to be one kind of secondary education. . . . But proclaiming the unity of secondary education did not unify it; the reform [of 1902] did not put an end to the battle of ancients and moderns" (Talbott, *Politics of Educational Reform*, pp. 15–21).

78. "German achievements set the standards by which French performance was judged," concludes Weisz (*Universities*, p. 224).

Chapter 10

1. "I will, if I remain in office, conduct the Kulturkampf to the bitter end." Bismarck's statement was recorded in the diary of Adalbert Falk, entry for 6 Oct. 1877, quoted by Stürmer, ed., *Bismarck und die preussisch-deutsche Politik*, pp. 383–86. French fears were meanwhile expressed by, among others, the French ambassador to the Vatican: "It would be too painful for me . . . to imagine that we could someday be involved in a reconciliation between the Holy See and Germany that

would be accomplished at our expense" (Gabriac to Waddington, 29 May 1879, MAE Paris, Rome 1065). See Hanotaux, *Histoire de la France contemporaine*, 4:503–14.

2. Saint-Vallier to Waddington, 6 June 1879, MAE Paris, Mémoires et documents, Allemagne 166 bis.

3. Hohenlohe to Bismarck, 27 Mar. 1879, AA Bonn, I.A.B.c 87, Bd. 3; Auswärtiges Amt to Falk, 31 Mar. 1879, ibid., 77, Bd. 16; Falk to Bismarck, 5 Apr. 1879, ibid.; Gabriac to Waddington, 9 July 1879, MAE Paris, Rome 1066; Saint-Vallier to Waddington, 14 Nov. 1879, ibid., Allemagne 31.

4. At the Hôtel de Ville in Paris it was not uncommon to hear speeches about "the declaration of war by the Syllabus against secular society," as in the "Rapport présenté par M. Hovelacque au nom de la 4e commission . . . tendant à la transformation des écoles communales congréganistes en écoles laïques," CMP, *procès-verbaux*, 7 Dec. 1878, AN Paris, F^{17} 9196.

5. The retort to Lockroy was by the conservative deputy Baudry d'Asson (JORF, 20 May 1879).

6. Waddington to Gabriac, 9 Apr. 1879, MAE Paris, Rome 1065; Gabriac to Waddington, 10 Apr. 1879, ibid.; *La république française*, 20 June 1879.

7. Gabriac to Waddington, 5 July 1879, MAE Paris, Rome 1066.

8. Hohenlohe to Bismarck, 29 July 1879, AA Bonn, I.A.B.c 79, Bd. 3.

9. "La liberté d'enseignement: discours de M. Jules Ferry à l'association philotechnique," 2 July 1882, RIE 4 (1882):101–4.

10. "[Jules Ferry] recognizes that the rigorous application of the law would be the only solution if all municipal councils resembled the Municipal Council of Paris. Yet it is incontestable . . . that the law needs to become established. We must adhere to the principle of the separation of church and school, but the rest is trivial" (CSIP [section permanente], *procès-verbaux*, 20 Oct. 1882, AN Paris, F^{17} 12980).

11. Petition of 1 May 1882, ibid., 9125^{1}. One of the principal movers of this campaign was the Comte de Mun, according to the prefect of the Gironde to Ferry, 26 May 1882, ibid. See Martin, *Count Albert de Mun*, pp. 44–46.

12. See Sedgwick, *Ralliement*, p. viii.

13. Directives from Lepère to the prefects, 3, 28 Apr. 1879, AN Paris, F^{19} 1958.

14. "The conflict between the French regime and the clergy is progressing in its development," commented Hohenlohe to Bismarck, 27 Apr. 1879, AA Bonn, I.A.B.c 87, Bd. 3. See Gadille, *La pensée et l'action*, 2:148.

15. Directive from Lepère to the prefects, 3 June 1879, AN Paris,

F[1a] 2140a. Later that year, while evaluating the admirable performance of Edwin von Manteuffel as chief administrator in the new *Reichsland* of Alsace-Lorraine, Saint-Vallier commented that the German general was profiting from "the tendency of the government in Berlin to abandon or at least to mitigate the Kulturkampf" and, at the same time, from "the tendency of some French ministers and their prefects, under pressure from advanced [political] factions and certain municipal councils, to pursue the clergy" (Saint-Vallier to Waddington, 27 Nov. 1879, MAE Paris, Allemagne 31).

16. Comte d'Aunay to Freycinet, 19 Mar. 1880, ibid., Rome 1067; Desprez to Freycinet, 28 Mar. 1880, ibid. Among the other orders not specifically authorized by the Concordat were Franciscans, Dominicans, Augustinians, Trappists, and Marists.

17. Freycinet to Desprez, 28 Mar. 1880, ibid.

18. Desprez to Freycinet, 31 Mar. 1880, ibid. See Acomb, *French Laic Laws*, pp. 137–46, 229–36; and Padberg, *Colleges in Controversy*, pp. 249–72.

19. Comte d'Aunay to Gambetta, 9 Apr. 1880, MAE Paris, Papiers Aunay; Freycinet to Desprez, 10, 14 Apr. 1880, ibid., Rome 1067. This was no slip of the pen because ten days later Freycinet reiterated: "If the Holy See does not take care, as I have said, it will mean the beginning of a rupture between church and state" (Freycinet to Desprez, 24 Apr. 1880, ibid.).

20. Freycinet to Desprez, 12 May 1880, ibid.

21. Desprez to Freycinet, 22 Apr. 1880, ibid.; Freycinet to Desprez, 3, 10 May 1880, ibid.

22. Desprez to Freycinet, 15 May 1880, ibid.; two telegrams from Freycinet to Desprez, 16 May 1880, ibid.

23. Directives from Lepère to the prefects, 3, 28 Apr. 1879, AN Paris, F[19] 1958; Lepère to Grévy, [?] May 1879, ibid., 2446; Lepère to Desprez (archbishop of Toulouse), [?] 1879, ibid.

24. See Gadille, *La pensée et l'action*, 2:130–34.

25. Freycinet to Gabriac, 6 Jan. 1880, MAE Paris, Rome 1067.

26. Flourens to Freycinet, 11 Jan., 7 Feb., 6 Mar. 1880, ibid. Emile Flourens was the very active director general of "cultes" under Jules Ferry, whom he advised regularly on matters pertaining to the implementation of laws passed in the parliament.

27. Barthélémy Saint-Hilaire to Constans, 17 Nov. 1880, AN Paris, F[19] 1958.

28. Mourney to Flourens, 15 Mar. 1881, ibid., 2450.

29. Bert to Cazot, 30 Nov. 1881, ibid., 5580; Bismarck to Busch, 2 Dec. 1881, GW VIc:231.

30. "Observations présentées au nom de l'épiscopat à messieurs les

sénateurs et les députés par les cardinaux," May 1882, AAP Paris, 4 B I-1.

31. The French chargé in Rome reported to the Quai d'Orsay concerning the church's attitude toward secular governments: "Consequently it condones all of them and has a marked predilection for none of them in particular" (Moubel to Duclerc, 21 Oct. 1882, AN Paris, F¹⁹ 1943).

32. All of these measures could be voluminously documented, but a few characteristic examples may suffice: Prefect of the Vosges to Duvaux, 7 Nov. 1882, ibid., F¹⁷ 9125²; Goblet to Ferry, 2 Dec. 1882, ibid.; "Rapport fait au nom de la commission du budget . . . par Mr. Ribot, député," 19 Dec. 1882, ibid., F¹⁹ 2446; Martin-Feiullée to Ferry, 17 Mar., 12 May 1883, ibid., F¹⁷ 9125². See Capéran, *Laïcité française,* 2:14–22.

33. Challemel Lacour to Lefebvre de Béhaine, 20 May 1883, AN Paris, F¹⁹ 1943. See Weber, *Peasants into Frenchmen,* pp. 361–64.

34. Courcel to Challemel Lacour, 11 June 1883, ibid., 6233; Ferry to Lefebvre de Béhaine, 24 Sept. 1883, ibid., 1943; Jacobini to Moubel, 4 Dec. 1883, ibid.

35. "Lettre des évêques de France à sa Sainteté le Pape Léon XIII en réponse à l'encyclique Nobilissima Gallorum Gens du 8 février 1884," AAP Paris, 4 B I-1. See Sedgwick, *Ralliement,* pp. 6–8.

36. Lefebvre de Béhaine to Ferry, 20 Mar., 27 Aug. 1884, AN Paris, F¹⁹ 1943; telegram from Ferry to Lefebvre de Béhaine, 3 Sept. 1884, ibid.

37. The separation of church and state was favored by 80 percent of the deputies elected in 1885. See Watson, *Georges Clemenceau,* p. 113.

38. Lefebvre de Béhaine to Ferry, 13 Sept. 1884, AN Paris, F¹⁹ 1943.

39. This theme has been a commonplace since the appearance of Wienefeld, *Franco-German Relations,* and Mitchell, *Bismarckian Policy of Conciliation.*

40. Among the important general works on the subject are Baumont, *L'essor industriel;* Brunschwig, *Myths et réalités;* Pisani-Ferry, *Jules Ferry;* Ganiage, *L'expansion coloniale;* and Grupp, *Deutschland, Frankreich und die Kolonien.* The renewal of public interest in the colonies was directly related to the lost war and the felt need to restore French prestige and economic growth after the loss of Alsace-Lorraine, argues Valette, "Note sur l'idée coloniale."

41. Confidential note from Barthélémy Saint-Hilaire to Constans, 1 June 1881, AN Paris, F¹⁹ 1943. See O'Donnell, "Cardinal Charles Lavigerie." Even earlier, at the Congress of Berlin in 1878, the French diplomatic delegation had been expressly requested by the Vatican to assist in

defense of Christian interests in "the Orient" (Gabriac to Waddington, 7 June 1878, MAE Paris, Rome 1064).

42. Challemel Lacour to Lefebvre de Béhaine, 20 May 1883, AN Paris, F^{19} 1943.

43. Lefebvre de Béhaine to Ferry, 10 Feb. 1885, ibid.

44. Lefebvre de Béhaine to Ferry, 16 Mar. 1885, ibid.; Jacobini to Lefebvre de Béhaine, 25 Mar. 1885, ibid.; Goblet to Freycinet, [?] Apr. 1885, ibid.

45. Lefebvre de Béhaine to Freycinet, 30 June 1885, ibid., 2446.

46. *Moniteur de Rome*, 26 Aug., 7–8 Oct. 1885. The Fulda conference preceded the first *Friedensgesetz* of 21 May 1886, which reestablished Catholic religious orders in Germany—except the Jesuits—and ended other legal restrictions on the Roman church.

47. Quoted from Kohn, ed., *Modern World*, pp. 152–53.

48. The text was published in France as "Lettre encyclique de N.T.S.P. Léon XIII, pape par la providence divine, aux archevêques et évêques de Prusse," *Le Monde*, 20 Jan. 1886. See Schmidt-Volkmar, *Kulturkampf*, pp. 299–300.

49. Lefebvre de Béhaine to Freycinet, 19 Feb. 1886, AN Paris, F^{19} 1943.

50. Freycinet to Goblet, 22 Mar. 1886, ibid.; Francis Charmes to Goblet, 29 Mar. 1886, ibid.

51. *L'Univers*, 18 Apr. 1886.

52. Freycinet to Lefebvre de Béhaine, 12 May 1886, AN Paris, F^{19} 1943. A particular target was of course Jules Ferry, who was accused of being "Bismarck's valet" and of marrying a Prussian (his wife was in fact Alsatian). See Pisani-Ferry, *Monsieur l'instituteur*, pp. 272–74.

53. Germany's interaction with France during the Boulanger crisis is outlined in Mitchell, *Bismarck and the French Nation*, pp. 99–105.

54. Auguste Vacquerie, "Les élections allemandes," *Rappel*, 9 Feb. 1887; Eugène Spuller, "Le pape et l'Allemagne," *La république française*, 8 Feb. 1887. Such pertinent editorials are collected in AN Paris, F^{19} 1947.

55. Robert Mitchell, "Puissance morale," *Souveraineté*, 8 Feb. 1887.

56. Albert de la Berge, "Les conditions de la trêve," *Le Siècle*, 6 May 1887.

57. The exception cited was the cabinet of Maurice Rouvier (30 May–12 Dec. 1887), in an unsigned editorial entitled "La république et le 'Kulturkampf,'" *Moniteur de Rome*, 30 Aug. 1888.

58. See Mayeur, *Les débuts*, pp. 197–203; Sedgwick, *Ralliement*, pp. 39–41; Ozouf, *L'école, l'église et la république*, pp. 167–90; and McManners, *Church and State in France*, pp. 64–80.

59. For a narrative see Ligou, *Histoire du socialisme*, pp. 5–175; for

a critical review of the literature see Moss, *Origins*, pp. 201–10; and for a local study (of the Var) see Judt, *Socialism in Provence*, pp. 217–38.

60. Lafargue strenuously objected to Christian Socialism and thus advocated more than the separation of church and state: "We demand something else. . . . Even before separating church and state, it is crucial to separate church and factory to assure the freedom of conscience of the working class" ("Proposition de loi tendant à la séparation des Eglises et de l'Etat présentée par M. Paul Lafargue," 17 Dec. 1891, AN Paris, F⁷ 12389; JORF, 18 Dec. 1891).

61. The archives are well stocked with data showing the steady progress of the republican campaign: e.g., "Enquête sur les laïcisations d'écoles publiques," 10 Jan. 1889, ibid., F¹⁷ 9176; and "Tableau récapitulatif des états de situation des écoles primaires, année scolaire 1887–1888," 10 Jan. 1889, ibid., 10725.

62. For example, Direction des Cultes to the archbishop of Sens, 17 Jan. 1889, AN Paris, F¹⁹ 5613.

63. "Lettre pastorale de monseigneur l'évêque d'Angers sur les devoirs des chrétiens dans l'exercice du droit de suffrage," *La semaine religieuse du diocèse d'Angers*, 10 Mar. 1889, ibid., 5618; Lefebvre de Béhaine to Spuller, 21 Mar. 1889, ibid., 5613; Spuller to Thévenet, 28 Mar. 1889, ibid.; Spuller to Thévenet, 3 Apr. 1889, ibid., 2447. A similar incident involved the archbishop of Aix-en-Provence, who drew a warning from the Ministry of Justice and Religion: directive from Thévenet to the French bishops, 4 Sept. 1889, AAP Paris, 3 B-4.

64. Charles Dumay, "Note pour Monsieur le Garde des Sceaux," 27 Mar. 1889, AN Paris, F¹⁹ 5611.

65. "Illusions et vanités," *L'Estafette*, 23 Oct. 1889. The Ministry of Justice and Religion later attempted to repress the pilgrimages on the grounds that they had caused "regrettable incidents" in Rome (directive from Fallières to archbishops and bishops, 4 Oct. 1891, AN Paris, F¹⁹ 5563). See Martin, *Count Albert de Mun*, pp. 86–128; and McManners, *Church and State*, pp. 81–103.

66. Quoted from Kohn, ed., *Modern World*, pp. 153–56. For an appreciation of *Rerum Novarum* as a momentous document and yet one that "complicated an already very difficult situation," see Latreille et al., *Histoire du catholicisme en France*, 3:472–80.

67. "Exposé de la situation faite à l'église en France et déclarations des eminentissimes cardinaux," 16 Jan. 1892, AN Paris, F¹⁹ 5613. The five French cardinals (Desprez, Foulon, Langénieux, Place, and Richard) were immediately notified by the cabinet that a copy of their offensive statement was being forwarded to the Conseil d'Etat for possible legal action (directive from Fallières to the archbishops of Toulouse, Lyon, Reims, Rennes, and Paris, [?] Jan. 1892, ibid.).

68. The archbishop of Paris, for instance, circumspectly expressed

his regrets in declining an invitation to a republican celebration at the Panthéon: "I hasten to add ... that this abstention bears no hint of hostility to republican institutions" (Monsignor François Richard to Louis Richard [minister of justice and religion], 21 Sept. 1892, ibid., 5582).

69. To cite only one instance among many, a recently published account of the heroic resistance of a persecuted Alsatian abbot was glowingly praised in the following terms: "In reading these pages—so vital, so vibrant—we feel strengthened, we understand the purpose of struggle, we see clearly the possibility of victory, we blush at the pittance that has been accomplished in France until now, we await the onset of the battle. . . . The moment to act has come. The value of [abbot] Kannengieser's work is to suggest for us the example of a clergy and a people who have spoken little and acted much. Let us imitate them" (Henry Boissard, "Catholiques allemands," L'Univers, 20 Mar. 1892).

70. See Digeon, La crise allemande, pp. 324–27.

71. Lefebvre de Béhaine to Develle, 27 Jan., 19 May, 9 June 1893, AN Paris, F¹⁹ 2447; and later, Poincaré to Hanotaux, 4 May 1895, ibid.

72. See Digeon, La crise allemande, pp. 332–33, 538–42; and Seager, Boulanger Affair, pp. 47–69.

73. See Johnson, France and the Dreyfus Affair, pp. 13–53; Mitchell, "Xenophobic Style," pp. 424–25; and Wilson, Ideology and Experience, pp. 290–300, 422–24.

74. A police report about the appearance by a Capucine monk "of German origin" was indicative of such ugly talk: "He made a parallel between the persecutions of which Catholics have been victim and the favors reserved for Jews. . . . He made allusion to the Dreyfus Affair by saying that the Jews wanted at any cost to save a culprit [who was] in complicity with the Freemasons. . . . Finally, he pointed out all the small property owners ruined by these miserable Jews and Freemasons, [who] should be exterminated" (police commissioner of Avallon to the prefect of the Yonne, 24 Dec. 1898, AN Paris, F¹⁹ 5613). See McManners, Church and State, pp. 118–28; and Wilson, Ideology and Experience, pp. 145–59, 390–94, 415–22, 679–84.

75. For the rest of the story, consult such standard works as Mayeur, La séparation; Sorlin, Waldeck-Rousseau; Partin, Waldeck-Rousseau, Combes, and the Church; Larkin, Church and State; or (in the moderate Catholic perspective and lucid prose of René Rémond) Latreille et al., Histoire du catholicisme en France, 3:487–530.

Bibliography

Manuscript Sources

Archives de l'archevêché, Paris
  1 D IX Papiers Guibert
  1 J   Direction de l'enseignement: actes, circulaires, corre-
          spondance
  3 B   Rapports avec le pouvoir civil
  4 B   Episcopat de France: correspondance avec les évêques
Archives de la préfecture de police, Paris
  B A/86–87 Rapports quotidiens
  B A/311–37 Rapports de correspondants . . . principalement
                 à l'étranger
  B A/1280 Thiers
Archives de la Seine, Paris
  Procès-verbaux du Conseil Municipal de Paris
Archives du seminaire de Saint-Sulpice, Paris
  Fonds Dupanloup
Archives nationales, Paris
  F^1 Administration générale
  F^7 Police générale
  F^{17} Instruction publique
  F^{19} Cultes
  F^{30} Finances, administration générale
  AB XIX Documents entrés aux Archives nationales par des voies
         extraordinaires
             Papiers Dupanloup
  AP   Archives privées
             Papiers Jules Simon
             Papiers Scheurer-Kestner
Archivio Segreto Vaticano (Segretaria di Stato), Rome
  Rubrica 242 Guerra di Francia

Rubrica 248 Nunciatura di Parigi
Rubrica 255 Questioni religiosa: Germanica
Rubrica 261 Francia ministro
Rubrica 283 Vescovi esteri: Francia
Rubrica 291 Francia consoli
Auswärtiges Amt, Bonn
    I.A.B.c 70–87 Frankreich
    I.D.44   Militärangelegenheiten
    II.B.10   Frieden
Baker Library, Harvard Business School, Cambridge, Mass.
    Bleichröder Nachlass
Bayerische Staatsbibliothek, Munich
    Döllinger Nachlass
Bibliothèque nationale, Paris
    Papiers Dupanloup (NAF 24711–15)
    Papiers Rémusat (NAF 14414–71)
    Papiers Thiers (NAF 20601–84)
    Miscellaneous
Bibliothèque Thiers, Paris
    Papiers Decazes (681–751)
Bundesarchiv, Koblenz
    Bülow Nachlass
    Hohenlohe Nachlass
Ministère des affaires étrangères, Paris
    Correspondance politique, Allemagne (1–38)
    Correspondance politique, Bavière (250–60)
    Correspondance politique, Rome (1052–67)
    Mémoires et documents, Allemagne (156–67 bis)
    Papiers Aunay
    Papiers Favre
    Papiers Gambetta
    Papiers Hanotaux
    Papiers Waddington
Schloss Friedrichsruh, near Hamburg
    Bismarck Nachlass
Service historique de l'armée de terre, Vincennes
    Conseil Supérieur de la Guerre (1 N 2–4)
    Cabinet du ministre (5 N 1–2)
    Etat-major de l'armée (7 N 1–46, 653–77, 1106–22, 1736–1826)
    Directions, commissions et inspections (9 N 4, 26, 40)
    Mémoires et reconnaissances (MR 1983, 1998–99, 2008, 2032, 2120–21, 2128–30, 2136–37, 2150)
    Correspondance générale (G^8 177–79)
    Organisation générale (XS 163–64)

Published Documents

Annuaire statistique de la France.
Bismarck: die gesammelten Werke. Edited by Herman von Petersdorf et al. 15 vols. Berlin, 1924–35.
Die Grosse Politik der europäischen Kabinette, 1871–1914. Edited by Johannes Lepsius et al. 40 vols. Berlin, 1922–27.
Documents diplomatiques français, 1871–1914. Edited by the Ministère des affaires étrangères. 1st series (1871–1900). 15 vols. Paris, 1929–59.
Journal officiel de la république française.
Le moniteur universel.

Contemporary Journals and Newspapers

L'Autorité.
Le Bulletin militaire de l'étranger.
L'Estafette.
Impressions.
Journal des débats.
Journal des sciences militaires.
La Libre parole.
Le Monde.
Le Moniteur de Rome.
Norddeutsche Allgemeine Zeitung.
Le Pèlerin.
Le Rappel.
La République française.
Revue d'artillerie.
Revue des deux mondes.
Revue internationale de l'enseignement.
Revue militaire de l'étranger.
Le Siècle.
La Souveraineté.
Le Spectateur militaire.
Le Temps.
L'Univers.

Memoirs, Letters, and Polemics

L'armée nouvelle. Etude sur la réorganisation de notre force publique. Paris, 1871.
Bonaparte, Louis. *Oeuvres de Napoléon III.* 2 vols. Paris, 1856.
Bonnal, General. *L'art nouveau en tactique.* Paris, 1904.

———. *Note posthume sur les grandes manoeuvres du 6e corps en 1888.* Paris, 1912.

Bréal, Michel. *Quelques mots sur l'instruction publique en France.* Paris, 1872.

Broglie, Duc Albert de. *Mémoires.* 2 vols. Paris, 1938–41.

Chabaud-Latour, Ernest. *Etude militaire sur la division de la France en régions territoriales.* Paris, n.d.

Choppin, Henri (Charles Delacour). *L'armée française, 1870–1890.* Paris, 1900.

Cluseret, Gustave-Paul. *Armée et démocratie.* Paris, 1869.

———. *Mémoires.* 3 vols. Paris, 1887–88.

Conzemius, Victor, ed. *Ignaz von Döllinger—Lord Acton: Briefwechsel.* 3 vols. Munich, 1963–71.

Derrécagaix, Captain. *Etude sur les état-majors des armées étrangères, suivie d'un projet de réorganisation de l'état-major français.* 2d ed. Paris, 1871.

Dessoye, Arthur. *Jean Macé et la fondation de la ligue de l'enseignement.* Paris, 1883.

Doumer, Paul. *Note sur la réorganisation de l'armée française, présentée à la commission sénatoriale de l'armée.* Paris, 1919.

Dreyfus-Brisac, Edmond. *L'éducation nouvelle. Etudes de pédagogie comparée.* 3 vols. Paris, 1882–97.

———. *L'université de Bonn et l'enseignement supérieur en Allemagne.* Paris, 1879.

Du Barail, General. *Mes souvenirs.* 3 vols. Paris, 1894–96.

Ducrot, General. *De l'état-major et des differentes armes.* Paris, 1873.

Duruy, Victor. *Administration de l'instruction publique (de 1863 à 1869).* Paris, n.d.

———. *Notes et souvenirs.* 2 vols. Paris, 1901.

Farre, General. *Observations sur les réformes militaires à l'étude.* Paris, 1882.

Ferneuil, Théodore. *La réforme de l'enseignement public en France et les nouveaux programmes adoptés par le Conseil Supérieur de l'Instruction Publique.* 2d ed. Paris, 1881.

Ferron, General. *Etudes sur l'armée nouvelle.* Paris, 1872.

La France est-elle prête? Paris, 1884.

La France est prête! Paris and Limoges, 1885.

Freycinet, Charles de. *La guerre en province pendant le siège de Paris, 1870–1871.* 14th ed. Paris, 1894.

———. *Souvenirs, 1848–1878.* 6th ed. Paris, 1914.

———. *Souvenirs, 1878–1893.* 4th ed. Paris, 1913.

Gilbert, Captain Georges. *Lois et institutions militaires. Six études organiques.* Paris, 1895.

Gillon, Edouard. *Le nouveau soldat du service obligatoire.* Paris, 1873.

Girardin, Saint-Marc. *Notice sur le général de division Baron de Chabaud-La-Tour.* Paris, 1885.

Guibert, Archbishop Joseph. *Les trois lettres de Son Eminence le Cardinal Guibert, Archevêque de Paris, à M. le Garde des Sceaux, Ministre du Conseil et des Cultes, à l'occasion de la discussion du budget pour l'année 1877.* Paris, 1876.

Jacqmin, François. *Les chemins de fer pendant la guerre de 1870–1871.* Paris, 1872.

Langlois, Captain. *Les artilleries de campagne de l'Europe en 1874.* Brussels and Paris, 1875.

Lemoyne, Captain. *La mobilisation. Etude sur les institutions militaires de la Prusse.* Paris, 1872.

Lewal, Jules. *Etudes de guerre.* Paris, 1873.

_____. *La réforme de l'armée.* Paris, 1871.

Liard, Louis. *Universités et facultés.* Paris, 1890.

Lill, Rudolf, ed. *Vatikanische Akten zur Geschichte des deutschen Kulturkampfes.* Vol. 1. Tübingen, 1970.

Lois annotées sur le recrutement, l'organisation et la composition des cadres et des effectifs de l'armée. Paris, 1878.

Macé, Jean. *La ligue de l'enseignement à Beblenheim, 1862–1870.* Paris, 1890.

Maillard, General. *Cours de tactique d'infantrie, 1884–1885.* Paris, 1885.

_____. *Cours de tactique générale et d'infantrie (2e partie), 1889–90.* Paris, 1890.

Martin, Louis. *Le maréchal Canrobert.* Paris and Limoges, 1895.

Moch, Gaston. "La poudre sans fumée et la tactique." *Revue d'artillerie* 35 (1889–90):297–341, 393–416, 498–522.

_____. *L'armée d'une démocratie.* 2d ed. New York and London, 1972.

Monod, Gabriel. "Du progrès des études historiques en France depuis le XVIe siècle." *Revue historique* 1 (1876):5–38.

_____. *Portraits et souvenirs.* Paris, 1897.

Noix, Lt.-Colonel. *Géographie militaire.* Vol. 3: *Allemagne.* 2d ed. Paris, 1885.

Ollivier, Emile. *Journal, 1846–1869.* 2 vols. Paris, 1961.

Pesch, Captain. *Histoire de l'Ecole de Saint-Cyr.* Paris, 1886.

Pinet, G. *Histoire de l'Ecole Polytechnique.* Paris, 1887.

Pourquoi la France n'est pas prête. Paris, 1885.

Préparation à l'école supérieure de guerre: conseils au candidats. Paris, n.d.

Prévost, Lt.-Colonel. *Des fortresses françaises pendant la guerre de 1870–1871.* Paris, 1873.

Projet de réorganisation du corps d'état-major présenté par la commission instituée par décision ministerielle en date du 5 février 1872. Paris, 1872.

Randon, Marshal. *Mémoires.* 2 vols. Paris, 1875–77.

Recueil des lois, décrets, circulaires et décisions portant organisation du service d'état-major. 2d ed. Paris and Limoges, 1895.

Reinach, Joseph, ed. *Discours et plaidoyers politiques de M. Gambetta.* 11 vols. Paris, 1880–85.

Rémusat, Charles de. *Mémoires de ma vie.* 5 vols. Paris, 1958–67.

Réorganisation du corps d'état-major. Projet présenté par la minorité de la commission de réorganisation. Paris, 1872.

Rossel, Louis-Nathaniel. *Papiers posthumes.* Paris, 1871.

Simon, Jules. *La réforme de l'enseignement secondaire.* Paris, 1874.

———. *L'école.* Paris, 1865.

———. *Le gouvernement de M. Thiers.* 2 vols. Paris, 1879.

Stoffel, Baron Eugène. *Rapports militaires écrits de Berlin, 1866–1870.* Paris, 1871.

Thiers, Adolphe. *Notes et souvenirs, 1870–1873.* Paris, 1904.

Titeux, Eugène. *Saint-Cyr et l'école spéciale militaire en France.* Paris, 1898.

Trochu, Louis Jules. *L'armée française en 1867.* Paris, 1867.

———. *L'empire et la défense de Paris devant le jury de la Seine.* Paris, 1872.

Vinoy, Joseph. *L'armée française en 1873.* Paris, 1873.

Wolseley, Garnet Joseph. "France as a Military Power in 1870 and 1878." *Nineteenth Century* 3 (1878):1–21.

Books and Articles

Acomb, Evelyn M. *The French Laic Laws, 1879–1889: The First Anti-Clerical Campaign of the Third French Republic.* New York, 1941.

Albisetti, James C. *Secondary School Reform in Imperial Germany.* Princeton, 1983.

Anderson, R. D. *Education in France, 1848–1870.* Oxford, 1975.

Armengaud, André. *L'opinion publique en France et la crise nationale allemande en 1866.* Paris, 1962.

Aubert, Roger. "Das vatikanische Konzil." In *Handbuch der Kirchengeschichte,* edited by Hubert Jedin, 6:744–91. 7 vols. Freiburg, Basel, and Vienna, 1963–79.

Auspitz, Katherine. *The Radical Bourgeoisie: The Ligue de l'Enseignement and the Origins of the Third Republic, 1866–1885.* New York, 1982.

Barnett, Corelli. "The Education of Military Elites." *Journal of Contemporary History* 2 (1967):15–35.

Baumont, Maurice. *Aux sources de l'affaire.* Paris, 1959.

―――. *L'échiquier de Metz: empire ou république, 1870.* Paris, 1971.

―――. *L'essor industriel et l'impérialisme colonial, 1878–1904.* Paris, 1937.

Becker, Josef. *Liberaler Staat und Kirche in der Aera von Reichsgründung und Kulturkampf.* Mainz, 1973.

Ben-David, Joseph. *The Scientist's Role in Society: A Comparative View.* Englewood Cliffs, N.J., 1971.

Bertocci, Philip A. *Jules Simon: Republican Anticlericalism and Cultural Politics in France, 1848–1886.* Columbia, Mo., 1978.

Blackbourn, David, and Eley, Geoff. *Mythen deutscher Geschichtsschreibung. Die gescheiterte bürgerliche Revolution von 1848.* Frankfurt-am-Main, 1980.

Boivin, Marcel. "Les origines de la ligue de l'enseignement en Seine-Inférieure, 1866–1871." *Revue d'histoire économique et sociale* 46 (1968):203–31.

Bond, Brian. *The Victorian Army and the Staff College, 1854–1914.* London, 1972.

Broc, Numa. "La géographie française face à la science allemande, 1870–1914." *Annales de géographie* 86 (1977):71–94.

Brunschwig, Henri. *Mythes et réalités de l'impérialisme colonial français, 1871–1914.* Paris, 1960.

Bury, J. P. T. *Gambetta and the Making of the Third Republic.* London, 1973.

―――. *Gambetta and the National Defence: A Republican Dictatorship in France.* 2d ed. New York, 1970.

Caemmerer, Lt.-General von. *The Development of Strategical Science during the 19th Century.* London, 1905.

Canini, G. "Géographie militaire de la France de l'est, 1875–1914." *Revue historique de l'armée* 29 (1973):19–28.

Capéran, Louis. *Histoire contemporaine de la laïcité française.* 3 vols. Paris, 1957–61.

Carrias, Eugène. *La pensée militaire française.* Paris, 1960.

―――. *Le danger allemand.* Paris, 1952.

Case, Lynn. *French Opinion on War and Diplomacy under the Second Empire.* Philadelphia, 1954.

Casevitz, Jean. *Une loi manquée: la loi Niel, 1866–1868. L'armée française à la veille de la guerre de 1870.* Paris, 1959.

Chabanier, Jean. "La garde nationale mobile en 1870–1871: la loi Niel." *Revue historique de l'armée* 27 (1971):43–61.

Challéat, General. *Histoire technique de l'artillerie de terre en France pendant un siècle, 1816–1919.* Paris, 1933.

Challener, Richard D. *The French Theory of the Nation in Arms, 1866–1939.* 2d ed. New York, 1965.

Chalmin, Pierre. "Les écoles militaires françaises jusqu'en 1914." *Revue historique de l'armée* 10 (1954):129–66.

———. *L'officier français de 1815 à 1870.* Paris, 1957.

Chapman, Guy. *The Dreyfus Case: A Reassessment.* London, 1955.

———. *The Third Republic of France: The First Phase, 1871–1894.* London, 1962.

Chevallier, Pierre. *Histoire de la franc-maçonnerie française.* 3 vols. Paris, 1975.

———. *La séparation de l'église et de l'école.* Paris, 1981.

——— et al. *L'enseignement français de la révolution à nos jours.* 2 vols. Paris and The Hague, 1968–71.

Choisel, Francis. "Du tirage au sort au service universel." *Revue historique des armées* 8, no. 2 (1981):43–60.

Cipolla, Carlo M. *Literacy and Development in the West.* London, 1969.

Contamine, Henry. *La revanche, 1871–1914.* Paris, 1957.

———. *La victoire de la Marne.* Paris, 1970.

Coutrot, Aline, and Dreyfus, François. *Les forces religieuses dans la société française.* Paris, 1965.

Craig, Gordon. *The Politics of the Prussian Army, 1640–1945.* New York and Oxford, 1956.

Crozier, Michael. *The Bureaucratic Phenomenon.* Chicago, 1964.

Dansette, Adrien. *Histoire religieuse de la France contemporaine.* 2d ed. Paris, 1965.

———. *Le boulangisme.* 16th ed. Paris, 1946.

Day, C. R. "Technical and Professional Education in France: The Rise and Fall of l'Enseignement Spécial, 1865–1902." *Journal of Social History* 6 (1972):177–201.

———. "The Making of Mechanical Engineers in France: The Ecoles d'Arts et Métiers, 1803–1914." *French Historical Studies* 10 (1978):439–60.

Defrasne, Jean. "L'armée française devant l'alerte de 1875." *Revue historique de l'armée* 26 (1970):37–57.

De Gaulle, Charles. *La France et son armée.* Paris, 1938.

Demeter, Karl. *Das deutsche Offizierkorps in Gesellschaft und Staat, 1650–1945.* 4th ed. Frankfurt-am-Main, 1965.

Dessal, Marcel. *Un révolutionnaire jacobin: Charles Delescluze, 1809–1871.* Paris, 1952.

Digeon, Claude. *La crise allemande de la pensée française, 1870–1914.* Paris, 1959.

Doise, Jean. "La deuxième ligne en fortification sur les frontières nord et est de la France, 1815–1940." *Revue historique des armées* 6, no. 1 (1979):123–52.

Durosoy, General. *Saumur. Historique de l'école d'application de l'ar-*

mée blindée de la cavalerie. Paris, 1965.

Duveau, Georges. *La pensée ouvrière sur l'éducation pendant la seconde république et le second empire*. Paris, 1948.

———. *Les instituteurs*. 2d ed. Paris, 1961.

Edwards, Stewart. *The Paris Commune 1871*. London, 1971.

Ellis, Jack D. *The Early Life of Georges Clemenceau, 1841–1893*. Lawrence, Kan., 1980.

Ellis, John. *The Social History of the Machine Gun*. New York, 1975.

Elwitt, Sanford. *The Making of the Third Republic: Class and Politics in France, 1868–1884*. Baton Rouge, La., 1975.

Encrevé, André, and Richard, Michel, eds. *Les protestants dans les débuts de la troisième république, 1871–1885*. Paris, 1979.

Feine, Hans Erich. *Kirchliche Rechtsgeschichte*. 4th ed. Cologne and Graz, 1964.

Fox, Robert, and Weisz, George, eds. *The Organization of Science and Technology in France, 1800–1914*. Cambridge, 1980.

Franz, Georg. *Kulturkampf: Staat und katholische Kirche in Mitteleuropa von der Säkularisation bis zum Abschluss des preussischen Kulturkampfes*. Munich, 1954.

Frauenholz, Eugen von. *Das Heerwesen des XIX. Jahrhunderts*. Munich, 1941.

Freyssinet-Dominjon, Jacqueline. *Les manuels d'histoire de l'école libre, 1882–1959*. Paris, 1969.

Fuchs, Walther Peter, ed. *Staat und Kirche im Wandel der Jahrhunderte*. Stuttgart, 1966.

Furet, François, and Ozouf, Jacques, eds. *Lire et écrire. L'alphabétisation des français de Calvin à Jules Ferry*. 2 vols. Paris, 1977.

Gadille, Jacques. *La pensée et l'action politiques des évêques français au début de la IIIe république, 1870–1883*. 2 vols. Paris, 1967.

Ganiage, Jean. *L'expansion coloniale et les rivalités internationales de 1871 à 1914*. 2 vols. Paris, 1975.

Gaudemet, Y. H. *Les juristes et la vie politique de la troisième république*. Paris, 1970.

Gerbod, Paul. *La condition universitaire en France au XIXe siècle*. Paris, 1965.

———. *La vie quotidienne dans les lycées et collèges au XIXe siècle*. Paris, 1968.

Geuss, Herbert. *Bismarck und Napoleon III.: ein Beitrag zur Geschichte der preussisch-französischen Beziehungen, 1851–1871*. Cologne and Graz, 1959.

Giesberg, Robert I. *The Treaty of Frankfort: A Study in Diplomatic History, September 1870–September 1873*. Philadelphia, 1966.

Gilpin, Robert. *France in the Age of the Scientific State*. Princeton, 1968.

Girard, Louis. *La garde nationale, 1814–1871.* Paris, 1964.

Girardet, Raoul. *La société militaire dans la France contemporaine, 1815–1939.* Paris, 1953.

Gonjo, Yasuo. "Le 'Plan Freycinet,' 1878–1882: un aspect de la 'grande dépression' économique en France." *Revue historique* 248 (1972): 49–86.

Grasser, Jacques. "Un exemple de fortifications dites 'Séré de Rivières': le camp retranché d'Epinal entre 1871 et 1914." *Revue historique de l'armée* 29 (1973):116–34.

Greenberg, Louis M. *Sisters of Liberty: Marseille, Lyon, Paris, and the Reaction to a Centralized State, 1868–1871.* Cambridge, Mass., 1971.

Grupp, Peter. *Deutschland, Frankreich und die Kolonien.* Tübingen, 1980.

Guerlac, Henry E. "Science and French National Strength." In *Modern France: Problems of the Third and Fourth Republics,* edited by Edward Mead Earle, pp. 81–105. New York, 1964.

Hanotaux, Gabriel. *Histoire de la France contemporaine, 1871–1900.* 4 vols. Paris, 1903–8.

Harrigan, Patrick J. "Historians and Compilers Joined: The Historiography of the 1970s and French Enquêtes of the Nineteenth Century." In *The Making of Frenchmen: Current Directions in the History of Education in France, 1679–1979,* edited by Donald N. Baker and Patrick J. Harrigan, pp. 3–21. Waterloo, Ontario, 1980.

―――. *Mobility, Elites, and Education in French Society of the Second Empire.* Waterloo, Ontario, 1980.

―――. "Secondary Education and the Professions in France during the Second Empire." *Comparative Studies in Society and History* 17 (1975):349–71.

Harvey, David. "Monument and Myth." *Annals of the Association of American Geographers* 69 (1979):362–81.

Hasler, August Bernhard. *Pius IX. (1846–1878), Päpstliche Unfehlbarkeit und 1. Vatikanisches Konzil: Dogmatisierung und Durchsetzung einer Ideologie.* Stuttgart, 1977.

Hébert, M., and Carnec, A. *La loi Falloux et la liberté d'enseignement.* La Rochelle, 1953.

Hittle, J. D. *The Military Staff: Its History and Development.* 3d ed. Harrisburg, Pa., 1961.

Horvath-Peterson, Sandra. *Victor Duruy and French Education: Liberal Reform in the Second Empire.* Baton Rouge, 1984.

Houtin, Albert. *Le père Hyacinthe, réformateur catholique.* Paris, 1922.

Howard, Michael. "The Armed Forces." In *The New Cambridge Modern History.* Vol. 11: *Material Progress and World-Wide Problems,* edited by F. H. Hinsley, pp. 204–42. Cambridge, 1967.

_____. *The Franco-Prussian War.* 2d ed. New York, 1969.

_____. *War in European History.* London, 1976.

Hutchison, Graham S. *Machine Guns: Their History and Tactical Employment.* London, 1938.

Irsay, Stephen d'. *Histoire des universités françaises et étrangères.* 2 vols. Paris, 1933–35.

Isambert-Jamati, Viviane. *Crises de la société, crises de l'enseignement.* Paris, 1970.

Israël, Alexandre. *L'école de la république: la grande oeuvre de Jules Ferry.* Paris, 1931.

Jauffret, Jean-Charles. "Monsieur Thiers et le Comité de Défense." *Les cahiers de Montpellier* 5 (1982):27–45.

Johnson, Douglas. *France and the Dreyfus Affair.* New York, 1966.

Judt, Tony. *Socialism in Provence, 1871–1914: A Study in the Origins of the French Left.* Cambridge, 1979.

Kehr, Eckart. *Der Primat der Innenpolitik: Gesammelte Aufsätze zur preussisch-deutschen Sozialgeschichte im 19. und 20. Jahrhundert.* Edited by Hans-Ulrich Wehler. Berlin, 1965.

Kennan, George F. *The Decline of Bismarck's European Order: Franco-Russian Relations, 1875–1890.* Princeton, 1979.

Kessel, Eberhard. *Moltke.* Stuttgart, 1957.

Keylor, William R. *Academy and Community: The Foundation of the French Historical Profession.* Cambridge, Mass., 1975.

Kitchen, Martin. *A Military History of Germany from the Eighteenth Century to the Present Day.* Bloomington and London, 1975.

Kohn, Hans, ed. *The Modern World: 1848 to the Present.* New York, 1963.

Kovacs, Arpad F. "French Military Institutions before the Franco-Prussian War." *American Historical Review* 2 (1945):217–35.

Kuntz, François. *L'officier français dans la nation.* Paris, 1960.

La Gorce, Paul-Marie de. *La république et son armée.* Paris, 1963.

Larkin, Maurice. *Church and State after the Dreyfus Affair.* London, 1974.

Latreille, André, et al. *Histoire du catholicisme en France.* 3 vols. Paris, 1957–62.

Laulan, Robert. *L'école militaire et l'école supérieure de guerre.* Paris, 1937.

Lavisse, Ernest. *Un ministre: Victor Duruy.* Paris, 1895.

Legrand, Louis. *L'influence du positivisme dans l'oeuvre scolaire de Jules Ferry: les origines de la laïcité.* Paris, 1961.

Léon, Antoine. *Histoire de l'enseignement en France.* Paris, 1967.

Léonard, Emile G. *Le protestant français.* Paris, 1953.

Ligou, Daniel. *Dictionnaire universel de la franc-maçonnerie.* 2 vols. Paris, 1974.

———. *Histoire du socialisme en France, 1871–1961*. Paris, 1962.

———. "Les protestants et la franc-maçonnerie aux débuts de la troisième république." In *Les protestants dans les débuts de la troisième république, 1871–1885*, edited by André Encrevé and Michel Richard, pp. 229–41. Paris, 1979.

Lill, Rudolf. "Die Entstehung der altkatholischen Kirchengemeinschaft." In *Handbuch der Kirchengeschichte*, edited by Hubert Jedin, 6:792–96. 7 vols. Freiburg, Basel, and Vienna, 1963–79.

Locke, Robert R. "Industrialisierung und Erziehungssystem in Frankreich und Deutschland vor dem 1. Weltkrieg." *Historische Zeitschrift* 225 (1977):265–96.

Lösch, Stefan. *Döllinger und Frankreich: Eine geistige Allianz, 1823–1871*. Munich, 1955.

Lundgreen, Peter. "Bildung und Besitz—Einheit oder Inkongruenz in der europäischen Sozialgeschichte? Kritische Auseinandersetzung mit einer These von Fritz Ringer." *Geschichte und Gesellschaft* 7 (1981):262–75.

———. *Sozialgeschichte der deutschen Schule im Ueberblick*. 2 vols. Göttingen, 1980.

———. "The Organization of Science and Technology in France: A German Perspective." In *The Organization of Science and Technology in France, 1800–1914*, edited by Robert Fox and George Weisz, pp. 311–32. Cambridge, 1980.

Luvaas, Jay. "European Military Thought and Doctrine, 1870–1914." In *The Theory and Practice of War*, edited by Michael Howard, pp. 69–93. Bloomington and London, 1965.

McClelland, Charles E. *State, Society and University in Germany, 1700–1914*. Cambridge, 1979.

McManners, John. *Church and State in France, 1870–1914*. New York, 1973.

Marrus, Michael R. "Pilger auf dem Weg. Wallfahrten in Frankreich des 19. Jahrhunderts." *Geschichte und Gesellschaft* 3 (1977):329–51.

Martin, Benjamin F. *Count Albert de Mun: Paladin of the Third Republic*. Chapel Hill, 1978.

Mayeur, Françoise. *L'éducation des filles en France au XIXe siècle*. Paris, 1979.

———. *L'enseignement secondaire des jeunes filles sous la troisième république*. Paris, 1977.

Mayeur, Jean-Marie. "Albert Dumont et les transformations de l'enseignement supérieur au début de la troisième république." *Bulletin de correspondance hellénique* 1 (1976):7–10.

———. *La séparation de l'église et de l'état*. Paris, 1966.

———. *Les débuts de la IIIe république, 1871–1898*. Paris, 1973.

Messerschmidt, Manfred. *Militär und Politik in der Bismarckzeit und im wilhelminischen Deutschland.* Darmstadt, 1975.

Michel, Henry. *La loi Falloux.* Paris, 1906.

Mitchell, Allan. " 'A Situation of Inferiority': French Military Reorganization after the Defeat of 1870." *American Historical Review* 86 (1981):49–62.

―――. *Bismarck and the French Nation, 1848–1890.* New York, 1971.

―――. "Crucible of French Anticlericalism: The Conseil Municipal de Paris, 1871–1885." *Francia* 8 (1980):395–405.

―――. "German History in France after 1870." *Journal of Contemporary History* 2 (1967):81–100.

―――. "Partners in Failure: Dupanloup, Döllinger, and the Doctrine of Papal Infallibility." *Francia* 10 (1982):381–90.

―――. "The Freycinet Reforms and the French Army, 1888–1893." *Journal of Strategic Studies* 4 (1981):19–28.

―――. *The German Influence in France after 1870: The Formation of the French Republic.* Chapel Hill, 1979.

―――. "The Xenophobic Style: French Counterespionage and the Emergence of the Dreyfus Affair." *Journal of Modern History* 52 (1980):414–25.

―――. "Thiers, MacMahon, and the Conseil Supérieur de la Guerre." *French Historical Studies* 6 (1969):232–52.

Mitchell, Pearl Boring. *The Bismarckian Policy of Conciliation with France, 1875–1885.* Philadelphia, 1935.

Monteilhet, Joseph. *Les institutions militaires de la France, 1814–1924.* Paris, 1926.

Moody, Joseph N. *French Education since Napoleon.* Syracuse, 1978.

Moss, Bernard H. *The Origins of the French Labor Movement, 1830–1914: The Socialism of Skilled Workers.* Berkeley, 1976.

Mours, Samuel, and Robert, Daniel. *Le protestantisme en France du XVIIIe siècle à nos jours, 1685–1970.* Paris, 1972.

Müller, Detlef K. *Sozialstruktur und Schulsystem: Aspekte zum Strukturwandel des Schulwesens im 19. Jahrhundert.* Göttingen, 1977.

Nora, Pierre. "Ernest Lavisse, son rôle dans la formation du sentiment national." *Revue historique* 228 (1962):73–106.

Nye, Mary Jo. "The Scientific Periphery in France: The Faculty of Sciences at Toulouse (1880–1930)." *Minerva* 13 (1975):374–403.

O'Brien, Patricia. "L'Embastillement de Paris: The Fortification of Paris during the July Monarchy." *French Historical Studies* 9 (1975):63–82.

O'Donnell, J. Dean, Jr. "Cardinal Charles Lavigerie: The Politics of Getting a Red Hat." *Catholic Historical Review* 63 (1977):185–203.

Ornano, Roland d'. *Gouvernement et haut-commandement en régime parlementaire français, 1814–1914.* Aix-en-Provence, 1958.

Ozouf, Jacques, and Ozouf, Mona. "Le thème du patriotisme dans les manuels primaires." *Mouvement social* 49 (1964):5–32.

Ozouf, Mona. *L'école, l'église et la république.* Paris, 1963.

Padberg, John W. *Colleges in Controversy: The Jesuit Schools in France from Revival to Suppression, 1815–1880.* Cambridge, Mass., 1969.

Partin, Malcolm O. *Waldeck-Rousseau, Combes, and the Church: The Politics of Anticlericalism, 1899–1905.* Durham, N.C., 1969.

Paul, Harry W. "The Issue of Decline in Nineteenth-Century French Science." *French Historical Studies* 7 (1972):416–50.

————. *The Sorcerer's Apprentice: The French Scientist's Image of German Science, 1840–1919.* Gainesville, Fla., 1972.

Pflanze, Otto. "Bismarcks Herrschaftstechnik als Problem der gegenwärtigen Historiographie." *Historische Zeitschrift* 234 (1982):561–99.

Pisani-Ferry, Fresnette. *Jules Ferry et le partage du monde.* Paris, 1962.

————. *Monsieur l'instituteur: L'école primaire a 100 ans.* Paris, 1981.

Poidevin, Raymond, and Bariéty, Jacques. *Les relations franco-allemandes, 1815–1975.* Paris, 1977.

Ponteil, Félix. *Histoire de l'enseignement en France, 1789–1965.* Paris, 1965.

Porch, Douglas. *The March to the Marne: The French Army, 1871–1914.* Cambridge, 1981.

Prost, Antoine. *Histoire de l'enseignement en France, 1800–1967.* Paris, 1968.

Ralston, David B. *The Army of the Republic: The Place of the Military in the Political Evolution of France, 1871–1914.* Cambridge, Mass., and London, 1967.

Rémond, René. *L'anticléricalisme en France de 1815 à nos jours.* Paris, 1976.

Ringer, Fritz K. *Education and Society in Modern Europe.* Bloomington and London, 1979.

Ritter, Gerhard. *Der Schlieffenplan: Kritik eines Mythos.* Munich, 1956.

————. *Staatskunst und Kriegshandwerk: das Problem des 'Militarismus' in Deutschland.* 4 vols. Munich, 1954–68.

Rohr, Jean. *Victor Duruy, ministre de Napoléon III: Essai sur la politique de l'instruction publique au temps de l'empire libéral.* Paris, 1967.

Ropp, Theodore. *War in the Modern World.* Durham, N.C., 1959.

Rüdt von Collenberg, Ludwig. *Die deutsche Armee von 1871 bis 1914.* Berlin, 1922.

Schmidt-Volkmar, Erich. *Der Kulturkampf in Deutschland, 1871–1890.* Göttingen, 1962.

Schnapper, Bernard. *Le remplacement militaire en France: Quelques aspects politiques, économiques et sociaux du recrutement au XIXe siècle.* Paris, 1968.

Schram, Stuart R. *Protestantism and Politics in France.* Alençon, 1954.
Seager, Frederic H. *The Boulanger Affair: Political Crossroad of France, 1886–1889.* Ithaca, 1969.
Sedgwick, Alexander. *The Ralliement in French Politics, 1890–1898.* Cambridge, Mass., 1965.
Serman, William. *Les officiers français dans la nation, 1848–1914.* Paris, 1982.
_____. *Les origines des officiers français, 1848–1870.* Paris, 1979.
Shinn, Terry. "Des corps de l'état au secteur industriel: genèse de la profession d'ingénieur, 1750–1920." *Revue française de sociologie* 19 (1978):39–71.
_____. *Savoir scientifique et pouvoir social: l'école polytechnique, 1794–1914.* Paris, 1980.
Silvestre de Sacy, Jacques. *Le maréchal de MacMahon, duc de Magenta, 1808–1893.* Paris, 1960.
Sor, Daniel. *Les fusils d'infantrie européens à la fin du XIXe siècle.* Paris, 1972.
Sorlin, Pierre. *Waldeck-Rousseau.* Paris, 1966.
Stadelmann, Rudolf. *Moltke und der Staat.* Krefeld, 1950.
Strieter, Terry W. "The French Army's Problem of Numbers: The Recruitment of Sous-officiers in Industrializing France." *Third Republic* 6 (1978):211–36.
Stürmer, Michael, ed. *Bismarck und die preussisch-deutsche Politik, 1871–1890.* Munich, 1976.
_____. "Staatsstreichgedanken im Bismarckreich." *Historische Zeitschrift* 209 (1969):556–615.
Suleiman, Ezra. *Politics, Power, and Bureaucracy in France.* Princeton, 1974.
Sussman, George D. "The Glut of Doctors in Mid-Nineteenth Century France." *Comparative Studies in Society and History* 19 (1977): 287–304.
Talbott, John E. *The Politics of Educational Reform, 1918–1940.* Princeton, 1969.
Thadden, Rudolf von. "Les protestants allemands face à la controverse entre laïcs et cléricaux français." In *Les protestants dans les débuts de la troisième république, 1871–1885,* edited by André Encrevé and Michel Richard, pp. 501–11. Paris, 1979.
Thomas, T. H. "Armies and the Railway Revolution." In *War as a Social Institution,* edited by Jesse D. Clarkson and Thomas C. Cochran, pp. 88–94. New York, 1941.
Thoumas, General. *Les transformations de l'armée française.* 2 vols. Paris, 1887.
Truttmann, Philippe. "La fortification en VIe région militaire." *Revue*

historique de l'armée 29 (1973):55–79.

Vagts, Alfred. *A History of Militarism.* 2d ed. New York, 1959.

Valette, Jacques. "Note sur l'idée coloniale vers 1871." *Revue d'histoire moderne et contemporaine* 14 (1967):158–72.

Vovelle, Michel. *Piété baroque et déchristianisation en Provence au XVIIIe siècle.* Paris, 1973.

Watson, D. R. *Georges Clemenceau: A Political Biography.* London, 1974.

——. "The Politics of Educational Reform in France during the Third Republic, 1900–1940." *Past and Present* 34 (1966):81–99.

Weber, Eugen. "Comment la Politique Vint aux Paysans: A Second Look at Peasant Politicization." *American Historial Review* 87 (1982): 357–89.

——. *Peasants into Frenchmen: The Modernization of Rural France, 1870–1914.* Stanford, 1976.

Wehler, Hans-Ulrich. *Bismarck und der Imperialismus.* 5th ed. Frankfurt, 1983.

——. " 'Deutscher Sonderweg' oder allgemeine Probleme des westlichen Kapitalismus?" *Merkur* 5 (1981):478–87.

——. "Die Sozialgeschichte zwischen Wirtschaftsgeschichte und Politikgeschichte." In *Sozialgeschichte und Strukturgeschichte in der Schule,* pp. 13–25. Bonn, 1975.

——. "Moderne Politikgeschichte oder 'Grosse Politik der Kabinette.' " *Geschichte und Gesellschaft* 1 (1975):344–69.

Weill, Georges. *Histoire de l'enseignement secondaire en France, 1802–1920.* Paris, 1921.

Weiss, John. *The Making of Technological Man: The Social Origins of French Engineering Education.* Cambridge, Mass., 1982.

Weisz, George. "Reform and Conflict in French Medical Education, 1870–1914." In *The Organization of Science and Technology in France, 1800–1914,* edited by Robert Fox and George Weisz, pp. 61–94. Cambridge, 1980.

——. *The Emergence of Modern Universities in France, 1863–1914.* Princeton, 1983.

Weitlauff, Manfred. "Pius IX. und die Dogmatisierung der päpstlichen Unfehlbarkeit." *Zeitschrift für Kirchengeschichte* 91 (1980):94–105.

Wienefeld, Robert H. *Franco-German Relations, 1875–1885.* Baltimore, 1929.

Williamson, Samuel R., Jr. *The Politics of Grand Strategy: Britain and France Prepare for War, 1904–1914.* Cambridge, Mass., 1969.

Wilson, Stephen. *Ideology and Experience: Antisemitism in France at the*

Time of the Dreyfus Affair. Rutherford, Madison, and Teaneck, 1982.

Wright, Gordon. "Public Opinion and Conscription in France, 1866–70." *Journal of Modern History* 14 (1942):26–45.

Zaniewicki, Captain. "L'oeuvre de Freycinet au ministère de la guerre, 1888–1893." *Revue historique de l'armée* 19 (1963):55–72.

Zeldin, Theodore. *France, 1848–1945*. 2 vols. Oxford, 1973–77.

————. "Higher Education in France, 1848–1940." *Journal of Contemporary History* 2 (1967):53–80.

Index

A

Acton, John, 140
Adam, Juliette, 77
Administration, 20, 35, 83, 88, 138, 147, 186, 195, 223, 233. *See also* Bureaucracy; Prefectoral corps
Agriculture, 13, 276 (n. 87)
Ajaccio, vacant bishopric of, 130
Algeria, 50–51, 93, 103, 261 (n. 2), 276 (n. 86)
Allain-Targé, Henri, 178, 301 (n. 59)
Allocations. *See* Budget
Alps, 57, 151, 293 (n. 35)
Alsace-Lorraine, 43, 57, 147, 176, 178, 230, 242, 244, 247, 260 (n. 32), 314 (n. 15), 315 (n. 40), 316 (n. 52), 318 (n. 69)
Ambulance corps, 79
Amiens, 126
Amnesty. *See* Communards
Anticlericalism, 138–39, 142, 149, 151, 159–60, 167–68, 170–73, 175–80, 182–84, 186, 188, 194, 196, 220, 222, 225, 227, 234–36, 238, 241, 243, 299 (n. 35), 301 (n. 50)
Antigermanism. *See* Germanophobia
Anti-Semitism, 242, 318 (n. 74). *See also* Dreyfus Affair
Antonelli, Monsignor Giacomo (papal secretary of state), 132–34, 139, 162, 164–65, 168, 172, 181, 285 (n. 31), 299 (n. 31)
Appropriations. *See* Budget; Finances
Ardennes, 113–14
Aristocracy, 33, 89

Armament. *See* Weaponry
Armistice of 1871, 17, 124–25
Army (French), xii, xiv; reorganization of, 4–8, 24–25, 39, 41, 45–47, 50–51, 61–62, 64–65, 75, 78, 89, 96, 105–107, 115, 168, 253 (n. 44), 255 (n. 68); reserve, 6–10, 12, 15, 19, 22, 29–30, 33–37, 41, 47–48, 66, 73–74, 76–77, 81, 110, 251 (nn. 14, 15, 16), 253 (n. 47); regular, 7–8, 10, 12–13, 16, 22, 29, 34–35, 37, 39, 45–46, 72, 110, 258 (n. 2); professional, 8–13, 15–19, 22, 25–27, 31, 36, 39, 71, 73, 103, 108, 261 (n. 35); of Versailles, 19, 126; territorial, 29, 39, 45, 47, 73–74, 79, 81, 95, 100, 109–10. *See also* Artillery; Cavalry; Infantry; Militia; Reform; Weaponry
Army (Prusso-German), 4–6, 8, 14–15, 20–22, 25–26, 30, 35, 37–38, 127, 279 (nn. 33, 34)
Arnim, Harry von, 172
Artillery, xiv, 9, 16, 18, 32, 41, 49–51, 55–56, 59, 64–71, 77, 79, 92, 95, 99–100, 102–3, 109, 111–14, 252 (n. 35), 266 (n. 53), 267 (n. 68), 268 (nn. 70, 71), 280 (n. 44). *See also* Weaponry
Artisans, 247
Assembly, 19, 24–29, 32–33, 36, 40–42, 45–47, 56, 62, 125–26, 132, 136–37, 139, 152, 154, 157, 160–61, 173, 254 (n. 54), 255 (nn. 61, 65), 258 (n. 91), 262 (n. 17), 287 (n. 49). *See*

Charlemont, 114
Chassepot rifle, 71–72
Chauvinism, 20, 160, 248. *See also* Nationalism; Patriotism; Revanchism
Cherbuliez, Victor, 147
Chesnelong, Charles, 162, 165, 197
Chigi, Monsignor Flavio (nuncio in Paris), 122, 125, 128–29, 135, 137–38, 162, 172, 284 (n. 24), 298 (n. 21)
China, 235
Christianity, 136, 170, 196–97, 231, 316 (n. 41). *See also* Catholicism; Protestantism
Christian Socialism, 239, 317 (n. 60)
Church, Roman Catholic, xi–xii, 136, 138, 144, 146, 154, 171–72, 188, 236–37, 289 (n. 5), 298 (n. 21); hierarchy of, xi–xii, 136, 159–60, 166, 171, 175, 184, 188, 191–92, 222, 225–28, 231, 237–38, 243, 284 (nn. 21, 24); cooperation with state, 121–27, 135, 137, 141, 160, 184, 187, 190–92, 223, 231, 234, 239, 286 (n. 38), 305 (n. 103), 315 (n. 31), 316 (n. 46); conflict with state, 128–36, 140, 142, 149, 151, 158–59, 164, 167–70, 176, 180–83, 185, 189, 220, 224, 226–29, 232–33, 235, 238, 287 (n. 51); separation from state, 170, 175, 178–79, 181, 184, 193, 222, 225, 227, 230, 232, 237–43, 313 (n. 10), 314 (n. 19), 315 (n. 37), 317 (n. 60). *See also* Catholicism; Concordat; Kulturkampf; *Ralliement*
Cissey, General Ernest de, 19, 32–33, 38–39, 41–42, 44, 50–51, 64–65, 83, 88, 267 (n. 58), 278 (n. 24)
Cities. *See* Urbanization
Città Vecchia, 140, 167
Classics, 145, 150, 155–56, 158, 194, 201–8, 215–18, 246, 295 (nn. 45, 49), 308 (n. 44), 309 (n. 51), 312 (n. 77). *See also* Education; *Gymnasium*; *Lycée*
Clemenceau, Georges, 90, 178, 194–95, 225, 237, 301 (n. 59)
Clergy, 124–25, 129, 136–37, 146, 168, 175, 177, 183, 188, 221–28, 232, 237–41, 243, 285 (n. 28), 287 (n. 44), 299 (n. 31), 300 (n. 42), 313 (n. 14), 314 (n. 15). *See also* Catholi-

cism; Priests
Clericalism, 136, 144, 148–49, 159–63, 167, 175–77, 179, 183, 186, 188, 192, 194–96, 198, 201, 221, 225, 228, 238, 289 (n. 5), 293 (n. 30), 296 (n. 4), 306 (n. 12). *See also* Anticlericalism; Ultramontanism
Club Alpin Français, 151
Cluseret, General Gustave-Paul, 14, 18, 254 (n. 56)
Collèges, 152, 155, 201, 204, 234
Colonialism, 8, 231–32, 234, 315 (n. 40). *See also* Imperialism
Comité de Défense, 53, 106, 262 (n. 17), 280 (n. 44)
Comité de l'Artillerie, 50, 66–68, 270 (n. 30)
Comité diocésain des écoles chrétiennes, 196–97
Commerce, 63, 94, 96, 150, 176, 203
Commission Supérieure de l'Artillerie, 68
Commission Supérieure des Chemins de Fer, 60–61, 63, 66
Communards, 18–19, 179, 194, 235
Commune (Paris), 14–15, 18, 64, 126, 134, 137–38, 148, 150, 154, 170, 175, 193, 237, 254 (nn. 55, 58), 283 (n. 15), 292 (n. 28)
Communications, 16, 75
Comte, Auguste, 87
Concordat, 121–22, 125–26, 131–35, 179–80, 184, 224, 229, 232–33, 238, 240, 285 (n. 31), 286 (n. 36), 314 (n. 16). *See also* Church
Condé, 114
Conscription, xiii, 5, 8, 11, 16–17, 29, 38, 50, 71–72, 74–75, 109, 216, 259 (n. 4), 279 (n. 32); universal, xi, 4, 6, 10, 13, 15, 19, 22–23, 26–28, 30–31, 36, 47, 71, 76, 146, 194, 255 (n. 61), 258 (n. 93); exemption from, 5–6, 12, 30, 108, 250 (n. 11); exoneration from, 6, 30, 108; seven-year, 9–10, 31; five-year, 10, 12, 20–28, 30–32, 42, 77, 79, 108, 259 (n. 5), 270 (n. 31), 277 (n. 13); three-year, 28, 75–80, 101–3, 106, 108, 252, 270 (nn. 28, 30), 271 (n. 39). *See also* Laisant proposal
Conseil d'Etat, 7, 11, 132–33, 135, 286 (n. 35), 292 (n. 26)

Naquet, Alfred, 152–53
National Assembly. *See* Assembly
National guard, 6, 12, 16, 18–19, 254
 (n. 58)
Nationalism, xii, 12, 14, 17, 22, 27, 33,
 60, 108, 136, 170, 200, 218, 230–31,
 236–38, 241, 244, 246–48, 258
 (n. 93), 291 (n. 22). *See also* Chauvin-
 ism; Patriotism; Revanchism
Nationalization. *See* Railways
Navy, 19
Near East, 232, 234, 316 (n. 41)
Needle-gun, 72
Newspaper press, xiii, 3, 21, 32, 78–79,
 81, 102, 161, 169, 180–81, 185, 187,
 220, 222, 235–36, 238, 240–41, 251
 (n. 17), 299 (n. 31). *See also* Public
 opinion
Niel, Marshal Adolphe, 7–9, 13–14, 82,
 143–44, 147, 252 (nn. 28, 29, 30)
Niel law, 3, 7–9, 11–13, 22. *See also* Re-
 form
Nîmes, 176
Noailles, Marquis de, 304 (n. 87)
Noirot, Henri, 80
Nomination. *See* Investiture controversy
Non-commissioned officers, 9, 31, 50, 75,
 77, 79–81, 103, 258 (n. 2), 259
 (n. 8), 270 (n. 30), 271 (n. 37). *See
 also* Cadres
Norddeutsche Allgemeine Zeitung, 28, 163
Normandy, 176
North Africa, 94, 232
North German Confederation, 3, 6–7, 35,
 245, 260 (n. 32). *See also* Germany;
 Prussia
Notables, 36
Nouvelle Revue, 103
Nuns, 124, 136, 148, 184, 196

O

Occupation, 16, 25, 27–28, 72, 125–27,
 137, 160
Officers, 19, 21–22, 32, 40–41, 50–51,
 65–66, 74–75, 77, 80–81, 83–87,
 89–91, 93, 104–5, 108–9, 125, 157,
 175, 255 (n. 64), 258 (n. 2), 260
 (n. 26), 272 (nn. 42, 49), 273 (n. 63),
 274 (n. 71), 275 (n. 75), 277 (n. 11),
 281 (n. 50). *See also* Army; Etat-Major; General staff; High command

Old Catholics, 123, 171–72, 174. *See also*
 Catholicism
Ollivier, Emile, 124, 252 (n. 36)
Opportunism, 176, 178. *See also* Gam-
 betta
Orénoque, 140–41, 164–67, 288 (n. 59),
 298 (n. 18)
Orléans, 17, 124, 130
Oxford University, 214

P

Papacy, 123, 129–34, 136, 139–41, 162–
 65, 168, 172–74, 180–81, 184, 186–
 87, 190–91, 221–23, 225–26, 230–
 31, 239–41, 288 (n. 55), 298 (n. 23).
 See also Catholicism; Church; Holy
 See; Leo XIII, Pius IX; Rome; Vatican
Papal encyclical, 168, 237; *Immortale Dei*,
 191, 233; *Nobilissima Gallorum
 Gens*, 229; *Jampridem Nobis*, 233–
 34; *Rerum Novarum*, 239–40, 317
 (n. 66)
Papal infallibility, doctrine of, 123, 130,
 136, 171, 283 (n. 7), 299 (n. 37)
Papal nuncio: in Paris, 122, 125, 128–29,
 135, 137, 139, 165–68, 172, 180,
 184, 228, 238, 284 (n. 25), 288
 (n. 59), 297 (n. 15), 298 (n. 21); in
 Munich, 181, 185, 287 (n. 51), 298
 (n. 21); in Vienna, 185
Paris, 22, 26, 96, 140, 151, 193, 200, 222,
 230, 232, 234, 238, 242, 283 (n. 15);
 insurrection in, 18, 137, 150; military
 parade in, 20–21; press of, 27; military governor of, 32, 105, 281
 (n. 52); CSG meets in, 42, 46; military defense of, 55–56, 98, 116, 124,
 253 (n. 50); military academy in, 86–
 87; archbishopric of, 122, 128–32,
 135, 140, 229, 284 (n. 26), 285
 (n. 27), 317 (n. 68); cabinet officers
 in, 127, 134, 143; preeminence of,
 145, 213, 215, 247; theater and opera
 of, 146–47; medical school in, 153,
 214–15, 218; German embassy in,
 159, 187, 191, 220, 296 (n. 55), 276
 (n. 86); Church officials in, 165, 167,
 171, 227–28, 298 (n. 21); elections
 in, 175, 301 (n. 50); Protestants in,
 176; Freemasons in, 177; Radicals in,
 178; police of, 179; German agents